ORIENTATION to COLLEGE
for the Students of St. Charles Community College

St. Charles
COMMUNITY COLLEGE
www.stchas.edu

Second Custom Edition

Taken from:
Cornerstone: Building on Your Best, Fourth Edition
by Robert M. Sherfield, Rhonda J. Montgomery, and Patricia G. Moody

PEARSON
Custom Publishing

PEARSON
Prentice Hall

Cover photos courtesy of St. Charles Community College.

Taken from:

Cornerstone: Building on Your Best, Fourth Edition
by Robert M. Sherfield, Rhonda J. Montgomery, and Patricia G. Moody
Copyright © 2005, 2002, 2000, 1997 by Pearson Education, Inc.
Published by Prentice-Hall
Upper Saddle River, New Jersey 07458

Copyright © 2006, 2005 by Pearson Custom Publishing
All rights reserved.

This copyright covers material written expressly for this volume by the editor/s as well as the compilation itself. It does not cover the individual selections herein that first appeared elsewhere. Permission to reprint these has been obtained by Pearson Custom Publishing for this edition only. Further reproduction by any means, electronic or mechanical, including photocopying and recording, or by any information storage or retrieval system, must be arranged with the individual copyright holders noted.

All trademarks, service marks, registered trademarks, and registered service marks are the property of their respective owners and are used herein for identification purposes only.

Printed in the United States of America

10 9 8 7 6 5 4 3

ISBN 0-536-20751-8

2006420072

AK/KL

Please visit our web site at *www.pearsoncustom.com*

PEARSON Custom Publishing
PEARSON CUSTOM PUBLISHING
75 Arlington Street, Boston, MA 02116
A Pearson Education Company

GREETINGS FROM THE PRESIDENT

Welcome to St. Charles Community College!

We hope you will enjoy our beautiful campus, the small class sizes, our top-notch faculty and staff, and all of the wonderful resources available here to increase your opportunities for success.

I'd like to introduce you, specifically, to COL 101, a program that will help you to better know your own strengths and interests as well as the direction you want your life to take, both now and after you leave SCC. I hope you will devote time and effort to reviewing the concepts in this textbook and to interacting with your instructor and fellow students in order to get the most out of COL 101. Take the opportunity to learn about services open to you and get to know the people who provide them -- you'll find out how to use the Career Center, library, and tutoring services. You'll learn what faculty expect of you.

By enrolling at SCC, you have begun a new experience, similar in some ways to your previous education but different in many other ways. COL 101 will help you explore these differences and discover the range of opportunities offered to you by the college; it will help you begin planning your future. The COL 101 course will also teach you the study skills and critical thinking you need to be successful in college. We want your time at SCC to be an exhilarating and life-changing experience!

America's community colleges enroll almost half of the nation's first-time freshmen and conduct nearly half of all workforce training. Our graduates are well prepared for rewarding jobs and well prepared for transfer to a four-year college or university. They go on to become teachers, managers, business owners, health professionals, law enforcement officers, information technology specialists, counselors, college professors, and legislators. The sky really is the limit for students who are successful at SCC!

Let COL 101 open the doors to a world of opportunity that lies ahead of you.

Sincerely,

John M. McGuire, Ph.D.
President

Contents

AN INVITATION . . . viii

TO OUR STUDENTS . . . x

TO THE INSTRUCTOR . . . xi

ABOUT THE AUTHORS   xiii

ACKNOWLEDGMENTS   xv

1 CHANGE 3

Preparing for and Dealing with Change

Where Are You . . . At This Moment	6
Goals . . . For Change	7
Questions for Building on Your Best	7
Why College?	8
The Significance of Your College Experience	10
● **WORLD OF WORK:** Brian R. Epps	12
What Do You Want? Thinking About Your Choices	13
Changes in the Days to Come	14
What's Happening to Me? Physical and Emotional Reactions to Change	18
Attitudes that Hinder Change	20
So, I Want to Change: How Do I Do It?	20
● **ACTIVITY:** The Change Implementation Model	23
● **Blueprints for Change**	25
● **CASE STUDY:** Tomer Perry	26
● **JOURNALS**	28
● **ADVICE TO GO**	29

2 GROW 31

Motivation, Goal Setting, and Self-Esteem

Where Are You . . . At This Moment	34
Goals . . . For Change	35
Questions for Building on Your Best	35
The Impact of Values	36
The Impact of Attitude	36
Are You Hanging Out with Toxic People?	37
Overcoming Doubts and Fears	38
Motivation: What Is It and How Can I Get It?	40
Building a New You: The Goal-Setting Process	41
● **WORLD OF WORK:** Kevin Todd Houston	45
● **ACTIVITY:** Setting Goals	47
● **ACTIVITY:** Develop Your Motivational Plan	49

Do You Love Yourself? The Impact of Self-Esteem on Your Motivation	50
Influences on Self-Esteem: How Did You Get to Be Who You Are?	51
Loving You More! Improving Your Self-Esteem	52
● **Blueprints for Change**	55
● **CASE STUDY:** Jamie Juul	56
● **JOURNALS**	58
● **ADVICE TO GO**	59

3 PERSIST 61

Things You Need to Know About College But Might Never Ask

Where Are You . . . At This Moment	64
Goals . . . For Change	65
Questions for Building on Your Best	65
To Be Successful, You Have to Last: Persistence in College	66
What You Need to Know Up Front: College Policies and Procedures	66
Nutty or Nurturing? The College Professor	67
Success on a Platter: Academic Success Centers and Services	70
Don't Panic . . . There's Something for Everyone: Student Success Centers and Services	71
The Golden Rule—or Just a Crock? Classroom Etiquette and Personal Decorum	73
Writing Your First-Year History: Tips for Journaling	75
Journaling Beyond *Cornerstone*	76
Gotta Get Out of Here! Dropping Classes, Dropping Out, Stopping Out	76
Where Is It Written? Your College Catalog	77
Let Me Give You a Piece of Advice: The Academic Advisor/Counselor	77
You're Not in Kansas Anymore: Transfer Issues	78
Does 1 + 1 Really Equal 2? How to Calculate Your Grade Point Average	79
From The Far Away Nearby: Succeeding in Distance Education and Independent Study Courses	80
But I'm Not Even Finished with This One Yet! Preregistration for Next Term	81
● **WORLD OF WORK:** Andre Bauer	82
Pennies from Heaven: The Secret World of Financial Aid	83
Playing It Safe: Protecting Yourself on Campus	87
Won't You Stay for a While? Persisting in College	88

iii

CONTENTS

- *Blueprints for Change* — 91
- CASE STUDY: Vanessa Santos — 92
- JOURNALS — 94
- ADVICE TO GO — 95

4 PRIORITIZE — 97
Managing Your Time and Money Wisely

Where Are You . . . At This Moment	100
Goals . . . For Change	101
Questions for Building On Your Best	101
You Have All the Time There Is	102
Working Hard and Playing Hard	103
The "P" Word: Procrastination	103
WORLD OF WORK: Timothy Spencer Rice	**104**
Managing Time So You Can Have More Fun	105
When to Do What: Using Your Body's Cycles to the Best Advantage	111
Planning and Organizing for School	112
Planning and Organizing for Work	115
Planning and Organizing at Home	116
"B" Is for Budgeting	118
Practicing Fiscal Fitness	119
Facts You Need to Know about Credit Cards	120
Student Loans: A Day of Reckoning Will Come	122
Protect Yourself from Identity Theft	124
The Pitfalls of Payday Loans and Car Title Loans	126
Blueprints for Change	127
CASE STUDY: Coretta Hooks	128
JOURNALS	130
ADVICE TO GO	131

5 READ — 133
Building Active Reading and Comprehension Skills

Where Are You . . . At This Moment	136
Goals . . . For Change	137
Questions for Building on Your Best	137
Is Reading FUNdamental or Just Pure Torture?	138
I Feel the Need . . . the Need for Speed! Determining Your Personal Reading Rate	140
Why We Read	143
Your Don't Have to Be a Logodaedalian to Enjoy Words	143
It's Not Just a Door Stop: Using Your Dictionary	146
Improving Speed and Comprehension	147
WORLD OF WORK: Robin Baliszewski	**148**
Get to the Point, Would You! Finding the Topic and Main Ideas in Paragraphs and Sections	150
Doing It Right the First Time: SQ3R to the Rescue	154
I Think I've Got It! Testing Your Reading Comprehension Through Bloom	160
He Turned to Her and Ever So Gently . . . Reading for Pleasure	164
Blueprints for Change	165
CASE STUDY: Joey Luna	166
JOURNALS	168
ADVICE TO GO	169

6 LEARN — 171
Multiple Intelligences, Learning Styles, and Personality Typing

Where Are You . . . At This Moment	174
Goals . . . For Change	175
Questions for Building on Your Best	175
Understanding Your Strengths	176
Looking for Treasures: Discovering and Polishing Your Talents	176
WORLD OF WORK: Bryan Delph	**177**
A New Way of Looking at Yourself: Understanding Multiple Intelligences	180
Making it Work for You: Using Multiple Intelligences to Enhance Studying and Learning	181
Understanding Learning Styles Theory	183
What Can You Learn About Personality?	186
Why Personality Matters: Functions of Typology	189
Making Your Personality Work For You: Enhancing Your Learning	190
Blueprints for Change	195
CASE STUDY: LaDondo Johnson	196
JOURNALS	198
ADVICE TO GO	199

7 LISTEN — 201
The Art of Active Listening

Where Are You . . . At This Moment	204
Goals . . . For Change	205
Questions for Building on Your Best	205

The Importance of Listening	206
The Difference Between Listening and Hearing	206
What Did You Say? Obstacles to Listening	210
● **WORLD OF WORK: Maritza E. Rudisill**	**211**
Listening for Key Words, Phrases, and Hints	213
Listening When English Is Your Second Language: Suggestions for ESL Students	214
How Do I Get Others to Listen to Me? Tips for Creative Communicating	215
● *Blueprints for Change*	*217*
● CASE STUDY: Melpo Kardon	218
● JOURNALS	220
● ADVICE TO GO	221

8 RECORD — 223
Note-Taking Systems that Work

Where Are You . . . At This Moment	226
Goals . . . For Change	227
Questions for Building on Your Best	227
Why Take Notes?	228
Writing It Right: Tips for Effective Note Taking	228
● **WORLD OF WORK: Garcia Mills Tate**	**229**
You'll Be Seeing Stars: The L-Star System	230
Something for Everyone: Three Common Note-Taking Systems	233
It's as Simple as A, B, C—1, 2, 3: The Outline Technique	233
It's a Split Decision: The Cornell (Modified Cornell, Split Page, or T) System	234
Going Around in Circles: The Mapping System	235
What to Do When You Get Lost	237
Using Your Laptop Computer for Note Taking	238
● *Blueprints for Change*	*241*
● CASE STUDY: Rebekah Bicknell	242
● JOURNALS	244
● ADVICE TO GO	245

9 REMEMBER — 247
Empowering Your Memory

Where Are You . . . At This Moment	250
Goals . . . For Change	251
Questions for Building on Your Best	251
Why Study? I Can Fake It	252

The Importance of Your Study Environment	252
I Forgot to Remember! Understanding Memory	252
● **WORLD OF WORK: Coleman Peterson**	**253**
This Isn't Your Daddy's VCR: Using VCR3 to Increase Memory Power	257
What Helps? What Hurts? Attending to Your Memory	259
Ready, Set, Go! Memory and Studying	263
Studying with Small Children in the House	269
What Do You Mean the Test Is Tomorrow? Studying in a Crunch	270
● *Blueprints for Change*	*273*
● CASE STUDY: Martin Zavala	274
● JOURNALS	276
● ADVICE TO GO	277

10 ASSESS — 279
Strategies for Test Taking

Where Are You . . . At This Moment	282
Goals . . . For Change	283
Questions for Building on Your Best	283
Controlling Test Anxiety	284
Three Types of Responses to Test Questions	287
Test-Taking Strategies and Hints for Success	288
● **WORLD OF WORK: Zheng Gu**	**293**
Academic and Personal Integrity: Making the Right Decisions	296
● *Blueprints for Change*	*299*
● CASE STUDY: Oscar Bowser, Jr.	300
● JOURNALS	302
● ADVICE TO GO	303

11 THINK — 305
Critical- and Creative-Thinking Skills

Where Are You . . . At This Moment	308
Goals . . . For Change	309
Questions for Building on Your Best	309
Thinking About Thinking	310
What Is It Anyway? A Working Definition of Critical Thinking	310
When Will I Ever Use It? The Importance of Critical Thinking	311
A Plan for Critical Thinking: Making It Work for You	313
● **WORLD OF WORK: Glenn E. Montgomery**	**314**
Creative Thinking: From Ridiculous to Possible	326

- *Blueprints for Change* — 329
- CASE STUDY: Deepa Bhalla — 330
- JOURNALS — 332
- ADVICE TO GO — 333

12 COMMUNICATE — 335
Practical Steps for Writing and Speaking

- Where Are You . . . At This Moment — 338
- Goals . . . For Change — 339
- Questions for Building on Your Best — 339
- Your Chance to Shine — 340
- The Power of Words — 340
- WORLD OF WORK: Roger Dow — 341
- Step 1: Topic Selection — 344
- Step 2: Audience Analysis — 345
- Step 3: Writing a Thesis Statement — 346
- Step 4: Researching Your Speech or Paper — 347
- Step 5: Organizing Your Paper or Speech — 350
- Step 6: Writing Your Paper or Speech — 352
- Step 7: Documenting Your Paper or Speech — 358
- Step 8: Outlining Your Notes for Delivery — 360
- Step 9: Using Audiovisual Aids — 361
- Step 10: Rehearsal and Delivery — 362
- *Blueprints for Change* — 365
- CASE STUDY: Lauren Stock — 366
- JOURNALS — 368
- ADVICE TO GO — 369

13 RELATE — 371
A Celebration of People, Cultures, and Self

- Where Are You . . . At This Moment — 374
- Goals . . . For Change — 375
- Questions for Building on Your Best — 375
- Relationships — 376
- Why Are Relationships Important? — 376
- Communities — 376
- Types of Relationships — 377
- ACTIVITY: Building a Friend — 379
- When Relationships Go Sour — 381
- Sexual Harassment — 381
- Rape — 383
- Relationships with Diverse Others — 384
- The Ties That Bind: Components of Culture — 385
- Who Are You? — 387
- Conflict Is Inevitable: How Do You Deal with It? — 388
- The Golden Rule for Celebrating Diversity — 390
- WORLD OF WORK: James E. Farmer — 394
- Slamming the Door on Hate: What Can You Do to Make a Difference? — 397
- *Blueprints for Change* — 399
- CASE STUDY: Forrest Evans — 400
- JOURNALS — 402
- ADVICE TO GO — 403

14 LIVE — 405
A Plan for Wellness, Stress Reduction, and Personal Responsibility

- Where Are You . . . At This Moment — 408
- Goals . . . For Change — 409
- Questions for Building on Your Best — 409
- What Does It Mean to Be Healthy? — 410
- The Mind, Soul, and Body: A Holistic Approach to Wellness — 410
- The Mind's Effect on Wellness — 410
- The Soul's Effect on Wellness — 412
- The Body's Effect on Wellness — 414
- Are You What You Eat? The Body and Food — 415
- Stress and Wellness — 416
- WORLD OF WORK: Charles Steve Spearman — 417
- What You Do Matters: Personal Responsibility and Wellness — 419
- I Love the Night Life: It's All the Rave! — 420
- Out on a Binge: When Drinking Goes Awry — 423
- Goin' Out of My Head Over You: The Residual Damage of Drugs and Alcohol — 424
- Sexually Transmitted Diseases — 424
- ACTIVITY: Your Action Plan for Wellness — 429
- *Blueprints for Change* — 431
- CASE STUDY: Natasha Yearwood — 432
- JOURNALS — 434
- ADVICE TO GO — 435

15 DREAM — 437
Career and Life Planning

- Where Are You . . . At This Moment — 440
- Goals . . . For Change — 441

Questions for Building on Your Best	441
What Am I Going to Do for the Rest of My Life?	442
The Coming Job Boom: Your Future Looks Incredibly Bright	442
Your Career May Change Frequently: Prepare for Flexibility	443
● **ACTIVITY: What Do You Know About What You Want to Become?**	**444**
Career Planning: Where the Jobs Are	446
Plan for a Career—Not a Series of Jobs	447
What Do You Want to Be When You Grow Up? Your Career Self-Study	447
Help Me: I'm Undeclared	452
Nine Steps to Career Decision Making	453

Networking: The Overlooked Source for Career Development	454
Mentors	455
● **WORLD OF WORK: Tanya Stuart Overdorf**	**455**
Bringing It All Together	457
● *Blueprints for Change*	459
● **CASE STUDY: Nailah Robinson**	**460**
● **JOURNALS**	**462**
● **ADVICE TO GO**	**463**

GLOSSARY	G-0
REFERENCES	R-0
INDEX	I-0

An Invitation. . .

Today, you will begin preparing for the many opportunities and adventures that lie ahead. You might realistically think of this time as "the first day of the rest of your life." Regardless of what you have experienced in the past—good or bad—this is a new day and it brings many exciting opportunities and challenges. It might take a while, but soon you will begin to understand yourself better, and as a result, you will also begin to understand others.

The secret to life is not finding yourself. The secret to life is creating yourself. —GEORGE BERNARD SHAW

Chances are good that you have already begun to change and grow. Perhaps you have begun to understand that what you are at this moment is not what you were yesterday, and is not what you will be tomorrow. All your life you have been evolving and becoming. The pace is about to pick up! Some days you may feel like you are on a runaway train. At first, you might think you can't keep up. Be patient with yourself as you focus on discovering your greatest strengths and shaping your ambitions.

Throughout your college career you will always be changing and creating yourself anew. As you work toward becoming who and what you want to become—the person you were meant to become—we invite you to build on your best.

We also invite you to . . .

BUILD ON YOUR OPEN-MINDEDNESS

A truly educated person learns to consider a person's character rather than the color of one's skin, or one's religion, or sexual orientation, or ethnic background. As you become more open-minded, you will begin to work on understanding before judging, reasoning before reacting, and delving deeper before condemning. As you build on your best character, strive hard to develop a habit of practicing open-mindedness.

BUILD ON YOUR COMPETENCE

You have already established a certain level of competence or you wouldn't be here. Now is the time to push yourself to learn more than you ever have before. Your future depends on the knowledge you are gaining today. Settling for mediocrity can be the death of the search for your greatest self. Work to acquire knowledge about the world, other cultures, events that impact and shape humanity, and most importantly, work hard to understand yourself and your place in the world.

BUILD ON YOUR ABILITY TO QUESTION

It has been said, "Sometimes, the question is more important than the answer." As you move through the coming months and years, don't be afraid to ask questions of others, especially your professors. Questioning is the first step in becoming a more critical and logical thinker. If you ask the right questions and listen, you will learn.

BUILD ON YOUR SUPPORTIVE NATURE

Education is more than facts and figures. It involves learning how to support others in the world around you—learning how to be a member of a larger community than your own. An ancient Chinese quote may help you in building on your best supportive nature: "Help thy brother's boat across and lo, Thine own has reached the shore."

...to build on your best

BUILD ON YOUR ABILITY TO GIVE

As you build on your best, you will have more to give than ever before. Writer and educator Leo Buscaglia once said that you want to make yourself the most creative, educated, wonderful, caring person in the world so that you can give it away. Strive hard to find a need in the world and devote your best to it. It's a strange but true phenomenon—the more you give, the more you get.

BUILD ON YOUR NEED TO BE CHALLENGED

The easy road will never lead to greatness or to your best. Winston Churchill said, "It is from adversity that we gain greatness." When you are struggling, remember that you are getting stronger. You are preparing for becoming the person you were meant to be. As you register for classes, search for professors, volunteer for projects, and explore internships, choose those that will challenge you, make you stretch, and ultimately lead you to another level in the search to be your best.

BUILD ON YOUR CREATIVITY

In building on your best, don't forget to let your creativity shine. You may say that you are not a "creative person," but that would be an unfair statement. Everyone has creative genius on some level. By allowing yourself to wander, dream, explore, and yes, even fail, your creativity will develop and soar. Try new ideas, experience new adventures, engage in activities with new people. Build your creativity!

BUILD ON YOUR ABILITY TO BALANCE

No ONE thing will ever bring you joy, peace, or prosperity. Try to include family, friends, cultural events, social activities, work, and service in your daily life. Seek balance between work and play. You will never be happy unless there is a sense of balance in your life. Harmony and balance in life help you to be your best.

BUILD ON YOUR PROSPERITY

While money won't make you happy, you need a certain amount to take care of yourself and your family. Your definition of success may or may not involve money and material possessions. It is not a sin, however, to pursue financial success. Prosperity can afford you the opportunity to give back to your community, your family, and fellow citizens in need. Money, used properly, can bring great happiness if you share it with others.

BUILD ON YOUR SUCCESS

You need to define exactly what success means to you so you know what you are working toward. Whatever success is for you, pursue it with all of the passion and energy you have. Set your goals high and work hard to create a life that you can ultimately look back on with pride, satisfaction, and joy and be able to say, "I did my best. I have no regrets."

build on your best

To Our Students

We chose the title *Cornerstone* because a cornerstone is the fundamental basis for something—the first building block—laid to establish a firm foundation. Often, a ceremony takes place when a cornerstone is laid and sometimes treasured documents and valuables are placed within the cornerstone of the building. *Today is a celebration; a celebration of your success,* your future, your hopes, your challenges, your potential and, yes, a celebration for building on your best.

It is our hope that this book will help you to see the possibilities of your future, anticipate and cope with new situations, guide you through difficult days, discover more about yourself and your unique gifts, develop study and learning habits that help you succeed in every class, come to understand and appreciate more about diverse cultures, hone your creative and critical thinking skills, and learn more about careers and the countless opportunities available to you. It is our ultimate hope that you will use this book as a steppingstone to obtain your college degree.

As you begin reading *Cornerstone,* pay special attention to the features because these will assist you in mastering the content and applying the information to other classes and "real world" situations.

Journaling. Each chapter will offer you many chances to stop and reflect on where you have been, where you are now, and where you want to be—insights discovered through "**At This Moment**" and other journaling opportunities. You will be asked questions about your personal and academic life. You will be asked to interact with other members of your college community and to share your own views and personal experiences. By participating in these activities, your college experience will be enriched.

Blueprints for Change. The "Blueprints for Change" are perhaps the most important feature in the text because they allow you the opportunity to apply the chapter's content to your specific goals, major, and dreams.

Critical Thinking. This chapter will help you prepare for classes and projects from biology to philosophy to English. It will also help you think more critically when making major purchases, establishing relationships, and making major life decisions regarding your future.

Reading Comprehension. This chapter will help you learn to read faster and more efficiently. As the semester progresses and assignments pour in, learning to read more effectively and better comprehend the texts, journals, magazines, and the Internet will be essential. This chapter can literally turn your academic life around.

Real Stories. Academic concepts make more sense when put into real life situations. *Cornerstone* provides two features that show how these concepts relate directly to your life. Each chapter contains a "Case Study" that shares the stories of actual students and a "World of Work" feature that allows you to interact with professionals from companies across the country.

To the Instructor

What *Cornerstone* can do for your students . . . We have spent the past ten years researching, reading, exploring and, most important, listening. We have listened to colleagues at our respective institutions, to students from around America, and we have listened to *you*. We are honored and privileged that you have chosen to use *Cornerstone: Building on Your Best, Fourth Edition*. We thank you for your confidence in this book, in the *Cornerstone* program, and in us. We think that you will be excited and pleased with the additions and changes that have resulted from your advice.

You will find new and exciting features in this edition along with your favorite and tested material from the past three editions. In the past, the focus of *Cornerstone* has been:

- Self-discovery
- Change
- Motivation
- Goal setting
- Personal responsibility

This focus has not changed. We still believe that the fundamental success of any first-year course is helping students understand the importance of being responsible for their own learning, their own success, and indeed, their own actions. We have enhanced activities to help students *build on their best*. The following sections discuss the salient features of this edition.

Critical Thinking

The chapter "Think: Critical- and Creative-Thinking Skills" has been totally revised and updated to include

- **practical applications** for critical and creative thinking
- **specific examples** of when critical and creative thinking are needed in college, work, and life,
- how critical thinking can assist with **decision making, problem solving, and conflict management**
- applications for distinguishing **fact from opinion**

Retention

The chapter "Persist: Things You Need to Know About College But Might Never Ask" grew from listening to students and colleagues across the United States discuss the challenges that first-year students face beyond academics. This chapter deals frankly with the topics of:

- college policy
- grading
- success centers on campus
- personal decorum
- counselor–student relationships
- faculty–student relationships
- financial aid
- campus safety

The chapter "Read: Building Active Reading and Comprehension Skills" was developed to help students cope with one of the fastest growing and most serious academic problems on campus today—comprehension and reading speed. For years, we have heard colleagues across the country lament about students' inability to read and comprehend texts. This chapter covers material such as:

- dictionary usage
- vocabulary building
- finding main ideas
- improving concentration

This chapter also includes a reading speed calculator.

Application

This edition also has a totally revised end-of-chapter section. Materials and activities at the end of each chapter include the following:

- **Blueprints for Change:** This revised feature now includes "Reflection," an opportunity for students to read the authors' final thoughts on the chapter's content, and "Get Real," in which readers are asked to apply chapter content to academic life, social settings, and careers.
- **Case Study:** Real college students from across the United States have contributed their stories related to the chapter content. Students will have the opportunity to read the case study and answer questions about the situation and apply the case to their own lives.
- **At This Moment:** Students will have the opportunity to reflect back on their goals for the chapter, evaluate the progress made toward those goals, and revise them to be more realistic and concrete.
- **Online Journal:** By visiting the Cornerstone Website, students will be able to submit journal entries directly to you related to pre-set questions or questions/situations that you assign.
- **Advice to Go, Cornerstones:** This succinct poster offers one-sentence summary statements of the chapter's most important points.

Again, it is with sincere gratitude that we welcome you to the *Cornerstone* program. Thank you for choosing *Cornerstone* and know that we wish you much success in your course.

About the Authors

ROBERT M. SHERFIELD, PH.D.

Robert Sherfield has been teaching public speaking, theater, and study skills and working with first-year orientation programs for over 20 years. Currently, he is a professor at the Community College of Southern Nevada, teaching student success, public speaking, technical writing, and drama.

An award-winning educator, Robb was recently named Educator of the Year at the Community College of Southern Nevada. He twice received the Distinguished Teacher of the Year Award from the University of South Carolina Union, and has received numerous other awards and nominations for outstanding classroom instruction and advisement. In 1998, 1999, and 2000, he was nominated by students for, and named to, *Who's Who Among American Educators*.

Robb's extensive work with student success programs includes experience with the design and implementation of these programs—including one program that was presented at the International Conference on the Freshman Year Experience in Newcastle upon Tyne, England.

In addition to his coauthorship of *Cornerstone: Building on Your Best*, he has also coauthored *Roadways to Success* (Prentice Hall, 2001), the trade book *365 Things I Learned in College* (Allyn & Bacon, 1996), *Capstone: Succeeding Beyond College* (Prentice Hall, 2001), *Case Studies for the First Year: An Odyssey into Critical Thinking and Problem Solving* (Prentice Hall, 2004), and *The Everything® Self-Esteem Book* (Adams Media, 2004).

Robb's interest in student success began with his own first year in college. Low SAT scores and a mediocre high school ranking denied him entrance into college. With the help of a success program, Robb was granted entrance into college, and went on to earn a doctorate and become a college faculty member. He has always been interested in the social, academic, and cultural development of students, and sees this book as his way to contribute to the positive development of first-year students across the nation.

Visit www.robertsherfield.com.

RHONDA J. MONTGOMERY, PH.D.

Rhonda Montgomery is an Associate Professor in the William F. Harrah College of Hotel Administration at the University of Nevada, Las Vegas, and has been teaching in higher education for 18 years. Rhonda has been responsible for developing and incorporating first-year orientation/study skills curricula into existing introductory courses and programs.

Currently, Rhonda is teaching a first-year orientation/study skills course as well as hospitality education. Because she believes in the holistic development of first-year students, she volunteers to teach first-year students each semester and uses a variety of experiences such as field trips, exercises, and case studies to aid in their retention and success.

Rhonda has received several awards for her teaching and advising. She is also an active member of Phi Eta Sigma, a National Freshman Honorary

Association. Rhonda is the coauthor of seven texts, including *Cornerstone: Building on Your Best, Roadways to Success* (Prentice Hall, 2001), *365 Things I Learned in College* (Allyn & Bacon, 1996) *Capstone: Succeeding Beyond College* (Prentice Hall, 2001), and *Case Studies for the First Year: An Odyssey into Critical Thinking and Problem Solving* (Prentice Hall, 2004). She has also presented at The National Conference on the Freshman Year Experience and spoken extensively to first-year students and educators about building success into their curriculum.

PATRICIA G. MOODY, PH.D.

Patricia G. Moody is Dean of the College of Hospitality, Retail and Sport Management at the University of South Carolina, where she has been a faculty member for over 25 years. An award-winning educator, Pat has been honored as Distinguished Educator of the Year at her college and as Collegiate Teacher of the Year by the National Business Education Association, and has been a top-five finalist for the Amoco Teaching Award at the University of South Carolina. In 1994, she was awarded the prestigious John Robert Gregg Award, the highest honor in her field of over 100,000 educators.

Pat frequently speaks to multiple sections of first-year students, incorporating personal development content from her trademark speech, "Fly Like an Eagle," as well as numerous strategies for building self-esteem and for achieving success in college. She also works with first-year classes on subjects such as goal setting, priority management, and diversity.

A nationally known motivation speaker, Pat has spoken in 42 states, has been invited to speak in several foreign countries, and frequently keynotes national and regional conventions. She has presented "Fly Like an Eagle" to thousands of people, from Olympic athletes to corporate executives to high school students. Her topics include Thriving in the Changing Corporate Environment, Perception Is Everything: Powerful Communications Strategies, Gold Star Customer Service, and The Great Balancing Act: Managing Time at Home and at Work.

An avid sports fan, she follows Gamecock athletics and chairs the University of South Carolina Athletics Advisory Committee.

Acknowledgments

Professional Acknowledgments

First, we would like to thank the following individuals for their support: Dr. Carol Harter, President, University of Nevada–Las Vegas; Dr. Charles Mosley, Department Chair, Community College of Southern Nevada; Dr. Robert Palinchak, Vice President, Community College of Southern Nevada; Dr. Stuart Mann, Dean, University of Nevada–Las Vegas; Dr. Jerome Odom, Provost, University of South Carolina; Dr. Ron Remington, President, Community College of Southern Nevada; Professor Patti Shock, Department Chair, University of Nevada–Las Vegas; Dr. Don Smith, Dean of Arts and Letters, Community College of Southern Nevada; Dr. Andrew A. Sorensen, President, University of South Carolina.

Contributor Acknowledgments

Our sincere thanks to Paul Billings, Community College of Southern Nevada, for *At This Moment* assessments; Janet Lindner, Midlands Technical College, for developing the *Companion Website;* Julie Boch, Massasoit Community College, for consulting on the development of the *Online Class Component.*

Our sincere thanks also to the following faculty, who recommended students for the case studies: Julie Boch, Massasoit Community College; Irma Camacho, El Paso Community College; Chloe Carson, Southwest Texas State University; Sharon Cordell, Roane State University; JoAnn Credle, Northern Virginia Community College; Faye Johnson, Middle Tennessee State University; Janet Lindner, Midlands Technical College; Cheryl Rohrbaugh, Northern Virginia Community College; JoAnne Reinke, Central Missouri State University; Pat Thomas, Middle Tennessee State University; Anna E. Ward, Miami-Dade Community College; Kay Young, Jamestown Community College; Marie Zander, New York Institute of Technology.

We offer our heartfelt thanks to our contributors for *World of Work:* Brian Epps, Barona Valley Ranch Resort and Casino; Todd Houston, Alexander Graham Bell Association for the Deaf and Hard of Hearing; Andre Bauer, Lt. Governor, South Carolina; Tim Rice, Waddell and Reed Financial Services; Robin Baliszewski, Pearson Education/Prentice Hall; Bryan Delph, BPH Billition; Maritza Rudisill, Disneyland; Garcia Tate, University of South Carolina; Coleman Peterson; WalMart Stores, Inc.; Zheng Gu, University of Nevada–Las Vegas; Glenn Montgomery, Montgomery Consultants; Roger Dow, Marriott International; James Farmer, General Motors; Steve Spearman, Bank One; and Tonya Overdorf, Attorney, Indianapolis, IN.

And thanks to our students who shared their real-life stories for Case Studies: Tomer Perry, University of Nevada, Las Vegas; Jamie Juul, Jamestown Community College; Vanessa Santos, Miami Dade Community College; Coretta Hooks, University of South Carolina; Joey Luna, El Paso Community College; LaDondo Johnson, Houston Community College; Melpo Kardon, Central Missouri State University; Rebekah Bicknell, Roane State University; Martin Zavala, Southwest Texas State University; Oscar Bowser, Midlands Technical College; Deepa Bhalla, New York Institute of Technology; Lauren Stock, Massasoit

Community College; Forrest Evans, University of Maryland, University College; Natasha Yearwood, Community College of Southern Nevada; and Nailah Robinson, Northern Virginia Community College.

Our Wonderful and Insightful Reviewers

For the Fourth Edition. Fred Amador, Phoenix College; Kathy Bryan, Daytona Beach Community College; Dorothy Chase, Community College of Southern Nevada; JoAnn Credle, Northern Virginia Community College; Betty Fortune, Houston Community College; Doroteo Franco Jr., El Paso Community College; Cynthia Garrard, Massasoit Community College; Joel Jessen, Eastfield College; Peter Johnston, Massasoit Community College; Steve Konowalow, Community College of Southern Nevada; Janet Lindner, Midlands Technical College; Carmen McNeil, Solano College; Joan O'Connor, New York Institute of Technology; Mary Pepe, Valencia Community College; Bennie Perdue, Miami-Dade Community College; Ginny Peterson-Tennant, Miami Dade Community College; Anna E. Ward, Miami-Dade Community College; Wistar M. Withers, Northern Virginia Community College; and Marie Zander, New York Institute of Technology.

For the Previous Editions. Joanne Bassett, Shelby State Community College; Sandra M. Bovain-Lowe, Cumberland Community College; Carol Brooks, GMI Engineering and Management Institute; Elaine H. Byrd, Utah Valley State College; Janet Cutshall, Sussex County Community College; Deborah Daiek, Wayne State University; David DeFrain, Central Missouri State University; Leslie L. Duckworth, Florida Community College at Jacksonville; Marnell Hayes, Lake City Community College; Elzora Holland, University of Michigan, Ann Arbor; Earlyn G. Jordan, Fayetteville State University; John Lowry-King, Eastern New Mexico University; Charlene Latimer; Michael Laven, University of Southwestern Louisiana; Judith Lynch, Kansas State University; Susan Magun-Jackson, The University of Memphis; Charles William Martin, California State University, San Bernardino; Jeffrey A. Miller; Ronald W. Johnsrud, Lake City Community College; Joseph R. Krzyzanowski, Albuquerque TVI; Ellen Oppenberg, Glendale Community College; Lee Pelton, Charles S. Mott Community College; Robert Rozzelle, Wichita State University; Penny Schempp, Western Iowa Community College; Betty Smith, University of Nebraska at Kearney; James Stepp, University of Maine at Presque Isle; Charles Washington, Indiana University–Purdue University; and Katherine A. Wenen-Nesbit, Chippewa Valley Technical College.

The Creative and Supportive Team

Without the support and encouragement of these people at Prentice Hall, this book would not be possible. Our sincere thanks to Robin Baliszewski, Jeff Johnston, Sande Johnson, Christina Quadhamer, Cecilia Johnson, Kim Lundy, and Erin Anderson.

And finally, to a few people whose creative talents have helped us greatly over the years: Nancy Forsythe of Pearson Education/Allyn and Bacon, who gave us a chance; Gay Pauley of Holcomb Hathaway and John Wincek and Rhonda Wincek of Aerocraft Charter Art Service, who continually amaze us with their design and production talents; and Amy Gehl, Bev Kraus, and others at Carlisle Communications, our typesetter.

CORNERSTONE

Building on Your Best

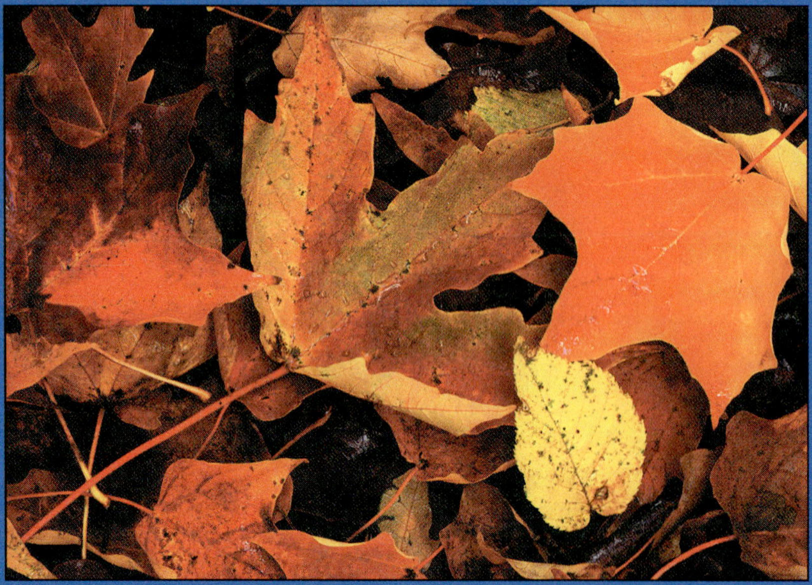

1 Change

Life is about change, and about movement, and about becoming something other than what you are at this very moment.

CHAPTER 1
CHANGE

Mark was the son of textile workers. Both of his parents had worked in the cotton mill for almost 30 years. They lived in the rural south about 35 miles from the nearest metropolitan area. His high school graduated a small number of students yearly. Mark had decided to attend a community college some 30 miles from home for his first two years and then transfer to a larger, four-year college. Money, time, grades, goals, and family commitments led to his decision.

Mark was not a good student in high school. He finished with a D– average and his SAT scores and class rank *were in the lowest 25th percentile.* In fact, initially he had been *denied entrance to the community college.* The college granted him provisional acceptance only if he enrolled in, and successfully completed, a summer preparatory program. During the summer, Mark enrolled in the prep program, *never realizing what lay ahead.*

Mark's first class that semester was English. The professor walked in, handed out the syllabus, called the roll, and began to lecture. Lord Byron was the topic for the day. The professor sat on a stool by the window, leaned his elbow on the ledge, and sipped a cup of coffee as he told the story of how Byron's foot had been damaged at birth. He continued to weave the details of Byron's life poetically, through quotes and parables, until the 50-minute period had quietly slipped away. After an hour's break, Mark headed across campus for history. The professor entered with a dust storm behind her. She went over the syllabus, and before the class had a chance to blink, she was involved in the first lecture. "The cradle of civilization," she began, "was Mesopotamia." The class scurried to find notebooks and pens to begin taking notes. *Already they were behind, Mark included.* Exactly 47 minutes after she had begun to speak, the professor took her first breath. "You are in history now. You elected to take this class and you will follow my rules," she told the first-year students sitting in front of her. "You are not to be late, you are to come to this class prepared, and you are to read your homework. If you do what I ask you to do, you will learn more about Western civilization than you ever thought possible. *If you do not keep up with me, you will not know if you are in Egypt, Mesopotamia, or pure hell!* Class dismissed!"

Without a moment to spare, Mark ran to the other end of campus for his next class. He walked into the room in a panic, fearing he was late. To his surprise, the instructor was not yet in class. *The class waited for more than 10 minutes before the professor entered.* "You need to sign this roster and read chapter one for Wednesday," he said. "You can pick up a syllabus on your way out." *Mark was shocked. Was the class over?* What about the bell? The students in the class looked at each other with dismay and quietly left the room, wondering what Wednesday would hold. On the 30-mile trip home, Mark's mind was filled with new thoughts . . . *Lord Byron, Mesopotamia, professors who talked too*

4

Preparing for and Dealing with Change

fast, professors who did not talk at all, the cost of tuition, the size of the library. He knew that something was different, *something had changed.* He couldn't put his finger on it. It would be years later before he would realize that the change was not his classes, not his schedule, not the people, not the professors—but himself; *Mark had changed.* In one day, he had tasted something intoxicating, something that was addictive. *He had tasted a new world.*

> **Mark was not a good student in high school. He finished with a D- average...**

Mark had to go to work that afternoon, and even his job had changed. He had always known that he did not want to spend the rest of his life in the factory, but this day the feeling was stronger. His job was not enough, his family was not enough, the farm on which he had been raised was not enough anymore. *There was a new light for Mark, and he knew that because of one day in college, he would never be the same.* It was like tasting Godiva chocolate for the first time—Hershey's kisses were no longer enough. It was like seeing the ocean for the first time and knowing that the millpond would never be the same. *He couldn't go back. What he knew before was simply not enough.*

My name is Robert Mark Sherfield, and 27 years later, as I coauthor your text, I am still addicted to that new world. Spartanburg Methodist College changed my life, and I am still changing—with every day, every new book I read, every new class I teach, every new person I meet, and every new place to which I travel, I am changing.

QUESTIONS FOR REFLECTION

Consider responding to these questions online in the Questions for Reflection module of the Companion Website.

1. Mark knew that his life was changed from the first day of college. You may not have experienced this type of change yet, but look ahead a few months or even years. What changes do you hope college will help make in your life?

2. What were your expectations for your first days of college? Contrast your expectations of your first days with what you actually experienced.

3. Discuss the class you currently take that most excites you about learning.

Where are you... AT THIS MOMENT

Before reading this chapter, take a moment and respond to the following 10 questions. Consider each one carefully before answering, and then respond by circling the number in the appropriate box. When you have answered the questions, add your points and find your total score on the feedback chart below.

STATEMENT	STRONGLY DISAGREE	DISAGREE	DON'T KNOW	AGREE	STRONGLY AGREE	SCORE
1. I am aware of the expectations that my school and teachers have of me.	1	2	3	4	5	
2. I don't know what I want to get out of college.	5	4	3	2	1	
3. I don't foresee many changes in my life and myself as a result of college experiences.	5	4	3	2	1	
4. I am enthusiastic about the challenges and opportunities that will be presented to me in college.	1	2	3	4	5	
5. I enjoy the challenge of learning new things.	1	2	3	4	5	
6. I have difficulty adapting and adjusting to changes in my life.	5	4	3	2	1	
7. I am confident in my ability to integrate my study habits, computer skills, and interpersonal skills to be successful in school.	1	2	3	4	5	
8. I have thought about what it means to be "successful" in college.	1	2	3	4	5	
9. Being open-minded about the subjects I will be exposed to in school is not important to being a successful student.	5	4	3	2	1	
10. I avoid asking other people for help when I need it.	5	4	3	2	1	
TOTAL VALUE						

SUMMARY

10–17 Your ability to cope with change is limited, and your expectations of your college experiences are unfocused. You will need to spend significant time exploring your expectations for your school career, as well as developing strategies to help cope with the coming life changes.

18–25 Your expectations for your college experiences are somewhat unclear, and your ability to prepare for and adjust to change is limited. Your direction in school needs refinement, and you'd benefit from having strategies to help cope with the changes you will face.

26–34 You are average in your level of coping skills for dealing with life changes. You likely have a general notion of what you want to get for yourself as a result of your college education. Some fine-tuning of your expectations and adaptive strategies would likely be helpful.

35–42 Your ability to deal effectively with life changes is above average. You likely have a solid sense of why you are in college and what you want to get out of being in school.

43–50 You are exceptional in your ability to adapt to changes, and you know how to recover from setbacks. You likely have a clear understanding of what college life has in store for you, and you are eager to meet those experiences head-on.

Goals . . . FOR CHANGE

Based on your total points, what is one goal you would like to achieve related to making a positive change in your life?

Goal _____
_____

List three actions you can take that might help you move closer to realizing this goal.

1. _____
2. _____
3. _____

Questions FOR BUILDING ON YOUR BEST

As you read this chapter, consider the following questions. At the end of the chapter, you should be able to answer all of them. You are encouraged to ask a few questions of your own. Consider asking your classmates or professors to assist you.

1. Why is it important to learn how to usher change into my life and cope with the unexpected changes that may come my way?
2. Why is thinking about and preparing for change a positive way to handle and cope with some of the negative side effects that may accompany change?
3. What attitudes and/or behaviors do I currently have that hinder my ability to change?
4. What steps can I take to develop a positive attitude about change?
5. What concrete steps can I take to change my opinions and behaviors to ensure success in college and life?

What additional questions might you have about change in college and life?

1. _____
2. _____
3. _____

Why College?

Well, here you are, in college. Time to party? Time to get away from the children? Time to find a significant other? Time to study? Time to ponder the meaning of life? All these may be reasons to attend college. There are more than three and a half million first-year students in the nation's colleges right now; each one may have a different reason for being there. Some students are pursuing a high-paying job, developing a specific skill, retraining for the job market, following an old dream. Others are recently divorced and trying to acquire skills that were not taught 15 years ago. Some are in college because of pressure from their parents. And yes, there are those who say that they are in college to party and have a good time. Perhaps you've met a few of them already. And let us not forget the tens of thousands who say they are enrolled to experience developmental, interactive pedagogy and scientific relativity . . . NOT!

The college experience is different for every person. Some people love every minute of it, some people see it as a necessary evil to getting that wonderful job. Some see the college experience as a way of expanding horizons, and others see it as a two- or four- (or five-) year prison sentence!

List the major reasons why you are in college today. Be honest with yourself!

1. _____
2. _____
3. _____
4. _____

The college experience is different for every person.

Were all four blanks easy to fill? Did you do it quickly? As you discuss these reasons in class, you will find that many of your classmates are at-

> The real object of education is to give one resources that will endure as long as life endures; habits that time will not destroy; occupations that will render sickness tolerable, solitude pleasant, age venerable, life more dignified and useful, and death less terrible. —S. SMITH

tending college for many of the same reasons you listed. If your class holds true to form, most of your classmates responded, "to get a better job and make more money."

According to *The Chronicle of Higher Education* (Aug. 2003), one of the leading research sources in higher education, 70.5 percent of students polled stated that their **primary reason** for going to college was "to be able to get a better job" and "make more money" (p. 17).

Depending on how you approach college, it can, and should, be one of the most exciting, rewarding, challenging, and wonderful times of your life. Certainly, college brings about stressful times, tearful times, and life-altering times, but college can give you rewards of the mind, rewards of the soul, and yes, rewards of a more lucrative future.

According to the 2000 U.S. Census, Department of Commerce, people with a bachelor's degree earn considerably more money each year than people without the degree. Men with a bachelor's degree earn $31,647 per year more than men with only a high school diploma. Women with a bachelor's degree earn $16,256 more than women with only a high school diploma.

As you review the annual earning chart shown in Figure 1.1, you may find the graph somewhat shocking. The first thing that you will notice is that income increases with education, but perhaps the most eye-opening revelation is the degree to which the salaries differ by gender. Look at the Professional Degree column. Men with a professional degree earn almost double the salary of women with a professional degree.

Involvement in extracurricular activities can enhance your college experience and help you adjust to change.

Annual earnings by education level and gender. — FIGURE 1.1

Education Level	Female	Male
less than 9th grade	$10,561	18,282
9th–12th grade	12,728	24,988
H.S. graduate (includes equivalency)	18,501	33,276
Some college, no degree	23,514	41,595
Associate degree	25,486	45,073
Bachelor's degree	34,757	64,923
Master's degree	45,025	77,184
Professional degree	59,291	107,943
Doctorate degree	54,962	92,440

1 unit = $10,000/year

Source: U.S. Census, Dept. of Commerce, 2001.

Below, list a few reasons why you feel men and women have such salary differences.

_____
_____
_____

This discrepancy in salary can be disheartening, but the figures have grown closer over the years. Granted, there are still monumental steps to be taken, but as more and more women enter the "traditional fields" once held exclusively by men, and as more and more companies recognize and adjust the discrepancy, hopefully, the gap will close even further in the near future.

By focusing on money in this section, we do not mean to suggest that the only reason for attending college is to make more money. As a matter of fact, we feel that it is a secondary reason. Many people without college degrees earn great money each year. Many reasons beyond money constitute success, contribute to happiness, and provide altruistic appeal.

One response you probably didn't find on your list of reasons for attending college—or on the lists of your classmates—is "I want to change." Although most people do not come to college for the express purpose of changing, change is certain to happen during your college years. The key to dealing with change is to realize that change is the only thing in this world that is assured, short of death and taxes.

Whatever your reasons for attending college, if you embrace the notion that change is going to occur and respond to change by guiding it along, nurturing your new relationships with peers and professors, learning to study effectively, becoming involved in campus activities, and opening your mind to different views and ideologies, college will be a "moment in time" that you can carry with you for the rest of your life. You will be building on your best.

The Significance of Your College Experience

In your lifetime many events, people, places, and things will alter your views, personality, goals, and livelihood. Few decisions, people, or travels will have a greater influence on the rest of your life than your decision to attend college and the years you spend in structured higher learning. College can mean hopes realized, dreams fulfilled, and the breaking down of social and economic walls that may be holding you captive.

Every student entering an institution of higher learning will soon understand that education is a two-way street. Not only do you have expectations of your college, but also your college has expectations of you. Successful students understand quickly that what was expected from them in high school is vastly different from what is expected of them in college.

The successful completion of college requires that you accept substantially more responsibility for your own learning. By accepting admission into the institution you are attending, you have voluntarily agreed to be a part of their community. This agreement means that you have a responsibility to follow the institution's codes of academic and moral conduct. You have also committed yourself to the pursuit of knowledge and respecting your fellow classmates, faculty, administrators, and staff while adhering to the institution's procedures and guidelines.

Before reading further, jot down some thoughts about what you want to achieve in college, what you value about being in college, what you expect from your institution, and what your college expects from you.

While in college, I want to achieve . . .
___
___
___
___

Regardless of your background or reasons for attending college, the experience of change is something you'll share with everyone. Will you be able to open yourself up to new people and new situations?

I feel college is significant to my life because . . .
___
___
___
___

From my college, I expect . . .
___
___
___
___

Education is the knowledge of how to use the whole of oneself. Many use one or two faculties out of a score with which they are endowed. One is educated who knows how to make a tool of every faculty; how to open it, how to keep it sharp, and how to apply it to all practical purposes.   —H. W. BEECHER

My college expects me to . . .
___
___
___
___

WORLD OF WORK

Starting college is an instrumental change in your life. It is preparing you for all the possibilities ahead, but it cannot prepare you for the personal knowledge that you will gain as you mature and grow. When I consider how change has affected me, I realize that my career did not progress as I had planned while in college. During that time, I thought the changes I was experiencing were incredible and some of the most difficult of my life. But by enduring those changes, and accepting some of the hard lessons I've learned along the way because of them, I realize how much they helped me grow personally and professionally.

Change is such an important thing in our lives. Our whole destiny is affected by it. I think it is important that we consider change a friend, not an enemy. Sometimes, things that occur in our lives seem cruel, overwhelming, or hopeless, but they really are not. In my experience, change has always brought something positive. Sometimes, you have to look a little harder and give it time, but the growth experience is rewarding.

A career in the hospitality industry has always been something I have enjoyed. Years ago, many people believed that their careers would be like their fathers' and grandfathers'—they worked their entire lives at one company and then they retired with the gold watch. However, that is not the case anymore. I read lately in *The Wall Street Journal* that the average college graduate will experience 7 to 10 career changes during their work life—not just job changes, but career changes. That powerful statement indicates how necessary it is for a person to be able to adapt to change.

As I made my career choices and changes, I grew in ways I never imagined possible. For me personally, I seek knowledge. When I have mastered something in my current position, I tend to become restless and thirst for more knowledge. I think it is fine to recognize this as a need for change. If you cannot get what you are seeking in your current position, you need to explore how to achieve what you are looking for.

QUESTIONS FOR REFLECTION

Consider responding to these questions online in the World of Work module of the Companion Website.

1. What have you experienced in your life that at the time made you feel hopeless, but in reality became a growth opportunity?
2. What did this experience teach you about using change as a positive force in your life?
3. What do you have to do to prepare yourself for multiple career changes?

Brian R. Epps, *Executive Director of Hotel Operations,* Barona Valley Ranch Resort and Casino, San Diego, CA

Noted authors and experts on the first-year student experience John Gardner and Jerome Jewler (2000) suggest that students undergo several life-altering changes and developments during their college years. Some of the changes they cite are:

- Your self-esteem grows
- Your political sophistication increases
- Your intellectual interests expand
- Your views become more flexible
- You become more concerned with wellness and health care

Our observations of college students reveal these changes also. If your professor were to make a video of you as a first-year student and allow you to view it as a senior, you would be astounded at the changes in you. Beyond changes in appearance you would see development in attitudes, values, judgment, and character. Generally, college tends to teach students to be more gentle, more accepting, more open, and more willing to get involved in their community and to share their resources; often, college creates in students the desire to continue to learn. Many college professors utilize a class portfolio to grade a student's progress. Keeping your class portfolios will give you a visual record of your educational progress.

No one, not all the researchers in the world, not your authors, not your professors, not even your friends, can put a real value on the experience that college provides or the degree of change you will undergo. The value differs for each student, and it is private. You may share with others the benefits of your higher education, but fundamentally, the results of these years are quietly consumed by your character, your actions, and your values. Some people will change a little, some people will change a lot. For all, however, change is coming.

Take a moment to reflect on the opening story about Mark. How do you think his excitement and enthusiasm for starting his educational experience improved his chance for success? How much do you believe you are responsible for your success or failure in college? Why is your positive attitude regarding your education important to your success?

> **DID YOU KNOW?**
>
> **77.8%**
>
> The percentage of students who stated that their reason for attending college was "to learn more about things that interest me."
>
> Source: *The Chronicle of Higher Education*, 49(1), August 30, 2002.

What Do You Want?
THINKING ABOUT YOUR CHOICES

Today, you face many decisions. Some of them will affect the rest of your life. Some changes and decisions will be of your own making; others will be beyond your control. Some will be easily altered; others will hold for the long run.

Before you read further, think about where you are at this very moment and where you want to be in the coming years. Remember the quotation, "If you don't know where you are going, that's probably where you'll end up." The following activity is one of the first cornerstones of this book. It requires you to look at your current status, your peers, your past, and your aspirations and is intended to guide you in evaluating your life, attitudes, and thoughts. Take your time, be honest with yourself, and think in terms of realistic goals.

1. *Define success.*

   _____
   _____

2. *Name one person you deem successful. Why is that person successful?*

   _____
   _____

3. *List one accomplishment that might signify your success.*

_____
_____

4. *What will you have to change to achieve this accomplishment?*

_____
_____

5. *How will you approach these changes?*

_____
_____

6. *What part will your college experience and education play in helping you reach this accomplishment?*

_____
_____
_____

Changes in the Days to Come

One of the first changes you will notice about college is the degree of freedom you are given. There are no tardy notes to be sent to the principal's office, no hall passes, no mandates from the state regarding attendance, and, usually, no parent telling you to get up and get ready for school. You may have only one or two classes in a day. "Great!" you say, and maybe you're right. This freedom can be wonderful, but it can also be dangerous. Many people do their best when they are busy and have a limited amount of time to accomplish a task. College can give you more freedom than you are used to. You need to learn how to handle it quickly, before the freedom that is intended to liberate you destroys you. Learning how to set priorities for your time, money, and resources is a critical step to successfully handling this freedom. Chapter 4 will help you with priority management.

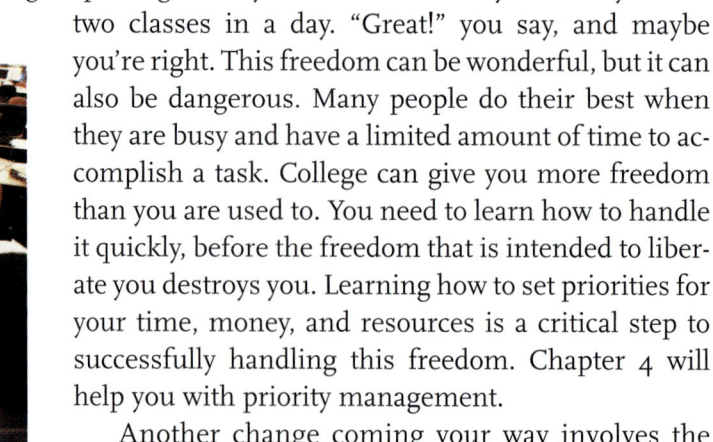

Another change coming your way involves the workload for your courses. The workload is likely to be greater than what you are used to. You may be assigned a significant amount of reading as homework. Although you may have only two classes in one

Understanding and using technology can help you research, write, and communicate.

day, the rule of thumb is that for every hour spent in class, a minimum of 2 hours should be spent in review and preparation for the next class. Quick math: if you are taking 5 classes and are in class for 15 hours per week, you need to spend 30 hours studying; this makes a 45-hour week—5 hours more than a normal work week for most people! Not I, you may say, and you may be right. It all depends on how wisely you use your time and how difficult the work is. However tempting, don't make the mistake of putting off assignments for very long. Waiting until the last minute may cause serious problems for you sooner or later; probably sooner. And, think about your schedule before you register to make sure that you have enough time to deal with the demands of the courses you have selected. Many professors now have their syllabi on the Web, thus enabling you to review their course requirements before you schedule their class. Talk to friends, residence hall assistants, and returning students about your schedule; see what they think about it. Make informed decisions about your class schedules.

> You gain strength, experience, and confidence by every experience where you really stop to look fear in the face. . . .You must do the thing you think you cannot. —ELEANOR ROOSEVELT

As you begin to understand the differences between high school and college classes, the increased amount of time required, and other changing expectations, review Figure 1.2 and compare these differences and expectations to high school, college, and work environments. As you study the chart, notice the difference in possible penalties from high school to college to work.

Another change of paramount importance is the increased focus and attention paid to technology by your college professors. Your high school will probably have introduced you to many different computing concepts and applications. However, if you are returning to college after a few years in the workforce or if your high school did not have a strong computer emphasis, take every opportunity to learn as much about computers and technology as possible. You may be asked to submit assignments electronically, conduct research on the Internet, use a CD-ROM with one of your textbooks, or design your own statistical program for a research project. If you do not know how to type, this is the first order of business. Enroll in a keyboarding class or a continuing education class in typing. You'll thank yourself for this essential skill.

You have probably already noticed a difference between your college professors and your high school teachers in terms of teaching style and relationships with students. You may have encountered a teaching assistant, usually a graduate student who serves as an instructor in first-year and sophomore-level classes. Unlike teaching assistants, college professors take on many different roles. They are involved in research, community and college service, teaching, and committee work.

A significant change you may face in the days and weeks to come is the amount of diversity in the people around you. You may have come from a high school with a fairly homogeneous student body. If you went to school in a metropolitan area such as New York, Atlanta, Los Angeles, Boston, Chicago, Dallas,

FIGURE 1.2 A guide to understanding expectations.

	HIGH SCHOOL	COLLEGE	WORK
PUNCTUALITY AND ATTENDANCE	Expectations: • State law requires a certain number of days you must attend • The hours in the day are managed for you • There may be some leeway in project dates Penalties: • You may get detention • You may not graduate • You may be considered a truant • Your grades may suffer	Expectations: • Attendance and participation in class are strictly enforced by many professors • Most professors will not give you an extension on due dates • You decide your own schedule and plan your own day Penalties: • You may not be admitted to class if you are late • You may fail the assignment if it is late • Repeated tardiness is sometimes counted as an absence • Most professors do not take late assignments	Expectations: • You are expected to be at work and on time on a daily basis Penalties: • Your salary and promotions may depend on your daily attendance and punctuality • You will most likely be fired for abusing either
TEAMWORK AND PARTICIPATION	Expectations: • Most teamwork is assigned and carried out in class • You may be able to choose teams with your friends • Your grade may reflect your participation Penalties: • If you don't participate, you may get a poor grade • You may jeopardize the grade of the entire team	Expectations: • Many professors require teamwork and cooperative learning teams or learning communities • Your grade will depend on your participation • Your grade may depend on your entire team's performance • You will probably have to work on the project outside of class Penalties: • Lack of participation and cooperation will probably cost you a good grade • Your team members will likely report you to the professor if you do not participate and their grades suffer as a result	Expectations: • You will be expected to participate fully in any assigned task • You will be expected to rely on coworkers to help solve problems and increase profits • You will be required to attend and participate in meetings and sharing sessions • You will be required to participate in formal teams and possess the ability to work with a diverse workforce Penalties: • You will be "tagged" as a non-team player • Your lack of participation and teamwork will cost you raises and promotions • You will most likely be terminated

FIGURE 1.2 — A guide to understanding expectations, continued.

	HIGH SCHOOL	COLLEGE	WORK
PERSONAL RESPONSIBILITY AND ATTITUDE	Expectations: • Teachers may coach you and try to motivate you • You are required to be in high school by law regardless of your attitude or responsibility level Penalties: • You may be reprimanded for certain attitudes • If your attitude prevents you from participating, you may fail the class	Expectations: • You are responsible for your own learning • Professors will assist you, but there is little "hand holding" or personal coaching for motivation • College did not choose you, you chose it and you will be expected to hold this attitude toward your work Penalties: • You may fail the class if your attitude and motivation prevent you from participating	Expectations: • You are hired to do certain tasks and the company or institution fully expects this of you • You are expected to be positive and self-motivated • You are expected to model good behavior and uphold the company's work standards Penalties: • You will be passed over for promotions and raises • You may be reprimanded • You may be terminated
ETHICS AND CREDIBILITY	Expectations: • You are expected to turn in your own work • You are expected to avoid plagiarism • You are expected to write your own papers • Poor ethical decisions in high school may result in detention or suspension Penalties: • You may get detention or suspension • You will probably fail the project	Expectations: • You are expected to turn in your own work • You are expected to avoid plagiarism • You are expected to write your own papers • You are expected to conduct research and complete projects based on college and societal standards Penalties: • Poor ethical decisions may land you in front of a student ethics committee or a faculty ethics committee, or result in expulsion from the college • You will fail the project • You will fail the class • You may face deportation if your visa is dependent on your student status	Expectations: • You will be required to carry out your job in accordance with company policies, laws, and moral standards • You will be expected to use adult vision and standards Penalties: • Poor ethical decisions may cause you to be severely reprimanded, terminated, or in some cases could even result in a prison sentence

STRATEGIES
FOR BUILDING ON YOUR BEST

Consider the following strategies for adjusting to change in the days to come:

- Approach change with an open mind.
- If you haven't done so, take an afternoon and explore all the resources on your campus such as the library, the academic support center, counseling/advising office, etc.
- Don't be afraid to ask people in your class or your professors questions about things that are confusing or unclear.
- So you won't fall behind, adjust your study habits to accommodate more rigorous assignments.
- Join a club, organization, or study group so you can start building a network of friends.
- If you are not technologically savvy, find out if there are any resources that can help you catch up.

or Washington, D.C., you may be used to a diverse student body. Regardless of your background, you will meet students, peers, and classmates whose views, values, customs, language, sexual orientation, race, ethnicity, and origin are 100 percent different from yours. You will encounter people who are atheistic and people who are ultra-religious; people who are pro-life and people who are pro-choice; people who are against the death penalty and people who support capital punishment; people who abhor interracial relationships and people to whom race does not matter. If you come from a region or from a family in which these positions are not openly expressed, you must prepare yourself for change and realize how much you can learn from diversity. Chapter 13 is dedicated to understanding relationships and diversity.

Remember, the healthiest way to deal with change is to realize that it happens daily and to prepare for it.

What's Happening to Me?
PHYSICAL AND EMOTIONAL REACTIONS TO CHANGE

By the time you've read this far, you've probably gone through a few changes. Were they exciting? Were they stressful? When you experience change, your body typically goes through a process of physical and emotional change as well. Learning to recognize these symptoms in order to control them can help you control the stress that can accompany change. You may already have experienced some of these emotional and physical changes since arriving at your college. Take a moment now to reflect on your first few days in your new surroundings.

1. *How did you feel on entering your first class in college?*

   _____
   _____
   _____
   _____

2. *If you are married or have children, how did you feel when you had to leave your family today?*

   _____
   _____

> The real voyage of discovery consists not in seeing new lands, but in seeing with new eyes. —M. PROUST

3. How did you feel when you received your first syllabus outlining the content of a course?

_____

_____

_____

4. If you are living on campus, what physical changes occurred just before you met your new roommate? If you are living at home, how did you feel leaving today?

_____

_____

_____

These events cause a degree of stress and anxiety because they mean you are experiencing change. Chapter 14 will help you learn to deal with the stress associated with college and everyday events.

Don't be shocked if your body and spirit begin to feel:

- Nervousness
- Stress
- A sense of being on the edge
- Fear
- Fatigue
- Guilt
- Homesickness
- Denial
- Anger
- Depression

These feelings are normal when you go through a powerful change, but they are temporary. If any of these feelings become overwhelming or life-threatening, seek counseling, talk to your friends, go to your advisor, or speak with your professors. These people are your support group; use them. Don't wait until it is too late to ask for help. Don't hide your feelings and pretend that nothing is wrong. Change is not easy. One of the most crucial steps in successfully dealing with change is realizing that it can cause problems, but you can plan to overcome these negative feelings.

Not all reactions to change will be negative. You may also begin to experience some of the following emotions:

- A renewed sense of excitement
- Heightened awareness
- A more dynamic energy level
- Increased sensitivity to others
- Greater optimism
- A feeling of belonging
- Happiness

Change can introduce you to new people, ideas, cultures, and experiences.

More than likely, you will find that you are going through a wide range of emotions and feelings. This is normal; don't get overwhelmed.

> In human life there is a constant change of fortune; and it is unreasonable to expect an exemption from this common fate. —PLUTARCH

Attitudes that Hinder Change

You can develop attitudes that hinder change and stop growth. Such attitudes are dangerous because they rob you of opportunity, happiness, growth, and goals. These attitudes include:

- The "I can't" syndrome
- Apathy, or the "I don't care" syndrome
- Closed-mindedness
- Unfounded anxiety
- Fear of taking chances
- Loss of motivation
- The "let someone else deal with it" syndrome

If you can learn to watch out for and control these negative attitudes, you will begin to view change as a wonderful and positive lifelong event.

So, I Want to Change
HOW DO I DO IT?

After reading and reflecting thus far, you may have identified several changes that you need to make. Further, changes may have been thrust upon you by choices you or those around you have made. The following model provides a method for dealing with and implementing change in your life and might be helpful in bringing about positive results.

After studying the model, consider the following example in which Jeremy uses the change implementation model to bring about positive change in his life.

THE CHANGE IMPLEMENTATION MODEL

1. Determine what you need or want to change and why.

2. Research your options for making the desired changes and seek advice and assistance from a variety of sources.

3. Identify the obstacles to change and determine how to overcome them.

4. Establish a plan by outlining several positive steps to bring about the changes you identified.

5. Implement your plan for bringing about the desired change:
- Focus on the desired outcome.
- View problems as positive challenges.
- Turn your fears into energy by reducing anxiety through physical exercise, proper nutrition, and stress-management strategies.
- Associate with positive and motivated people.

The Change Implementation Model: *Jeremy's Example*

Consider the following example (p. 22), in which Jeremy uses the *Change Implementation Model* to bring about positive change in his life.

Jeremy entered his Accounting 101 class eager to take the first course in his major field. He was shocked to find that his professor began lecturing on the first day. Not only was the material difficult to understand, so was the professor, whose first language was not English.

The professor assigned two chapters per session, but the lectures were not based on material found in the text. Jeremy tried to study as he had in high school and felt overwhelmed and isolated.

After three weeks and a failed first test, Jeremy noticed that the students who passed the test had formed study groups, something that Jeremy once thought only the brightest students practiced.

Using the *Change Implementation Model,* Jeremy decided to make positive changes in his study habits. His plans for change are shown in the chart on the following page.

1	Determine what you need or want to change and why.	Jeremy realizes that he must change his study habits or fail the class. His high school study methods are not working.
2	Research your options for making the desired changes and seek advice and assistance from a variety of sources.	Jeremy looks around campus to determine what services are available to him such as tutoring, learning centers, and learning communities. He also makes an appointment to speak with the professor. He talks to one of the members of a study group in class to see what benefits she is getting from the group.
3	Identify the obstacles to change and determine how to overcome them.	In the past, Jeremy has been afraid to get involved. He realizes that he has never adjusted his time-management practices to college life; he is still studying on a "high school time frame." He realizes that he has never reached out to classmates before. By listing the problems on paper, Jeremy sees that he has to change his habits and take a risk by asking to join a study group.
4	Establish a plan by outlining several positive steps to bring about the changes you identified.	Jeremy spends a quiet evening thinking about steps that he can take to become a better student. He decides that he needs to (1) approach members of the study group to ask permission to join, (2) make an appointment at the tutoring center, and (3) make a commitment to reading the assigned material every night.
5	Implement your plan for bringing about the desired change: • Focus on the desired outcome.	Jeremy knows that he wants and needs to pass the class. This is the ultimate desired outcome, but he also knows that he must change his study habits for other classes and this group may help him do so. He realizes that if he can change his time and study practices, he will be successful in other areas.
	• View problems as positive challenges.	Instead of concentrating on the amount of time and energy required for the study group, he decides to look at it as a way to learn more, study better, and make new friends who have the same goals.
	• Turn your fears into energy by reducing anxiety through physical exercise, proper nutrition, and stress-management strategies.	Jeremy learns that two people from the study group also run every other morning. He decides to ask them if he can join them. He also decides that instead of going off campus to the Burger Hut, he will bring his own lunch and use this time to study for other classes.
	• Associate with positive and motivated people.	Jeremy notices that his attitude toward the class and life in general is improving because of the positive attitudes in the group. He can't believe how much he has changed in a few short weeks just by concentrating on the positive and associating with people who are motivated to succeed.

The Change Implementation Model: *Activity*

TRY IT OUT!

After studying the Change Implementation Model, complete the following activity. Focus on a few things that you might want to change about your own academic life. Even if you do not fill them all in, give serious consideration to each category.

STUDY HABITS. *If I could, I would change...*

MOTIVATIONAL LEVEL. *If I could, I would change...*

ATTITUDE. *If I could, I would change...*

TIME MANAGEMENT ABILITIES. *If I could, I would change...*

MONEY MANAGEMENT ABILITIES. *If I could, I would change...*

The Change Implementation Model: *Activity*

Now, choose one of the major changes you wish to incorporate into your life. Using the Change Implementation Model, devise a strategy to effect this change. Write your steps for implementing change below.

1 What do you need or want to change? Why?
_____
_____

2 Research your options for making the desired changes and seek advice and assistance from a variety of sources. List possible options here.
_____
_____

3 Identify the obstacles to change. How will you overcome them?
_____
_____

4 Establish a plan: outline several positive steps to bring about the changes you identified.
_____
_____

5 Implement your plan for bringing about the desired change.

   a. Focus on the desired outcome. List it here.
_____
_____

   b. View problems as positive challenges. Summarize them here.
_____
_____

   c. Turn your fears into energy by reducing anxiety through physical exercise, proper nutrition, and stress-management strategies. List your strategies here.
_____
_____

   d. Associate with positive and motivated people. Who are they?
_____
_____

BLUEPRINTS FOR CHANGE

NAME

DATE

REFLECTION

A Moment in Time

The transition from one place to another is never easy, even when it is what you want. Entering college has forced you to assume new roles, develop new friendships, meet new people, work under different circumstances, and perhaps adjust your lifestyle. These changes form the very essence of the college experience; they create wonderful new experiences. Now is the time for you to seek new truths, associate with new and different people, read books that you will never have time to hold in your hands again, develop a solid philosophy of life, explore new religions, go to plays, buy season football tickets, join a club, read a book of poetry, go on a picnic with friends, sing, laugh, cry, write home, and love much.

The winds of change are coming—fly!

GET REAL

Below are a few questions to help you think about change in college and in life. Study each question carefully and respond.

In what areas of your life have you experienced the most changes since starting college?

How can successfully dealing with change affect your life beyond college?

How can the suggestions for changing behavior discussed in this chapter be implemented in your life today?

When change brings on negative feelings, how will you deal with them?

How will you deal with the responses from people who knew you "back when" as they see the changes in your life?

Case Study

NAME: Tomer Perry
SCHOOL: University of Nevada, Las Vegas
MAJOR: Hotel Administration   AGE: 21

Below is a real-life situation faced by Tomer. Read the brief case and respond to the questions.

My first year of college was full of changes—massive changes. I decided that I needed to move out of my parents' home and on to another part of the country. So, I moved from New York City to Las Vegas, Nevada. Not only was this a geographic change, but it was also a change of attitude, a change of pace, a change of culture, and a total change in my support network. The hardest change that I had to deal with, however, was the loneliness. I was totally alone for the first time in my life; I had never known the emotion of being "alone." I was socially connected and very active in my high school, and this was a completely new experience for me.

Upon moving to Las Vegas, I had to start from scratch. I had to make new friends, find a new job, and adjust to a new way of life in a new city. All of these changes were positive, but they were not without their stresses. Little did I know that more change and stress was coming.

I began classes at the University of Nevada, Las Vegas as a computer programming engineer. A few weeks into the semester, I knew that I had chosen the wrong career path. Now, not only was I going through changes with geography, attitude, pace, and friends, but my MAJOR was changing. If I had ever doubted the old quote, "*Change is the only constant in life,*" I did not doubt it now.

After my first semester, I changed to an undeclared major. Later, I declared psychology as my major. That changed too. I went back to undeclared, then to pre-medicine, and now I'm in hotel management. I'm beginning to wonder if change is all I'll ever know.

Why is a support network important to you and your success?

_____
_____
_____
_____

How can learning to deal with change help you deal with your college experience and future employment?

_____
_____
_____
_____

What has been the most difficult change you have faced since beginning college? Why?

_____
_____
_____
_____

If you had met Tomer during the first week of classes and he shared his story with you, how might you have helped him adjust to his "new life"?

_____
_____
_____
_____

What steps could Tomer have taken to avoid changing majors several times?

_____
_____
_____
_____

If Tomer was on your campus, where could he go to find help with his career decision?

_____
_____
_____
_____

If you are having trouble adjusting to the changes in your life at the moment, where can you go on your campus for assistance?

_____
_____
_____

Phone # _____

at this moment Journal

Refer to page 7 of this chapter. Having read and reflected upon the information in the chapter, consider how you might revise your goal to make it more:

REASONABLE

BELIEVABLE

MEASURABLE

ADAPTABLE

CONTROLLABLE

DESIRABLE

See page 43 of Chapter 2 for a detailed explanation of these terms.

ONLINE JOURNAL

To complete an online journal entry, log onto the Companion Website at www.prenhall.com/sherfield. Go to Chapter 1 and click on the link to the Online Journal. You can respond to the questions provided or to questions assigned by your professor, or you may journal about your own experiences.

ADVICE TO GO

CORNERSTONES

for dealing with change

Remember, *challenges* can be *opportunities*.

Get involved and direct the change.

Embrace changes as *worth the effort*.

Keep your sense of *humor*.

Talk to friends and family.

Change can increase *energy*.

Change means growth.

Focus on the *positive*.

Be *courageous*.

Be *objective*.

CHANGE

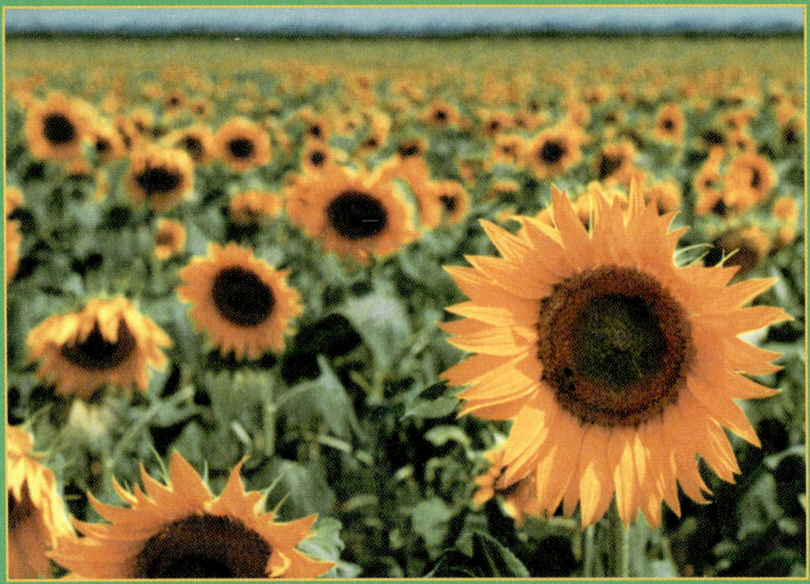

2 Grow

Our world is a college, events are teachers, happiness is graduation, and character is the diploma. —N.D. Hillis

CHAPTER 2

GROW

This story began about ten years ago, when I met Leeah, a shy, sullen, withdrawn young woman, the daughter of an acquaintance. I had met Leeah's mother, a hotel housekeeper, while conducting training for the hotel staff, and knew that Leeah's mother had high hopes for her daughter. I thus took an interest in Leeah.

Leeah's family lived under *difficult circumstances.* Her father had abandoned the family when Leeah was a small child; her mother had supported the seven of them by working as a housecleaner. Leeah's mother was concerned for her daughter's future. Leeah had had few opportunities, little direction, and little encouragement—*almost everything was working against her.*

I asked Leeah about her plans after graduation from high school. Leeah responded that she would like to go to college but could not afford it. I asked to see Leeah's transcript and learned that she was ranked very high in her graduating class. *Leeah had more opportunities to go to college than she could imagine.*

I helped Leeah apply for grants and scholarships and gave her a job as a student assistant. It soon became obvious that Leeah was a *serious student.* She studied at every opportunity; she read voraciously, from classics to current events; she asked questions; and she observed everything. *She was like a sponge, literally soaking up knowledge.* Gradually, she began to change. She became more friendly and outgoing, her confidence seemed to increase, and she smiled more often. *Leeah was becoming a classic example of the powerful difference that education plus motivation, goal setting, and improved self-esteem can make in a person's life.*

Leeah matured rapidly and began to take on more responsibility. Although she had been awarded an endowed scholarship, which provided full tuition and room and board, she worked two jobs. She upgraded her wardrobe, bought a car, and became totally independent. She still conferred with me occasionally, but Leeah made most of her own decisions. She was *growing quickly and positively,* and she was beginning to know who she was and what she wanted. *More important, she began to realize what she could become.* All her professors quietly marveled at the dramatic changes in her.

When Leeah took my class as a junior, she was introduced to goal setting, motivation strategies,

Motivation, Goal Setting, and Self-Esteem

and using adversity as a strength. She listened quietly, asked questions, and quickly designed her own blueprint for success. Her self-esteem was at a high level. *Leeah was on her way because she had a clearly defined plan and she was willing to pay the price to reach her goals.*

Prior to graduation, Leeah applied to several prestigious graduate schools and was accepted at *every one.* She graduated *with honors* and was awarded several scholarships for graduate school. She continued to work two jobs during the summer;

> **I asked Leeah about her plans . . . Leeah responded that she would like to go to college but could not afford it.**

she wanted to save money for her expenses so that she would not have to work during the semester and could concentrate on her studies. Leeah was *highly motivated, goal directed, and focused* on her plans.

Several years later, Leeah stopped by my office. She had earned her CPA credentials and was a full-fledged accountant working for a Big Eight accounting firm. Dressed in a classic suit and carrying a briefcase, Leeah stood up straight, smiled with confidence, and spoke assertively. I was struck by the awesome difference between this Leeah and the one I had met those many years ago. *Today, Leeah owns her own accounting firm, and several CPAs work for her.* She is a great example of the power of motivation and goal setting.

QUESTIONS FOR REFLECTION

Consider responding to these questions online in the Questions for Reflection module of the Companion Website.

1. What might have happened to Leeah if she had not gone to college?

2. How do you think Leeah developed staying power in spite of a family background that had not prepared her to be successful in college?

3. How do you think Leeah developed her attitude and skills to succeed despite a family background that did not prepare her for college?

Where are you... AT THIS MOMENT

Before reading this chapter, take a moment and respond to the following 10 questions. Consider each one carefully before answering, and then respond by circling the number in the appropriate box. When you have answered the questions, add your points and find your total score on the feedback chart below.

STATEMENT	STRONGLY DISAGREE	DISAGREE	DON'T KNOW	AGREE	STRONGLY AGREE	SCORE
1. My self-esteem has no influence over my successes and failures.	5	4	3	2	1	
2. When things go wrong, it is usually not my fault.	5	4	3	2	1	
3. I am ambitious in the goals I have set for my future.	1	2	3	4	5	
4. I actively work toward the goals I have set for my future.	1	2	3	4	5	
5. I am motivated by goals that are challenging.	1	2	3	4	5	
6. I tend to give up easily when frustrated.	5	4	3	2	1	
7. The fear of failure usually stops me from even trying.	5	4	3	2	1	
8. I am more motivated by the pleasure I feel when successful than from the outside rewards I receive for success.	1	2	3	4	5	
9. I have little control over my emotions.	5	4	3	2	1	
10. I know I can count on my own strengths to help me get through hard times.	1	2	3	4	5	
TOTAL VALUE						

SUMMARY

10–17 Your motivational level is low, you lack confidence, and lack the skills to set goals for yourself. Significant reshaping of your sense of self-worth and self-direction is needed to help you be successful in college.

18–25 Your motivational level is somewhat low, and your ability to set goals for yourself and to reach them is limited. Your self-confidence in relation to being successful needs boosting.

26–34 You are average in your level of motivation. You are likely aware of your personal goals and have had some success reaching goals. You possess a fair level of self-esteem.

35–42 Your levels of motivation, self-esteem, and success are above average. You are probably skilled in setting goals for yourself and have the persistence and confidence to be successful frequently.

43–50 You are exceptional in your ability to set goals and achieve them. You also enjoy the positive self-esteem that comes with persistence, success, and the certainty that you can hit the target you aim for.

Goals... FOR CHANGE

Based on your total points, what is one goal you would like to achieve related to goal setting, motivation, or self-esteem?

Goal _____
_____

List three actions you can take that might help you move closer to realizing this goal.

1. _____
2. _____
3. _____

Questions FOR BUILDING ON YOUR BEST

As you read this chapter, consider the following questions. At the end of the chapter, you should be able to answer all of them. You are encouraged to ask a few questions of your own. Consider asking your classmates or professors to assist you.

1. What are my personal core values?
2. How do my values influence goals that I set for myself?
3. How has adversity strengthened or discouraged me in my life?
4. How will goal setting help me be a better student?
5. How does self-esteem impact my ability to achieve my goals?

What additional questions do you have about goal setting, motivation, and self-esteem?

1. _____
2. _____
3. _____

The Impact of Values
MOTIVATION, GOAL SETTING, AND SELF-ESTEEM

If you have been highly motivated to accomplish a goal in the past, this achievement was probably tied to something you valued a great deal. Most of what you do in life centers around what is truly important to you. You cannot get excited about achieving a goal or be disciplined enough to stick to it unless you definitely want to make it happen. If you really want to make the swim team, for example, you have to pay the price of long hours of practice, getting up early in the morning, and swimming when others are sleeping or playing. If you hate swimming, but you set a goal to make the swim team because your father was a champion swimmer and expects the same of you, you are not likely to achieve this goal. Your goals must relate to your personal value system.

Values, self-esteem, motivation, and goal setting are all mixed up together, making it difficult to separate one from the other. What you try to accomplish is directly connected to those things, ideas, and concepts that you value most.

Values are central beliefs and attitudes that make you a unique person, while greatly impacting your choices and your personal lifestyle. If you cherish an attitude or belief, many of your actions will be centered around this ideal.

You were not born with your basic values. Your values were shaped to a great extent by your parents, the school you attended, the community where you grew up, and the culture that nourished you. Because of your personal background, you have developed a unique set of values. To make good decisions, set appropriate goals, and manage your priorities, you must identify those values that are central to who you are today. Until you clarify what you really value, you may try to accomplish what is important to someone else, and you will tend to wander around and become frustrated. Values, goals, and motivation bring direction to your life and help you get where you want to go.

> You are likely to achieve goals that relate to your own personal value system and that are truly important to you. Have you thought much about your own goals? Are they your goals, or has someone else set them for you?

The Impact of Attitude
MOTIVATION, GOAL SETTING, AND SELF-ESTEEM

How many people have you met who turned you off immediately with their negative attitudes? They whine about the weather or their parents; they verbally attack people who differ from them; they degrade themselves with negative remarks. Listen for the negative comments people make, and the

> When a man's willing and eager, the gods join in. —AESCHYLUS

messages they send out about themselves. When people continually feed their brains negative messages, their bodies respond accordingly.

You may feel that you have had enough of attitude. Your parents talked to you about it, your teachers hounded you about it. But it is important! The impact of a bad attitude on your motivation and self-esteem is overpowering, and the importance of a good attitude should not be underestimated. Focusing on the positive can bring dramatic changes in your life.

We all know that life sometimes deals bad blows, but your goal should be to be positive much more often than you are negative. Positive attitudes go hand in hand with energy, motivation, and friendliness. People with positive attitudes are more appealing; negative people drive others away.

Listen to yourself for a few days. Are you whining, complaining, griping, and finding fault with everything and everybody around you, including yourself? Do you blame your roommate for your problems? Is your bad grade the professor's fault? Are your parents responsible for everything bad that ever happened to you? If these kinds of thoughts are coming out of your mouth or are in your head, your first step toward improved motivation and self-esteem is to clean up your act.

To be successful at anything, you have to develop a winning attitude. You have to eliminate negative thinking. Begin today: tell yourself only positive things about yourself; build on those positives; focus on the good things; work constantly to improve.

Winners get up early with an attitude of "I can't wait for this day to start so I can have another good day." OK, OK—so you may not get up early, but you can get up with a positive attitude. Tell yourself things that will put you in the right frame of mind to succeed. When you are talking to yourself—and everybody does—feed your brain positive thoughts. Think of your brain as a powerful computer; you program it with your words, and your body carries out the program.

Pay attention to the messages you send out to others as well. What kinds of remarks do you make about yourself and about others when you are with your friends? Do you sound positive or negative? Do you hear yourself saying positive things? Avoid gossiping about people. Gossips usually say negative things about others because it makes them feel important.

> Gossips pick up more dirt with a telephone than they do with a vacuum cleaner. —LILLIAN GLASS

Are You Hanging Out with Toxic People?

CHOOSE YOUR FRIENDS CAREFULLY

Although your motivation and attitude belong to you and are uniquely yours, they can be greatly influenced by the people with whom you associate. People do tend to become like the people with whom they spend time.

As a new college student, you have a clean slate where friends are concerned. You need to choose your very best friends carefully. Of course you want to spend time with people who have interests in common with yours. That's a given. But you should also want your friends to have ambition, good work habits, positive attitudes, and high ethical standards. Seek out people who read good books, watch educational television programs, are goal oriented, and don't mind taking a stand when they believe strongly about something. Find friends who will work out with you, go to the library with you, attend plays and concerts with you. One of the best ways to make the most of your college education is to befriend people who have interests and hobbies that are new to you. Staying focused is much easier if you surround yourself with positive, motivated, goal-oriented people. Add some people to your circle of friends who are from a different culture.

How are the friends you are making in college influencing your decisions?

Overcoming Doubts and Fears

Fear is a great motivator; it probably motivates more people than anything else. Unfortunately, it motivates most people to hold back, to doubt themselves, to accomplish much less than they could, and to hide the person they really are.

One of the biggest obstacles to reaching your potential may be your own personal fears. If you are afraid, you are not alone; everyone has fears. It is interesting to note that our fears are learned. As a baby, you had only two fears: a fear of falling and a fear of loud noises. As you got older, you added to your list of fears. And, if you are like most people, you let your fears dominate parts of your life, saying things to yourself like: "What if I try and fail?" "What if people laugh at me for thinking I can do this?" "What if someone finds out that this is my dream?"

You have two choices where fear is concerned. You can let fear dominate your life, or you can focus on those things you really want to accomplish, put your fears behind you, and go for it. The people most successful in their fields will tell you that they are afraid, but that they overcome their fear because their desire to achieve is greater. Barbra Streisand, recording artist and stage performer, becomes physically nauseated with stage fright when she performs, yet she faces these fears and retains her position as one of the most popular entertainers of our time.

MOVING OUT OF YOUR COMFORT ZONE

Successful people face their fears because their motivation and ambition force them out of their comfort zones. Your comfort zone is where you know you are good, you feel confident, and you don't have to stretch your talents far to be successful. If you stay in your comfort zone, you will

T*hey who have conquered doubt and fear have conquered failure.* —JAMES ALLEN

never reach your potential and you will deny yourself the opportunity of knowing how it feels to overcome your fears.

Deciding to go to college probably caused you some level of discomfort and raised many fears: "What if I can't make good grades?" "What if I flunk out?" "What if I can't make the team?" "What if I can't keep up with the kids just out of high school?" "What if I can't do my job, go to school, and manage a family at the same time?" The mere fact that you are here is a step outside your comfort zone—a very important step that can change your life dramatically.

Everyone has a comfort zone. When you are doing something that you do well, and you feel comfortable and confident, you are in your comfort zone. When you are nervous and afraid, you are stepping outside your comfort zone. When you realize you are outside your comfort zone, you should feel good about yourself because you are learning and growing and improving. You cannot progress unless you step outside your comfort zone.

DEALING WITH ADVERSITY AND FAILURE

To be motivated, you have to learn to deal with failure. Have you ever given up on something too quickly, or gotten discouraged and quit? Can you think of a time when you were unfair to yourself because you didn't stay with something long enough? Did you ever stop doing something you wanted to do because somebody laughed at you or teased you? Overcoming failure makes victory much more rewarding. Motivated people know that losing is a part of winning: the difference between being a winner and being a loser is the ability to try again.

If you reflect on your life, you may well discover that you gained your greatest strengths through adversity. Difficult situations make you tougher and more capable of developing your potential. Overcoming adversity is an essential part of success in college and in life.

Think of a time in your life when you faced difficulties but persisted and became stronger as a result. Perhaps you failed a course, didn't make an athletic team, lost a school election, had a serious illness, broke up with a long-term boyfriend or girlfriend, or experienced your parents' divorce. If you are a nontraditional student, you may have been fired from a job or passed over for a promotion, suffered through a divorce, or experienced a death in the family.

STRATEGIES FOR BUILDING ON YOUR BEST

Consider the following strategies for dealing with adversity and failure:

- Accept the fact that EVERYONE experiences failure and adversity.
- Make a commitment to yourself that you will not walk away when things get tough.
- Identify the reasons that you have experienced adversity or failure.
- Determine if a certain person or people in your life contributed to this failure.
- Be honest and truthful with yourself and determine what role, if any, you played in bringing about this adversity or failure.
- If you played a role in your own failure, devise a plan or set a goal to eliminate the behavior that caused the problem.
- Develop the mind-set that every new minute brings new hope. You can start over at any moment you choose.

Describe your experience of adversity.

_____
_____
_____

What did you learn from this experience?

_____
_____
_____

How can you use this experience as a reminder that you can overcome adversity, learn to grow from it, and become a better person as a result of it?

_____
_____
_____

Motivation
WHAT IS IT AND HOW CAN I GET IT?

Quite often you hear people talk about their lack of motivation or you hear someone else referred to as a "motivated person." You might wish you were more motivated, but aren't sure how to get to that point. You see people who are highly self-disciplined and you would like to be more like them, but you don't have a clue how to get started. You've probably heard that old cliché, "A journey of a thousand miles begins with a single step." It may be old and sound a little corny, but actually, it's the truth.

Becoming motivated is a process—it's not one giant leap to becoming something you want to be. Motivation rarely comes overnight; rather, you become motivated by experiencing one small success after another as your confidence grows, and gradually, you try something bigger and more challenging.

There are only two broad categories that will ever motivate you: a **dream** you have or a **problem** you are trying to overcome. Every goal and everything regarding motivation will fit into one of these two categories. Either dreaming of something or wanting to solve a problem is the first part of the formula for motivation. The other part is about making it happen—an action plan. Dreaming or wanting to solve a problem without action will get you nowhere. Nothing works unless you do! Motivation can be broken down into:

Desire+Courage+Goals+Discipline=Motivation

In order to stay motivated, you have to become committed to doing something. You need to face your fears and not let them become bigger than your dreams. You need to be willing to write your dream or desire down as a goal and say it out loud to your friends and family. You need to put those goals or commitments somewhere you can see them often in order to to keep you on track. You need to take the initiative to get started. You have to be willing to form good habits and replace bad habits. For example, if you are a procrastinator, you have to work hard to change the habit that gets you in trouble over and over and over again. You need to be determined to take responsibility for yourself and your habits. In other words, you need to discipline yourself. If you can keep up a good practice for 21 days, it usually becomes a habit. Tell yourself, "I can do anything for 21 days."

No one can do any of this for you. Motivation comes from within, and you are the only one in control of your personal motivation. The choice to be motivated, to be successful, to reach your potential is up to you. Blaming others, making excuses, using difficult circumstances as a crutch, or quitting will never get you anywhere. If you want to be motivated and successful, *get up and get started*.

When you are sure that you are becoming more disciplined, that your work habits are getting better, your grades are improving, and you are focused on success, reward yourself. Do something that you have really wanted to do for a long time. Share your successes with a few people who really care. Be careful not to boast. If you are good, people will know it. As you grow and become more successful, you will begin to make wiser choices; you will reach bigger goals; you will be on your way to accomplishing your dreams!

As you begin to think about your own ambitions and motivational level, consider Figure 2.1. Think about your own life and determine how the stages of motivation apply to your dreams or hope of solving a problem.

Building a New You
THE GOAL-SETTING PROCESS

Goal setting itself is relatively easy. Many people make goals, but fail to make the commitment to accomplish those goals. Instead of defining their goals in concrete, measurable terms, they think of them occasionally and have vague, unclear ideas about how to attain them. The first step toward reaching a goal is the commitment to pay the price to achieve it. Opportunities abound everywhere; commitment is a scarce commodity.

There is only one definition of success . . . to be able to spend your life in your own way.
—CHRISTOPHER MORLEY

FIGURE 2.1 — Developmental stages of a motivated person.

Unmotivated Person—academically unsuccessful, no direction, unchallenged, no ambition, floundering, no goals, undisciplined, poor habits, allows friends to drag student down, afraid of failure

Stages of Motivation

Stage 1: Recognizes desire. Begins to realize that motivation is a process. Has aspirations for improvement. Begins to dream. Has a yearning to be proud of one's work. Likes the feeling of winning. Has aspirations of making accomplishments.

Stage 2: Faces fear. Begins to understand the paralyzing effects of fear. Determines to overcome irrational fears. Begins to share fears with other people.

Stage 3: Moves further out of comfort zone. Meets new people. Gains confidence by expanding academic, cultural, and social horizons. Begins to overcome fear of embarrassment by trying new ventures.

Stage 4: Becomes goal setter in all aspects of life. Motivated to get out of comfort zone every day. Challenged to do more, be more, and have more. Has direction in life, has plan for the future, is focused on success. States goals aloud to friends and family.

Stage 5: Becomes highly disciplined. Focuses on desired outcomes every day. Stays focused even during setbacks. Refuses to allow people or events to interfere. Overcomes difficult circumstances and refuses to give up.

Becoming Motivated

Strategy 1: How do I recognize desire? Make a list of the top five things you truly want in life. Think about such things as where you want to be, what you want to have, and with whom you want to share your successes. Set a simple goal.

Strategy 2: How do I face fear? Identify irrational fears; set slightly more challenging goals; select the least fearful thing in your life and develop simple steps to address this fear. Take chances. Ask close friends and family to help you.

Strategy 3: How do I move further out of my comfort zone? Interact with one new person every week; select one social or cultural event a month to attend; deliver a presentation on a topic that you have avoided in the past; travel to one place you have never been.

Strategy 4: How do I become a goal setter in every aspect of life? Choose five areas (such as financial, physical, social, health, education). Set one realistic goal in each area. Develop steps to achieve each goal. Post your goals so that you see them every day.

Strategy 5: How do I become more disciplined? Select one goal that you started and quit and re-tackle it with renewed discipline. Identify circumstances in the past that caused you to quit and develop a plan to overcome old habits. Spend more time with positive, disciplined people.

Motivated Person—goal setter, visionary, focused, engaging, confident, disciplined, risk taker, courageous, compassionate

When you are ready to make a commitment to achieve your goals, write them down, along with steps for accomplishing deadlines that must be honored. These goals are your targets. Now you are ready to act, to begin accomplishing your goals, and you need to do so without delay. Be prepared to fail, because you surely will fail some of the time, but you must be equally committed to getting up and trying again. Your commitment to success must be so strong that quitting would never even occur to you.

CHARACTERISTICS OF ATTAINABLE GOALS

It is usually easier to set goals than to achieve them. To be able to set attainable goals, you need to know their characteristics. Attainable goals must be:

- **Reasonable.** Your goals need to be based on your abilities, desires, and talents. If you made terrible grades in English composition and hate to sit at a computer, you shouldn't set a goal to become a writer. On the other hand, if you are a star athlete and love to work with young people, your goal might be to become a coach.

- **Believable.** To achieve a goal, you must really believe it is within your capacity to reach it. You may want a sailboat very badly, but the cost may be prohibitive. If you want it, but don't believe you can get it, you are probably fooling yourself—at least at this stage of the game.

> The thing always happens that you really believe in; and the belief in a thing makes it happen. —FRANK LLOYD WRIGHT

- **Measurable.** A goal needs to be concrete and measurable in some way. If you set a vague goal, such as "I want to be happy," you cannot know if you've attained your goal, because you have no way of measuring it.

- **Adaptable.** Your goals may need to be adapted to changing circumstances in your life. You may begin with a goal and find that you have to change direction for one reason or another. Maybe you don't like this goal once you learn more about it, or perhaps some insurmountable obstacle arises. You might have to adjust your expectations and the goal itself in order to achieve it.

- **Controllable.** Your goals should be within your own control; they should not depend on the whims and opinions of anyone else. For example, if your goal is to learn to play golf well enough to score 90, you need to control your practice and the times you play; you do not want to practice based on the needs of your roommate, who may have strengths and weaknesses different from yours.

- **Desirable.** To attain a difficult goal, you must want it very badly. You cannot make yourself work for something just because someone else wants it. If you have always dreamed about becoming a teacher of young children, set this as your goal; it will be extremely difficult for you to stay on course to become a medical researcher because your parents want you to follow in their footsteps.

All things are possible until they are proved impossible—and even the impossible may only be so, as of now. —PEARL S. BUCK

HOW TO WRITE GOALS

According to Boldt (2001), "It is difficult to act without a clear picture of where you are going." The process of goal setting involves deciding what you want and working to get it, just as Leeah did in the opening story. Goals can be short term or long term. Short-term goals can usually be accomplished within six months or a year, although they could be accomplished in a much shorter time. "Within six months, I will save enough money to spend a week skiing in Vail" is a short-term goal; "Within six years, I will become a certified public accountant (CPA)" is a long-term goal.

When you write goals, you need to include a *goal statement, action steps, target dates,* and a *narrative statement*. The goal statement should be specific and measurable; that is, it should entail some tangible evidence of its achievement. An example of a goal statement is "I will lose 10 pounds in six weeks." You can make goal statements from intangibles if you can devise a way to measure the desired outcome. For example, "I will develop a more positive attitude by the end of six weeks as evidenced by at least three people commenting on my improved attitude and by my dealing positively with at least three negative situations weekly."

After you write the goal statement, you'll need to create specific action steps that explain exactly what you are going to do to reach your goal. Then, decide on a target date for reaching your goal.

The next step is to write a narrative statement about what your goal accomplishment will mean to you and how your life will change because of reaching this goal. For example, if your goal is to lose 50 pounds, paint a "verbal picture" of how your life is going to look once this goal has been reached. Your verbal picture may include statements such as: "I'll be able to wear nicer clothes." "I'll feel better." "I'll be able to ride my bicycle again." "My self-esteem will be stronger." If your goals don't offer you significant rewards, you are not likely to stick to your plan. Finally, write down two reasons *why* you deserve this goal. It may seem simple, but this is a complex question. Many people do not follow through on their goals because deep down, they don't feel they deserve them. The narrative statement helps you understand why you deserve this goal.

When you have accomplished your goal, you need to begin the process again. Successful people never get to a target and sit down; they are always becoming. They reach one goal and begin dreaming, planning, preparing for the next accomplishment. Goal setting and follow-through are major components of your personal staying power as a college student.

Now you are ready to begin the exciting adventure known only to goal setters, using the activity on the following pages. To help you get started, listed below are some common areas for which you might want to set goals. Think about goals in these terms: you can have a boat, you can be a member of the student

WORLD OF WORK

Growing up in rural South Carolina in a family with very modest means taught me lessons that I continue to appreciate today. My parents were extremely hard workers; my mother worked in a cotton mill, and my father was a carpenter at a cable manufacturing plant. They encouraged me to always "do my best" no matter what the task was that lay ahead. Whether I was finishing one of my chores or bringing home a report card from school, I would always get the same question from my parents: "Son, did you do your best?"

That scenario has stayed with me over the years. On occasion, I've not done my best in certain situations, and I've lived to regret the results. My parents had high expectations for me and—by extension—I grew to have high expectations for myself. My own path to success began with simply believing in myself. Granted, there were times when I experienced self-doubt, but I would always remember my parents asking, "Did you do your best?" That would usually "snap" me out of my temporary funk.

Unfortunately, simply believing you can be successful won't ensure that you'll achieve the goals you've set for yourself. Sure, you have to believe in yourself, but you must also establish clear, attainable goals and then focus on them like a laser beam. Don't become distracted. Others will try to derail your efforts, and there are always temptations that can throw a monkey wrench into any plan. I've learned to use the power of focus—there's no greater satisfaction than working hard to achieve a goal that others have said was impossible or unobtainable.

Along that path to success, you must be willing to take risks. You will encounter naysayers and other roadblocks along the way. Remain focused but be willing to take chances that could help you to reach your goals. Of course, taking risks demands that you maintain a certain level of self-confidence. Failure is always a possibility, but without taking calculated risks, you may never achieve the level of success you were destined to obtain.

Your journey to greatness has been traveled by countless others. I've also learned to seek the knowledge and guidance of individuals who have experienced wonderful success in their chosen endeavors. I've been extremely fortunate to have the counsel of very wise teachers and mentors from the time I was in high school through college and graduate school and even today. We're never too old to learn from others.

Just as my own mentors have done with me over the years, you must learn to give back. That is, you must share your own knowledge and expertise with others who have less experience and are struggling. In this universe, I firmly believe that what you unselfishly give to others will come back to you tenfold.

Finally, one must maintain a balance in life. Set clear goals for yourself academically and professionally, but don't forget about the importance of the loved ones in your life. Seek out companionship, live in the moment, laugh out loud, and find joy in everyday occurrences.

QUESTIONS FOR REFLECTION

Consider responding to these questions online in the World of Work module of the Companion Website.

1. How can you use the "power of focus," as Dr. Houston did, to improve your life as a college student?
2. How can you (or do you) avoid distractions so that you may stay focused on achieving your goals?
3. What person has been a mentor to you? How has this person helped you grow and become better?

Kevin Todd Houston, Ph.D., *Executive Director,* The Alexander Graham Bell Association for the Deaf and Hard of Hearing, Washington, DC

government, you can play a musical instrument—a goal can apply to any area of your life. After reviewing these categories, use the goal sheets on pages 47 and 48 to develop your own goals and action plan.

CATEGORIES FOR GOALS
- Personal or self-improvement
- Academic
- Family
- Career
- Financial
- Community service
- Social
- Health
- Spiritual

You have just read the section on motivation, studied the developmental stages of a motivated person, and learned how to set realistic, attainable goals. The activity on pages 49 and 50 will allow you to develop your own motivational plan. Carefully read, study, and answer each question. When answering the questions, move across the columns from 1 to 2 and then to 3. Take your time and concentrate on the desired outcome.

Evaluation Plan for Your Goals

- Do I really want to achieve this goal enough to pay the price and to stick with it?
- What is the personal payoff to me if I achieve this goal?
- Who will notice if I achieve this goal? Does that matter to me?
- How realistic is this goal? Am I way over my head for this stage of my development?
- Do I need to reduce my expectations so I won't be disillusioned in the beginning, and then increase the difficulty of my goal only after I have reached the first steps?
- Can I control all the factors necessary to achieve this goal?
- Is this goal specific and measurable?
- Does this goal contribute to my overall development? Is this goal allowing me to spend my time in the way that is best for me right now?
- How will I feel when I reach this goal?
- Will my parents and friends be proud that I accomplished this goal?
- Will the achievement of this goal increase my self-esteem?

If you refuse to accept anything but the best out of life, you very often get it. —SOMERSET MAUGHAM

SETTING GOALS

Activity

Name _____

GOAL STATEMENT _____
_____

ACTION STEPS

1. _____
2. _____
3. _____
4. _____

TARGET DATE _____

NARRATIVE STATEMENT

_____
_____
_____
_____
_____
_____
_____
_____
_____

I DESERVE THIS GOAL BECAUSE:

1. _____
_____

2. _____
_____

I HEREBY MAKE THIS PROMISE TO MYSELF.

date _____ signature _____

SETTING GOALS *Activity*

Name _____

GOAL STATEMENT _____

ACTION STEPS

1. _____
2. _____
3. _____
4. _____

TARGET DATE _____

NARRATIVE STATEMENT

_____
_____
_____
_____
_____
_____
_____
_____
_____
_____
_____

I DESERVE THIS GOAL BECAUSE:

1. _____
   _____
2. _____
   _____

I HEREBY MAKE THIS PROMISE TO MYSELF.

date _____ signature _____

DEVELOP YOUR MOTIVATIONAL PLAN

COLUMN 1

Where Are You?

1. Identify the biggest realistic desire you have.

1. What are your fears associated with the desire you listed?

1. On a scale of 1 to 10 (10 being the highest), rate your current motivation level toward reaching this desire. How can you improve this score?

1. Write one goal statement to achieve your desire. It should include action steps, target date, and a narrative statement.

COLUMN 2

Why Are You There?

2. Why is this a desire?

2. Why do you think you have these fears?

2. What would help you step further out of your comfort zone to address your desire and fears?

2. What problems have you had in the past while working toward this desire (or any desire)?

COLUMN 3

What Do You Plan to Do About It?

3. What are your first steps to achieve this desire?

3. List three ways you can overcome these fears.

3. What steps do you plan to take to move outside of your comfort zone?

3. What steps do you plan to take to bring this desire to fruition?

Activity

COLUMN 1

Where Are You?

1. What personal habit, weakness, or trait has hampered your discipline level in the past?

COLUMN 2

Why Are You There?

2. Why has this habit, weakness, or trait affected your discipline level in the past?

COLUMN 3

What Do You Plan to Do About It?

3. What do you plan to do to maintain consistent discipline while working to accomplish this desire?

Do You Love Yourself?

THE IMPACT OF SELF-ESTEEM ON YOUR MOTIVATION

If you were asked to name all the areas of your life that are impacted by self-esteem, what would you say? The correct answer is, "Everything. All areas of your life." Self-esteem and self-understanding are two of the most important components of your personal makeup! In other words, you have got to know and love yourself! There are many highly accomplished people who never truly know themselves and never learn to believe their personal worth. Many people who are in therapy are there simply because they cannot accept the fact that they are OK. Self-esteem is a powerful force in your life and is the source of your joy, your productivity, and your ability to have good relationships with others.

Did you know that your IQ score might not be as important as knowing your own talents and strengths and having healthy self-esteem? A student can be brilliant in terms of mental ability, but may perform at a very low capacity because of unhealthy self-esteem. Unhealthy self-esteem and a lack of self-understanding are also connected to loneliness and depression. "Self-esteem is the armor that protects kids from the dragons of life: drugs, alcohol, delinquency and unhealthy relationships" (McKay and Fanning, 2000).

The foundation for love and friendship begins with self-understanding and healthy self-esteem. Feeling a part of things, believing that you are liked and accepted, is possible only when you know yourself and feel deserving. Studies have shown that "socially uncertain college students had lower levels of self-esteem as well as higher levels of depression, stress, and loneliness" (Salmela-Aro and Nurmi, 1996). It has further been proven that how students treat others is related to how they feel about themselves. In other words, the bullies, taunters, and jerks really don't like themselves. People who love themselves can love others easily and feel comfortable allowing other people to be themselves without judging. Romantic relationships that are fulfilling and last for a long time are also built on the fact that the two people involved feel good about themselves. If one suffers from unhealthy self-esteem, then jealousy, a controlling personality, or violence may cause the relationship to fail.

Finally, self-esteem manifests itself in the workplace. If you feel good about yourself, you will interview well, you will seek out jobs that offer the kinds of rewards you are seeking, and you will most likely advance on the job. Self-esteem and self-understanding are the foundations on which your personal happiness and success are built.

You might think of self-esteem as a photograph of yourself that you keep locked in your mind. It is a cumulative product developed through many experiences and through relationships with many people.

People who demonstrate healthy self-esteem and confidence usually have five characteristics:

Five Characteristics of Self-Esteem

1. A sense of security
2. A sense of identity
3. A sense of belonging
4. A sense of purpose
5. A sense of personal competence

DID YOU KNOW?

55.8%

The percentage of students who rated themselves above average in the category of self-understanding.

Source: Rooney, M. "Freshmen show rising political awareness and changing social views." *The Chronicle of Higher Education,* January 31, 2003.

These characteristics are considered key to a person's ability to approach life with confidence, maintain self-direction, and achieve outstanding accomplishments. As a high school senior or on the job, you might have felt pretty good about yourself, but since you have entered a new environment, you may find that your self-esteem is not as strong. It is natural to be nervous or to feel threatened as you move into a new environment. If your self-esteem is healthy, you will soon feel comfortable again.

Influences on Self-Esteem
HOW DID YOU GET TO BE WHO YOU ARE?

The concept of the child within has been a part of our culture for more than 2000 years. Psychotherapists have used different names for this concept: Donald Winnicott called it the "true self," Carl Jung used the "divine child," and Emmett Fox used the "wonder child"; many others refer to it as simply the inner child.

The child within is the very best part of us. It is our joy, enthusiasm, energy, and spontaneity; it determines whether we are fun-filled and happy, as well as fulfilled and productive. Troubled, dysfunctional families damage the inner child, resulting in anxiety, fear, emptiness, confusion, and low self-esteem. No matter what your past, however, you can learn to improve your self-esteem and, along with it, your happiness and success.

Many people, especially women, are unhappy with their appearance, and these feelings often engender unhealthy self-esteem. Bulimia and anorexia may arise when thinness is inextricably linked to a person's feeling good about herself—these disorders are found primarily in women. College students carry the extra baggage of a societal value that links self-esteem and appearance, again, particularly for women. Sandra Haber, a New York City psychiatrist, specializes in eating disorders. Haber believes that what we see in the mirror is what we take into all our roles. In other words, how we see ourselves equates to our self-esteem.

Many people are obsessed with their outer shell and believe that if they can be thin enough or wear the right clothes or have big muscles, they will somehow miraculously be loved by others. Recently, there has been an increase in the number of young men taking steroids to pump themselves up, even though they know it can be dangerous to their health. Paying attention to physical appearance is important and can improve your feelings about yourself, but emphasis on appearance without attention to mental and emotional well-being will rarely bring about lasting change.

Alcoholism, drug dependency, abusive relationships, and promiscuous sexual behavior are other symptoms of unhealthy self-esteem. No one is born with unhealthy self-esteem. Many of the root causes of unhealthy self-esteem begin in childhood and are often in the form of "messages" given to us by parents, teachers, peers, and others. Since many of these thoughts related to unhealthy self-esteem originated many years ago, you need to realize that correcting these problems may take time. The result is worth the effort, however, if you learn to love and value yourself.

Loving You More!
IMPROVING YOUR SELF-ESTEEM

You may be wondering what the point of all this is—why should you worry about self-esteem when you already have concerns about grades, work, laundry, relationships, and a million other things? Who has time for all this extra stuff? Maybe you think you can wait to worry about your self-esteem when you finish college. The reason you need to be concerned now is that your grades, work, social life—everything—are tied up with your self-esteem.

Several outstanding psychiatrists and professors stress the importance of addressing self-esteem in the educational process, believing that self-esteem goes hand in hand with academics. Carl Rogers (1972), a noted psychiatrist who has developed many psychological theories and ideas about self-esteem, wrote, "Sometimes I feel our education has as one of its major goals the bringing up of individuals to live in isolation cages." Leo Buscaglia (1982), a well-known professor who taught for years on the subjects of love and relationships, asked, "How many classes did you ever have in your entire educational career that taught you about you?"

Your relationships with others—friends, parents, children, professors, bosses, spouse—depend on how well you have developed your own self-esteem. You are not an isolated human being. Every day you must relate to others, and your self-esteem will influence the kinds of relationships you build. You will continue to meet new people and face new challenges with the people you know as you grow and mature, and these challenges are likely to increase in complexity. Unless you are planning to live a life alone in the woods, you will rely on your ability to relate positively to all kinds of people. The basis for those relationships lies within you, in your self-esteem.

Your relationships with others depend on how well you have developed your own self-esteem.

TEN WAYS TO INCREASE YOUR SELF-ESTEEM

Take control of your own life. If you let other people rule your life, you will always have unhealthy self-esteem. You will feel helpless and out of control as long as someone else has power over your life. Part of growing up is taking control of your life and making your own decisions. Get involved in the decisions that shape your life. Seize control—don't let life happen to you!

Adopt the idea that you are responsible for you. The day you take responsibility for yourself and what happens to you is the day you start to develop your self-esteem. When you can admit your mistakes and celebrate your successes knowing you did it your way, you will learn to love yourself much better.

Refuse to allow friends and family to tear you down. You may have family or friends who belittle you, criticize your decisions, and refuse to let you make your own decisions. Combat their negativity by admitting your mistakes and shortcomings to yourself and by making up your mind that you are going to overcome them. By doing this, you are taking their negative power away from them. Spend less time with people who make you feel small and insecure and more time with people who encourage you.

Control what you say to yourself. "Self-talk" is important to your self-esteem and to your ability to motivate yourself positively. Your brain is like a powerful computer and it continually plays messages to you. If these self-talk messages are negative, they will have a detrimental impact on your self-esteem and on your ability to live up to your potential. Make a habit of saying positive things to yourself: "I will do well on this test because I am prepared." "I am a good and decent person, and I deserve to do well." "I will kick the ball straight."

Take carefully assessed risks often.   Many people find risk taking very hard to do, but it is one of the very best ways to raise your self-esteem level. If you are going to grow to your fullest potential, you will have to learn to take some calculated risks. While you should never take foolhardy risks that might endanger your life, you must constantly be willing to push yourself out of your comfort zone. Every day, force yourself to take a little step outside your comfort zone.

Don't compare yourself to other people.   You may never be able to "beat" some people at certain things. But it really does not matter. You only have to beat yourself to get better. If you constantly tell yourself that you "are not as handsome as Bill" or "as smart as Mary" or "as athletic as Jack," your inner voice will begin to believe these statements, and your body will act accordingly. One of the best ways to improve self-esteem and to accomplish goals is simply to get a little better every day without thinking about what other people are doing. If you are always practicing at improving yourself, sooner or later you will become a person you can admire—and others will admire you, too!

Develop a victory wall or victory file.   Many times, you tend to take your accomplishments and hide them in a drawer or closet. Put your certificates, letters of praise, trophies, and awards out where you can see them on a daily basis. Keep a file of great cartoons, letters of support, or friendly cards so that you can refer to them from time to time.

Keep your promises and be loyal to friends, family, and yourself.   If you have ever had someone break a promise to you, you know how it feels to have your loyalty betrayed. The most outstanding feature of one's character is one's ability to be loyal, keep one's promises, and do what one has agreed to do. Few things can make you feel better about yourself than being loyal and keeping your word.

Win with grace—lose with class.   Everyone loves a winner, but everyone also loves a person who can lose with class and dignity. On the other hand, no one loves a bragging winner or a moaning loser. If you are engaged in sports, debate, acting, art shows, or math competitions, you will encounter winning and losing. Remember, whether you win or lose, if you're involved and active, you're already in the top 10 percent of the population.

Set goals and maintain a high level of motivation.   Find something that you can be passionate about; set a realistic goal to achieve this passion, and stay focused on this goal every day. By maintaining a high level of motivation, you will begin to see your goals come to fruition and feel your self-esteem soar. Setting a goal and achieving it is one of the most powerful ways to develop healthy self-esteem.

BLUEPRINTS FOR CHANGE

NAME

DATE

REFLECTION

Making goal setting a part of your life can dramatically change your success in college and in the workplace. You are guaranteed to see progress in yourself in many areas if you will follow the strategies suggested regarding goal setting. Leeah used goal setting as one of several ways to overcome a difficult and deprived past. She continues to use goal setting today as she builds a competitive and successful accounting practice. Goal setting is a valuable skill that you can use for the rest of your life.

Most people have experienced some difficult times that impacted their self-esteem in adverse ways. Personal strength can be gained from overcoming the bad memories that caused self-doubts. The more adept you become at setting goals and forcing yourself out of your comfort zone, the more your self-esteem will improve.

GET REAL

Below are a few questions to help you think about your motivation, goals, and self-esteem. Study each question carefully and respond.

Name one past goal that caused you to reach. How did the accomplishment of that goal make you feel?

Discuss one experience you had this semester where your self-esteem caused you to hold back and not take a chance on doing something you really wanted to do.

How can you use the information provided in this chapter to improve your college success?

How can you apply what you have learned in this chapter to work?

If you become a dedicated goal setter and a highly motivated person, how will your life as a college student improve?

If you resolve your long-term self-esteem problems (or work to strengthen your self-esteem), how do you think your life will be happier and more productive?

How will becoming a stronger and more dedicated goal setter in college impact your future in the workforce?

Case Study

NAME: Jamie Juul
SCHOOL: Jamestown Community College, Jamestown, NY
MAJOR: Medical Technology   AGE: 18

Below is a real-life situation faced by Jamie. Read the brief case and respond to the questions.

My dream is to work in the field of medical technology. There I will work to diagnose blood diseases and abnormalities through cultures and research. I've always wanted to help people, and this is the way I want to do it.

My long-term goal of working in this profession is pretty solid. I've known for some time that this is what I want to do. I even shadowed a medical technologist several years ago. So, it would seem that I have had no trouble with goal setting, but I did.

I found that when I started college, I was so focused on my long-term goal that I had trouble with my short-term goals, like studying and passing tests. I was so "fixed" on my career that I missed many opportunities to set and achieve short-term goals. For example, I had problems in math and I was offered help, but I felt that I did not need help. I did not set any short-term goals for improving my math skills until it became painfully obvious that I had missed the boat. At midterm, we received our grades, and I was not doing as well as I wanted.

By learning to set short-term goals that reinforced my long-range goal, I have improved my academic performance greatly. Short-term goals helped me develop a study plan, get a tutor in math, and still have time for my friends. I finally saw the forest *and* the trees.

Why are short-term goals sometimes more important than long-term goals?

Why are long-term goals important?

If Jamie was your friend, what advice would you have shared with her when she was struggling in math class?

What is a long-term goal of yours and how do you plan to achieve it?

_____
_____
_____
_____
_____

List three short-term goals that are directly tied to your long-term career goal.

1. _____
_____
2. _____
_____
3. _____
_____

If you (or a friend of yours) are having trouble with goal setting or self-motivation, where can you go on your campus for assistance?

_____
_____

Phone # _____

at this moment Journal

Refer to page 35 of this chapter. Having read and reflected upon the information in the chapter, consider how you might revise your goal to make it more:

REASONABLE

BELIEVABLE

MEASURABLE

ADAPTABLE

CONTROLLABLE

DESIRABLE

ONLINE JOURNAL

To complete an online journal entry, log onto the Companion Website at www.prenhall.com/sherfield. Go to Chapter 2 and click on the link to the Online Journal. You can respond to the questions provided or to questions assigned by your professor, or you may journal about your own experiences.

ADVICE TO GO

CORNERSTONES

for motivation, goal setting, & self-esteem

Develop a *high standard* of academic, personal, and social *integrity*.

Use the power of *positive thinking*.

Step *outside* your comfort zone.

Base your goals on your *values*.

Broaden your circle of friends.

Seek professional counselling for *long-term* self-esteem problems.

Turn negative thoughts *loose*.

Don't give in to defeat.

Picture yourself *happy*.

Know what you want.

GROW

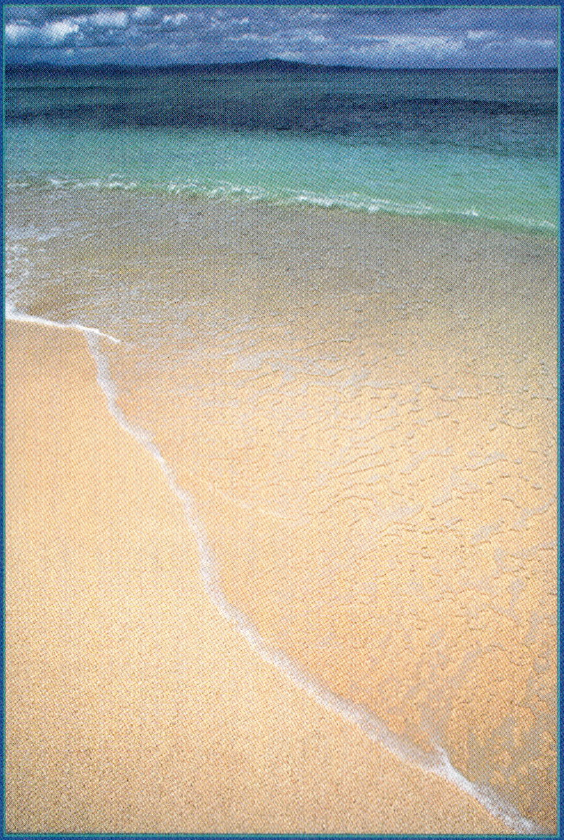

3 Persist

I'm a great believer in luck, and I find the harder I work, the more I have of it.

— Thomas Jefferson

CHAPTER 3
PERSIST

Vonda was beyond excited. She had waited for this day for 15 years. Today was the day that she had set aside to visit Clarkson College and tie up all of the loose ends that might hinder her from being successful in her first semester as an elementary education major.

Vonda had begun college 15 years ago, but dropped out to marry her high school sweetheart. Shortly after their marriage, she found herself pregnant with their first child. When Ben was only one and a half, she found herself pregnant with Jannyce. For the past 14 years, Vonda had been a mother, a wife, a daughter, a clerk at the grocery store, and a dreamer.

She dreamed of becoming a first-grade teacher, but her dreams were put on hold while her husband completed his engineering degree and they raised Ben and Jannyce. *But she never let go of the dream that one day she would be standing in front of first graders,* helping them learn about the world.

Today was that day. Vonda had received her acceptance letter to Clarkson last week. Her dream was really going to happen. Ben and Jannyce had started high school, her husband was behind her, she had given notice at the grocery store, and finally, the dream was no longer deferred.

Vonda drove to Clarkson with more excitement than she had felt in years. If the truth was known, more excitement than she had ever felt, with the exception of having her children. Her plans for the day were to attend the early morning orientation session, drop by financial aid to apply for a work-study position, meet her advisor, register for four classes, buy her books, find her classrooms, and have lunch in the dining hall. *She just wanted things to go smoothly.*

When Vonda turned onto the campus of Clarkson, she was stunned to see so many people. *Stunned!* She had arrived almost an hour early, but the student parking lot was beyond full. She drove to the back of the campus only to find that lot full as well. She circled for a while and finally decided to park down the road in an overflow lot. By the time she parked and walked back to campus, she only had five minutes before orientation started.

She ran to the auditorium, checked in, received her packet, and entered to find that there was standing room only, and not much of that. Shortly after she entered, the session began. The students were welcomed and for the next hour, person after person stood before them talking about college policies, vaccines, financial aid, parking, academic

Things You Need to Know About College But Might Never Ask

success centers, and student responsibilities. Vonda thought that her head would explode with so much new information. *But she was elated to be in this atmosphere of learning and growing.*

After the session was over, Vonda found her advisor, discovered the classes she needed to take first, bought her textbooks, found her classrooms, and then decided to have lunch before she went to the financial aid office. She found the dining hall, purchased her lunch, and decided to sit at an outside table to soak in the environment. *"I'm in college,"* she thought. She was ready to scream with joy.

Sitting there on that concrete bench, Vonda knew that things were not going to be easy. "I couldn't even park," she laughed to herself. "But *nothing is going to stop me now.*" She watched other students moving about the campus, talking, laughing—some walking alone, others with rolling suitcases full of books and fliers and dreams.

> **She dreamed of becoming a first-grade teacher, but her dreams were put on hold**

"Monday is it." As she sat there, her mind wandered. "Fifteen long years I've waited. I don't know what is down the road, but I'm ready to take the drive. I'm ready to jump any hurdle that is in front of me." She finished her lunch, took a few steps onto the campus green, and in her mind, she knew that she was home.

QUESTIONS FOR REFLECTION

Consider responding to these questions online in the Questions for Reflection module of the Companion Website.

1. Have you ever put a dream on hold? How did this affect your life?

2. Vonda was shocked over the parking situation. What is the biggest logistical shock you've had since beginning college?

3. Do you feel "at home" at your college like Vonda? Why or why not?

Where are you... AT THIS MOMENT

Before reading this chapter, take a moment and respond to the following 10 questions. Consider each one carefully before answering, and then respond by circling the number in the appropriate box. When you have answered the questions, add your points and find your total score on the feedback chart below.

STATEMENT	STRONGLY DISAGREE	DISAGREE	DON'T KNOW	AGREE	STRONGLY AGREE	SCORE
1. I have read and understand my college catalog.	1	2	3	4	5	
2. I am uncomfortable talking with professors.	5	4	3	2	1	
3. When I need help with my studies, I don't really know where to go to get that help.	5	4	3	2	1	
4. I do not enjoy participating in class discussions.	5	4	3	2	1	
5. I know what my professors' office hours are, and how to contact them.	1	2	3	4	5	
6. If I must stop attending a course, I know what actions I should take.	1	2	3	4	5	
7. I have spoken with an academic advisor or counselor more than once.	1	2	3	4	5	
8. I know what it means to be prepared to attend class.	1	2	3	4	5	
9. I do not know how the courses I intend to take will or will not transfer to other degree programs or other schools.	5	4	3	2	1	
10. I have investigated my options for financial aid, scholarships, grants, and loans.	1	2	3	4	5	
TOTAL VALUE						

SUMMARY

10–17 You seem to be lacking many of the skills and strategies necessary to successfully stay in school. You need to pay careful attention to the ideas and exercises you will encounter in this course, as well as visit your school's academic counseling department for additional guidance.

18–25 Your level of preparedness for college is limited; additional skills for successfully staying in school are needed. Make connections with your teachers and academic advisors and listen carefully to their suggestions.

26–34 You are average in your knowledge of what it takes to successfully stay in school. You likely have had successful school experiences, but some additional guidance and knowledge about your school's policies would benefit you.

35–42 You likely have an above average knowledge of how your school operates and how to get assistance when you need it. Continue to access the people and services at your school for on-going guidance and success.

43–50 You are exceptional in your knowledge of your school's support services and relate well with your instructors. When you need assistance, you're not afraid to seek it out and use it to your maximum benefit.

Goals . . . FOR CHANGE

Based on your total points, what is one goal you would like to achieve related to persisting in college?

Goal _____

_____

List three actions you can take that might help you move closer to realizing this goal.

1. _____
2. _____
3. _____

Questions FOR BUILDING ON YOUR BEST

As you read this chapter, consider the following questions. At the end of the chapter, you should be able to answer all of them. You are encouraged to ask a few questions of your own. Consider asking your classmates or professors to assist you.

1. How can I establish a positive relationship with my professors?
2. Where can I go on my campus if I need some serious academic help?
3. What is a grade point average (GPA), and how do I calculate it?
4. Where can I go to learn more about financial aid and scholarships?
5. Why is it important to get involved in campus life, and where can I go to find more information about clubs and organizations?

What additional questions might you have about the nuts and bolts of persisting in college?

1. _____
2. _____
3. _____

To Be Successful, You Have to Last
PERSISTENCE IN COLLEGE

Have you ever given up on something in the past and regretted it later? Do you ever think back and ask yourself, "What would my life be like if only I had done X or Y?" Have you ever made a decision or acted in a way that cost you dearly? If you see yourself in any of these statements, then you now know the value of persistence.

Persistence. The word itself means that you are going to stay—that you have found a way to stick it out, found a way to make it count, and found a way *to not give up*. That is what this chapter is all about—finding out how to make college work for you. It is about alerting you to the ins and outs of college life. It is about giving you advice up front that can save your college education and your future dreams.

Dropping out of college is not uncommon. As a matter of fact, over 40 percent of the people who begin college never complete their degrees. Don't be mistaken in thinking that they dropped out because of their inability to learn. Many leave because they made serious and irreparable mistakes early in their first year.

Before everything else, **getting ready** is the secret to success.   —HENRY FORD

Some students leave because they did not know how to manage their time. Some leave because they could not manage their money and didn't know how to look for scholarships and other funding sources. Some leave because they couldn't get along with a professor. And still, some leave because they simply could not figure out how "the system" worked, and frustration, anger, disappointment, and fear got the better of them.

You do not have to be one of these students. This chapter and *indeed this book and this course* are geared to help you NOT make those mistakes. They are geared to help you make the decisions that will lead to becoming a college graduate.

This chapter will offer you information and advice about professors, support services, activities, personal decorum, journaling, advising, preregistration, financial aid, and a host of other topics important to your success.

As you read through this book, you will find that very often we talk about *choices*. The choices you make in your first year can greatly help you persist to your second year and on to your degree.

What You Need to Know Up Front
COLLEGE POLICIES AND PROCEDURES

Familiarizing yourself with the policies and procedures of the college that you are attending can save you a great deal of grief and frustration in the long run.

Vonda was able to familiarize herself with many policies by reading the college catalog and attending orientation.

Policies and procedures vary from institution to institution, but regardless, it is your responsibility to know what you can expect from your institution and what your institution expects from you. These policies can be found in the college catalog (traditional and online) or student handbook or schedule of classes, depending on your college.

Some universal college policies include:

- Students must meet certain residence requirements for a degree (even if you transfer into the college).
- All students are subject to the Federal Privacy Act of 1974 (this ensures your privacy, even from your parents).
- Most institutions require placement tests (these are different from admission tests). They are used to properly advise you into the correct English, math, foreign language, reading, and/or vocabulary classes.
- Most colleges adhere to a strict drop/add date. Always check your schedule of classes for this information.
- Most colleges have an attendance policy for classroom instruction.
- Most colleges have a strict refund policy.
- Many colleges will not allow you to take over a certain number of credit hours per semester (18 semester hours is usually the upper limit).
- Most every college in America has an Academic Dishonesty Policy (this is discussed further in Chapter 10).
- Most colleges have a standing drug and alcohol policy.

Colleges do not put policies into place to hinder your degree completion; rather, the purpose is to ensure that all students are treated fairly and equitably.

Nutty or Nurturing?
THE COLLEGE PROFESSOR

The college teaching profession is like no other profession on earth. There are certain rights and privileges that come with this profession that are not granted to any other career; however, there are also demands that no other profession faces.

Unlike high school teachers, college professors are charged with much more than just classroom instruction. Many are required to research, write articles and books, attend and present at academic conferences, advise students, and keep current in their ever-changing fields of study.

Many of your college professors attended college for 7 to 12 years preparing to teach you. College professors, for the most part, must have at least a master's degree in their field, but many are required to have a doctorate. A professor who has obtained a bachelor's, a master's, and a doctorate may have spent as many as 12 or more years in higher education.

THE FREEDOM TO TEACH AND LEARN

Professors are granted something called **academic freedom**. Most high school teachers do not have this privilege. Academic freedom means that a professor has the right to teach controversial issues, topics, subjects, pieces of literature, scientific theories, religious tenets, and political points of view *without* the threat of termination.

Whereas you may not have been able to read Lillian Hellman's *The Children's Hour* in your high school drama class because of its homosexual overtones, you would be able to study it uncensored in a college literature or drama class. This is the right of the college professor—to teach and guide in an unobstructed atmosphere free from parental, administrative, trustee, or public pressure.

Because of academic freedom, you too have the right to speak your mind and disagree with issues ranging from politics to religion to social ills to controversial health and science matters. You can even disagree with your professors. If you choose to do so, be certain that you do so respectfully and in an assertive manner, not an aggressive one.

F? WHAT DO YOU MEAN AN F?

There will be times when you are disappointed with a grade that you receive from a professor. What do you do? Threaten? Sue? Become argumentative? Those techniques usually cost you more than they gain for you.

First, remember that the grade given by a professor is usually impervious. This means that seldom is the grade changeable. If you made a less than sterling grade, there are several things that you need to do. First, be truthful with yourself and examine the amount of time you spent on the project. Did you really give it your best? Next, review the requirements for the assignment. Did you miss something? Did you take an improper or completely wrong focus? Did you omit some aspect of the project? Did you turn the project in late?

Next, consider the following questions, as they can contribute to your total understanding of material, projects, and expectations.

- Did you attend class regularly?
- Did you come to class prepared and ready for discussion?
- Did you ask questions in class for clarification?
- Did you meet with the professor during office hours?
- Did you seek outside assistance in places such as the writing center or math lab?
- Did you ask your peers for assistance or join a peer study/focus group?

These activities can make the difference between success and failure with a project or a class.

If you are truly concerned about the grade, talk to the professor about the assignment. Ask him or her what is considered to be the most apparent problem with your assignment, and ask how you might improve your studying or preparing for the *next* assignment.

Above all, don't get into a verbal argument over the grade. In 99 percent of the cases, this will not help. Also, make sure that *the professor is your first point of contact*. Unless you have spoken with him or her *first* and exhausted all options with him or her, approaching the department chair, the dean, the vice president, or the president will more than likely result in your being sent directly back to the professor.

CLASSROOM CHALLENGES

When the professor doesn't show. At times during your college career, a professor will not show up for class. This will be rare, but it will happen. Sometimes, a note on the board or door will explain the circumstances of the professor's absence. If there is no note, assume that the professor is running late. Do not leave class just because the professor is not there on time. You should normally wait at least 15 minutes for a professor. Use common sense and wait long enough to see whether the professor is just running late or is truly not going to show up for the class.

You might consider starting a roster for students to sign before they leave so that you all have proof that you attended the class. You can present the list to the professor if there is a question about attendance.

Consult your college catalog or your class syllabus for details regarding a policy for waiting when a professor does not arrive.

When professors don't speak English well. Yes, you will have professors who do not speak English well. Universities often hire professors from around the world because of their expertise in their subjects. You may be shocked to find that it is difficult to understand a professor's dialect or pronunciation. If you have a professor with a foreign accent, remember these hints:

- Sit near the front of the room.
- Watch the professor's mouth when you can.
- Follow the professor's nonverbal communication patterns.
- Use a tape recorder if allowed.
- Read the material beforehand so that you will have a general understanding of what is being discussed.
- Ask questions when you do not understand the material.

Understanding what professors want. College professors are unique. They all value and appreciate different things. What makes one professor the happiest person on earth will upset another. One professor may love students who

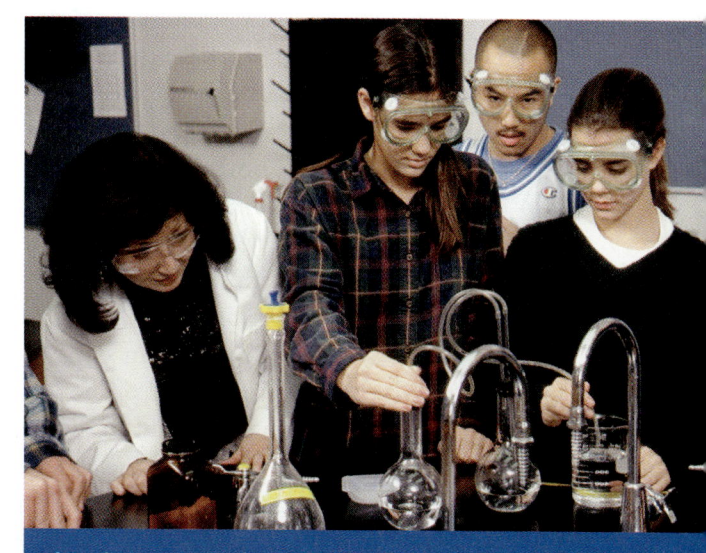

Large lecture classes often have a lab component, also, in which instruction is much more focused.

STRATEGIES
FOR BUILDING ON YOUR BEST

Consider the following strategies for making the most of your relationships with your college professors:

- Make an effort to get to know your professors outside the classroom if possible.
- Come to class prepared, bringing your best to the table each class session.
- Answer questions and ASK questions in class.
- Ask for help if you see things getting difficult.
- Never make excuses; talk and act like an adult.
- Volunteer for projects and co-curricular opportunities.
- Be respectful, and it will most likely be returned.

ask questions and another professor will think these students are trying to be difficult. One professor may enjoy students who have opposing points of view, while the next professor may consider them troublemakers. One professor may be stimulated when students stop by the office to chat, while another may consider this an infringement on his or her time.

The best way to deal with your professors is as individuals, on a one-to-one, class-by-class basis. Take some time at the beginning of the semester to make notes about what you see in class, how students are treated who do certain things, and how the professor reacts in certain situations. This exercise will assist you in decoding your professors and in making the most out of your relationship with them.

There are, of course, certain characteristics that all professors cherish in students, so keep in mind that all professors like students who read the text, come to class and come on time, and hand in assignments on time.

Success on a Platter
ACADEMIC SUCCESS CENTERS AND SERVICES

Most colleges offer you assistance for academic success outside the classroom. Your tuition or student activities fee may fund many of these centers. You've paid for them; you should take full advantage of their services.

Academic success centers usually provide one-on-one or group study sessions, private tutoring, specialized instruction, and self-paced tutorials. These centers can help you if you feel yourself falling behind, want to understand the material better, or want to enhance your study strategies.

Computer labs offer students the opportunity to use e-mail, Internet services, and other online applications usually free of charge. These centers are also usually staffed with trained professionals who can help you with problematic programming issues.

Writing Centers are staffed with professionals who are trained to assist you with your writing skills. They will not rewrite your paper for you, but they can give you advice on how to strengthen your project, properly document information, and add to the overall quality of your work. This can really help your grade in the classes where writing is important.

The very first step toward success in ANY ENDEAVOR is to become interested in it. —WILLIAM OSLER

Math Centers are staffed with professionals and usually student tutors. They are in place to help you with complex math problems, one-on-one or group tutoring, and study sessions. Traditionally, math is the single most difficult course for first-year students—even for those students who did well in high school math. Make use of this service before your first test or homework project. Even if you just drop by to confirm that what you've done is correct, it could save you grief later on.

Tutoring or Mastery Learning Centers usually are staffed by student tutors and offer assistance in almost any subject matter. Many colleges offer this service free of charge (or for a very nominal fee), whereas an outside tutor may charge upward of $30.00 to $45.00 per hour.

Language Labs are in place to help you if you are taking a foreign language or sign language. There may be "live" tutors to assist you or, more traditionally, there are computer-based tutorials that drill you in the respective language.

With all of the help available on your campus, you should begin to feel better even about the most difficult subjects that lie ahead. Colleges, and yes professors too, wish for your success, and these centers are just one way to help you become more successful.

Don't Panic . . . There's Something for Everyone

STUDENT SUCCESS CENTERS AND SERVICES

Unlike Academic Success Services, Student Success Services do not usually concentrate on the academic life of students; rather, they focus on the social, personal, career, and spiritual success of students.

These services range from campus clubs and organizations to legal services to chaplains to your college records (transcripts). Below, you will find a brief description of some of the major student services on most campuses.

Transcripts. This office keeps a record of all of your academic work from every college that you have attended. This is the office that you will visit to have your transcript sent to another institution if you choose to transfer.

Veteran affairs. This is the office that offers assistance to people who have served in the armed forces. They are experts at financial aid and regulations for veterans.

Re-entry or adult learning centers. The Re-Entry center is in place to assist returning adult students with making the transition to college. They can assist with child care, financial aid, and work-study programs.

International student services. This office is in place to assist students who have traveled to the United States from another country. They can help

DID YOU KNOW?

5,614,000

The number of students served annually in programs for the disabled.

Source: *The World Almanac and Book of Facts, 2002.* New York: World Almanac Books, 2003.

---

with language barriers, cultural barriers, federal and state regulations, and a variety of issues faced only by international students.

Minority student services. This office can offer assistance to minority students on campus. They can assist with financial aid and cultural issues, and may provide support and social groups for minority students.

Security. Most every campus has some form of campus security. Many campuses have their own police force. They are in place to assist you with security and safety issues. Upon request, they can even walk you to your car if you are taking a night class.

Career services. This office is invaluable to first-year students and graduating students alike. They can assist you in finding employment on campus or off campus, and they can assist you in determining a major and ultimate career. This service is usually free to currently enrolled students.

Disabled student services. If you have a documented disability, colleges and universities across America are required by law to offer you "reasonable accommodations" to ensure your success (Americans with Disabilities Act, Sec. 504). If you are visually impaired, colleges will assist you with appropriate texts in Braille or on tape. If you are deaf or hard of hearing, colleges will work to provide you an interpreter. If you are physically challenged, colleges will make every effort to see that your classes are accessible. Some of the other services offered by the college might include:

- Handicapped parking
- Special testing centers
- Extended time on tests and timed projects
- Textbook translations and conversions
- Interpreters
- Note-taking services
- TTY/TDD services
- Closed captioning

Health services. Many campuses offer the assistance of doctors and/or nurses. They can assist with health issues ranging from a cold to referring you for further medical advice. Many offer forms of contraception and some can even dispense medicine.

Mental/emotional health services. Some colleges offer mental health counseling on campus. If you feel that you need to speak with someone about troubling issues, this could be a great place to start. If your college does not offer mental health services, the counseling department may be able to offer you a referral.

Celebrate GOOD TIMES

As you begin to search for ways to get involved, think about the following clubs and organizations . . .

Student Newspaper	Intramural Sports
Student Literary Magazine	Music or Band
Student Yearbook	Medical Associations
Art Club	Nursing
Hiking Club	Radiology
Biology Club	Physical Therapy, etc. . .
Astronomy Club	Language Clubs
Student Business Association	Speech Club
Student Government	Technology Clubs
Accounting Club	Preprofessional Organizations

IF YOUR CLUB OF INTEREST DOES NOT EXIST, TALK WITH A FACULTY MEMBER AND START IT!

Student activities. Most every college offers some type of student activity. From the newspaper to the hiking club, if you want to be involved, there is usually something to do. Student activities offer more than a place to play or hike or draw—they are an opportunity to be around people with similar interests, great places to find a mentor, and a fantastic time to network and begin making connections for career opportunities. You can do this and have fun, too!

The Golden Rule—or Just a Crock?

CLASSROOM ETIQUETTE AND PERSONAL DECORUM

You may be surprised, but the way you act in (and out) of class can mean as much to your success as what you know. No one can make you do anything or act in any way that you do not want. The following tips are provided from years of research and actual conversations with thousands of professors teaching across America. You have to be the one who chooses whether or not to use this advice.

- Bring your materials to class daily: texts, notebooks, pens, calculators, and syllabi.
- Come to class prepared: read your text and handouts, do the assigned work at home, bring questions to be discussed.

- Turn in papers, projects, and assignments on time. Many professors do not accept late work.
- Participate in class. Ask questions, bring current events to the discussion, and contribute with personal experiences.
- Visit professors during office hours. The time before and after class may not be the most appropriate time for you or the professor. Your professor may have "back-to-back" classes and may be unable to assist you.
- If you are late for class, enter quietly, DO NOT walk in front of the professor, don't let the door slam, don't talk on your way in, and take the seat nearest the door. Make every effort not to be late to class.
- Wait for the professor to dismiss class before you begin to pack your bags to leave. You may miss important information or you may cause someone else to miss important information.
- Never carry on a conversation with another student while the professor or another student is talking.
- Do not sleep in class. If you are having problems staying awake, you should consider dropping the class and taking it at another time next semester.
- If for any reason you must leave during class, do so quietly and quickly. It is customary to inform the professor that you will be leaving early before class begins.
- If you make an appointment with a professor, keep it. If you must cancel, a courtesy call is in order.
- If you don't know how to address your professor; that is, by Mr., Mrs., Miss., Ms., or Dr., ask them which they prefer, or simply call them "Professor _____."

> Tain't no law on earth dat kin make a man be decent if it ain't in 'im. —ZORA NEALE HURSTON

- You should not wear sunglasses, oversized hats, strong cologne or perfume, skates, or earphones to class.
- Be respectful of other students. Profanity and obscene language may offend some people. You can have strong, conflicting views without being offensive.
- Turn off your cell phone or beeper. If you have a home or work situation that requires that you "stay connected," put the device on vibrate.
- If you act like an adult (which you are), you'll be treated as one.

Remember that respect for others on your part will afford you the opportunity to establish relationships that otherwise you might never have had.

Writing Your First-Year History
TIPS FOR JOURNALING

It may seem a little crazy at the moment, but keeping a journal during your first year of college can be an amazing trip. If you write just one entry per week, you'll be amazed how much you've changed when you read the entries just 16 weeks later at the end of the term. With journaling, you are, in essence, creating a history of your first year in college. You will be able to look back years later and reminisce about the issues, policies, and social ills of the day. And most interestingly, it will be your personal account of what was happening at the time.

Journaling has been around as long as humans have been around. Early cave dwellings are filled with drawings and designs that tell stories and share information about people and their past. Your journaling efforts will do no less. Properly used, this text will allow you to create a history of your first year in college. You will, in essence, be creating a written history of who you were, what you believed, and how you felt during your first-year experience.

Journaling is an important aspect of the *Cornerstone* program. Each chapter suggests that you consider journaling in your online journal.

WHY JOURNAL?
- To recover from the past
- To explain the present
- To interact with our feelings
- To dream about the future
- To assess where we are at the present moment
- To nurture our spiritual lives

HOW LONG DOES JOURNALING TAKE?
- As long as it takes. There is no time limit, and journaling will be different for every person.
- If you have never kept a journal before, set aside at least 20 minutes for each journaling project.
- Know that the more you journal, the more time it usually takes.

WHEN SHOULD I JOURNAL?
- Regularly
- At least three times per week
- During a time when you are least likely to be interrupted

WHAT SHOULD I JOURNAL?
- The truth, and only the truth
- Your feelings
- Your desires and dreams and wishes
- Your fears and challenges

Journaling Beyond Cornerstone

Cornerstone asks you to reflect on the material in the text or on the website. You may wish to consider creating your own first-year journal in a separate binder or online. If you choose to do so, you may want to consider the following topics or headings for your writings:

- Daily thoughts and actions
- Your history
- Pilgrimage (your personal growth)
- Dreams
- Musings
- Family
- School
- Finances

Gotta Get Out of Here!
DROPPING CLASSES, DROPPING OUT, STOPPING OUT

Sometimes, students have to drop a class or their entire schedule because of family problems, medical reasons, work, or other reasons. We mention this because some students simply leave college, thinking that if they do not come back, their classes will automatically be dropped and everything will be fine. Then, when they return or transfer to another college, they are horrified to see five F's on their transcript. Never assume that your classes have been dropped from your records. At most colleges, classes are not automatically dropped. You must take care of this process. To make matters worse, some colleges never remove grades from your transcript, even if you repeat the course a thousand times and make an A every time. If you leave your classes without taking care of the paperwork, your grade of F can be with you and be calculated in your GPA for the rest of your college years.

If you have to drop all your classes, it is best to talk with each professor and explain why you are leaving. An open and honest relationship with your professors could help you when you return. Leaving your classes for an entire semester is called *dropping out*; if you decide not to return to college, the same term applies. Leaving college for one semester because of problems, work, or military service and planning to return is called by some colleges *stopping out*. Whether you drop a class, drop out for the semester, or stop out for a year, make sure your records are in order before you go. This will save you money, time, effort, and frustration on your return to college. Consult your college catalog for information dealing with dropping out, dropping courses, or stopping out.

Where Is It Written?
YOUR COLLEGE CATALOG

Every college in the nation has a different catalog. Don't make the mistake of thinking that these catalogs are advertising tools and not that important. Your college catalog is one of the most important publications you will read during your college years. It describes the rules, regulations, policies, procedures, and requirements of the college and your academic degree. It is imperative for you to keep the college catalog that was issued during your first year because college degree requirements can change from year to year. Most colleges require that you graduate under the rules and requirements stated in the catalog under which you entered the college. This policy is sometimes referred to as the grandfather clause.

The college catalog includes information about adding and dropping classes, auditing, probation, plagiarism, attendance, honors, course descriptions, graduation requirements, faculty credentials, and college accreditation, and usually includes a campus map. It is an important tool.

Let Me Give You a Piece of Advice
THE ACADEMIC ADVISOR/COUNSELOR

Your academic advisor is one of the most important people you will meet at college. You may never have your advisor for a class or even see your advisor except at registration time each semester, but he or she can be of enormous assistance to you throughout your college career.

Advisors are usually appointed by the college, although a few colleges allow students to select their own advisors. A good advisor will be of tremendous value to you; a poor advisor is one of the worst things that could happen to you. If you find that you and your advisor are completely incompatible, do not hesitate to ask for a reassignment.

Recognize that you are the person most responsible for the completion of your degree. You should know as much as your advisor about your degree.

Your roommates, friends, and peers can help you in the advising and registration process, but the last word should always come from your advisor. Your decisions about classes and scheduling should be made with the advice of faculty, staff, and the administration of the college.

If you do not know why you have to take certain courses or in what sequence courses should

Your academic advisor is one of the most important people you will meet at college.

be taken, don't leave your advisor's office until you find out. Lack of understanding of your course sequence, your college catalog, or the requirements for graduation could mean the difference between a four-year degree, a five-year degree, or no college degree at all.

Academic advisors are not psychological counselors. They are assigned to assist students in completing their academic programs of study. They may offer advice on personal or career matters, but they are not trained to assist with psychological and emotional matters. However, if you are having problems not related to your academic studies, your academic advisor may be able to direct you to the professional on campus who can best help you address certain issues and problems. Your academic advisor may be the first person to contact in times of crisis.

MAKING THE MOST OF YOUR STUDENT–ADVISOR RELATIONSHIP

- Locate your advisor as soon as you arrive on campus and introduce yourself. Begin your relationship on a positive note.
- Stop by to say hello if you see your advisor in his or her office. Don't stay for a long time without an appointment, but a brief hello can help you build your relationship.
- Prepare a list of questions before you go to your advisor. This will help ensure that you have all the answers you need when you leave.
- Call your advisor if you have a problem that can be dealt with over the phone.
- Don't go to your advisor unprepared. You should have an idea of which classes you would like to take or need to take for the upcoming semester.

You're Not in Kansas Anymore . . .
TRANSFER ISSUES

Many students enroll with the notion that they will one day transfer to another institution, perhaps after a semester, a year, or after earning a two-year degree.

First, your "Survival Guide for Transfer" is the college catalog; not only the catalog from your current institution, but also the catalog from the institution to which you plan to transfer. They are both helpful, but you need to be as mindful of the receiving college's requirements and policies as those of your current college.

You also need to be aware that most colleges WILL NOT accept grades below a "C" (2.0) from another institution. Also, you will find that your future college DOES NOT transfer your grade point average (GPA). When you transfer to your future college, your GPA will start anew. This can be a double-edged sword. If you have a 4.0 at your current college, sadly, you must start again at

There are no secrets to success. It is the result of preparation, hard work and learning from failure. —GENERAL COLIN POWELL

the future college. However, if you had a 2.0, you get to start again at your future college. GPAs are explained later in this chapter.

Finally, and maybe *most* importantly, you need to speak with an informed, qualified TRANSFER advisor or counselor before registering for any course or degree if you plan to transfer. Your relationship with your advisor or counselor holds as much importance as your relationship with your professors and peers.

Does 1 + 1 Really Equal 2?
HOW TO CALCULATE YOUR GRADE POINT AVERAGE

The grade point average (GPA) is the numerical grading system used by almost every college in the nation. GPAs determine if a student is eligible for continued enrollment, financial aid, or honors. Most colleges operate under a 4.0 system. This means that:

Each A earned is worth 4 quality points

Each B is worth 3 points

Each C is worth 2 points

Each D is worth 1 point

Each F is worth 0 points

For each course, the number of quality points earned is multiplied by the number of credit hours carried by the course. For example, if you are taking

English 101 for 3 semester hours of credit

Speech 101 for 3 semester hours of credit

History 201 for 3 semester hours of credit

Psychology 101 for 3 semester hours of credit

Spanish 112 for 4 semester hours of credit

then you would be enrolled for **16 hours** of academic credit. Your calculation would look like this:

	GRADE	SEMESTER CREDIT		QUALITY POINTS		TOTAL POINTS
ENG 101	A	3 hours	×	4	=	12 points
SPC 101	C	3 hours	×	2	=	6 points
HIS 201	B	3 hours	×	3	=	9 points
PSY 101	D	3 hours	×	1	=	3 points
SPN 112	B	4 hours	×	3	=	12 points
		16 hours				**42 Total Points**

42 total points divided by **16 semester hours** equals a **GPA of 2.62** (or C+ average).

Lowering a GPA is very easy, but raising one is not as easy. Examine how just one grade can affect your GPA. As in the example below, the Spanish grade is lowered to an F from a B.

	GRADE	SEMESTER CREDIT		QUALITY POINTS		TOTAL POINTS
ENG 101	A	3 hours	×	4	=	12 points
SPC 101	C	3 hours	×	2	=	6 points
HIS 201	B	3 hours	×	3	=	9 points
PSY 101	D	3 hours	×	1	=	3 points
SPN 112	F	4 hours	×	0	=	0 points
		16 hours				**30 Total Points**

30 total points divided by **16 semester hours** equals a **GPA of 1.87** (or D+ average).

From the Far Away Nearby

SUCCEEDING IN DISTANCE EDUCATION AND INDEPENDENT STUDY COURSES

Independent study courses or courses taught by distance learning are great for students who work or have families and small children. These courses have flexible hours and few, if any, class meetings and allow you to work at your own pace. Do not let anyone try to tell you that these courses are easier than regular classroom offerings; they are not. Independent study and distance-learning courses are usually more difficult for the average student. Some colleges reserve independent study and distance-learning courses for students with GPAs of 3.0 or higher. You need to be a self-starter and highly motivated to complete and do well in these courses.

Consider the following tips when registering for independent study or distance education classes:

- If at all possible, review the material for the course before you register. This may help you in making the decision to enroll.
- Begin before the beginning! If at all possible, obtain the independent study packet or distance-learning materials before the semester begins and start working. You may think you can wait because you have the whole semester, but time will quickly slip by.
- Make an appointment to meet the professor as soon as possible. Some colleges will schedule a meeting for you. If it is not possible to meet, at least phone the professor and introduce yourself.
- Communicate with your advisor from time to time via e-mail if your campus is equipped for you to do so.
- Develop a schedule for completing each assignment and stick to it! Don't let time steal away from you. This is the biggest problem with these courses.

- Keep a copy of all work mailed, e-mailed, or delivered to the professor or the college. When possible, send your materials by certified mail to ensure their delivery.
- Always mail, e-mail, or deliver your assignment on time or even early if possible. Remember that you have deadlines and the mail system can be slow. Allow time in your schedule for revisions.
- Try to find someone who is registered for the same course so that you can work together or at least have a phone number to call if you run into a problem.

But I'm Not Even Finished with This One Yet!

PREREGISTRATION FOR NEXT TERM

Sounds simple: preregister, "to register beforehand." Preregistration is a process by which you reserve your seat in classes for the upcoming semester. Although it sounds simple, a large number of students fail to preregister or pay fees. If you are at a large institution, preregistration is a must. If 300 people want to take a class that has 45 seats, logic will tell you that you can't walk in on the first day of class and expect to get a seat. Your graduation may hinge on preregistration; if you are not able to enroll in certain classes, your course sequence could be thrown off and you may have to wait an entire year before a required class is offered again.

It is equally important to pay your fees on time to ensure that your seat is held until the semester begins. Many colleges have a purge date. If you do not pay your fees by the end of fall term exams, for instance, your schedule of classes for spring semester and your seats in those classes are purged from the computer and another student will get your seat. You may have to pay a late fee and go through the registration process again. More important, the classes you need may be full, and if so, you will have to wait another year to take them. Preregister and pay your fees! Consult your college schedule of classes to determine registration dates and fee payment dates.

TIPS FOR PREREGISTERING

- Don't wait until the last day of preregistration to begin the process.
- Think ahead. If preregistration begins on October 15, you should review the college catalog before that date to begin planning your schedule.
- Make an appointment with your advisor early. Keep the appointment and be on time.
- When developing your schedule, work with several plans. If one class happens to be full, what are your alternatives? The students who graduate on time are those who know how to plan alternatives.
- Present your advisor with options. Don't suggest only one class or time. You may have to rearrange your life to get the class you need. Do it!
- There is no need to pay your fees on the first day of fee payment, but make sure that you do not miss the deadline.

WORLD OF WORK

One of the main reasons I have been able to accomplish a great many goals at a relatively young age can be attributed to one word—persistence. I have always listened to people who are wiser and older than I am and tried to learn from them if they are positive. On the other hand, I have not let negative people influence me. There's always someone to tell you something can't be done. If I had listened to them, I would have just given up before I even got started. There have been many people who have told me I couldn't do something. "You are too young." "You don't have enough experience." "You need to wait awhile and learn more before you try this." My advice to students is to ignore negative people and persist at accomplishing your goals. Only you know what you can do and what price you are willing to pay.

I wasn't a 4.0 college student, but I consistently went to class, took good notes, and turned in my work on time. While I was in college, I started a T-shirt business that paid for my college expenses. I also started buying and selling cars. While I was still in college, I sold an idea to Wal-Mart that did very well. Of course, I had to use creativity, and I had to work very hard to be a college student and an entrepreneur. Here again, the main thing that kept me going was persistence and a great desire to be successful.

When I was 26, I decided to run for the South Carolina House of Representatives against an incumbent who was entrenched and considered unbeatable. I'm sure many people thought I was crazy, but I thought, "What have I got to lose?" Building on what I had learned in college and business, I just rolled up my sleeves and went to work. My friends and I literally fixed potholes in the streets in one of the towns in the district where I was running for the House. I walked door-to-door every day, calling on the voters in my district. Persistence was the key to my victory to the House of Representatives, and persistence in serving my constituents got me re-elected.

After a few years, the Senate seat for the South Carolina legislature in my district came open, and I tossed my hat in the ring. Again, I had advice to wait, to think hard about this decision, etc. Again, I did what I have always done. I worked hard and I used persistence. I won that race and worked hard for my constituents, always keeping a goal of a statewide race in mind. In 2002, I announced for the Lieutenant Governor's race and began the hardest year of my life. I traveled all over the state meeting people, raising money, studying the issues, shaking hands, improving my speaking ability—persisting day after day after day.

I was sworn in at age 33 as Lieutenant Governor of South Carolina. I am very fortunate to have the honor of serving the people of South Carolina. I will do this job as I have done every job—keeping persistence high on my list of priorities that led to past successes.

QUESTIONS FOR REFLECTION

Consider responding to these questions online in the World of Work module of the Companion Website.

1. Have there been times when you wanted something very badly, but you listened to people who told you that you could not succeed? How did this affect your life?
2. Discuss one time in your life where you persisted against all odds and won.
3. How can you use Lieutenant Governor Bauer's story to help you increase your staying power in college?

Andre Bauer, *Lieutenant Governor,* Columbia, SC

Pennies from Heaven
THE SECRET WORLD OF FINANCIAL AID

You may feel that it is crazy to talk about financial aid at this point. After all, you had to have found the money to enroll in college or you would not be in this orientation class. Still, financial aid comes in many forms, and there may be some sources of aid you have not yet thought about that can help you through the rest of your college years.

The most well-known sources of financial assistance are the federal and state governments. Federal and state financial aid programs have been in place for many years and are a staple of assistance for many college students. Sources of aid include:

- Federal and state loans
- Federal and state grants
- Scholarships (local, regional, and national)
- Work study

Not every school takes part in every federal assistance program. To determine which type of aid is available at your school, you need to contact the financial aid office.

Some students may be confused about the differences between loans, grants, and work-study programs. The following definitions are supplied by *The Student Guide,* published by the U.S. Department of Education:

- Grants—Monies that you don't have to repay
- Work Study—Money earned for work that you do at the college that does not have to be repaid
- Loans—Borrowed money that you must repay with interest

An undergraduate may receive any of these types of assistance, whereas graduate students cannot receive Pell Grants or FSEOGs.

One of the biggest mistakes students make when thinking about financial aid is forgetting about scholarships from private industry and social or civic organizations. Each year, millions of dollars are unclaimed because students do not know about these scholarships or where to find the necessary information. Below, you will find resources that can help you research and apply for all types of financial aid.

FEDERAL FINANCIAL AID TYPES

Pell Grant. This is a need-based grant awarded to qualified undergraduate students who have not been awarded a previous degree. Amounts vary based on need and costs.

Federal Supplemental Educational Opportunity Grant (FSEOG). This is a need-based grant awarded to institutions to allocate to students through their financial aid offices.

Stafford Loan (formerly known as the Guaranteed Student Loan). The Stafford Direct Loan Program is a low interest, subsidized loan. You must show need to qualify. The government pays the interest while you are in school, but you must be registered for at least half-time status. You begin repayments six months after you leave school.

Unsubsidized Stafford Loan. This Stafford Loan is a low interest, NON-subsidized loan. You DO NOT have to show need to qualify. You are responsible for the interest on the loan while you are enrolled. Even though the government does not pay the interest, you can defer the interest and the payment until six months after you have left school.

PLUS Loan. This is a federally funded, but state administered, low interest loan to qualified parents of students in college. The student must be enrolled at least half-time. Parents must pass a credit check and payments begin 60 days after the last loan payment.

Work Study. Work study is a federally funded, need-based program that pays students an hourly wage for working on (and sometimes off) campus. Students earn at least minimum wage.

Hope Scholarship Tax Credit. This tax credit is for students in their first two years of college and who are enrolled at least half-time in a degree or certificate program. For each student, taxpayers may receive a 100 percent tax credit for each year for the first $1000.00 of qualified out-of-pocket expenses. They also may claim a 50 percent credit on the second $1000.00 used for qualified expenses (U.S. Bank, 2002).

Perkins Loan. This is a need-based loan where the amount of money you can borrow is determined by the government and the availability of funds. The interest rate is 5 percent and repayment begins nine months after you leave school or drop below half-time status. You can take up to 10 years to repay the loan. (Note: The Federal Government may have eliminated this program by the publication time of this book.)

DRUGS AND MONEY

What do drugs and money have in common? More than you might think! Did you know that when applying for federal financial aid, you must complete a drug conviction worksheet? This worksheet will be used to determine if you can receive ANY type of federal aid. Be warned!

The questions on the worksheet include:

- Have you ever been convicted of selling or possessing drugs?
- Have you completed an acceptable drug rehab program since your last conviction?
- Do you have more than two convictions for possessing drugs?
- Do you have more than one conviction for selling drugs?

Financial Aid Glossary

Borrower— The person who borrows the funds and agrees to repay them.

COA— Cost of Attendance. This is the total amount it will cost you to go to college.

Cosigner— A person who signs a promissory note and agrees to repay the debt should the borrower default.

Default— The term used when you do not repay your student loans. This will prevent you from receiving any further funding. Your wages can be garnished until full restitution is made. Your tax refunds will also be held until full payment is made. This default will also be reported to credit agencies and your credit will be scarred for seven to ten years.

Deferment— A period of time when you do not have to make loan payments. This period usually applies to education loans and usually lasts only six to nine months.

EFC— Expected Family Contribution. The amount of money your family contributes to your educational costs.

FAFSA— Free Application for Federal Student Aid. The application that you (or your parents) fill out to determine your financial needs. This is the first step in any financial aid process.

FAT— Financial Aid Transcript. A record of your financial assistance from all institutions.

Gross income— Your income before taxes and deductions.

Interest— The fee (or amount of money) charged to you to borrow money.

Late fee— A fee charged to you if you do not make your payment on time.

Need analysis— A formula established by Congress to determine your financial need. This is based on your FAFSA form.

Net income— Your income after taxes and deductions.

Payoff— The total amount owed on a loan if you were to pay it off in one lump sum.

Principal— The exact dollar amount that you borrowed and the amount on which interest is charged.

Promissory note— A legal document that obligates the borrower to repay funds.

Selective Service Registration— If you are required by law to register with Selective Service, you must do so before you can qualify for federal student aid.

There are three ingredients in the good life: learning, earning, and yearning. —CHRISTOPHER MORELY

Student Eligibility for Federal Financial Aid[*]

To receive aid from the major federal student aid programs, you must:

- Have financial need, except for some loan programs.
- Hold a high school diploma or GED, pass an independently administered test approved by the U.S. Department of Education, or meet the standards established by your state.
- Be enrolled as a regular student working toward a degree or certificate in an eligible program. You may not receive aid for correspondence or telecommunications courses unless they are a part of an associate, bachelor, or graduate degree program.
- Be a U.S. citizen.
- Have a valid Social Security number.
- Make satisfactory academic progress.
- Sign a statement of educational purpose.
- Sign a statement of updated information.
- Register with the Selective Service, if required.

[*]Some federal financial aid may be dependent on your not having a previous drug conviction.

Source: Adapted from *The Student Guide: Financial Aid from the U.S. Department of Education*. U.S. Dept. of Education, Washington, DC, 2002-2003.

SCHOLARSHIPS

Each year, millions and millions of scholarship dollars go unclaimed simply because no one applied for them. Scholarships are given to students based on academic excellence, talent, need, affiliation, sporting abilities, social interests, community involvement, and a variety of other attributes.

When looking for scholarships, use the Internet as a tool for tracking down appropriate sources. Your local bookstore will also carry many books that offer sources and even applications.

TIPS FOR APPLYING FOR FINANCIAL AID

- *Do not miss a deadline*. There are *no* exceptions for making up deadlines for federal financial aid!
- *Read all instructions* before beginning the process.
- Always fill out the application completely and have someone proof your work.
- If documentation is required, submit it according to the instructions. Do not fail to do all that the application asks you to do.
- Never lie about your financial status.
- Begin the application process as soon as possible. Do not wait until the last moment. Some aid is given on a first come, first served basis. Income tax preparation time is usually financial aid application time.
- Talk to the financial aid officer at the institution you will attend. Person-to-person contact is always best. Never assume anything until you get it in writing.

- Take copies of fliers and brochures that are available from the financial aid office. Private companies and civic groups will often notify the financial aid office if they have funds available.
- Always apply for admission as well as financial aid. Many awards are given by the college to students who are already accepted.
- If you are running late with an application, find out if there are electronic means of filing.
- Always keep a copy of your tax returns for each year!
- To receive almost any money, including some scholarships, you must fill out the Free Application for Federal Student Aid form.
- Apply for everything possible. You will get nothing if you do not apply.

FINANCIAL AID RESOURCES

Consider the following books when looking for money for college. Also log onto *Cornerstone's* Companion Website at www.prenhall.com/sherfield for some really great websites about financial aid and scholarships.

- *How to Go to College Almost for Free*
- *Paying for College Without Going Broke*
- *Don't Miss Out: The Ambitious Student's Guide to Financial Aid*
- *The Best Way to Save for College*
- *Winning Grants, Step By Step*, 2nd edition
- *The A, B, C's of Academic Scholarships*
- *Free College and Training Money for Women*
- *Kaplan Scholarships, 2005*
- *College Financial Aid: How to Get Your Fair Share*
- *Get Free Cash for College*
- *Cash for College*
- *The Student Aid Game*

Financial aid and scholarships may not be easy money to find, but it is certainly worth the effort. With combined federal and state aid, scholarships, work study, and tax credits, you may very well have most of your tuition and books covered. Good luck in your search!

Playing It Safe
PROTECTING YOURSELF ON CAMPUS

Each year, colleges and universities around the nation are required to report and publish the number of crimes committed on campus. Those crimes include homicide, rape, forcible sex offenses, assaults, robberies, and burglaries. These statistics may be found in your student handbook, class schedule, or college catalog.

The following tips are provided to assist you in protecting yourself against simple or violent crimes (Business and Legal Reports, Inc., 1995).

- Allow campus security to escort you to your car or residence hall if you are taking a night class.
- Walk in groups at night or in poorly lit places.
- Don't bring valuables to campus.
- Whereever you live: lock your doors and windows when you are sleeping, don't prop your door open, pull the blinds or curtains in the evenings, never give your key to anyone, and never invite strangers into your residence.
- Protect your belongings by taking out a renter's insurance policy.
- When walking around campus, walk confidently and not like a victim.
- Lock your car doors and always have your keys ready when you approach your car.
- Park in well-lit areas close to buildings.
- Lock valuables in your trunk.
- Never carry a lot of money with you.
- Use an ATM that is outside, well lit, and in a populated area.
- Never leave your book bag unattended.
- Always lock your bicycle to something that can't be moved.
- If you are robbed, never fight back, let them have what they want.
- NEVER go anywhere with a person who attacks you; try every means possible to get away.
- Lock your car doors every time you are in the car.
- If someone is following you, try to "lose" them by making unexpected turns.
- Always date in groups until you get to know new people.
- Always let someone know where you are going and with whom.
- Be very careful where you use alcohol—it can cloud your judgment.

Won't You Stay for a While?
PERSISTING IN COLLEGE

It is estimated that each year, nearly 40 percent of the people who begin their college career do not enroll for a second year. The national college dropout rate for public two-year colleges is 48 percent. The average college dropout rate for public four-year colleges is 32 percent (ACT, Inc., 2000).

The age-old "scare tactic" for first-year students, "Look to your left, look to your right—one of those people will not graduate with you," is not far from the truth. But the good news (actually, the great news) is that you do not have to become a statistic. You do not have to drop out of classes or college. You have the power to earn your degree. Sure, you may have some catching up to do. You may have to work harder and longer, but the beauty of college is that if you want help, you can get help.

Below, you will find some powerful, helpful tips for persisting in college. Using only a few of them can increase your chances of obtaining your degree. Using all of them virtually assures it!

- **Visit your advisor or counselor** frequently and establish a relationship with him or her. Take his or her advice. Ask him or her questions. Use him or her as a mentor.
- **Register for the classes in which you place.** It is unwise to register for Math 110 if you placed in Math 090 or English 101 if you placed in English 095. It will only cost you money, heartache, time, and possibly a low GPA.
- **Make use of every academic service** that you need that the college offers, from tutoring sessions to writing centers; these are essential tools to your success.

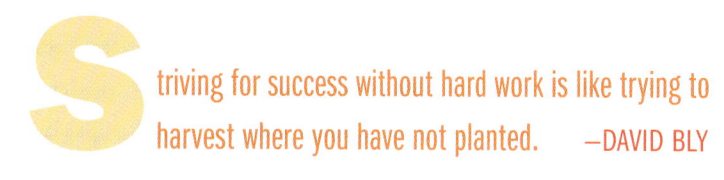

> Striving for success without hard work is like trying to harvest where you have not planted. —DAVID BLY

- Work hard to **learn and understand your "learning style."** This can help you in every class in which you enroll. Chapter 4 will assist you with this endeavor.
- Work hard to **develop a sense of community**. Get to know a few people on campus such as a special faculty member, a secretary, another student, or anyone that you can turn to for help.
- **Join a club or organization**. Research proves that students who are connected to the campus through activities drop out less.
- **Watch your finances carefully**. Don't get "credit-carditis." If you see yourself getting into financial trouble, seek counseling immediately! Poor financial management can cost you your degree as quickly as failing four classes.
- After reading Chapter 2, "Grow," concentrate on setting realistic, achievable goals. **Visualize your goals**. Write them down. Find a picture that represents your goal and post it so that you can see your goal every day.
- Work hard to develop and **maintain a sense of self-esteem and self-respect.** The better you feel about yourself, the more likely you will reach your goals.
- **Learn to budget your time** as wisely as you budget your money. You've made a commitment to college and it will take a commitment of time to bring your degree to fruition.
- **Use preregistration** time to reserve your classes. Don't wait until "after the holidays" or "after summer" to pre-enroll.
- If you have trouble with a professor, don't let it fester. Make an appointment to **speak with the professor** and work through the problem.
- If you get bored in class or feel that the class is not going to benefit you, remember that it is a required class and **you will always have a few boring classes** during your college career. Stick to it and it will be over soon.

- If you feel your professor doesn't care, it may be true. Some don't. This is where you have to **learn to care for yourself**. You must matter to you.
- **Find some type of strong, internal motivation** to sustain you through the tough times—and there will be tough times.
- **Focus on the future.** Yes, you're taking six classes while your friends are off partying, but in a few years, you'll have something that no party could ever offer, and something that no one can ever take away . . . your very own college degree.
- **Choose optimism.** Approach each day with a positive and upbeat attitude, even if it is Tuesday and you have your two hardest classes. Today is the day you're going to have a breakthrough!
- **Move beyond mediocrity**. Everyone can be average. If college were easy, everybody would have a college degree. You will need to learn to bring your best to the table for each class.
- **Focus on your career choice**. Can you do what you want to do without a college degree? That is perhaps the most important question when it comes to persistence. Can you have what you want, do what you want, be who you want to be without this degree?

As professors, we wish you every success imaginable. Use us as resources, contact us, ask us questions, trust us, visit us, and allow us to help you help yourself.

BLUEPRINTS FOR CHANGE

NAME DATE

REFLECTION

College can be a daunting and trying place, especially to a first-year student. There has never been a time when the old saying "knowledge is power" is more true. The more you know and understand about your institution, the less likely you will make mistakes that can cost you time, emotional distress, money . . . and your degree!

When you go to purchase a car, you spend time researching and considering. You want to make sure that you know as much as you can before you "take the leap." You should approach your education with the same type of fervor and understanding.

By simply taking the time to familiarize yourself with the workings of your college, you can eliminate many of the hassles that first-year students face. By doing this, you can enjoy your experience with more energy, excitement, and optimism. Good luck.

GET REAL

Below are a few questions to help you think about the nuts and bolts of life at your college. Study each question carefully and respond accurately.

If you failed a math test, where could you go to find assistance?

Phone # _____

If you have trouble writing and want to get advice before you turn your paper in to the professor, where could you find help?

Phone # _____

Where would you go to find out which clubs and organizations exist on your campus?

Phone # _____

If you would like to speak to someone about a health issue, is there a place on your campus?   Yes   No

Phone # _____

What is your internal motivation for staying in college?

How can financial aid affect your college success?

How can joining a club or organization affect your joy in life?

91

Case Study

NAME: Vanessa Santos
SCHOOL: Miami Dade Community College, Miami, FL
MAJOR: Pharmacy   **AGE:** 18

Below is a real-life situation faced by Vanessa. Read the brief case and respond to the questions.

The first two weeks of school were really bad for me. I wasn't actually prepared for the first day of classes. As a matter of fact, my mother had scheduled the "family vacation" on the weekend before classes started. I was not prepared or focused, and I missed the first week of classes. This set me apart from other students in my classes.

The first day that I did go to classes, I was so lost that I left the campus. I went home and asked my mom to come with me to help me find my classes and get my books and supplies. She agreed to help me.

I also work full time until 6:00 in the evening. This is really tough for me. I scheduled my classes for evenings and Saturdays, but I found that many things I need are closed on Saturday or when I get to the campus after 6:30. I was not able to get my ID card, which I needed for the library and to take my midterm exams. I did not get off to a great start.

What was Vanessa's first mistake?

___

Where could she have turned for help at the campus?

___

Why is preparation for college necessary to your success?

___

How can your work schedule affect your performance in college?

___

If you hold a job, how can you make sure you have the correct balance to succeed at both work and school?

_____
_____
_____
_____

What advice would you give to an entering, first-year student from your experience dealing with the first weeks of classes?

_____
_____
_____
_____

What preparation did you make for college that really helped you in your first few weeks? What do you wish you had done differently to prepare yourself for starting college?

_____
_____
_____
_____

at this moment Journal

Refer to page 65 of this chapter. Having read and reflected upon the information in the chapter, consider how you might revise your goal to make it more:

REASONABLE

BELIEVABLE

MEASURABLE

ADAPTABLE

CONTROLLABLE

DESIRABLE

ONLINE JOURNAL

To complete an online journal entry, log onto the Companion Website at www.prenhall.com/sherfield. Go to Chapter 3 and click on the link to the Online Journal. You can respond to the questions provided or to questions assigned by your professor, or you may journal about your own experiences.

ADVICE TO GO

CORNERSTONES

for persisting in college

Concentrate on your future.

Use *personal decorum* in and out of the classroom.

Establish a *relationship* with your professors.

Speak with your *advisor* or *counselor* frequently.

Know the *rules* and *policies* of your college.

Seek *academic assistance* when needed.

Join a *campus club* and get involved.

Apply for *financial aid* early and often.

Make use of *student services*.

Keep a *journal* of your first year.

PERSIST

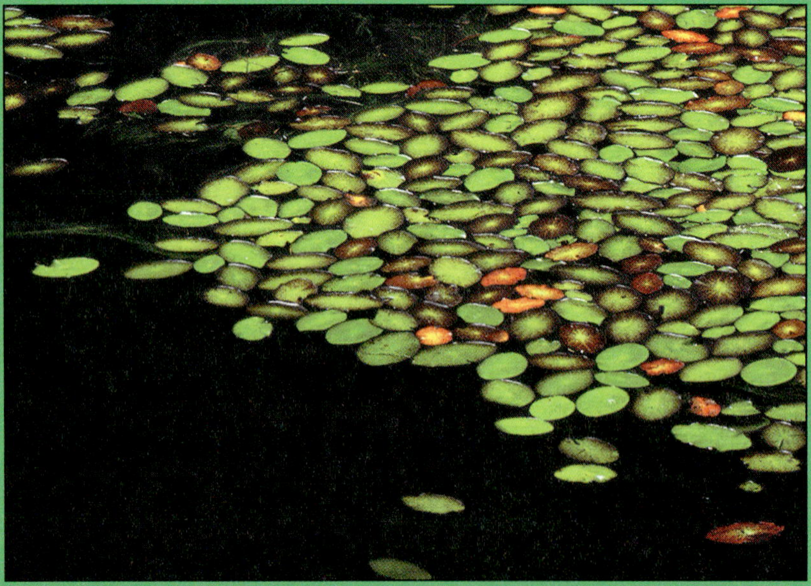

4 Prioritize

Do not squander time, for time is the stuff life is made of. — Ben Franklin

CHAPTER 4
PRIORITIZE

Yolandra was in my class several years ago. She impressed me as *the most organized person I had ever known.* She always had her calendar with her; she took meticulous notes and transcribed them every day; *and she never missed a deadline.* In her notebook, she had carefully written goals and objectives for every class. Yolandra recognized that she had to prioritize several components in her life: *her time, money, and resources.* She had a regular schedule, which she followed exactly, that detailed on which day she would do laundry, on which day she would shop for groceries, and at what time she would exercise. Yolandra adhered to a carefully organized schedule so she would have plenty of time for studying, reviewing her notes, and meeting with professors. She followed a budget because, as with most college students, resources were tight. Although she was not naturally outstanding academically, *through these efforts Yolandra was able to keep her grades among the highest in the class.* She organized herself to succeed and to maximize her staying power.

Her organization and adherence to her priorities also enabled Yolandra to serve on the student council, to be active in a sorority, and to work 15 hours a week. *I have never known a student to be more disciplined about her work.* One of the best things about her self-management style was that *she always took time to have fun and to be with her friends.* Yolandra noted in her calendar "Sacred Day." These were days that were reserved for her to have fun, to renew her spirit, *to do nothing*—days on which work was not on her agenda. Yolandra had learned some of the most important time-management and organizational strategies at a very young age: *make a plan, stick to the plan, work hard, play hard, and reward yourself when you have performed well.*

> **She impressed me as the most organized person I had ever known.**

You may think, "That's great for Yolandra, but it wouldn't work for me." And you may be right. The important thing to consider as you read this chapter *is how to design a plan that is right for you, a plan based on your schedule, your interests,*

Managing Your Time and Money Wisely

and your most productive times of day. You'll want to consider how to manage your time, money, and resources and how to set priorities based on you and your individual needs.

This chapter offers some pointers for getting things accomplished. Some of them will work for you and some of them won't, but when you have finished the chapter, *you should have a better handle on how to get the job done and still have time to play.*

If you can't follow a schedule as rigid as Yolandra's, that's fine. Design a schedule you can follow. You might have heard the old saying, *"All work and no play makes Jack a dull boy."* This statement is true, but so is *"All play and no work will make Jack flunk out of school."* The trick is to find a happy medium.

> If you really want to know what you value, look at your calendar and your check book.
> —HERB KELLEHER

QUESTIONS FOR REFLECTION

Consider responding to these questions online in the Questions for Reflection module of the Companion Website.

1. Would any of Yolandra's time-management techniques work for you? Why or why not?

2. How could you alter your current habits to maximize the use of your time?

3. Yolandra rewarded herself after she completed her assignments. What two rewards can you think of to give yourself after you have completed your assigned work for classes?

Where are you... AT THIS MOMENT

Before reading this chapter, take a moment and respond to the following 10 questions. Consider each one carefully before answering, and then respond by circling the number in the appropriate box. When you have answered the questions, add your points and find your total score on the feedback chart below.

STATEMENT	STRONGLY DISAGREE	DISAGREE	DON'T KNOW	AGREE	STRONGLY AGREE	SCORE
1. I am aware of when my "prime time" is (that time of day when I am most alert and productive).	1	2	3	4	5	
2. I don't schedule my most demanding tasks for attention during my prime time.	5	4	3	2	1	
3. I balance the time I spend for work, school, and play.	1	2	3	4	5	
4. I never use an organizer or calendar to plan my time.	5	4	3	2	1	
5. I have a history of being late in turning in assignments for school.	5	4	3	2	1	
6. When it comes to my work habits, I am an organized person.	1	2	3	4	5	
7. I never rely on credit cards and loans to cover my regular expenses.	1	2	3	4	5	
8. I feel that I need to work more and more hours to pay for my expenses.	5	4	3	2	1	
9. I make it a habit to put aside a portion of my earnings into a savings account.	1	2	3	4	5	
10. I avoid buying things I don't need when my budget is tight.	1	2	3	4	5	
TOTAL VALUE						

SUMMARY

10–17 You have little skill in setting priorities for yourself. You usually under plan, give in to distractions, and are impulsive. Significant changes need to be made in order to keep yourself on track and headed in the right direction.

18–25 Your skills in planning and prioritizing are somewhat low, and you probably have difficulty in organizing your time and budget. Additional learning in how to better schedule your time and set priorities is needed.

26–34 You are average in your ability to set priorities and stick to them. You have a fair sense of how to manage your time and balance the demands of your life. More consistent use of your skills would be beneficial.

35–42 You have an above average level of skill in determining your financial and scheduling priorities. You probably plan ahead for important tasks and have established a routine for study habits that others are aware and respectful of.

43–50 You are exceptional in your ability to set priorities and keep to them. You have an organized system in place for managing your time and money. You have struck a balance in your time for all the different facets of your life, including work and play.

Goals... FOR CHANGE

Based on your total points, what is one goal you would like to achieve related to managing your time or money more wisely?

Goal _____
_____

List three actions you can take that might help you move closer to realizing this goal.

1. _____
2. _____
3. _____

Questions FOR BUILDING ON YOUR BEST

As you read this chapter, consider the following questions. At the end of the chapter, you should be able to answer all of them. You are encouraged to ask a few questions of your own. Consider asking your classmates or professors to assist you.

1. How can I determine exactly how I am spending my time?
2. How can I manage a reasonable balance between school, work, family, and social life?
3. What techniques can I use to help me stop procrastinating?
4. How can I learn financial-management strategies that will help me now and after college?
5. How can I learn to control my spending habits?

What additional questions do you have about time management and financial planning?

1. _____
2. _____
3. _____

You Have All the Time There Is

TAKING CONTROL OF YOUR TIME AND YOURSELF

Have you ever tried to define time? This is an interesting exercise. If you stop now and try to define exactly what time is, you will probably find it difficult. It's almost like trying to catch a sunbeam or put your arms around a rainbow. Time is elusive and flexible and also restrictive and binding. Yet, we all know that time exists, and we all know how much trouble we can bring down on our heads when we use it poorly or waste it. The truth is, many college students' worst problems start with poor use of time. Staying power actually begins with how you manage your time and get control of your life.

Some people seem to be born with the ability to get so much more done than most other people. They appear to always be calm and collected, to have it together, to reach lofty goals. Many people from this group work long hours in addition to going to school. They never appear to be stressed out, and they seem to attend all the social functions. You are probably aware of others who are always late with assignments, never finish their projects on time, rarely seem to have time to study, and appear to have no concrete goals for their lives. This group also shows up at all the parties whether they have their work done or not. Many people from this second group never make it past the first semester of college, certainly not the second. There is no guarantee that you will finish college just because you had the good fortune to have been admitted. Many students lack staying power because they have no concept of how to manage themselves. Obviously, all these people have the same amount of time in their days and nights. The secret is that one group organizes for success, while the other never knows what happened to them.

Sometimes, we get the idea that one group of people accomplishes more because they have more time or because they don't have to work or they don't have children or they are smarter or wealthier. Actually, all of these reasons may be true, but it doesn't change the facts. We all have the same amount of time each week, and we decide how to spend most of it. Even if you are rich, you can't buy more time than the allotted 10,080 minutes that each of us is given every week.

Time is an unusual and puzzling resource. You can't save it in a box until you need it. You don't feel it passing by like wind in your face. It has no color. If you are in a hurry or if you are pressured to reach a deadline, time seems to fly. If you are bored or have nothing to do, it seems to creep at a very slow pace. Time is an invisible commodity. You can't get your arms around it; yet, you know it exists.

Corporate managers realize the value of time because they pay consultants millions of dollars to teach their employees to use their time more wisely. Time is money in the business world; employees who can produce excellent work by established deadlines are highly valued. Time must be considered one of your most valuable resources while you are in college and after you graduate.

Time management is actually about managing you, taking control. The sooner you get control of how you use your time, the quicker you will be on your way to becoming successful in college. Learning to manage your time is a lesson that you will use throughout your college career and beyond. Actually, you can't control time, but you can control yourself. Time management is really about self-management. Time management is paying attention to how you are spending your most valuable resource and then devising a plan to use it more effectively.

Working Hard and Playing Hard

Developing and perfecting priority-management skills are critical to your success as a college student. You have probably wondered how some people get so much done; how some people always seem to have it together, stay calm and collected, and are able to set goals and accomplish them. At the same time, you are aware of others who are always late with assignments and are unable to complete projects and live up to commitments.

Although college students' abilities vary greatly, most have the intellectual ability to succeed; the difference between success and failure is often the person's ability to organize and manage time and to set priorities. Have you ever thought about the statement "Life is a series of choices"? You can't do everything, so you have to make choices! Making choices is what priority and time management is all about.

> Ordinary people think merely how they will spend their time; people of intellect try to use it. —ARTHUR SCHOPENHAUER

This chapter presents guidelines to help you focus on managing your time so that you can devote a sufficient part of your day to your work and studies but still be able to have fun.

The "P" Word: Procrastination

HOW TO QUIT AVOIDING THE HARD JOBS AND GET YOUR PRIORITIES IN ORDER

We all procrastinate, then we worry and promise we'll never do it again if we can just get through this day. We say things to ourselves like, "If I can just live through this paper, I will never wait until the last minute again." But someone comes along with a great idea for fun, and off we go. Or there is a great movie on TV, and you reward yourself *before* you have done your work.

Most people don't have a clue how they spend their time. Many convince themselves they are working very hard; yet, the bottom line doesn't prove this to be true. College students need to learn early on that their courses will probably require much more time outside of class than high school. Some experts advise college students to count on spending at least three hours outside of class for every hour spent in class.

Some people actually do work hard, but their work habits are so poor that they still don't produce very much. Others try to work while they are simultaneously entertaining themselves. For example, they watch TV while they read ancient history that they don't like in the first place. Doesn't work! If you want to watch your favorite television show, you need to work in a quiet place where you can concentrate. Then, reward yourself with 30 minutes to watch your program.

The truth is simple: We all tend to avoid the hard jobs in favor of the easy ones. Even many of the list makers fool themselves. They mark off a long list of easy tasks while the big ones still loom in front of them. Many of us put off unpleasant tasks until our back is against the wall. So why do we procrastinate when we all know how unpleasant the results can be? Why aren't we disciplined and organized and controlled so we can reap the rewards that come from being prepared?

Procrastination is quite simply a bad habit formed after many years of practice. There are reasons, however, that cause us to keep doing this to ourselves when we all know better.

WHY IS IT SO EASY TO PROCRASTINATE?

Procrastination for most people is a habit that has been formed by years of perfecting the process. There are reasons, however, that cause us to keep doing this to ourselves when we know better.

WORLD OF WORK

I was fortunate in college; in addition to my academic pursuits, I was also involved in social and cultural activities. I also worked for a professor. I learned that the more I had to do, the more I could get done. The semesters that I was the busiest were the semesters that my grades were the highest. You have to learn how to do what you have to do, and when you have to do it. In college, there can be so many distractions. You have to deal not only with your schedule, but with the schedules of those around you.

As a Financial Advisor, I continually employ many of the *priority management skills* I learned in college. With the amount of information circulating around, you learn that you can't pay attention to everything. You quickly learn to prioritize and do the things that have to be done. I learned in college that you may not be able to do it tomorrow; tomorrow may be worse than today.

Technology has greatly impacted the way I conduct my personal and professional life. Learning to use this technology to help me prioritize has been both a challenge and a blessing. Technology is always changing. We had to upgrade our entire system in the office to deal with the Y2K problem. This caused our customer service to suffer somewhat, but in the long run, it will be worth it. It sometimes amazes me that we functioned without e-mail and ATMs. With each new invention, we wonder how we ever survived without it. However, technology can't replace human contact.

QUESTIONS FOR REFLECTION

Consider responding to these questions online in the World of Work module of the Companion Website.

1. Why do you think Mr. Rice was able to get more accomplished during the times that he had the most to do?

2. According to Mr. Rice, why is it risky to put things off until tomorrow? Do you agree or disagree?

3. In your opinion, why can't technology replace human contact?

Timothy Spencer Rice, *Financial Advisor,* Waddell & Reed, Inc., Shawnee Mission, KS

- **Superhuman expectations.** You simply overdo and put more on your calendar than Superman or Superwoman could accomplish.
- **Whining.** You tell yourself that smart people don't have to study, and everybody is smart but you. Smart people are studying or they have studied in the past and have already mastered the material you are struggling with now. Sooner or later, you must pay the price to gain knowledge. No one is born with calculus formulas totally mastered. So the sooner you quit whining, the sooner you will begin to master time management.
- **Fear of failing.** You have failed a difficult subject in the past, and you are scared it is going to happen again so you do the natural thing and avoid unpleasant experiences.
- **Emotional blocks.** It is time to get started and you have no routine and no past regimen to get you started. You are already feeling guilty because you have wasted so much time. You feel tired, depressed, and beaten.

> We have only this moment, sparkling like a star in our hand . . . and melting like a snowflake. Let us use it before it is too late. —MARIE RAY

HOW TO BEAT PROCRASTINATION

Not only is it important that you overcome procrastination for the sake of your college career—it is equally crucial to your success at work. Procrastination is a bad habit that will haunt you until you make up your mind to overcome it. The chart on the following pages offers some tips that might help.

Managing Time So You Can Have More Fun

WONDERFUL WORK = WONDERFUL EXPERIENCES

As you focus on managing and organizing your time, remember that you are not learning to manage yourself and your time just so you can do more work. Of course, you want to be more productive while using less time. But the real benefit of managing your time is so you can have more fun.

So how do you do this? Every 15 minutes for one week, you will record exactly how you spent that time. This exercise may seem a little tedious at first, but if you will complete the process over a period of a week, you will have a much better concept of where your most precious resource—time—is being used. Yes, that's right—for a week, you need to keep a written record of how much time you spend sleeping, studying, eating, working, getting to class and back, cooking, caring for children, watching television, doing yard work, going to movies, attending athletic events, hanging out, doing laundry, whatever.

Take your plan with you and keep track of your activities during the day. To make things simple, round off tasks to 15-minute intervals. For example, if you

25 Ways to Beat Procrastination

- **Face up to the results of procrastination.** What will happen if you procrastinate? How will you feel if you fail the test? How miserable will you be over the weekend if you have to write a last-minute paper while everyone else is at the big game?
- **Concentrate on the rewards of managing yourself and your time.** Think about the rewards that you will get when you finish a difficult task. You can go to a movie or a football game or hang out with friends. You can get a good grade. Think about how good you will feel when the weekend comes and your paper is finished and you don't have to spend all your time in the library. Focus on how good you will feel when you tell your parents or spouse or friends how well you did on a project. While you are working, stop periodically and focus on the rewards.
- **Break up big tasks into small ones.** If you have to write a paper, can you work on one segment tonight and another one tomorrow? If you start early and finish a small segment each day, a big paper is just a series of small tasks.
- **Give yourself a time limit to accomplish a task.** Work will expand to take up as much time as we allow it to. Push yourself to work faster and more efficiently.
- **Set a regular time for study, and do not vary from it.** Determine your personal "best time" and "best place."
- **Start studying with positive, realistic thoughts.** Push negative thoughts out of your mind. Tell yourself that you are growing and becoming more competent.
- **Establish study habits.** See Chapter 9 for a thorough discussion of study habits.
- **Set reasonable, concrete goals that you can reach in about 20–25 minutes.** Then, set others for the next block of time.
- **Face fear; look it right in the face.** Make up your mind you are going to overcome fear by studying and preparing every day.
- **Get help from your professor.** Show the professor what you have done and ask if you are on the right track.
- **Avoid whining and people who whine and complain.** You have this job to do, and it is not going away.
- **Allow yourself more time than you think you need to complete an assignment or to study for a test.**
- **Practice your new study habits for 21 days.** By then, you will have gone a long way toward getting rid of your procrastination habits.
- **Actually reward yourself when you have accomplished an important body of work.** Perhaps you spent two hours looking for research articles on the Internet. Now, you deserve a reward. Watch a TV program; visit a friend for a few minutes; talk on the phone; answer your e-mail; read a book to a child; if you are a nontraditional student, perhaps your entire family can go for a walk together. If you have not finished your work, push yourself to go back to work for a few more minutes. When you do this, you are building your discipline and staying power. Ask yourself: "Can I work just 15 more minutes?"
- **Look at this task in terms of your long-range goals.** Where does it fit in your plans of getting what you want? Does passing this calculus test get you admitted to the major you want? Does making a B+ on this accounting test take you one step closer to becoming a CPA? Does making a good grade on this speech move you toward overcoming your fear of public speaking?

(continued)

- **Don't get involved in too many organizations, accept too many commitments, or overextend yourself.** Stop and think about how much you really want to do something before you accept. How much time will it take? Does it help you grow and learn? Does it fit with your goals? It's better to say "no" than to accept something that will make you miserable before you finish. "NO!" is a powerful word—use it! Weed out activities that take too much of your time and provide you very little personal reward. You only have so much personal time. Fill that time with activities that give you pleasure and energy.

- **Force yourself to jump in.** Even if your initial work is not satisfactory, you have made a start and chances are you will get focused as you progress. Sometimes, you just have to plunge in. You can't jump off the high dive in small steps. Just do it!

- **Start on the difficult, most boring tasks first.** If you hate history, read that chapter first. Sometimes, it is effective to do these tasks early in the morning before breakfast. This depends on your personal "best time" to work.

- **Practice "do it now."** Do simple tasks as you get them. Practice multitasking. What things can you do at the same time? For example, you can read a chapter while the clothes are washing. You can take your children on a walk and get your own exercise at the same time.

- **Find a quiet place to study and concentrate.** Roommates may not need to study when you do. Dorms are notoriously noisy. Small children might not understand that mommy or daddy needs to study very badly. You may need to make regular visits to the library or to a computer laboratory so you can focus on your work.

- **If you are a nontraditional student, you will need to get cooperation from your family.** Going back to school for a mother or father requires help from the entire family. Establish clear rules for your study time. Reward the entire family when you have finished a big project. Promises of a picnic or a family movie can work wonders!

- **Weed out your personal belongings and living space.** Clean out and organize your closets and drawer space. Give things you no longer wear to charity. Buy fewer things that require waxing, polishing, recharging, cleaning, or storing. Things become monsters that take up your valuable time. Live a simpler life.

- **Prepare to be successful by getting ready the evening before.** Be sure your car has gas; select and press your clothes; put all your materials in your backpack; check to see if the children's materials and clothes have been organized. Often, the first few minutes of every day determine if you are going to have a good day. Program yourself for success!

- **Take time to smell the roses.** Part of every day should belong to you to do what you want to do. We all need to find time for regular exercise; we need to spend quality time with people we love and enjoy; we need to pay attention to friends and relationships; we need time to focus on spiritual development. Don't over-manage yourself to the point that you lose sight of what is really important—friends and family and self!

- **Balance your load.** If you are working full time and paying for all your expenses, you may need to take a lighter load so you can have a life. If you are a nontraditional student who is working and has small children and a home to take care of, you might need to rethink your schedule. Very few people will ever lament that they didn't do more work. But many will be sorry they didn't spend quality time with their parents, grandparents, or small children when they could have. It is true that you can do it all, but most of us can't do it all at one time. This race is just yours. You are not racing everyone else around you—just yourself.

start walking to the cafeteria at 7:08, you might want to mark off the time block that begins with 7:00. If you finish eating and return to your home at 7:49, you can mark off the next two blocks. You will also want to note the activity so you can evaluate how you spent your time later. Study the example that is provided for you in Figure 4.1.

In Figure 4.2 you will find daily time sheets for one week for you to use for this exercise. Remember to take these pages with you and record how you are spending your time during the day. As you progress through the week, try to improve the use of your time. When you finish this exercise, review how you spent your time. Answer the questions below regarding your personal time management:

1. What was your most surprising discovery about how you spent your time?

   _____
   _____

2. On what activities should you have spent more time?

   _____
   _____

3. On what things did you waste time?

   _____
   _____

FIGURE 4.1 *Evaluating how you really spend your time.*

Time	Activity	Time	Activity	Time
7:00	get up & shower	7:00		12:15
		7:15		12:30
	✗	7:30	Walked to Union	12:45
	Breakfast	7:45	1:00 Ate lunch	1:00
8:00		8:00		1:15
		8:15		1:30
	Read paper	8:30	Talked w/ Joe	1:45
	Walked to class	8:45	2:00	2:00
9:00	English 101	9:00	Went to book store	2:15
		9:15		2:30
		9:30	Walked to my room	2:45
		9:45	3:00	3:00
10:00		10:00	Called Ron	3:15
		10:15		3:30
		10:30		3:45
	Walked to class	10:45	4:00 Watched Friends	4:00
11:00	History 210	11:00		4:15
		11:15		4:30
		11:30	Walked to library	4:45
		11:45	5:00	5:00
12:00		12:00		5:15

Managing Your Time and Money Wisely   109

FIGURE 4.2 *Daily time sheets.*

Monday		Tuesday		Wednesday	
6:00	6:00	6:00	6:00	6:00	6:00
	6:15		6:15		6:15
	6:30		6:30		6:30
	6:45		6:45		6:45
7:00	7:00	7:00	7:00	7:00	7:00
	7:15		7:15		7:15
	7:30		7:30		7:30
	7:45		7:45		7:45
8:00	8:00	8:00	8:00	8:00	8:00
	8:15		8:15		8:15
	8:30		8:30		8:30
	8:45		8:45		8:45
9:00	9:00	9:00	9:00	9:00	9:00
	9:15		9:15		9:15
	9:30		9:30		9:30
	9:45		9:45		9:45
10:00	10:00	10:00	10:00	10:00	10:00
	10:15		10:15		10:15
	10:30		10:30		10:30
	10:45		10:45		10:45
11:00	11:00	11:00	11:00	11:00	11:00
	11:15		11:15		11:15
	11:30		11:30		11:30
	11:45		11:45		11:45
12:00	12:00	12:00	12:00	12:00	12:00
	12:15		12:15		12:15
	12:30		12:30		12:30
	12:45		12:45		12:45
1:00	1:00	1:00	1:00	1:00	1:00
	1:15		1:15		1:15
	1:30		1:30		1:30
	1:45		1:45		1:45
2:00	2:00	2:00	2:00	2:00	2:00
	2:15		2:15		2:15
	2:30		2:30		2:30
	2:45		2:45		2:45
3:00	3:00	3:00	3:00	3:00	3:00
	3:15		3:15		3:15
	3:30		3:30		3:30
	3:45		3:45		3:45
4:00	4:00	4:00	4:00	4:00	4:00
	4:15		4:15		4:15
	4:30		4:30		4:30
	4:45		4:45		4:45
5:00	5:00	5:00	5:00	5:00	5:00
	5:15		5:15		5:15
	5:30		5:30		5:30
	5:45		5:45		5:45
6:00	6:00	6:00	6:00	6:00	6:00
	6:15		6:15		6:15
	6:30		6:30		6:30
	6:45		6:45		6:45
7:00	7:00	7:00	7:00	7:00	7:00
	7:15		7:15		7:15
	7;30		7;30		7;30
	7:45		7:45		7:45
8:00	8:00	8:00	8:00	8:00	8:00
	8:15		8:15		8:15
	8:30		8:30		8:30
	8:45		8:45		8:45
9:00	9:00	9:00	9:00	9:00	9:00
	9:15		9:15		9:15
	9:30		9:30		9:30
	9:45		9:45		9:45
10:00	10:00	10:00	10:00	10:00	10:00
	10:15		10:15		10:15
	10:30		10:30		10:30
	10:45		10:45		10:45
11:00	11:00	11:00	11:00	11:00	11:00
	11:15		11:15		11:15
	11:30		11:30		11:30
	11:45		11:45		11:45
12:00	12:00	12:00	12:00	12:00	12:00

FIGURE 4.2 Continued.

Thursday	Friday		Saturday		Sunday	
6:00	6:00	6:00	6:00	6:00	6:00	6:00	6:00
	6:15		6:15		6:15		6:15
	6:30		6:30		6:30		6:30
	6:45		6:45		6:45		6:45
7:00	7:00	7:00	7:00	7:00	7:00	7:00	7:00
	7:15		7:15		7:15		7:15
	7:30		7:30		7:30		7:30
	7:45		7:45		7:45		7:45
8:00	8:00	8:00	8:00	8:00	8:00	8:00	8:00
	8:15		8:15		8:15		8:15
	8:30		8:30		8:30		8:30
	8:45		8:45		8:45		8:45
9:00	9:00	9:00	9:00	9:00	9:00	9:00	9:00
	9:15		9:15		9:15		9:15
	9:30		9:30		9:30		9:30
	9:45		9:45		9:45		9:45
10:00	10:00	10:00	10:00	10:00	10:00	10:00	10:00
	10:15		10:15		10:15		10:15
	10:30		10:30		10:30		10:30
	10:45		10:45		10:45		10:45
11:00	11:00	11:00	11:00	11:00	11:00	11:00	11:00
	11:15		11:15		11:15		11:15
	11:30		11:30		11:30		11:30
	11:45		11:45		11:45		11:45
12:00	12:00	12:00	12:00	12:00	12:00	12:00	12:00
	12:15		12:15		12:15		12:15
	12:30		12:30		12:30		12:30
	12:45		12:45		12:45		12:45
1:00	1:00	1:00	1:00	1:00	1:00	1:00	1:00
	1:15		1:15		1:15		1:15
	1:30		1:30		1:30		1:30
	1:45		1:45		1:45		1:45
2:00	2:00	2:00	2:00	2:00	2:00	2:00	2:00
	2:15		2:15		2:15		2:15
	2:30		2:30		2:30		2:30
	2:45		2:45		2:45		2:45
3:00	3:00	3:00	3:00	3:00	3:00	3:00	3:00
	3:15		3:15		3:15		3:15
	3:30		3:30		3:30		3:30
	3:45		3:45		3:45		3:45
4:00	4:00	4:00	4:00	4:00	4:00	4:00	4:00
	4:15		4:15		4:15		4:15
	4:30		4:30		4:30		4:30
	4:45		4:45		4:45		4:45
5:00	5:00	5:00	5:00	5:00	5:00	5:00	5:00
	5:15		5:15		5:15		5:15
	5:30		5:30		5:30		5:30
	5:45		5:45		5:45		5:45
6:00	6:00	6:00	6:00	6:00	6:00	6:00	6:00
	6:15		6:15		6:15		6:15
	6:30		6:30		6:30		6:30
	6:45		6:45		6:45		6:45
7:00	7:00	7:00	7:00	7:00	7:00	7:00	7:00
	7:15		7:15		7:15		7:15
	7;30		7;30		7;30		7;30
	7:45		7:45		7:45		7:45
8:00	8:00	8:00	8:00	8:00	8:00	8:00	8:00
	8:15		8:15		8:15		8:15
	8:30		8:30		8:30		8:30
	8:45		8:45		8:45		8:45
9:00	9:00	9:00	9:00	9:00	9:00	9:00	9:00
	9:15		9:15		9:15		9:15
	9:30		9:30		9:30		9:30
	9:45		9:45		9:45		9:45
10:00	10:00	10:00	10:00	10:00	10:00	10:00	10:00
	10:15		10:15		10:15		10:15
	10:30		10:30		10:30		10:30
	10:45		10:45		10:45		10:45
11:00	11:00	11:00	11:00	11:00	11:00	11:00	11:00
	11:15		11:15		11:15		11:15
	11:30		11:30		11:30		11:30
	11:45		11:45		11:45		11:45
12:00	12:00	12:00	12:00	12:00	12:00	12:00	12:00

4. *How will you spend your next week more wisely?*

   _____

   _____

5. *Could Yolandra improve her time-management practices by using a similar exercise?*

   _____

   _____

When to Do What
USING YOUR BODY'S CYCLES TO THE BEST ADVANTAGE

Priority management and the ability to concentrate are closely linked. Because many people are able to concentrate on visual or auditory stimuli for only about 20 to 30 minutes before they begin to make errors, cramming for tests rarely works. Some people are able to concentrate effectively for longer periods of time, and some people for shorter periods. You'll need to determine your own ability to concentrate and then plan short breaks to avoid making errors.

Other factors affect concentration in different ways.

- *Complexity of material* may lead to frustration.
- *Time of day* has an effect depending on type of task.
- *Noise* improves concentration for some people if it is not too loud.
- *Hunger* makes it difficult to concentrate.
- *Your social environment,* positive or negative feedback and support or lack of support, can affect concentration.
- *Pace,* if too fast, may result in errors; if too slow, may result in boredom.

You have a prime time when you are most capable of performing at your peak. For many people, even if they don't like to get up early, the peak performance time, is in the morning if they have had enough rest. Other people function best late at night. Of course, you want to work on the most important and demanding jobs at your peak working time. To determine your best working time, answer the following questions:

> **Y**ou have a prime time when you are most capable of performing at your peak.

1. Are you lethargic in the morning until you have been up for an hour or so?
2. Did you try to schedule your classes this semester after 10 A.M. so you could sleep later?
3. Do you feel a little down around 5 P.M. but feel ready to go again around 8 P.M.?
4. Have you pulled all-nighters in the past?
5. Do you wake up early and spring right out of bed?
6. Do you have a hard time being productive during the late afternoon hours?
7. Is it impossible for you to concentrate after 10 P.M.?
8. Are you one of those rare college students who love 8 A.M. classes?

If you answered yes to questions 1 through 4, or to most of them, you are a night person; if you answered yes to questions 5 through 8, or to most of them, you are a morning person. Being a morning person does not mean that you can never get anything done at night, but it does mean that your most productive time is morning. If you are a morning person, you should tackle difficult, complex problems early in the morning when you are at your peak. If you are a night person, you should wait a few hours after getting up in the morning before you tackle difficult tasks.

PLANNING—THE SECRET TO PRIORITY MANAGEMENT

"I don't have time to plan." "I don't like to be fenced in and tied to a rigid schedule." "I have so many duties that planning never works." No more excuses! To manage your time successfully, you need to spend some time planning. To plan successfully, you need a calendar that has a month-at-a-glance section as well as sections for daily notes and appointments.

Planning and Organizing for School

Each evening, you should take a few minutes (and literally, that is all it will take) and sit in a quiet place and make a list of all that needs to be done tomorrow. Successful time management comes from planning the NIGHT BEFORE! Let's say your list includes the following:

- Research speech project
- Study, finance test on Friday
- Read Chapter 13 for chem
- Meet with chem study group
- Attend English class, 8:00
- Attend mgt. class, 10:00
- Exercise
- Buy birthday card for mom
- Wash the car
- Take shirts to dry cleaner
- Buy groceries
- Call Janice about weekend

Now, you have created a list of tasks that you will face tomorrow. Next, separate this list into three categories: **MUST** Do, Would **LIKE** to Do, and **FUN** Breaks.

MUST DO
Read Chapter 13 for chem
Meet with chem study group
Study, finance test on Friday
Exercise
Attend English class, 8:00
Attend mgt. class, 10:00

WOULD LIKE TO DO
Research speech project
Buy a birthday card for mom
Take shirts to dry cleaner
Buy groceries

FUN BREAKS
Wash the car
Call Janice about weekend

Don't get too excited yet. Your time-management plan is NOT finished. You have not done the most important part yet. Now, you will need to rank the items in order of their importance. You will put a 1 by the most important, a 2 by the next most important, etc. in each category.

It may look something like this:

MUST DO
1 Attend English class, 8:00
1 Attend mgt. class at 10:00
1 Read Chapter 13 for chem
2 Meet with chem study group
2 Study, finance test on for Friday
3 Exercise

WOULD LIKE TO DO
1 Research speech project
2 Buy birthday card for mom
3 Take shirts to dry cleaner
2 Buy groceries

FUN BREAKS
2 Wash the car
1 Call Janice about weekend

Now, you have created a PLAN to get these tasks done! Not only have you created your list, but now you've made a written commitment to these tasks, and you know what needs to be done in what order.

Now, take these tasks and schedule them into your daily calendar (see Figure 4.3). You would schedule category 1 first (MUST DO), category 2 next

FIGURE 4.3 Daily calendar.

DAY Monday

Time	Task	Priority	Complete?
6:00			Yes No
6:30			Yes No
7:00	Study for finance		Yes No
7:30	↓		Yes No
8:00	English 101		Yes No
8:30			Yes No
9:00	↓		Yes No
9:30	Read Pg. 1–10 of Chem. Chapter		Yes No
10:00	Management 210		Yes No
10:30			Yes No
11:00	↓		Yes No
11:30	Finish Reading Chem. Chapter		Yes No
12:00			Yes No
12:30	↓		Yes No
1:00	Meet w/ Chemistry group (take lunch)		Yes No
1:30			Yes No
2:00			Yes No
2:30	↓		Yes No
3:00	Exercise at Golds		Yes No
3:30	↓		Yes No
4:00			Yes No
4:30	go th grocery store & get B/day card		Yes No
5:00	& drop off shirts		Yes No
5:30			Yes No
6:00			Yes No
6:30	Dinner		Yes No
7:00	↓		Yes No
7:30	Internet Research for speech		Yes No
8:00			Yes No
8:30	↓		Yes No
9:00	call Janice @ w/end		Yes No
9:30			Yes No

114 CHAPTER 4 PRIORITIZE

(WOULD LIKE TO DO), and category 3 (FUN BREAKS) next. Remember, *never* keep more than one calendar. Always carry it with you and always schedule your tasks immediately so that you won't forget them.

The more time we spend . . . on planning . . . a project, the less total time is required for it. Don't let today's busy work crowd planning time out of your schedule.   —EDWIN C. BLISS

If you are a very VISUAL person, you may want to create this type of calendar for the week or the month so that you can visualize what is coming. Your weekly calendar may look something like the one in Figure 4.4.

FIGURE 4.4 *Weekly calendar.*

Week of:	Mon	Tues	Wed	Thur	Fri	Sat	Sun
6–7 AM							
7–8 AM							
8–9 AM	Eng 101	Study	Eng 101	Study	Eng 101	↑	Study
9–10 AM							
10–11 AM	Mgt 210	Exercise	Mgt 210	Exercise	Mgt 210		
11–12 AM						Work	
12 (noon)–1 PM	Study	Math 110	Study	Math 110	Study		Exercise
1–2 PM	Chem group		Chem group		Chem group		
2–3 PM		Study		Study			
3–4 PM	Exercise	Phil 101	Exercise	Phil 101	Exercise		
4–5 PM							
5–6 PM		↑		↑	↑	↓	
6–7 PM	Dinner		Dinner				
7–8 PM		Work		Work	Work	Free Time	
8–9 PM	Study		Study				
9–10 PM							
10–11 PM		↓		↓	↓		
11 PM–12 (midnight)							

Now, put your plan to work! Today, focus on accomplishing the first priority item on your list.

- Push yourself to finish the first item in a specified amount of time.
- Move quickly to the next task.
- Focus on the fact that you will get a reward when you finish this task.
- Reward yourself with short, fun breaks—watch a brief TV program, call a friend (but limit your time), eat an apple, drink some juice. Then go back to work!
- Fun breaks for nontraditional students might be a time to talk to your spouse or spend time with your children, play a game, take a walk, ride bikes. You can't put everybody's life on hold while you go to school.
- Write appointments and meetings in a calendar (or electronic device) that you keep with you at all times. Choose a calendar or computerized device that works for you and avoid heavy, bulky items.
- Place stickers on your calendar to alert you to important tasks. Or use a colored pen for fun breaks, sacred days, and rewards. This gives you something to look forward to.

Planning and Organizing for Work

Some supermen and superwomen work full time and go to school full time while they juggle families and other responsibilities. *We don't recommend this schedule unless it is for one semester only, when you are pushing to graduate.* If kept up for a long period, you will burn out from the stress that such a pace imposes on your mind and body, and if you have children, they may be adversely affected by your overfull schedule. If you work less and, if necessary, take longer to graduate, you will have more opportunity to savor your college experience.

IMPORTANT PRINCIPLES FOR PRIORITY MANAGEMENT AT WORK

- Organize your materials at work as they are organized at home. If you have a desk in both places, keep your supplies in the same place in both desks. Simplify your life by following similar patterns at work and at home. Make your office or work space inviting, attractive, and stimulating. If you are a visual thinker and need to see different assignments, be considerate of others who may work close to you. Use clear plastic boxes, colored file folders, and colored file boxes to organize your projects.
- Write directions down! Keep a notebook for repetitive tasks. Keep a calendar, and be on time to meetings.
- Learn to do paperwork immediately rather than let it build up. File—don't pile!
- Never let your work responsibilities slide because you are studying on the job. Employers always notice.
- Leave the office for lunch, breaks, and short walks.

- When you are given projects that require working with others, plan carefully to do your work well and on time.
- Keep a Rolodex file or use a Palm Pilot for important phone numbers and addresses that you use frequently.
- Perform difficult, unpleasant tasks as soon as you can so you don't have them hanging over your head.
- When you plan your work schedule, allow for unexpected problems that might interfere with the schedule.
- Practice detached concern—care about your work but avoid taking it home with you.

Use these tips to help generate ideas for managing your time better, performing more effectively, and reducing stress at work. List your ideas in the space provided.

_____

_____

_____

_____

Planning and Organizing at Home

Some people organize effectively at work and school but allow things to fall apart at home. Whether you are a traditional student living in a residence hall or a nontraditional student living in a house with your family, your home should be pleasant and safe. It should be a place where you can study, relax, laugh, invite your friends, and find solitude. The following ideas about home organization will help you maximize your time.

IMPORTANT PRINCIPLES FOR PRIORITY MANAGEMENT AT HOME

For traditional students.

- Organize as effectively at home as you do at work.
- If you have roommates, divide the chores. Insist on everyone doing his or her share.
- Plan a rotation schedule for major household chores and stick to it—do laundry on Mondays and Thursdays; clean bathrooms on Saturdays; iron on Wednesdays; and so on.
- Organize your closet and your dresser drawers. Get rid of clothes you don't wear.
- Put a sign by your telephone that reads "TIME" to remind yourself not to waste it on the phone.
- If you can't study in your room because of drop-in visitors or loud roommates, go to the library.

- Pay bills twice monthly. Pay them on time so you don't ruin your credit rating.
- Practice sound money management so you are not stressed by too many bills and too little money.
- If you drive to class or work, fill up your tank ahead of time so you won't be late.
- Keep yourself physically fit with a regular exercise plan and nutritious meals.
- Get out of the house. Take a walk. Visit a friend.

For nontraditional students. If you are a nontraditional student and have children, teach them to be organized so they don't waste your time searching for their shoes, books, and assignments. Teach family members responsibility! You can't work, go to school, and hold everybody's hand all the time. Give each of your children a drawer in a filing cabinet. Show them how to organize their work. You will be preparing them to be successful.

Nontraditional students face special challenges and choices.

- If you are a perfectionist and want everything in your home to be perfect, get over it!
- Get rid of the clutter in your garage, basement, and closets.
- Establish a time for study hall in your home. Children do their homework, and you do yours.
- If you have a family, insist that all of you organize clothes in advance for school or work for several days.
- Put a message board in a convenient place for everyone to use.
- If your children are old enough to drive, have them run errands at the cleaners, post office, and grocery store.
- Carpool with other parents in your neighborhood.
- Delegate, delegate, delegate! You are not Superwoman or Superman. Tell your family you need help. Children can feed pets, make their own beds, fold clothes, vacuum, sweep, iron, and cut the grass if they are old enough.
- Schedule at least one hour alone with each of your children each week. Make this a happy, special time—a fun break!
- Make meals happy, relaxed times when each person's successes are shared and celebrated. Discuss current events.
- Plan special times with your spouse or partner if you have one so that he or she does not get fed up with your going to school.
- Tell your family and friends when you have to study; ask them to respect you by not calling or dropping by at this time.
- Post a family calendar where everyone can see it. Put all special events on it—for example, Janie's recital, Mike's baseball game, Jasmine's company party.
- Put sacred days on this calendar so that your entire family has something to look forward to.

"B" Is for Budgeting

PRIORITIZING YOUR FINANCES

When we talk about finances in our classes we've noticed that most college students do not budget. They have a reasonable idea of what they can spend and how much they require to cover their basic expenses, including tuition, books, housing, car payment, food, and utilities, but basically this is just a guesstimate. They have never sat down and decided to live within their income and to use their money wisely. As a result, many of the students we see are often strapped for money. The information in this section is intended to help you choose how to spend your money more wisely and to instill in you the belief that money management is an everyday process. If you are going to be financially secure, you cannot afford to live day to day and hand to mouth with no plan for accumulating wealth.

To fully maximize your financial resources, you need to establish a budget and learn to live within your means. According to Konowalow in his book *Cornerstones for Money Management* (1997),

> Watching and calculating how much money is coming in each month and how much you spend is important to taking control of your finances. While not having control of your income and expenditures may not be a problem this week or next, it is sure to become one soon if the money you are spending each month exceeds the money coming in.

When budgeting, you must first determine how much income you earn monthly. Complete the following chart.

SOURCE OF INCOME	ESTIMATED AMOUNT
■ Work	$_____
■ Spouse Income	$_____
■ Parental Contributions	$_____
■ Scholarships	$_____
■ Loans	$_____
■ Savings	$_____
■ Investments	$_____
■ Other	$_____
■ **Total Income**	$_____

Next, you must determine how much money you spend in a month. Complete the following chart.

■ Tuition	$_____
■ Books and Supplies	$_____
■ Housing	$_____
■ Utilities	$_____
■ Phone	$_____
■ Car Payment	$_____

- Insurance $\$$_____
- Gas $\$$_____
- Clothing $\$$_____
- Food $\$$_____
- Household Items $\$$_____
- Personal Hygiene Items $\$$_____
- Health Care and/or Health Insurance $\$$_____
- Entertainment/Fun $\$$_____
- Other $\$$_____
- **Total Expenditures** $\$$_____

If the amount of your total expenditures is smaller than your monthly income, you are on your way to controlling your finances. If your total expenditures figure is larger than your monthly income (as is the case for many of our students), you are heading for a financial crisis.

Practicing Fiscal Fitness

ARE YOU MANAGING YOUR MONEY OR IS IT MANAGING YOU?

Practicing fiscal fitness is as important as incorporating a regimen of physical fitness into your daily life! A very small percentage of the population learns to manage their money well, and many get themselves into serious trouble because of financial ignorance. According to the Federal Reserve, we have become a nation of debtors. Outstanding non-secured debt rose from $805 billion in 1990 to $1.65 trillion in 2001 (National Foundation for Credit Counseling, 2002).

The worst kind of debt is credit card debt! The sooner you learn this lesson and put it into practice, the better! According to Konowalow (2003), Americans paid $50 billion in finance charges in 2001. During the same year, 1.3 million credit card holders declared bankruptcy. Credit card debt now averages $8562 per household with a current average interest rate of 14.71% (National Foundation for Credit Counseling, 2002).

Credit card companies have been waiting on you to arrive at college. They have your name and address on file, and they will start sending you credit card applications right away. They want you to begin the dangerous habit of living off borrowed money. Don't let them get their tentacles wrapped around you and your money! Getting yourself too deeply in debt by abusing credit cards can bring you many sleepless nights and years of debt with high interest rates.

Most credit card companies charge a very high rate of interest—18 to 21 percent or higher. For every $1000 you charge, you will pay from $180 to $210 each year, states Konowalow (2003). Don't be fooled by the ploy of "1.5 percent interest." This means 1.5 percent each month, which equates to 18 percent per year. If you make only the minimum required payment, you will begin paying interest on interest before the debt is paid off. If you have an extra $180, invest it. Years from now, it most likely will have doubled and even tripled. On the other hand, if you owe $1000 and make only minimum payments, you will

DID YOU KNOW?

$2,226

The average credit card debt carried per student.

Source: Equifax.com. "Teaching students about money and credit." Accessed from www.equifax.com/CoolOnCredit/parent1.html.

---

probably still owe $1000 at the end of a year of making payments. Credit cards are a bad trap for people who use them unwisely.

According to statistics, the average college student is a better risk than the general adult population, with 67 percent of students sticking with one credit card. The bad news is that 33 percent have difficulty handling credit, according to Konowalow (2003). They fall into the instant gratification trap rather than saving until they can pay for something. Charging for extravagant items in the beginning, many people will begin charging for essentials because it seems like easy money. Nothing could be further from the truth!

Instead of using credit cards to pay for the expenditures that cause you to go over your budget, modify your expenditures. Almost every line on the expenditure chart can be modified. For example, adding a roommate or moving can lower your housing expense. You can change your car to a less expensive one or consider using public transportation or carpooling with colleagues. In the space below, list five ways you can modify your expenditures.

1. _____
2. _____
3. _____
4. _____
5. _____

Hints for cutting your expenses:

- Control impulse buying. (Don't buy anything that costs more than $15 until you have waited 72 hours; it is amazing how often you decide you don't need the item that you thought you had to have.)
- Carpool, take public transportation, or walk to classes.
- Don't eat out as often. Make your own meals. Make meals for several days on weekends to save time.
- Use coupons and buy during sales.
- Live more simply by getting rid of unnecessary items like cell phones, beepers, and cable television.

Facts You Need to Know about Credit Cards

WHAT YOU DON'T KNOW CAN WRECK YOUR CREDIT RATING AND RUIN YOUR LIFE

Listed below are some of the most important things you can learn about managing money:

- Understand that credit cards are nothing more than high interest loans—in some cases, very high!

- Carry only one or two credit cards so you can manage your debt and not get in over your head.
- Avoid the temptation to charge. You should use credit cards only when you absolutely must and only when you can pay the full amount before interest is added. "Buy now, pay later" is a dangerous game.
- When you pay off a card, celebrate and don't use that as a reason to charge again.
- If you have credit card debt, always pay more than the minimum.
- Pay your credit card payment early enough to avoid late charges, which now average $29.84. Send the payment at least five days in advance. Late fees now represent the third-largest revenue stream for banks. If you are assessed a late fee, call and complain. If you normally pay on time and don't max out your limit, you will probably get it removed. If you get more than two late fees in a year, you could be assessed a higher interest rate on your balance.

> Your credit card past is your credit future.
> —STEVE KONOWALOW

- Call the credit card company and negotiate a better rate. If they won't give you a better rate, tell them you are going to transfer the debt.
- If you have several credit card debts, consolidate all the amounts on the card where you have the lowest balance. Ask for a lower rate when you do. Destroy all the other cards so you don't accumulate debts again.
- If you pay off the full amount every month, some credit card companies allow you only 20 days from a purchase before they charge interest. If you carry a debt with them, however, they will allow you to have 25 days before your payment is due.
- Having a large number of credit cards with balances can seriously impact your credit rating. For example, what you do today may inhibit your ability to buy a car, purchase a house, and even get some jobs!
- You only need one or two credit cards. Destroy all applications that come to you in the mail.
- Handle your credit cards carefully. Write down the card account numbers and the phone numbers of the issuing company in case your cards are lost or stolen. Contact the company immediately if you cannot find your cards.
- Do not leave any personal information (credit cards, Social Security numbers, checking accounts) in places where roommates or other students have access to them. Purchase a metal file box with a lock and keep it in a secure place. Your roommates and friends may be very trustworthy, but everyone is not!
- Use your credit card only for plane tickets, hotel rooms, and other travel necessities that you can pay for within 20 days.
- If you have already gotten into credit card trouble, get counseling. One of the best agencies is the National Foundation for Credit Counseling

(NFCC). An ethical professional can help you reduce your interest rates, get control of your debt, and get relief from your creditors while you pay off the debt.

- Be very careful not to get involved with high pressure credit card counseling agencies who may cause you even more problems. Not all credit counselors are ethical.
- Be aware that using a credit card carelessly is similar to a drug addiction.
- Ask yourself these questions: "If I can't pay this credit card in full this month, what is going to change next month? Will I have extra income or will I reduce my spending enough to pay for this purchase?" If the answers are "No," you don't need to make the purchase.
- This may help you stop unnecessary spending: "How much do I have saved for fun, exciting plans for which I have a deadline?"
- Realize that you are building your future credit rating even though you are a student.

STRATEGIES FOR BUILDING ON YOUR BEST

Consider the following strategies for managing your time and money:

- Push yourself to use your time more wisely. Can you get more done in less time by focusing on what you have learned?
- Use your time-management practices at work and for school.
- Focus on doing hard, unpleasant jobs first, then reward yourself.
- Analyze how you are actually spending your time.
- Practice the strategies you have learned for avoiding procrastination.
- Map out your activities and tasks for a week and a month at a time.
- Think about your future and how your financial actions today are going to impact you.
- Practice delayed gratification.
- If you must use a credit card, don't charge more than you can pay off at the end of the month.

Student Loans
A DAY OF RECKONING WILL COME

The high cost of college makes tuition out of reach for many families. For many students, the only way to attend college is via student loans. If this is the only way you can go to college, borrow the money—but borrow no more than you absolutely must. Try not to borrow anything but tuition and perhaps room and board. Get a job, budget, cut out extras, work in the summers, take fewer credits even though it delays graduation—do everything possible not to borrow more money than you must.

If you have to borrow a great deal of money, ask yourself a few very important questions: "Am I majoring in a field that is going to pay me enough money to repay these loans and live? Will I ever be able to afford a house? Can I afford to get married and have a family?" You should have a good idea of how much money you can make when you get out of college. Be realistic. Can you pay this money back with the major you are in right now? If you owe a lot of money, should you rethink your future career choice? Perhaps a current major might

Glossary of Financial Terms

Annual fee— amount charged by a lender to keep a credit card

Annual percentage rate— the cost of credit at an annual rate.

Bankruptcy— Chapter 7 bankruptcy allows one's unprotected assets to be sold and disbursed to creditors. Chapter 13 allows the debtor time to pay debts.

Budget— a plan that takes into consideration one's income, expenses, and savings

Car title loans— loans made against one's car usually at a very high rate of interest.

Collateral— assets that may be used to secure a loan.

Credit— a promise to buy now and pay later.

Credit history— a record of one's history of loans and credit card debts and how one has repaid the debts.

Credit line— the amount of credit issued by a lender.

Credit report— your credit history, compiled by several companies and made available to banks, etc.

Debit card— card allows purchases to be charged directly to one's personal bank account.

Default— failure to repay a debt.

Delinquency— past due payment on a loan.

Discretionary income— amount of money one has left after all expenses have been paid.

Disposable income— money left over after taxes have been deducted.

Fixed expenses— expenses that remain the same every month.

Flexible expenses— expenses that vary from month to month.

Grace period— period one has to pay a debt before being charged finance charges.

Identity fraud— crime that occurs when someone assumes another person's identity.

Income taxes— a percentage of one's income that is assessed by the federal and some state governments and deducted from one's paycheck.

Installment loan— a debt in which the amount and number of payments are predetermined.

Interest— cost of borrowing or lending money.

Interest rate— percentage charged by the lender.

Investment— buying stock, real estate, art, bonds, etc. with the idea that the investment will appreciate in value.

Late Fee— charges made to a delinquent account.

Payday loans— loans made against one's next paycheck, usually at a very high rate of interest.

Principal— the outstanding balance of a loan exclusive of interest.

Repossession— creditor legally takes back something purchased and not paid for.

become a minor. It is very important to work at something you love; it is equally important to be able to pay your bills. According to Watson (2002), the median student loan debt is at record levels due to rising tuitions— $17,000 versus $2000 when baby boomers were in their 20s.

You will have to repay this money that you have borrowed. Even bankruptcy will not relieve you of this debt; so again, don't borrow any money you can do without.

The Latte Factor™

In his book *The Finish Rich Notebook* (2003), Bach states, "How much you earn has no bearing on whether or not you will build wealth." As a rule, the more we make, the more we spend. Many people spend far more than they make and subject themselves to stress, exorbitant debt, fear, and an ultimate future of poverty.

Bach uses the Latte Factor™ to call people's attention to how much money we carelessly throw away when we should be saving and investing for the future. He uses the story of a young woman who said she could not invest because she had no money. Yet, almost every day she bought a large latte for $3.50 and a muffin for $1.50. If you add a candy bar here, a drink there, a shake at the gym, you could easily be spending $10 a day that could be invested.

If you take that $10 per day and invest it faithfully at 10 percent, in 34 years, you will have $1 million. This is the power of compound interest! If you are a relatively young person, you will probably work that many years and more, so you could retire with an extra $1 million in addition to any other savings you might have accumulated.

The point is that most of us have the ability to become rich, but we either lack the knowledge or the discipline to do so. Remember the Latte Factor™ as you begin your college career and practice it if you want to become a millionaire.

Protect Yourself from Identity Theft

LIVING LARGE ON YOUR GOOD NAME

Every year thousands of people are victims of identity theft. In other words, someone uses their name and personal information and charges on their credit cards. Identity theft may also include filing fraudulent tax returns, accessing bank accounts, and committing other crimes. NEVER put any personal information in the garbage that has not been shredded. Buy an inexpensive shredder and use it! Many identity theft victims have spent over 175 hours and over $10,000 per incident to resolve their problems.

People who may steal your identity are roommates, relatives, friends, estranged spouses, and household workers who have ready access to your papers. Or they may steal your wallet, go through your trash, or take your mail. They can even legally photocopy your vital information at the courthouse if, for example, you have been divorced. The Internet provides thieves many other opportunities to use official-looking e-mail messages designed to obtain your personal information.

It is very difficult, if not impossible, to catch identity thieves. While you may not be liable, you still have to spend your time filing expensive legal affidavits, writing letters, and making telephone calls to clear your good name.

Victims of identity theft can suffer staggering consequences:

- They must resolve unauthorized debts and delinquent accounts.
- Some have lost their jobs.
- Some have faced criminal investigation, arrest, or conviction.
- Victims may not even know their identity has been stolen until, after several months, a negative situation arises and they realize they have a problem.

Order a credit report once a year to be sure you have no major problems!

HOW TO MINIMIZE IDENTITY THEFT RISK

Criminals are very clever, and many are adept at using electronic means to steal your information. Here are ways to avoid having this kind of problem:

- Carry only the ID and cards you need at any given time.
- Sign all new credit cards immediately with permanent ink.
- Do not make Internet purchases from sites that are unsecured (check for a padlock icon to ensure safety).
- Do not write your PIN number, Social Security number, or passcode on any information that can be stolen or that you are discarding.
- Try to memorize your passwords instead of recording them on paper or in the computer.
- Get someone you trust to check your mail in your absence.
- Destroy all carbons.
- Be aware of "shoulder surfers." Shield your numbers when using an ATM.
- Avoid providing your Social Security number to any organization until you have verified its legitimacy.
- Check your credit file periodically by requesting a copy of your report (*Identity Theft and Fraud*, 2003).

IF YOUR CREDIT CARDS ARE STOLEN:
- Contact your local police immediately.
- Notify your creditors immediately and request that your accounts be closed.
- Ask the card company to furnish copies of documents that show any fraudulent transactions.
- Refuse to pay any bill or portion of any bill that is a result of identity theft.
- Report the theft or fraud to credit reporting agencies.

IF YOU LOSE YOUR DRIVER'S LICENSE:
- Notify the state office of the Department of Motor Vehicles and place a fraud alert on your license number.
- Request a new driver's license.

The Pitfalls of Payday Loans and Car Title Loans

THERE'S SOMEONE ON EVERY CORNER TO TAKE YOUR MONEY

Many unsuspecting consumers have been duped into signing car title loans and payday loans that resulted in very high monthly payments and penalties. Some were told by their title loan broker before they signed the contract that they could make a partial payment if they needed to and this would be OK. Unfortunately, the unsuspecting victims find out too late that their car is going to be repossessed due to one late or partial payment. Others realize too late that on a loan of $400, they must pay back over $500 that month. According to recent reports from consumer affairs groups, some institutions have been charging as much as 250 percent interest on an annualized basis (Cojonet, 2003). In some instances interest rates as high as 900% have been charged due to poor government regulatory policies.

The main point that you need to remember is that you should only borrow money from a reputable bank or credit union. NEVER get involved in a payday loan or a car title loan. Not only could you lose your car, you can ruin your credit. There are indeed people on every corner who will take your money if you don't manage your affairs very carefully.

> If you can make a million by starting to invest after 45, how much more could you accumulate if you started at 25?   —PRICE PRITCHETT

BLUEPRINTS FOR CHANGE

NAME   DATE

REFLECTION

Priority and financial management are life skills that will serve you well during college. Learning to manage your time, stop procrastinating, control spending, and budget your money are important skills that will give you staying power as a college student.

The points that have been shared with you in this chapter will serve you well all through your college career. The greatest benefit of developing and improving these skills, however, will be realized when you graduate, go to work, and start a family. As technology and business practices continue to emerge and change, you will need to continually upgrade your personal management skills. College is truly the beginning of a journey where you will learn new skills and develop practices that will guide you for the rest of your life.

GET REAL

Below are a few questions to help you think about your priority management and financial practices and how they have impacted your college life so far. Study each question and respond honestly.

Describe one problem you have experienced this semester as a result of poor time management.

What have you done to resolve this problem as a result of studying this chapter?

How have you applied information you learned about credit cards and financial responsibilities?

How did *The Latte Factor*™ impact your thinking about saving for the future?

How can getting better control of your time help you become a successful student?

How can learning to control your credit card use impact you now and in the future?

How does priority management affect your ability to live a balanced life?

127

Case Study

NAME: Coretta Hooks
SCHOOL: University of South Carolina, Columbia, SC
MAJOR: Retail Management **AGE:** 21

Below is a real-life situation faced by one of Coretta's friends. Read the brief case and respond to the questions.

During my first semester, my friends and I were bombarded with credit card applications. They were in our orientation packets and they started showing up in our mailboxes. Unfortunately, one of my friends foolishly applied for—and received—several credit cards.

Marilyn spent a great deal of her time shopping. Before she knew it, she had accumulated three large balances on credit cards. She kept buying sweaters, shoes, and makeup. She ate out frequently and even took a trip to Atlanta that she charged on her credit card. She was living large! But a day of reckoning was coming!

Marilyn had never been taught a great deal about money management and nothing about the perils of credit card debt. Each of these cards charged 18 percent interest. Since she was late several times, she acquired four late fees of $29 each. When she finally realized what was happening, she was in a big mess! She couldn't tell her parents. Her dad would kill her. And her allowance wouldn't come close to paying off this debt. Marilyn cried and said over and over, "Why was I so dumb? What can I do?"

What was the first source of Marilyn's problems?
___
___
___

What do you think Marilyn should do immediately?
___
___
___

What can she do to get out of debt and get out of this mess?
___
___
___

How does Marilyn's story have real-world implications for you?
_____
_____
_____

If you are like Marilyn and have had little training in managing money, where can you go for assistance?
_____
_____
_____
_____

Is using a "credit repair" agency a good idea? Why or why not?
_____
_____
_____
_____

at this moment Journal

Refer to page 101 of this chapter. Having read and reflected upon the information in the chapter, consider how you might revise your goal to make it more:

REASONABLE

BELIEVABLE

MEASURABLE

ADAPTABLE

CONTROLLABLE

DESIRABLE

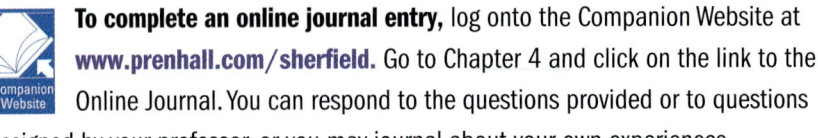

ONLINE JOURNAL

To complete an online journal entry, log onto the Companion Website at **www.prenhall.com/sherfield.** Go to Chapter 4 and click on the link to the Online Journal. You can respond to the questions provided or to questions assigned by your professor, or you may journal about your own experiences.

ADVICE TO GO

CORNERSTONES

prioritizing & money management

Manage your *time*, *money*, and *resources* carefully.

Know exactly how you are *spending* your time and your money.

Don't get caught in the *credit card trap*.

Protect your *credit rating* by using wise money management.

Prepare for success by investing for the future.

Spend more time with those who bring you *joy*.

Include *fun breaks, rewards,* and *sacred days* in your plans.

Plan for a *balanced life*.

Focus on *quality* and *joy*.

Make *to-do lists*.

PRIORITIZE

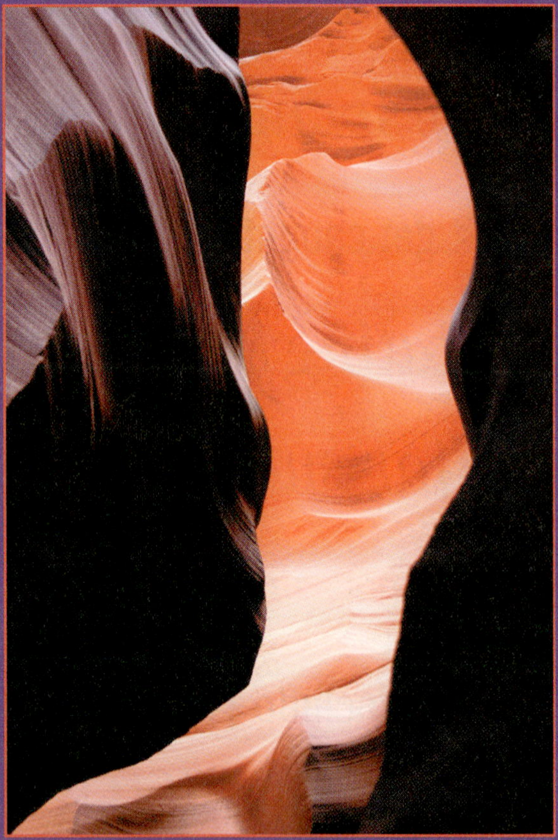

5 Read

The difference between the right word and the almost right word is the difference between lightening and the lightning bug.
—Mark Twain

CHAPTER 5
READ

Conrad wanted to go home to his wife and children, but he *just could not face them.* He couldn't. He knew that the first question out of their mouths would be, "How did you do, daddy? How did you do?"

He had just taken his placement test at Almanac College. His wife and children were excited that he was going back to college. They were excited, and he was horrified. *They seemed to have more faith in him than he had in himself.* This placement test did not determine whether Conrad was able to enter the college; it simply determined which courses he needed to take first.

He arrived on campus early, registered with the testing center, and took three placement tests before noon. First, he took the English placement test, then the math test, and finally the reading/vocabulary/spelling placement test. Since he had worked with numbers his whole life, he was not overly concerned with the math placement test. ==He was, however, very worried about the English and reading tests.==

After a lunch break, Conrad was told to return to the campus for his scores and to see an advisor. He went back to the testing center and waited for his appointment time at 1:30. As he sat in the testing lobby, he saw many students—some younger, some older, some with their children in tow, and some as carefree as the wind. "I wonder how they did," he thought. "What if I'm the only one who doesn't do well on these tests?"

His name was called, and an advisor greeted Conrad and escorted him to her office. She began to speak. "Mr. Hunter, you did very well on your math placement test and you are free to register for any curriculum math course. I would, however, advise you to start with the basic courses and work your way up. Math courses at Almanac are not easy. I know you'll do well. Mr. Hunter," she continued, "your scores in English and reading indicate the need for a great deal of remediation."

"What does that mean?" Conrad asked.

"It means that you will need to register for English 090 and complete that course with a C or better before you can take English 101, the course required for your major in small business management." She continued. "You will also need to register for Reading 100. This course will help you become a stronger reader and help you use a more dynamic vocabulary."

"Can I just not take the English 090 and reading courses? Can I opt out of them and just take the required courses?" Conrad asked.

"I'm afraid not, Mr. Hunter. These tests are very accurate when it comes to predicting your success in certain classes. In looking at your scores, you seem to have a problem with reading comprehension, analysis,

134

Building Active Reading and Comprehension Skills

and interpretation. To opt out of this reading class would be very detrimental to your success."

"But I need to finish my degree as quickly as possible because my family is depending on me," Conrad informed her.

"I do understand that, Mr. Hunter, but without this reading course, your scores indicate that you will have trouble in many of your classes. For example, you are required to take Psychology 101 for your major. Do you realize that the psychology book used for this course is written on the fourteenth grade level, and you're reading at the eighth grade level?"

> *"But I need to finish my degree as quickly as possible . . ."*

Conrad knew in his heart that she was right. He had never been strong in English, reading, spelling, or vocabulary. He knew that he had trouble in these areas. He knew that he had trouble concentrating and remembering what he had just read. "But how am I going to face my wife and children?" he thought. "How can I tell them that I don't read well?"

On the drive home, he struggled mightily with the questions in his head. "Should I just forget about this degree? Should I go to the dean and ask to be placed in the curriculum courses regardless of my scores? Should I tell my wife and children what happened? Should I just admit my shortcomings to my family and show them that I'm as determined as ever?"

Conrad pulled into the driveway still unsure of what he was going to tell his family. As he walked toward the front door, he heard his children yell, "Daddy's home! Daddy's home!" At that moment, he knew what he had to do.

QUESTIONS FOR REFLECTION

Consider responding to these questions online in the Questions for Reflection module of the Companion Website.

1. What decision do you think Conrad made? Why?

2. How could this be a positive experience for Conrad's entire family?

3. Has reading ever caused you problems in your academic work? If so, how have you dealt with this problem in the past?

Where are you... AT THIS MOMENT

Before reading this chapter, take a moment and respond to the following 10 questions. Consider each one carefully before answering, and then respond by circling the number in the appropriate box. When you have answered the questions, add your points and find your total score on the feedback chart below.

STATEMENT	STRONGLY DISAGREE	DISAGREE	DON'T KNOW	AGREE	STRONGLY AGREE	SCORE
1. I usually look up definitions in a dictionary when I read words I don't understand.	1	2	3	4	5	
2. Building a larger vocabulary isn't that important to me.	5	4	3	2	1	
3. I believe I can do well in school without reading the books and papers assigned by the professors.	5	4	3	2	1	
4. I am good at finding the main ideas of the paragraphs I read.	1	2	3	4	5	
5. When reading textbooks, I use the SQ3R strategy (or another strategy) to aid my comprehension.	1	2	3	4	5	
6. I know how to use a highlighter to aid me in my reading assignments.	1	2	3	4	5	
7. I do not usually take notes from my books while I read.	5	4	3	2	1	
8. It is not possible for me to become better at understanding what I read.	5	4	3	2	1	
9. I rarely give myself the time to reread materials that I don't understand.	5	4	3	2	1	
10. I often read books, magazines, or newspapers simply for pleasure.	1	2	3	4	5	
TOTAL VALUE						

SUMMARY

10–17 Your reading skills are limited. You need to learn reading strategies to help you understand what you read. Your dislike for reading doesn't mean you can't be successful in college, but it will be important to learn to get the needed information from what you read.

18–25 Your reading skills are below average, but can be improved with practice and patience. You will need to learn strategies for improving your reading skills. Your reading confidence will improve as you employ those strategies.

26–34 Your reading skills are likely average. You probably realize how important reading is for successful progress in school. You could brush up on strategies to maximize your reading comprehension.

35–42 Your reading skills and habits are above average. You likely enjoy reading and know how to read for comprehension. A few additional strategies will help you get even more benefit from the time you spend reading.

43–50 You are exceptional in your reading skills. You know how to read for comprehension by employing a variety of reading strategies and how to incorporate your reading into your larger study structure. You likely get much enjoyment from reading and use that to your advantage.

Goals... FOR CHANGE

Based on your total points, what is one goal you would like to achieve related to reading more effectively?

Goal _____
_____

List three actions you can take that might help you move closer to realizing this goal.

1. _____
2. _____
3. _____

Questions FOR BUILDING ON YOUR BEST

As you read this chapter, consider the following questions. At the end of the chapter, you should be able to answer all of them. You are encouraged to ask a few questions of your own. Consider asking your classmates or professors to assist you.

1. What is the relationship between reading and building a vocabulary?
2. Why is it important for me to read with a dictionary?
3. What role does note taking play in my reading success?
4. What is SQ3R and how can it help me read better?
5. How can I improve my concentration?

What additional questions might you have about reading and comprehension?

1. _____
2. _____
3. _____

Is Reading FUNdamental or Just Pure Torture?

THE ANSWER CAN CHANGE YOUR LIFE

Quick question: What are the top two academic problems among college students today? According to faculty members, assessments, national tests, and yes, even your peers around the nation, the two greatest problems students face today are math and reading comprehension—and some of the math problems can even be attributed to poor reading skills.

"I can read," you might say. "I've been reading since I was four years old!" You may even be asking at this point, "WHY would professors put a chapter in a COLLEGE textbook about reading?"

The answer is quite simple. There is a monumental difference between knowing and reading the words on a page and being able to comprehend, interpret, analyze, and evaluate those written words. Herein lies the problem; just because you have hands, this does not make you a mechanic. Just because you have a voice, this does not make you a singer, and just because you can read words, this does not mean that you comprehend what the author intended.

How many times have you read to the bottom of a page or completed a section in a textbook and said to yourself, "I don't know anything about what I just read, much less remember it." In actuality, all of us have done this at one time or another. This chapter is here to help you eliminate this problem from your academic studies. This chapter is here to help you learn how to read a page, a section, or an entire chapter so that when you reach the end, you will comprehend what you just read.

Finally! A Six-Pack that Can Actually Help You
The ingredients for successful reading:

The material you're reading

An open mind

Pencils

A highlighter

A tablet or loose-leaf paper

A dictionary

It may seem elementary, but without the tools shown above, you can't improve your reading comprehension, analysis, or speed. Enough said!

WOULD YOU RATHER DRIBBLE OR SHOOT?

Activity

Discover if You Are a Passive or an Active Reader

Estimate the following statements truthfully regarding your reading preferences right now.

1. I enjoy reading for pleasure.	TRUE	FALSE
2. College textbooks have little connection to my real life.	TRUE	FALSE
3. I look for the deeper meaning in words and phrases.	TRUE	FALSE
4. I seldom visualize what I am reading.	TRUE	FALSE
5. I look up words that I do not understand.	TRUE	FALSE
6. I read only what I have to read, and that is a stretch for me.	TRUE	FALSE
7. I stop reading to ponder what something means.	TRUE	FALSE
8. I never take notes when reading.	TRUE	FALSE
9. Reading brings me great joy.	TRUE	FALSE
10. My mind wanders constantly when I read.	TRUE	FALSE
11. I make time for reading even when I am not required to read.	TRUE	FALSE
12. Words are just words—they have no real meaning to my life or work.	TRUE	FALSE
13. I get excited about reading something new because I know I will learn something new and useful.	TRUE	FALSE
14. When reading, I just want to get it over with.	TRUE	FALSE
15. I usually have no trouble concentrating when reading.	TRUE	FALSE
16. I never look up words, I just read on.	TRUE	FALSE

TOTAL of *even* TRUE responses _____

TOTAL of *odd* TRUE responses _____

If you answered TRUE to more *even* numbers, you tend to be a more PASSIVE reader.

If you answered TRUE to more *odd* numbers, you tend to be a more ACTIVE reader.

Active reading is really nothing more than a mind-set. It is the attitude you have as you begin the reading process. For the next few days, try approaching your reading assignments with a positive, open-minded approach and notice the difference in your own satisfaction, understanding, and overall comprehension.

Now that you have discovered if you are an active or passive reader, the following section will help you determine your reading speed.

I Feel the Need . . . the Need for Speed!

DETERMINING YOUR PERSONAL READING RATE

You've heard the advertisements: "Breeze through a novel on your lunch hour," "Read an entire computer instruction book over dinner," or "Read *The New York Times* at a traffic light." Sure, there are people who do have an incredible gift for speed reading and a photographic memory, but those people are not the norm.

Speed is not everything. Most college professors agree that comprehension is *much* more important than speed. If you are a slow reader, does this mean that you are not intelligent? Absolutely not! Reading speeds will vary from person to person depending on training, frequency in reading, comprehension, and the complexity of the material.

This section is included in your text to give you some idea about how long it will take to read a chapter so that you can *plan your reading time* more effectively. There are an average of 450 words on a college textbook page. If you read at 150 words per minute, each page may take you an average of 3 minutes to read.

This is a *raw number* for just reading. It does not allow for marking, highlighting, taking notes, looking up words, or reflecting. When these necessary skills are coupled with basic reading, they can sometimes triple the amount of reading time required. So, that page that you estimated would take you 3 minutes to read may actually take you 9 to 10 minutes.

If your professor has assigned a chapter in your text that is 21 pages long and it takes you 9 minutes on average to read each page, you need to allow at least 189 minutes (or 3.15 hours) to read and comprehend the chapter.

In the following activity, you will find a passage from a later chapter in this book. Read the section at your normal pace. Use a stopwatch or a watch with a second hand to accurately record your time, and then calculate your rate and comprehension level using the scales provided.

CALCULATING YOUR READING RATE

Start Time _____   _____ **Minutes**   _____ **Seconds**

BINGE DRINKING

Binge drinking is classified as having more than five drinks at one time. Many people say, "I only drink once a week." However, if that one drinking spell includes drink after drink after drink, it can be extremely detrimental to your liver, your memory, your digestive system, and your overall health in general.

Most college students report that they do not mean to binge drink, but it is caused by the situation, such as a ballgame, a party, a campus event, or special occasions. Researchers at Michigan State University found that only 5 percent of students surveyed say they party to "get drunk" (Warner, 2002).

In their breakthrough work, *Dying to Drink,* Harvard researcher Henry Wechsler and science writer Bernice Wuethrich explore the problem of binge drinking. They suggest, "two out of every five college students regularly binge drink resulting in approximately 1,400 student deaths, a distressing number of assaults and rapes, a shameful amount of vandalism, and countless cases of academic suicide" (Wechsler and Wuethrich, 2002).

It is a situation reminiscent of the old saying, "Letting the fox guard the hen house." After a few drinks, it is hard to "self-police," meaning that you may not be able to control your actions once the drinking starts.

Perhaps the greatest tragedy of drug and alcohol abuse is the residual damage of pregnancy, sexually transmitted diseases, traffic fatalities, verbal/physical abuse, and accidental death. You know that drugs and alcohol lower your resistance and can cause you to do things that you would not normally do, such as drive drunk or have unprotected sex.

Surveys and research results suggest that students who participate in heavy episodic (HE) or binge drinking are more likely to participate in unprotected sex with multiple sex partners. One survey found that 61 percent of men who *do* binge drink participated in unprotected sex as compared to 23 percent of men who *do not* binge drink. The survey also found that 48 percent of women who *do* binge drink participated in unprotected sex as compared to only 8 percent of women who *do not* binge drink (Cooper, 2002).

These staggering statistics suggest one thing: alcohol consumption can cause people to act in ways in which they may never have acted without alcohol—and those actions can result in personal damage from which recovery may be impossible.

(387 words)

Finishing Time _____   _____ **Minutes**   _____ **Seconds**

Reading time in SECONDS = _____

Words per MINUTE (use the chart on the next page) = _____

(continued)

CONTINUED *Activity*

Example: If you read this passage in **2 minutes and 38 seconds,** your reading time in seconds would be **158.** Using the Rate Calculator Chart, your reading rate would be about **146 words per minute.**

RATE CALCULATOR FOR RELATIVELY EASY PASSAGES

Time in Seconds and Minutes	Words per Minute
40	581
50	464
60 (1 minute)	387
120 (2 minutes)	194
130	179
140	165
150	155
160	145
170	137
180 (3 minutes)	129
190	122
200	116
210	110
220	106
230	101

Source: *Breaking Through*, 6th ed., Smith, B. (2001).

Answer the following questions with T (true) or F (false) without looking back over the material.

_____ 1. Binge drinking has resulted in the deaths of students.
_____ 2. Men who binge drink have unprotected sex more often than men who do not binge drink.
_____ 3. Women who binge drink have unprotected sex no more often than women who do not binge drink.
_____ 4. "Self-policing" means that you are able to look out for yourself.
_____ 5. Binge drinking is classified as having more than three drinks at one time.

(Answers can be found on page 145.)

Each question is worth 20 percent.   Comprehension = _____%

Example: If you answered two correctly, your comprehension rate would be 40% (2 × 20%). If you answered four correctly, your comprehension rate would be 80% (4 × 20%).

WHAT DOES IT ALL MEAN?

According to Brenda D. Smith (1999), professor and reading expert, "rate calculators vary according to the difficulty of the material. Research indicates, however, that on relatively easy material, the average adult reading speed is approximately 250 words per minute at 70% comprehension. For college students, the rate is sometimes estimated at closer to 300 words per minute." The passage that you just read would be classified as relatively easy.

If you are reading below the average 250 word per minute rate, several factors could be contributing to this situation. They include:

- Not concentrating on the passage.
- Vocabulary words with which you are not familiar.
- Stopping too long on any given word (called fixations; discussed later).
- Not reading often enough to build your speed.

The remainder of this chapter is intended to assist you with improving your reading speed and comprehension.

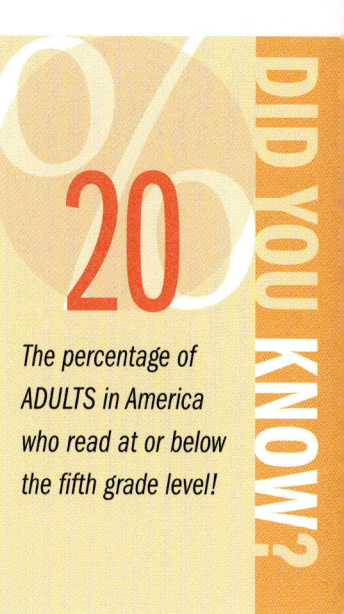

DID YOU KNOW?

20%

The percentage of ADULTS in America who read at or below the fifth grade level!

Source: Wurman, R. *Understanding.* New York: Donnelley & Sons, 1999.

Why We Read

There are really only two reasons that anyone reads—for learning and for pleasure. If you're lucky, you enjoy both. Realistically, some people do not enjoy reading and, therefore, do not do it for pleasure. We want to make the point that reading for pleasure can help you read better as a student seeking knowledge and understanding. We'll discuss reading for pleasure later in this chapter.

Reading for the sake of learning can be broken down into several categories. Sometimes, you read simply to **memorize information.** Sometimes, you read for **understanding,** and sometimes, you read for **application.** Reading college textbooks can be a rough and, yes, sometimes tedious exercise. Knowing WHY you are reading can help you become a more active reader and make reading more interesting and beneficial to you.

If you are reading simply to gather a few facts, you may tend to skim the section, chapter, or article very quickly. This type of reading can help you if you're in a crunch or if you just need a few ideas. However, this type of reading will do you little good in helping you gain a deep and clear understanding of the material. Reading for speed and scanning are discussed later.

If you are reading to use the information for a test, a paper, a speech, or to participate in a class discussion, you will need to allow more time for your reading activity, take notes as you read, ask yourself questions for comprehension, and review the material frequently. This type of reading is more apt to help you gain a clear understanding of the author's intent. The next sections will show you how to read for long-term comprehension.

You Don't Have to Be a Logodaedalian to Enjoy Words

THE POWER OF A DYNAMIC VOCABULARY

Thankfully, it is not every day you run across the word logodaedalian. (A *logodaedalian* is a person who has a great passion for unique, sly, and clever words and phrases.) Perhaps the best way to develop a dynamic vocabulary is by reading. By reading, you come across words that you may have never seen before. You are exposed to aspects of language that you may not have experienced in your family, neighborhood, or geographic location.

Of course, the words in a passage, section, or chapter with which you are unfamiliar will not become a part of your vernacular unless you STOP and look them up. This is the way to begin building a masterful vocabulary.

Let's start by looking up the word *vernacular*. Take a moment and jot down the definition. *Vernacular means*

_____

_____

See how simple that was? Now, you have a new word in your vocabulary—actually, you have two new words in just a few paragraphs: vernacular and logodaedalian. You're on your way to becoming a logophile!

PREFIXES AND SUFFIXES IN READING AND VOCABULARY DEVELOPMENT

Words can be made from combining parts of a word (prefixes, suffixes, or roots) into the whole word. If you understand what the prefixes and suffixes mean, this will make reading and vocabulary easier for you. Examine the prefixes and suffixes that follow.

PREFIX	MEANING	EXAMPLE
anti	against	anti-war, antidepressant
auto	self	autobiography, autocrat
bi	two	bicycle, binoculars
circum	around	circumference, circumstantial
de	away, undo	departure, demote
dis	not	dishonest, disbar
ex	out, former	ex-wife, extraordinary
in	not	incomprehensible, incorrect
inter	between	intersection, intercourse
intra	within, in	intramural, intragalactic
mal	bad, wrong	malfunction, malnutrition
mis	not, wrong	miscommunication, misdiagnose
mono	one	monorail, monocracy
post	after	postmortem, postpartum
pre	before	prerequisite, prefix
pro	before, forward	prospect, profess
non	not, no	noncredit, nonsense
re	back	regret, regain
sub	under	subway, submerge
super	above	supernatural, superstitious
tele	distance	telephone, telepathy
ultra	beyond, extreme	ultraviolet, ultrasound
un	not	unnecessary, ungrateful

Building Active Reading and Comprehension Skills   **145**

SUFFIX	MEANING	EXAMPLE
■ an	someone who	comedian
■ ne	someone who	comedianne, heroine
■ ee	someone who	employee
■ er	someone who	preacher
■ ess	someone who	hostess
■ ist	someone who	pianist
■ or	someone who	tailor
■ ship	referring to	ownership
■ hood	referring to	neighborhood
■ est	a condition	fairest
■ ic	a condition	allergic
■ ish	a condition	foolish
■ ive	a condition	festive
■ less	a condition	worthless
■ ness	a condition	kindness
■ ous	a condition	generous

> **Answers to Comprehension Test on p. 142:**
> 1=T, 2=T, 3=F, 4=T, 5=F

Being able to recognize these simple prefixes and suffixes can help you understand words without having to look them up. Consider the following sentences. Fill in the blanks with the missing prefix or suffix.

1. *If you are planning to become an engine_____ , you will need to have strong math and science skills.*
2. *She suffered from _____ partum depression after the birth of her child.*
3. *He _____ understood the entire movie.*
4. *The mean_____ and bloodi_____ of the murders was appalling.*
5. *She took a course in _____personal communication offered at the local college.*
6. *He was an _____ conservative member of the senate.*
7. *The house was a pigsty. It was in total _____array.*
8. *The field of _____communications is very hot right now. Fiber optics have gained attention worldwide.*
9. *Welcome to the brother_____ of Elks. We welcome you with open arms.*
10. *Nevada's legislature meets every two years and develops a _____annual budget.*

You will notice that with these sentences, you are able to pick up the correct prefix or suffix by hints within the sentence. Many times, you can clarify words in your text simply by paying close attention to the words used in the sentence.

Building a powerful and dynamic vocabulary will not happen overnight, but with a little work, some creativity, and a good dictionary, you will begin to notice how quickly you amass a more expansive array of common words and phrases.

It's Not Just a Doorstop
USING YOUR DICTIONARY

Your dictionary will become a good friend to you in college. There will be many words and phrases that you will not understand when reading texts that are written on the thirteenth and fourteenth grade levels. There is nothing to be ashamed of because you resort to "looking up" a word. You'll be smarter because of it.

When you look up a word in the dictionary, you are given more than just a definition (see Figure 5.1). You are given the phonetic pronunciation, the spelling, the meaning, the part of speech in which the word can be used, the origin of the word, and usually several definitions. You may have to choose the definition that best suits the context of the sentence.

Using the definition for *magnitude*, determine which definition would be best suited to this sentence:

*The **magnitude** of the power she had over him was truly amazing.*

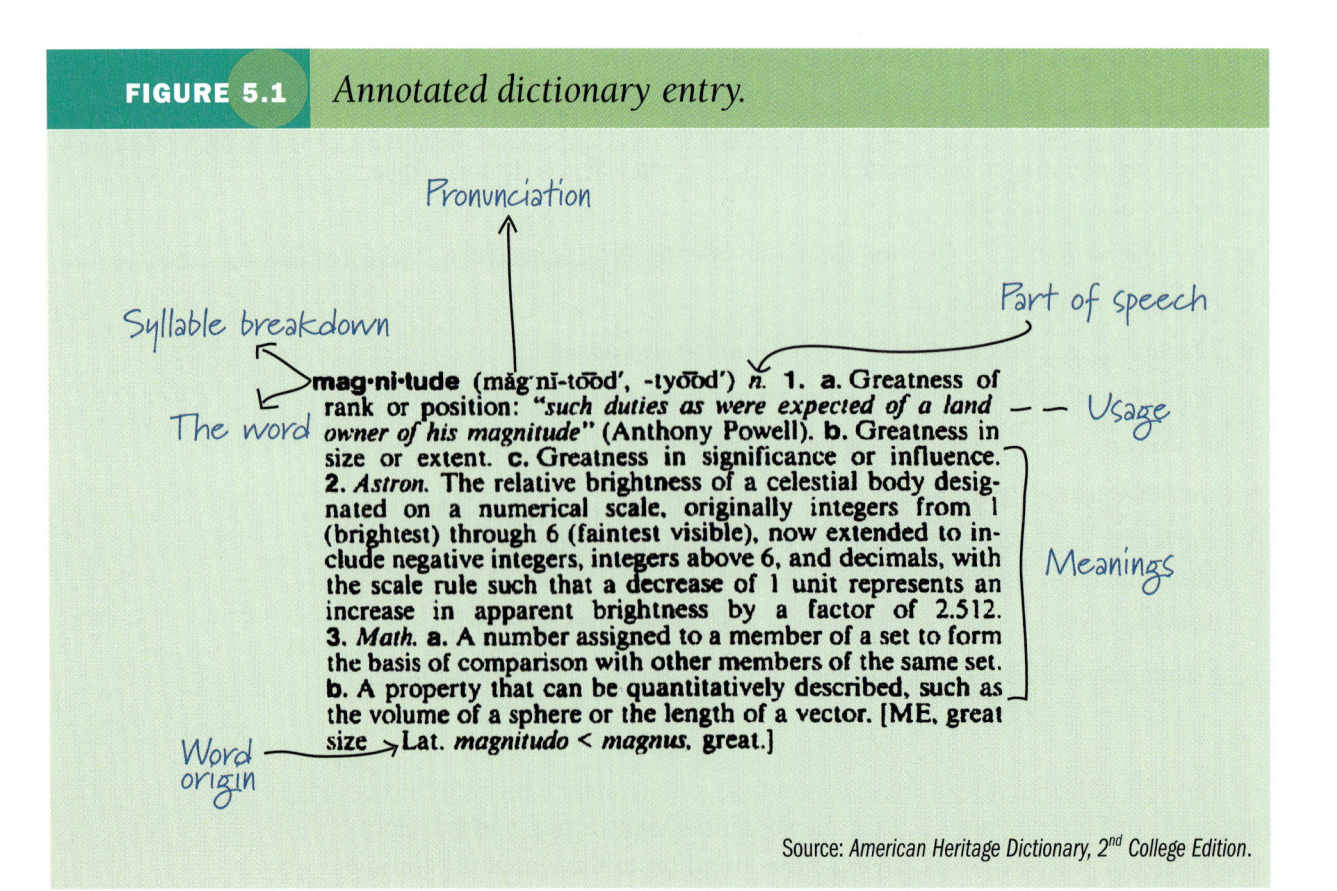

FIGURE 5.1 *Annotated dictionary entry.*

Pronunciation

Syllable breakdown

Part of speech

mag·ni·tude (măg'nĭ-tōōd', -tyōōd') *n.* **1. a.** Greatness of rank or position: "such duties as were expected of a land owner of his magnitude" (Anthony Powell). **b.** Greatness in size or extent. **c.** Greatness in significance or influence. **2.** *Astron.* The relative brightness of a celestial body designated on a numerical scale, originally integers from 1 (brightest) through 6 (faintest visible), now extended to include negative integers, integers above 6, and decimals, with the scale rule such that a decrease of 1 unit represents an increase in apparent brightness by a factor of 2.512. **3.** *Math.* **a.** A number assigned to a member of a set to form the basis of comparison with other members of the same set. **b.** A property that can be quantitatively described, such as the volume of a sphere or the length of a vector. [ME. great size ‹ Lat. *magnitudo* < *magnus*, great.]

The word

Usage

Meanings

Word origin

Source: *American Heritage Dictionary, 2nd College Edition.*

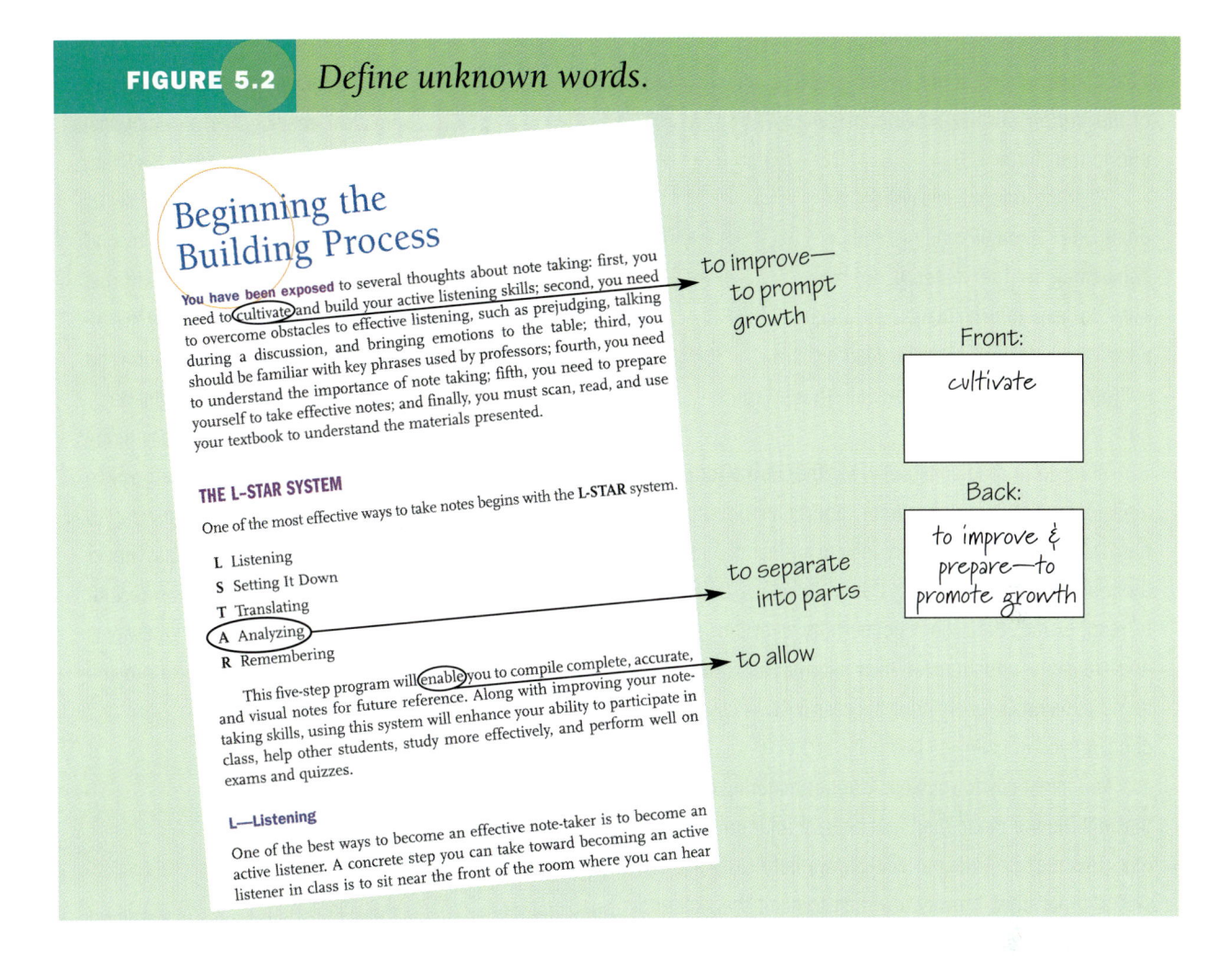

Building Active Reading and Comprehension Skills   147

FIGURE 5.2   *Define unknown words.*

Beginning the Building Process

You have been exposed to several thoughts about note taking: first, you need to (cultivate) and build your active listening skills; second, you need to overcome obstacles to effective listening, such as prejudging, talking during a discussion, and bringing emotions to the table; third, you should be familiar with key phrases used by professors; fourth, you need to understand the importance of note taking; fifth, you need to prepare yourself to take effective notes; and finally, you must scan, read, and use your textbook to understand the materials presented.

*to improve—
to prompt growth*

Front:
cultivate

THE L-STAR SYSTEM

One of the most effective ways to take notes begins with the **L-STAR** system.

L Listening
S Setting It Down
T Translating
A Analyzing
R Remembering

to separate into parts

Back:
to improve & prepare—to promote growth

This five-step program will (enable) you to compile complete, accurate, and visual notes for future reference. Along with improving your note-taking skills, using this system will enhance your ability to participate in class, help other students, study more effectively, and perform well on exams and quizzes.

to allow

L—Listening

One of the best ways to become an effective note-taker is to become an active listener. A concrete step you can take toward becoming an active listener in class is to sit near the front of the room where you can hear

---

There are several ways to begin your collection of unfamiliar words as you read. You can write them in the margin of the page in your text, you can put the word on an index card (word on the front, definition on the back), or you can put the definition in a special column when taking notes. Examples are shown in Figure 5.2.

Improving Speed and Comprehension

As you begin to practice your reading comprehension, review the following tips for helping you read the material more quickly and understand the material more clearly. Whenever you are faced with having to choose between comprehension and speed, choose comprehension every time.

CONCENTRATION

Speed and comprehension both require deep, mindful concentration. Neither can be achieved without it. Your body needs to be ready to concentrate. You

WORLD OF WORK

I have always been struck by the power of the written word to provide insight and to transform.

Reading informs everything we do in life. Through reading and by connecting to the material, we are able to experience things we might never know. In and of itself, reading is a solitary practice. It is what you do with what you have read that matters.

In my job I read constantly, whether in the form of e-mails, financial or management reports, or product proposals. Reading is the primary vehicle for learning and it is the foundation for everything I do in business. Being able to read, extract the salient points from what I'm reading, and translate and transfer that information into action items is the basis for ensuring success in business, and indeed, for you in college.

You might say to yourself, "I'm not majoring in a field that will require me to read and analyze information every day." This may be true, but it is always better to have the skill and not need it every day than to need the skill and not have it at all.

Reading and comprehending what you have read is not a luxury; it is a demand of the modern work world. Reading is important to everyone from auto mechanics who have to read and study manuals to nurses who have to read and comprehend charts and reports to graphic artists who have to read and analyze information to enable them to create the proper message in an advertisement or a poster.

In addition to being extremely practical, reading has an emotional component. In the same way that reading books for pleasure allows us to connect with characters, I try and connect with the writer and with the material being presented. Doing this allows me to personalize the information and make it come alive in a more meaningful way.

If I could pass along one thing to you, I'd pass along the concept that reading is a gateway. It is the gateway to learning, to compassion, to understanding, to growing, to experiencing parts of the world to which we may never have the privilege of traveling, and it is the gateway to your own self-enrichment. The beauty of having this gateway is that you don't have to depend on anyone else to provide it for you—it is yours simply by doing.

QUESTIONS FOR REFLECTION

Consider responding to these questions online in the World of Work module of the Companion website.

1. How can reading more effectively help you in your professional life like it helps Ms. Baliszewski?
2. Has reading ever taken you to another place and time? If so, how did this make you feel? If not, why?
3. What advantages do you believe improving your reading skills can have in your studies and in your future career?

Robin Baliszewski, President, Career, Health, Education, and Technology Division—Prentice Hall, Upper Saddle River, NJ

---

need sleep, rest, and proper nutrition. It will be nearly impossible to concentrate without them.

To increase your concentration for active reading, consider the following:

- Reduce outside distractions such as people talking, rooms that are too hot or cold, cell phones ringing, etc.
- Reduce internal distractions such as fatigue, self-talk, daydreaming, hunger, and emotions that cause you to think of other things.

- Set a goal for reading "X" amount of material by "Y" time. This goal can help you focus.
- Take a short break every 20 minutes. Don't get distracted and do something else; come back to your reading in 3–5 minutes.
- Take notes as you read. This helps reading become an active process.

VOCABULARY

Building a strong vocabulary is not easy and it does not happen overnight. However, it is very important that you work on this aspect of reading as often as possible. If you do not know a word, you must stop and look it up. Having to stop and look up a word that you do not know will slow you down and cause you to lose concentration; however, the more words you have in your vocabulary, the fewer times you will need to stop.

To increase your vocabulary for active reading, consider the following:

- Always stop and look up words you do not know or try to determine the meaning by the word's use in the sentence (its *context*).
- Keep those words on a list that you can review daily (so that you learn them and don't have to stop and look them up every time).
- Make time to study your vocabulary list.
- Work crossword puzzles or other word games to help you learn new words.

Building a strong vocabulary does not happen overnight—it takes effort.

FIXATION

Fixation is when your eyes stop on a single word to read it. Your eyes stop for only a fraction of a second, but those fractions add up over the course of a section or chapter. Your mind sees the words something like this:

Nutrition   is   important   to   good   health.

As you read this, you probably had six fixations because the words are spaced out. However, if they were not spaced, many people would still have six fixations. To increase your speed, try to see two words with one fixation; this will cut your reading time nearly in half. Try to see the sentence like this:

Nutrition is important   to good health.

Smith (1999) states that "research has shown that the average reader can see approximately 2.5 words per fixation."

To reduce your fixation time for active reading, consider the following:

- Practice seeing two or more words with one fixation.

- As you practice, try to read in phrases like the example below:

Nutrition is important   to good health.   Therefore,   you should work hard   to eat   proper meals   every day.   By doing this you can maintain   good health.

FREQUENCY

Not reading often enough to build your speed is a problem with many people. In order to build your speed and work on your concentration, you will need to read as much as possible. The more you read, the more you improve your skills. Quite simply, nothing helps you read better than actually reading.

To increase your frequency for active reading, consider the following:

- Read every chance you get.
- Read a variety of materials (texts, magazines, newspapers, novels).
- Don't read just for learning, read for pleasure as well.

Get to the Point, Would You!
FINDING THE TOPIC AND MAIN IDEAS IN PARAGRAPHS AND SECTIONS

Typically, each paragraph has a main idea. You're familiar with this through your English class. It is usually called a topic sentence. The topic statement is what the paragraph is about. Identifying the main idea of a paragraph can greatly aid your comprehension of that paragraph and eventually the entire section or chapter.

Read the following paragraph and determine the main idea—the point.

> Without exception, the conclusion should be one of the most carefully crafted components of your paper or speech. Long after your reader has finished reading or your listener has finished listening, the last part of your work is more than likely going to be the part they remember the most. Some writers and speakers suggest that you write your conclusion first, so that your paper or speech is directed toward a specific end result. That decision, of course, is up to you. However, a great piece of advice from writing experts tells us that captivating writers always know how their stories will end long before they begin writing them.
>
> —CORNERSTONE: BUILDING ON YOUR BEST

Can you determine **what the paragraph is about?** We know that the opening statement talks about writing the conclusion of a paper or speech. But it also talks about the importance of your conclusion and that some writers actually write their conclusions first. The main topic of this paragraph happens to be the first sentence. The remaining sentences simply add information and credibility to the topic sentence.

Read and study the following paragraph.

Can you remember how you found out that (O.J.) Simpson had been acquitted? Chances are that you don't remember, or that what you remember is wrong. Several days after the verdict, a group of California undergraduates provided researchers with detailed accounts of how they learned about the jury's decision. When the researchers probed students' memories again fifteen months later, only half recalled accurately how they found out about the decision. When asked again nearly three years after the verdict, less than 30 percent of students' recollections were accurate; nearly half were dotted with errors.

—*The Seven Sins of Memory* by D. Schacter

Circle the one option below that **best describes the topic sentence** of this paragraph.

1. The O.J. Simpson trial
2. Remembering the verdict in the trial
3. Time can be a deterrent to memory

Which did you choose? Statement one, although mentioned in the first sentence of the paragraph, has very little to do with the paragraph's intended message. It is simply a prompt. Statement two is closer, but it is too vague and does not adequately address the role of time in memory. Statement three is the correct topic for this paragraph.

According to Dorothy Seyler (2001), professor and reading expert, you can identify the topic of a paragraph in four easy steps:

- The topic is the **subject** of the paragraph.
- You can identify the topic by answering the question, "**What or who** is the paragraph about?"
- The topic statement should be **general enough** to cover all of the specifics of the paragraph.
- The topic statement should be **specific enough** to exclude other paragraphs on related topics.

Sometimes, you can determine the implied topic or main idea of a paragraph simply by making *connections from related words*. For example, if you read a paragraph that contained the following names, what would you suggest the main topic is about?

Ladybird Johnson
Laura Bush
Martha Washington
Bess Truman
Eleanor Roosevelt   **Topic?** _____

Find the implied main idea in these examples:

1	2	3
Dell	*People*	Pit Bull
Compaq	*Us*	Husky
Packard Bell	*O*	Terrier
IBM	*Vanity Fair*	Shepherd
Gateway	*Motor Trend*	Mix
Topic _____	**Topic** _____	**Topic** _____

Finding the topic sentence or main idea in a paragraph, section, or chapter is not hard, but it does take concentration and a degree of analytical skills. If you approach each paragraph as a detective searching for clues, you will soon find out how easy and effortless it is to determine main points.

Read the following paragraphs and identify the topic in your own words. Justify your answer. Then, identify the main idea of the paragraph. See if you can determine what the author really wants you to know. Finally, develop one test question for each paragraph.

You *will not* have to do this for every paragraph you read in college. As you become a stronger reader, you will do this type of analysis after each heading or chapter section. But for now, as you work on building your skills as a reader, take the time to learn how to fully analyze a small portion of a chapter.

Exercise 1

The origin of emotion is the brain. You might say that there are two minds—one that thinks (the thinking mind) and one that feels (the emotional mind). Think of thoughts and emotions as two different mechanisms for knowing and making sense of the world. The two minds are not adversarial or physically separate; rather, they operate interactively to construct your mental life. Passion (the heart) dominates reason (the mind) when feelings are intense.

—*Emotional Intelligence*, Nelson and Low

VOCABULARY BUILDER (DEFINE THE FOLLOWING)

mechanism _____

adversarial _____

dominate _____

The **TOPIC** of this paragraph is
_____
_____

Who or what is the paragraph about *(the* **MAIN IDEA***)?*
_____
_____

What does the author of the paragraph really want you **TO KNOW**?

_____
_____
_____

Develop one **TEST QUESTION** *from this paragraph.*

_____
_____
_____

Exercise 2

Many ancient Greek amphitheaters still survive—for example, the Theatre of Dionysus in Athens or the equally impressive theatres at Olympia and Epidaurus. These theatres were originally designed to accommodate musical performances as easily as plays, and they have excellent acoustics. A small coin dropped on the floor of the orchestra can be heard clearly in the audience, and even whispers carry to the farthest seat in the theater.

—DRAMA: CLASSICAL TO CONTEMPORARY, COLDEWEY AND STREITEBERGER

VOCABULARY BUILDER (DEFINE THE FOLLOWING)

orchestra _____

acoustics _____

Dionysus _____

The **TOPIC** *of this paragraph is*

_____
_____

Who or what is the paragraph about (the **MAIN IDEA**)?

_____
_____

What does the author of the paragraph really want you **TO KNOW**?

_____
_____

Develop one **TEST QUESTION** *from this paragraph.*

_____
_____

Doing It Right the First Time
SQ3R TO THE RESCUE

There are as many ways to approach a chapter in a textbook as there are students who read textbooks. Most would agree that there is no "right" or "wrong" way to begin the process. However, many would agree that there are a few ways of approaching a chapter that are more effective than others. One such approach is SQ3R.

The most basic and often-used reading and studying system is the SQ3R method, developed by Francis P. Robinson in 1941. This simple, yet effective, system has proved to be a successful study tool for millions of students. SQ3R involves five steps: Survey, Question, Read, Recite, and Review. The most important thing to remember about SQ3R is that it should be used on a daily basis, not as a method for cramming.

SURVEY

The first step of SQ3R is to survey, or pre-read, an assigned chapter. You begin by reading the title of the chapter, the headings, and each sub-heading. Look carefully at the vocabulary, time lines, graphs, charts, pictures, and drawings included in each chapter. If there is a chapter summary, read it. Surveying also includes reading the first and last sentence in each paragraph. Surveying is not a substitute for reading a chapter. Reading is discussed later. Before going any further, survey Chapter 6 of this text using the eight questions below.

CHAPTER SURVEY

1. *What is the title of the chapter?*

   _____
   _____

2. *What is the subheading of the chapter?*

   _____
   _____

3. *How many sections does the chapter have? List them.*

   _____
   _____

4. *What are the chapter objectives?*

   _____
   _____

5. Does the chapter include vocabulary words? List the words you will need to look up.

_____

_____

6. If the chapter contains quotations, which one means the most to you? Why?

_____

_____

7. What is the most important graph or chart in the chapter? Why?

_____

_____

8. Close your book and list five topics that this chapter will cover.

_____

_____

QUESTION

The second step is to question. There are five common questions you should ask yourself when you are reading a chapter: Who? When? What? Where? and Why? As you survey and read your chapter, try turning the information into questions and see if you can answer them. If you do not know the answers to the questions, you should find them as you read along.

Another way to approach the chapter is to turn the major headings of each section into questions (see an example in Figure 5.3). When you get to the end of the section, having carefully read the material, taken notes, and highlighted important information, answer the question that you posed at the beginning of the section.

READ

After you survey the chapter and develop some questions to be answered from the chapter, the next step is to read the chapter. Remember, surveying is not reading. There is no substitute for reading in your success plan. Read slowly and carefully. The SQ3R method requires a substantial amount of time, but if you take each step slowly and completely, you will be amazed at how much you can learn and how much your grades will improve.

Read through each section. It is best not to jump around or move ahead if you do not understand the previous section. Paragraphs are usually built on each other, and so you need to understand the first before you can move on to the next. You may have to read a chapter or section more than once, especially if the information is new, technical, or difficult.

Another important aspect of reading is taking notes, highlighting, and making marginal notes in your textbook. You own your textbook and should

FIGURE 5.3 Forming questions from headings.

Example: If you were describing the mall in Washington, D.C., you could begin with the Lincoln Memorial and then move on to the reflecting pond, the Washington Monument, and the Smithsonian.

Cause-Effect Organization is when you arrange your information in the cause-and-effect order. You would discuss the causes of a problem and then explore its effects. → *What is cause and effect? Why is it important?*

Example: If you were speaking about high blood pressure, you would first examine the causes of high blood pressure such as diet, hereditary factors, and weight and then move on to the effects such as heart attack and stroke.

Chronological Organization is presenting information in the order in which it happened. Speeches that deal with historical facts and how-to speeches often use chronological organization. → *When do I use chronological order? Why?*

> Order and simplification are the first steps toward mastery.
> —THOMAS MANN

Example: If you were giving a speech or writing a paper on the history of automobiles in America since 1950, you would begin with the 50s, move to the 60s, 70s, 80s, and 90s. If you were giving a how-to speech on refinishing a table, you would begin with the first process of stripping the old paint or varnish and move forward to the last step of applying a new coat of paint or varnish.

Problem-Solving Organization is often used in persuasive papers and speeches. Usually, you are trying to get your reader or audience to accept your proposal. You first begin by pointing out the major problem(s) and then move on to revealing the solutions, and the advantages of the solutions. → *Which speech would require problem solving as an organizational pattern?*

Example: If you were writing or speaking about crime on college campuses, you would begin by informing the reader or listener about the problems, the crime statistics, and the personal toll on students. You would then propose solutions and tell how the solutions would help all students.

Topical/Categorical Organization is when you group information into subdivisions or cluster information into categories. Some information naturally falls into specific categories, such as the different types of palm trees or the types of rollerblades available. → *What is Topical/Categorical Organization?*

Example: If you were writing a speech or paper on taxes in the United States, you might categorize your information into local taxes, state taxes, federal taxes, luxury taxes, "sin" taxes, and special taxes.

Compare/Contrast Organization is when you present your information in a fashion that shows its similarities to and differences from other information. → *When would I use compare/contrast? Why? What are the benefits?*

Example: You may be writing a paper or speech that compares the health care system in the United States to that of England or Canada.

Importance/Priority Organization allows you to arrange information from the most important issue to the least or the least important to the

Source: *Cornerstone: Building On Your Best.*

---

personalize it as you would your lecture notes. Highlight areas that you feel are important, underline words and phrases that you did not understand or that you feel are important, and jot down notes in the margins.

"If I mark in my text, I may not get much for it when I sell it back to the bookstore," you might say. Right now you need to be concerned with learning the information in the most beneficial and efficient way possible. Don't worry about selling your textbook after the class is over. You might even want to consider keeping your book until you have completed your degree, especially if it relates to your major field of study.

As you begin to read your chapter, mark the text, and take notes, keep the following in mind:

- Read the entire paragraph before you mark anything.
- Identify the topic or thesis statement of each paragraph and highlight it.
- Highlight key phrases.
- Don't highlight too much; the text will lose its significance.
- Stop and look up words that you do not know or understand.

Building Active Reading and Comprehension Skills 157

While reading, you will want to take notes that are more elaborate than your highlighting or marginal notes. Taking notes while reading the text will assist you in studying the material and committing it to memory. There are several effective methods of taking notes while reading (see Figure 5.4). They include:

- Charts
- Outlines
- Key words
- Mind maps
- Flash cards
- Summaries
- Time lines

FIGURE 5.4 *Sample note-taking methods.*

KEY WORDS

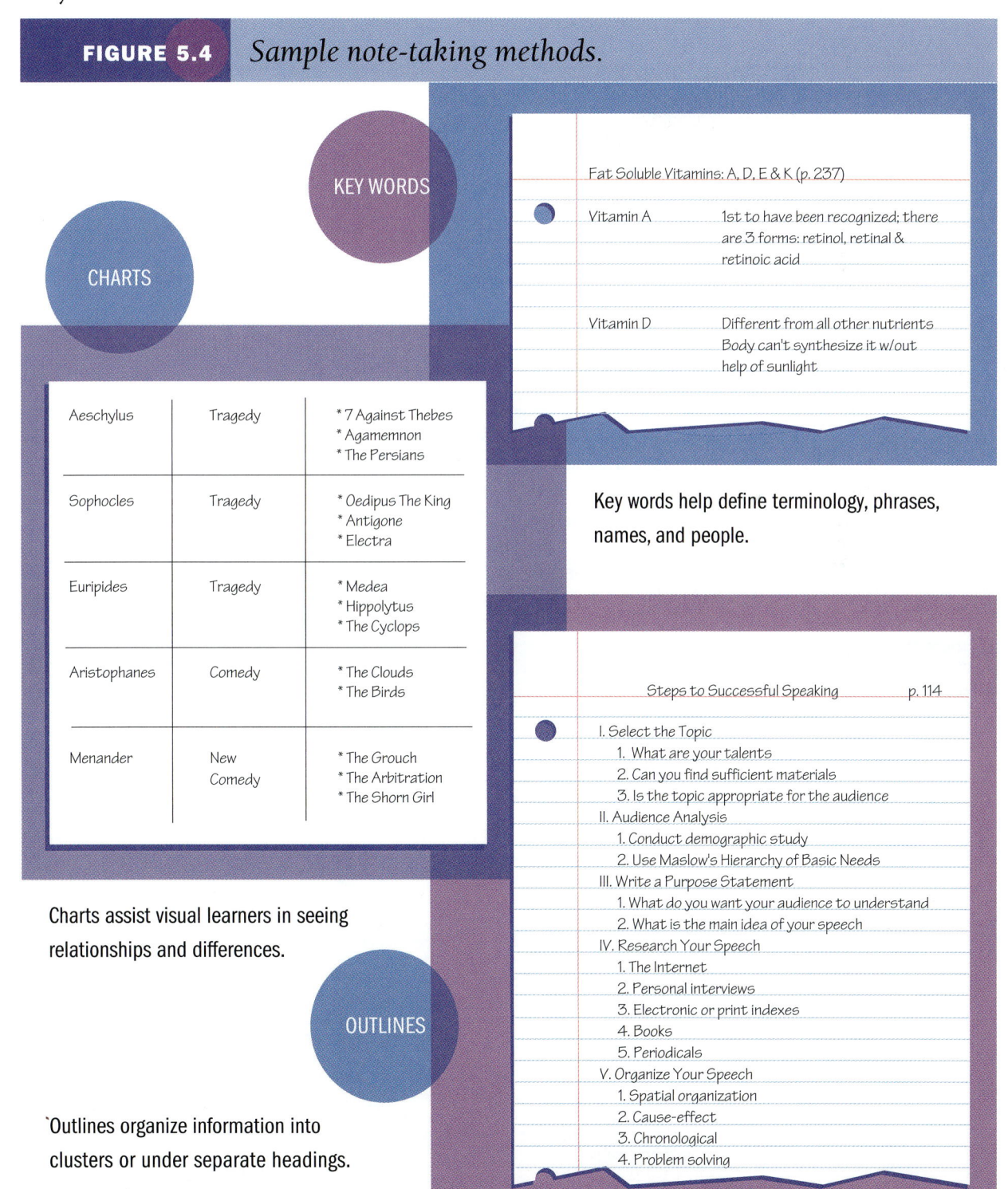

Fat Soluble Vitamins: A, D, E & K (p. 237)

Vitamin A — 1st to have been recognized; there are 3 forms: retinol, retinal & retinoic acid

Vitamin D — Different from all other nutrients Body can't synthesize it w/out help of sunlight

Key words help define terminology, phrases, names, and people.

CHARTS

Aeschylus	Tragedy	* 7 Against Thebes * Agamemnon * The Persians
Sophocles	Tragedy	* Oedipus The King * Antigone * Electra
Euripides	Tragedy	* Medea * Hippolytus * The Cyclops
Aristophanes	Comedy	* The Clouds * The Birds
Menander	New Comedy	* The Grouch * The Arbitration * The Shorn Girl

Charts assist visual learners in seeing relationships and differences.

OUTLINES

Steps to Successful Speaking   p. 114

I. Select the Topic
  1. What are your talents
  2. Can you find sufficient materials
  3. Is the topic appropriate for the audience
II. Audience Analysis
  1. Conduct demographic study
  2. Use Maslow's Hierarchy of Basic Needs
III. Write a Purpose Statement
  1. What do you want your audience to understand
  2. What is the main idea of your speech
IV. Research Your Speech
  1. The Internet
  2. Personal interviews
  3. Electronic or print indexes
  4. Books
  5. Periodicals
V. Organize Your Speech
  1. Spatial organization
  2. Cause-effect
  3. Chronological
  4. Problem solving

Outlines organize information into clusters or under separate headings.

As you read through a chapter in your textbook, you may find that you have to use a variety of these techniques to capture information. Try them for one week. Although taking notes while reading a chapter thoroughly is time consuming, you will be amazed at how much you remember and how much you are able to contribute in class after using these techniques.

While reading, always keep a dictionary handy. It is nearly impossible to read, comprehend, and remember a paragraph or section when you don't know or understand one or more words within the paragraph. For instance, it would be difficult to get at the meaning of the following sentence if you did not understand the words.

> It is easier to answer affirmatively to a question that even an anonymous respondent knows would evoke an excruciating response.

When you look up a word, circle it and write the definition in the margin.

> It is easier to answer affirmatively [TRUE] to a question that even an anonymous [UNKNOWN] respondent [a person who RESPONDS] knows would evoke [TO CALL TO MIND] an excruciating [PAINFUL] response.

As you are reading, especially if the material is difficult or very technical, you may want to break your reading down into smaller parts and stop after each paragraph to paraphrase the main idea of that paragraph. Again, this is time consuming, but few techniques will assist your comprehension more than this one. Consider the example in Figure 5.5.

IT'S NOT OVER UNTIL IT'S OVER

Finally, if you are reading material that is completely new to you—difficult to understand yet important to remember—you may have to disregard para-

---

FIGURE 5.5 *Breaking down the meaning.*

1. Infirmity = the lack of power, a disability
2. Continuum = a whole where all parts work together.
3. Debilitating = to make weak.

What Does It Mean to Be Healthy?

Most people consider themselves healthy. They believe that if they are not sick, they are healthy. However, the absence of illness does not mean that you are healthy; it simply means that you are currently without illness.

The World Health Organization defines health as "not merely the absence of disease or infirmity, but a state of complete physical, mental, and social well-being." Realistically, health is a continuum: on one end you have death, and on the other you have excellent health. Most students are somewhere in the middle of the continuum, experiencing neither excellent health nor debilitating diseases. Often students slip slowly into a state of unhealthiness, which if ignored, could lead to serious health problems. Most of us take our health for granted. We place undue stress on ourselves and assume that our bodies will continue to take this abuse. This chapter will afford you the opportunity to review your own health status and to explore some issues that might help you to lead a healthier lifestyle.

- Just because you are not sick, this does not mean you are healthy
- Wellness = a state of complete physical, mental, and social health.
- Health is a whole part of life—one end is excellent health, the other end is death.

graphs and paraphrase sections of a paragraph. This can be done with simple "tick marks" in your reading.

When you get to a point where you have "read enough," put a tick mark at that point. Continue reading until you get to the end of the paragraph, putting tick marks in the places where you feel you have read a complete thought.

When you get to the end of the paragraph, reread the first section that you marked off. Out to the side, paraphrase that section. Then go to the next section. Consider Figure 5.6.

Again, this is time consuming, but few techniques will assist your comprehension more than this one.

RECITE

Recitation is simple, but crucial. Skipping this step may result in less than full mastery of the chapter. Once you have read a section, ask yourself this simple question: "What was that all about?" Find a classmate, sit down together, and ask questions of each other. Discuss with each other the main points of the chapter. Try to explain the information to each other without looking at your notes. If you are at home, sit back in your chair, recite the information, and determine what it means. If you have trouble explaining the information to your friend or reciting it to yourself, you probably did not understand the section and you should go back and re-read it. If you can tell your classmate and yourself exactly what you just read and what it means, you are ready to move on to the next section of the chapter.

FIGURE 5.6 *Reading piece by piece.*

Negotiating Salary

If the company is interested in you, the interviewer might discuss salary and benefits with you on the second visit. Normally, you are advised not to bring up salary on the first interview. If, however, you detect that the company is not going to offer a salary that you can accept or if you have doubts that you are interested in working for that company, you might want to discuss this on the first interview.
→ Usually no salary discussions on 1st interview.
→ If there are doubts, you can discuss.

If you have several options and you are not quite sure about this company, you might say: "I know it's not considered good interviewing technique to discuss salary on the first interview, but I'm interested in knowing what the range is for this position. I want to be fair to you and not accept another interview and have you go to that expense if we're too far apart."
→ Talk to potential employer honestly about possibilities.

At the end of the second interview, if the interviewer hasn't mentioned salary, you should bring it up. You want the company to make the first move on salary. If the interviewer asks you, "If we are to make you an offer, what kind of salary are you looking for?" you can counter with this statement: "What is the range for this position?" This will give you something to go on.
→ If second interview comes and they do not discuss salary—you can bring it up by asking about the range.

If the interviewer then says, "The range is $27,000 to $32,000," you know if you are interested and you also know you want to go on the high side of this range. If ... tional grades and experience and you feel confi dent ... try for a sala...

Source: *Capstone: Succeeding Beyond College*, Sherfield, Montgomery, Moody (2001).

STRATEGIES
FOR BUILDING ON YOUR BEST

Consider the following strategies for making the most of your reading time:

- Reduce the distractions around you. Try to find an atmosphere that is comfortable and effective for you.
- Discover what time of day is best for you to read and concentrate on your material.
- Read with a healthy snack.
- Read in sections. Don't try to read an entire chapter in one sitting. Break it down and take breaks.
- Form questions about the material from headings as you are reading.
- Never just skip over words or phrases that you don't understand. Look them up in a dictionary.
- Allow yourself enough time to read the material effectively. Time management and reading comprehension go hand-in-hand.

Another way to practice reciting is to use the materials you produced as you READ the chapter. Hopefully, you took notes, highlighted passages, underlined phrases, and paraphrased sections. From these, you can create flash cards, outlines, mind maps, timelines, and key word note cards. Using these materials is another way to "recite" the material.

REVIEW

After you have read the chapter, immediately go back and read it again. "What?!! I just read it!" Yes, you did. And the best way to determine whether you have mastered the information is once again to survey the chapter; review marginal notes, highlighted areas, and vocabulary words; and determine whether you have any questions that have not been answered. This step will help you store and retain this information in long-term memory.

SQ3R can be a lifesaver when it comes to understanding material that is overwhelming. It is an efficient, comprehensive, and DOABLE practice that can dramatically assist you in your reading efforts.

*Only **you** can improve your reading skills, and reading is a skill—just like driving a car.*
—DOROTHY SEYLER

I Think I've Got It!
TESTING YOUR READING COMPREHENSION THROUGH BLOOM

In psychology or education classes, you will study about Benjamin Bloom. He developed a theory of learning called *Bloom's Taxonomy*. It is sometimes called *Bloom's Levels of Learning*. He felt that there were six levels on which we acquire knowledge and understand information, as summarized in the table below.

LEVEL OF UNDERSTANDING	WHAT YOU SHOULD BE ABLE TO DO AT EACH LEVEL
Level 1: **KNOWLEDGE**	Define, list, describe, identify, show, name, quote
Level 2: **COMPREHENSION**	Explain, describe, summarize, differentiate, discuss, interpret
Level 3: **APPLICATION**	Illustrate, use the information, apply, demonstrate, show, solve, classify, discover
Level 4: **ANALYSIS**	Break down, distinguish, infer, prioritize, order, justify, classify, arrange, divide

Building Active Reading and Comprehension Skills **161**

Level 5: **SYNTHESIS** — Integrate, modify, rearrange, substitute, plan, create, design, invent, incorporate

Level 6: **EVALUATION** — Decide, rank, test, measure, recommend, support, conclude, compare, appraise, defend

This theory, while not specifically designed for reading, can help you determine if you accurately and thoroughly understood what you read or if you simply picked up a few facts that may be forgotten in an hour's time. These six steps, used after you've read a section or a chapter, can increase your understanding of complex material.

Let's give it a try. In the following activity, you will find a longer selected reading. Read the passage carefully and do the following:

- Look up words you do not understand.
- Look for and identify the main idea of each paragraph.
- Paraphrase main points in your own words.
- Highlight the main ideas, key words, and points.

When you've read this passage, answer the six questions given. If you can answer them all, you know you've mastered this passage. By using this technique, you will assure yourself that you have fully understood the information presented. Good luck.

READ THIS SECTION, IDENTIFY UNFAMILIAR WORDS, HIGHLIGHT IMPORTANT WORDS AND PHRASES	LOOK UP YOUR IDENTIFIED WORDS THAT NEED TO BE DEFINED	PARAPHRASE THE MAIN IDEA IN YOUR OWN WORDS
THE LIFE AND DEATH OF HARVEY MILK		
More perplexing things have happened, but a Twinkie caused the death of Harvey Milk. That's right. In 1978, defense lawyers using the "Twinkie Defense" explained an inexplicable murder away. This was the first mainstream trial to use an "I am not responsible for my actions" defense.	Unfamiliar words and definitions _____ _____ _____ _____	The main idea of this paragraph is _____ _____ _____ _____
Harvey Milk was the first openly gay man elected to a significant office in America. In 1977, Milk was elected as a member of the San Francisco Board of Supervisors. This was quite arduous at this point in American history when most people, including many psychologists and religious leaders, still classified homosexuality as deviant and a mental illness.	Unfamiliar words and definitions _____ _____ _____ _____	The main idea of this paragraph is _____ _____ _____ _____
Harvey Milk is to the Gay Rights Movement what Martin Luther King, Jr. is to the Civil Rights Movement. Before King, little was happening with the CRM, and before Milk, little was happening with the GRM. He changed the face of California politics and paved the way for countless other gays and lesbians to enter the world of politica.	Unfamiliar words and definitions _____ _____ _____ _____	The main idea of this paragraph is _____ _____ _____ _____

Dan White, a staunch anti-gay advocate, served on the board with Milk. They were constantly at odds with each other and often engaged in verbal confrontations.

White had been a policeman and a fireman in San Francisco before running for office. While running for office, he vowed to restore "family values" to the city government. He vowed to "rid San Francisco of radicals, social deviants, and incorrigibles."

Dan White was one of the most conservative members of the board, and many proposals brought to the board by Milk and the mayor of San Francisco, George Moscone, were defeated because of the heavily conservative vote led by White.

At that time, the Board of Supervisors was made up of eleven members; six of them, including Dan White, were conservative and had the power to defeat most, if not all of the liberal measures brought before the board. This did not fare well with Harvey Milk and the other liberal members of the board.

Because the job offered diminutive wages, Dan White soon realized that he could not support his family on $9,800 per year, and he submitted his resignation to Mayor Moscone. This did not set well with the people who elected him. They urged him to reconsider and when he tried to rescind his resignation, Mayor Moscone refused. This decision was made, in part, because Harvey Milk convinced Moscone to deny his reinstatement.

In a fit of wrath over the decision, Dan White entered the San Francisco City Hall on the morning of November 27, 1978, through a basement window. He went to Mayor Moscone's office and shot him in the chest, and as he lay dying, shot him again in the head.

He then walked calmly down the hall and asked to see Harvey Milk. Once inside the office, he slew Milk with two bullets to the brain. He then left City Hall, called his wife, spoke with her in person at St. Mary's Cathedral, and then turned himself in.

It is reported that policemen representing the city of San Francisco shouted, cheered, and applauded when news of the murders reached the police department.

Dan White's defense lawyers used a "diminished capacity" defense suggesting that he was led to his actions by too much sugar from junk food. The lawyers convinced a jury that he was not himself and his senses were off kilter. This became known as the "Twinkie Defense."

Dan White was convicted of second degree manslaughter and was sentenced to only seven years for two premeditated murders. After serving only five years, he was released. The "Twinkie Defense" had worked.	Unfamiliar words and definitions _____ _____	The main idea of this paragraph is _____ _____
In 1985, after being released from Soledad Prison, Dan White walked into his garage, took a rubber hose, connected it to his car's exhaust, and killed himself with carbon monoxide poisoning. He was 39 years old. His tomb reads, "*Daniel J. White (1946–October 21, 1985), Sgt. U. S. Army, Vietnam. Cause of death: Suicide.*"	Unfamiliar words and definitions _____ _____	The main idea of this paragraph is _____ _____

Sources: "He Got Away with Murder" at www.findagrave.com; "Dan White" at www.backdoor.com/castro/milk; "The Pioneer Harvey Milk" at www.time.com; "Remembering Harvey Milk" at www.lambda.net.

Now answer the following questions:

Question 1	Knowledge	Identify two members of the Board of Supervisors and the mayor of San Francisco.
Question 2	Comprehension	Based on the story given, explain why Dan White killed Harvey Milk and George Moscone.
Question 3	Application	Demonstrate how homophobia plays a similar role in American society today as it did in the 1970s.
Question 4	Analysis	How can defense lawyers justify using the "I am not responsible for my own actions defense" in a premeditated murder case?
Question 5	Synthesis	Design a plan by which you would have *prosecuted* Dan White based on his homophobia, views, and politics.
Question 6	Evaluation	Recommend a policy or strategy by which members in a group could express their views without contempt, derogatory actions, degrading comments, or violence. How could you test this policy's effectiveness? Support your conclusions.

Another technique that you might consider when trying to get to the heart of a passage is answering the questions that were posed earlier in the chapter. This is not as detailed as analyzing your comprehension level through Bloom.

The **TOPIC** *of this passage is*

_____

_____

Who or what is the passage about (the **MAIN IDEA***)?*

_____

_____

What does the author of the passage really want you **TO KNOW***?*

_____

_____

Develop three **TEST QUESTIONS** *from this passage.*

_____

_____

Yes, these two techniques may be time consuming, but consider this: Would you rather spend an hour reading a chapter and not understand it or remember it (thus having to do it over or risk failing a test), or would you rather spend an hour and a half or two hours reading the same chapter and "get it" the first time? That choice is yours.

As you begin to work toward increasing your reading speed and comprehension, set goals to help you achieve this skill. Consider using the *Change Implementation Model* discussed in Chapter 1 to assist you with your reading goals.

A**s a college student, you will probably spend about a fourth of your waking hours reading textbooks.** —MAKER AND LENIER

He Turned to Her and Ever So Gently . . .
READING FOR PLEASURE

"Reading for pleasure? You've got to be kidding. I can barely keep up with what I'm supposed to read, let alone adding more . . . *for pleasure,*" you might say.

Reading for pleasure can involve anything from the daily newspaper to your favorite magazine to that "trashy" novel you have on your bedside table. It does not have to involve *War and Peace* or *The Economic and Philosophic Manuscripts of 1844*. Reading for pleasure is just that—it brings you joy.

Reading for pleasure can also help you read your academic work more effectively. It can help you with discussions in class. It can keep you abreast of current issues and trends. It can keep you on top of who is doing what and where. Reading for pleasure can also help you on your road to critical thinking.

That's right, just by picking up a newspaper or *Sports Illustrated* or *Motor Trend* or *Vogue* or *Ebony,* you increase your knowledge base and are able to make more informed judgments, compare and contrast, discuss issues more accurately, discern between fact and fiction, evaluate what information is essential to you or not, AND, all the while, increase your reading speed.

So, the next time you pass that newspaper or magazine, don't just say, "Oh, I haven't got the time." Sit down and enjoy a few minutes simply of reading for pleasure.

BLUEPRINTS FOR CHANGE

NAME

DATE

REFLECTION

Understanding the difference between reading the words on a page and comprehending the words and their meanings can literally save your academic life. Reading, while easy and fun for some, is daunting and torturous for others. Regardless of your situation at the moment, you can improve your reading ability, your comprehension, and your speed. But you are the only person on earth who can do it. You are the only one who can make these improvements, and you are the only one who can make the commitment to yourself to improve your skills. It has been said that if you can effectively read and write the English language, there is nothing that you can't understand in the world. Good luck in your journey. May the world be yours.

GET REAL

Below are a few questions to help you think about the nuts and bolts of reading and comprehension. Study each question carefully and respond accurately.

How can poor reading skills affect your career goals?

How can reading bring joy to your life?

What role can reading play in your ability to be open-minded?

How can reading affect your overall attitude about learning?

How can using Bloom's Taxonomy help with reading comprehension?

Having read the story of Harvey Milk in this chapter, where might you go in the library to find other interesting stories about important figures in history?

If you are having trouble reading, where can you go on your campus for assistance?

What technique discussed in this chapter will help you improve your reading the most? Why?

165

Case Study

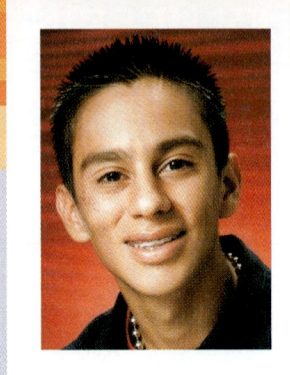

NAME: Joey Luna
SCHOOL: El Paso Community College, El Paso, TX
MAJOR: Biology   AGE: 19

Below is a real-life situation faced by Joey. Read the brief case and respond to the questions.

I have never enjoyed reading. I was not a good reader in high school and that trend continued when I first enrolled in college. I registered for 12 hours and, soon into the semester, dropped my English class because of the reading assignments. Later in the semester, I dropped two other courses and remained only in math.

The reason I stayed in the math course was that so little reading was required. I was able to do the work without a commitment to reading a textbook or reading outside materials.

I enrolled for 12 more hours the second semester and quickly dropped them all due to the reading assignments and my frustration with reading. I know how to read, but spent so little time doing it and never really thought about comprehending what I'd read. The classes were difficult.

This semester, I am enrolled in college again. I am learning to read and reread the assignments for comprehension. I'm taking notes while I read. I have my first test this Monday. I have high hopes of doing very well.

What advice would you give to Joey for Monday?

___
___
___
___

If Joey were enrolled at your campus, where could he have turned for help?

___
___
___
___

Why is note taking important to the reading process?

___
___
___

What relationship do reading and math have with each other?

_____
_____
_____
_____

Why do you think Joey is doing better since he started taking notes while reading?

_____
_____
_____
_____

What advice would you give to an entering, first-year student who has struggled with reading comprehension in the past?

_____
_____
_____
_____

at this moment journal

Refer to page 137 of this chapter. Having read and reflected upon the information in the chapter, consider how you might revise your goal to make it more:

REASONABLE

BELIEVABLE

MEASURABLE

ADAPTABLE

CONTROLLABLE

DESIRABLE

ONLINE JOURNAL

To complete an online journal entry, log onto the Companion Website at www.prenhall.com/sherfield. Go to Chapter 5 and click on the link to the Online Journal. You can respond to the questions provided or to questions assigned by your professor, or you may journal about your own experiences.

ADVICE TO GO
CORNERSTONES
for reading and comprehension

Commit yourself to becoming a better reader.

Approach the text, chapter, or article with an *open mind.*

Free your mind to focus on your reading.

Always read with your "*six pack*" at your side.

Underline and look up words you do not *understand.*

Write down your *vocabulary words,* and review them often.

Use *SQ3R* and *Bloom's Taxonomy* to increase and test your comprehension.

If you're having trouble, *get a tutor* to help you.

READ

Understand that *the more you read,* the better you'll become at it.

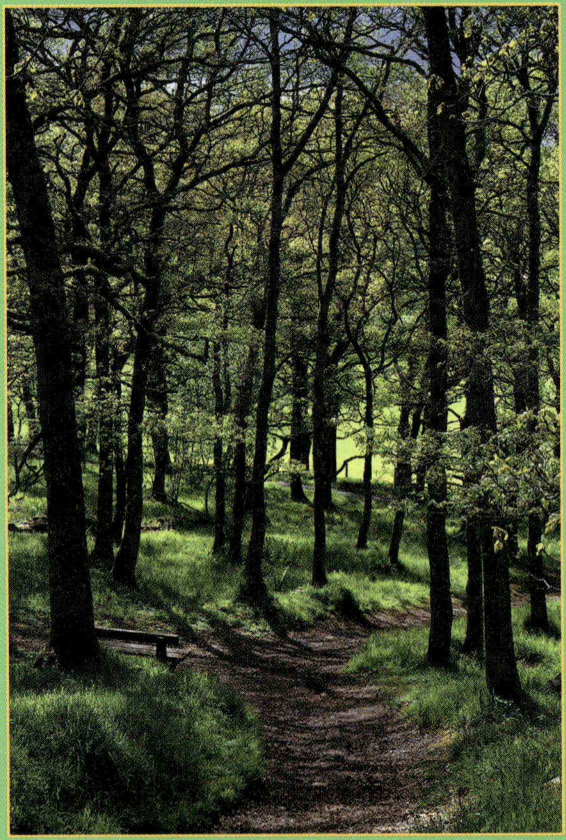

6 Learn

We are led to truth by our weaknesses as well as our strengths. — Parker Palmer

CHAPTER 6

LEARN

Paul was *nervous* about his first day in the history class *because he had never done very well in "lecture" classes.* As he entered the room of strangers, he chose a seat close to the window about halfway back from the professor's lectern. The professor arrived, issued and explained the syllabus, and true to form, *indicated that the class would be conducted in the lecture format* with very little chance for participation or activities. *Paul's anxiety grew even more.*

As the professor began to lecture on the causes of the Second World War, *it was all that Paul could do to keep up with the information,* and it was even harder for him to remain focused. He struggled through the first few classes *only to realize that this semester's history class was simply not going to get any better.* He wondered to himself, "Why can't my history class and professor be more like my poetry class and professor?"

Paul had never taken poetry before. In that class, the professor seldom lectured, *but often used music, posters, works of art, magic markers, copper wire, and even statues to teach* and impart the significance of the material. Paul had not wanted to take the poetry class, but it was the only literature alternative that would work in his schedule. It *turned out to be the class that he enjoyed the most* and the class in which he received the highest grade.

Paul was talking to some of his friends one evening about his classes, and he mentioned *how dynamic the poetry class had become.* "I never

> **Paul had not wanted to take the poetry class . . . it turned out to be the class he enjoyed the most.**

The ultimate mystery is one's own self. —Sammy Davis, Jr.

172

Multiple Intelligences, Learning Styles, and Personality Typing

thought that someone could take a handful of clay, some wire, and classical music and use it to make me understand poetry. One day," Paul said, "she read this poem called *Holocaust Museum*. There are lines in the poem that go like this:

> *Wandering through the bleak, dusk interior lighting,*
> *I was paralyzed coming upon the shoes . . .*
> *The shoes of millions dead, lying mateless, alone, brown and crumbling.*
> *Heaped in piles, mirroring the millions of bodies, burned and stacked like cords of wood.*

"When she finished the poem, she put on a CD of Rachmaninov's Symphony No. 2, threw some clay on our desks, gave us some wire and a square of cloth, and told us to sculpt those lines of the poem." Paul's friends were laughing now, not believing him. "I'm not blowin' smoke, that's what she did." His friends were in disbelief that this would happen in a poetry class.

Paul got very serious for a moment and said, "It was the first time in my life that I ever understood anything like that. *It was the first time that I ever held poetry in my hands.*"

"If only I could hold history in my hands," Paul thought, "this semester would be the best ever."

QUESTIONS FOR REFLECTION

Consider responding to these questions online in the Questions for Reflection module of the Companion Website.

1. From which teacher in your past have you learned the most? Why?

2. Have you noticed that you learn better by doing or seeing or hearing? How has this helped or hurt you?

3. Would you enjoy a class as dynamic and involved as Paul's poetry class? Why or why not?

Where are you... AT THIS MOMENT

Before reading this chapter, take a moment and respond to the following ten questions. Consider each one carefully before answering, and then respond by circling the number in the appropriate box. When you have answered the questions, add your points and find your total score on the feedback chart below.

STATEMENT	STRONGLY DISAGREE	DISAGREE	DON'T KNOW	AGREE	STRONGLY AGREE	SCORE
1. I know which teaching styles match my learning preferences.	1	2	3	4	5	
2. When I study, I use a variety of methods to learn new material.	1	2	3	4	5	
3. I don't know what my strengths and weaknesses are as a learner.	5	4	3	2	1	
4. I have devised study strategies that capitalize on my learning strengths.	1	2	3	4	5	
5. My personality type has no impact on my study strategies.	5	4	3	2	1	
6. There is little point in trying to improve my weaker learning styles.	5	4	3	2	1	
7. I have tried using different learning strategies in my studies.	1	2	3	4	5	
8. I do not know how I learn differently when I am seeing, hearing, or doing.	5	4	3	2	1	
9. There is no way to use my strengths in music, sports, or relationships to help me learn.	5	4	3	2	1	
10. When learning something new, I try to incorporate what I see with what I hear and to "do" or use the new information.	1	2	3	4	5	
TOTAL VALUE						

SUMMARY

10–17 Your knowledge of your own strengths, weaknesses, and styles of learning is limited. You don't seem to know much about how to use your personality traits, multiple intelligences, and study strategies together to learn. You will need to spend time exploring these issues.

18–25 You have a below average knowledge of your strengths and weaknesses as a learner. You need help putting together a set of strategies to integrate your personality and intelligence strengths for learning. Giving attention to improving your weaknesses will also be helpful for you.

26–34 You are average in your knowledge of your own learning preferences. You can see how different types of intelligence and personality affect your learning. You likely need to incorporate strategies for improving your weaknesses into your learning profile.

35–42 You are above average in knowing how to integrate your personality traits and different aspects of intelligence into your studies. You likely try different approaches to learning, but might still need improvement in addressing your weaknesses.

43–50 You are exceptional in your ability to bring together your various personality traits and multiple intelligences in your studies. You have likely spent time working to improve your weaknesses, routinely trying different approaches to learning material.

Goals... FOR CHANGE

Based on your total points, what is one goal you would like to achieve related to your learning style?

Goal _____
_____

List three actions you can take that might help you move closer to realizing this goal.

1. _____
2. _____
3. _____

Questions FOR BUILDING ON YOUR BEST

As you read this chapter, consider the following questions. At the end of the chapter, you should be able to answer all of them. You are encouraged to ask a few questions of your own. Consider asking your classmates or professors to assist you.

1. Why is it important for me to know my learning style?
2. How can my personality type affect my study habits?
3. What is the difference between a learning style and an intelligence?
4. How can I adapt the teaching style of my professor to my learning style?
5. How can understanding my learning style help me become a better student?

What additional questions might you have about your learning style, primary intelligence, or personality type?

1. _____
2. _____
3. _____

Understanding Your Strengths

Paul's situation is not uncommon. While many students do not like the lecture format, others relish it. Some students learn best by touching and doing, while others learn best by listening and reflecting. Some students learn best with a group of people sitting outside under the trees, while others must be alone in the library. There are many factors that may influence the way we learn and process information. Paul learned poetry best by "touching" it and getting involved with it. He began to use his tactile, or hands-on, skills to understand the poem's meaning. He may not have understood the depth of that poem if his only exposure to it had been a lecture.

> To be what we are, and to become what we are capable of becoming, is the only end in life. —ROBERT L. STEVENSON

You may be asking yourself, "Is there one 'best' way of learning?" The answer is no. The way one learns depends on so many variables. Learning styles, your personal intelligences, personality typing, your past experiences, and your attitude all play a part in the way you process new information. This chapter will explore the benefits of knowing your learning style and your personality type and the benefits of exploring your intelligences.

Looking for Treasures
DISCOVERING AND POLISHING YOUR TALENTS

This chapter will offer you the opportunity to complete three inventories: one to assess your learning style, one to assess your personality type, and one to help you better understand multiple intelligences. We must say up front that these assessments are in no way intended to label you. They are not a measure of your intelligence. They do not measure your worth or your capacities as a student or citizen. The three assessments are included so that you might gain a better understanding of your multiple intelligences and identify your learning styles and your personality type. There are no right or wrong answers and there is no one best way to learn. We hope that by the end of this chapter, you will have experienced a "Wow" or an "Ah-ha!" as you explore and discover new and exciting components of your education. We also hope that by the end of this chapter, you will have the skills needed to more effectively use your dominant traits and improve your less dominant traits.

Some educators and researchers do not even believe in the theory of learning styles or multiple intelligences. Anita Woolfolk (2001) states that "there has been considerable controversy over the meaning of intelligence.

There are many ways to learn how to ski. The learning technique that works best for you depends on many different factors, which may differ from situation to situation.

WORLD OF WORK

As a student, I didn't really know what my learning style was. I knew that I had certain strengths and interests, including intelligence for math and naturalistic sciences. I was years into college before I learned that I was an auditory learner.

When I began college, I knew exactly what I wanted to do. I knew that I wanted to use my aptitude for logic, math, and science. I was one of the lucky ones who chose a major, followed the course of study, and graduated into the profession of my dreams. Don't get me wrong, it was not easy and there were many stumbling blocks, but discovering my strengths and weaknesses early on really helped me excel.

One area on which I had to concentrate was interpersonal and verbal communication. I had always loved to talk and converse with my friends, but my profession demanded that I learn how to put all of my science and math talents into verbal and written form. That was not an easy job for me.

Today, my job at BPH Billiton is to develop ideas on how to find oil and gas around the world. Communicating those ideas is everything. If I can't communicate to my boss and my boss's boss, then I am useless to the company. Therefore, having identified my strengths early and spent time working on my less dominant areas paid off in my career.

QUESTIONS FOR REFLECTION

Consider responding to these questions online in the World of Work module of the Companion Website.

1. Bryan knew that he had an intelligence for math and science. What do you think are your primary academic strengths?

2. Bryan used his strengths as his major in college. Is your major in an area where you have strong interest and intelligence areas?

3. Should you concentrate on your strengths and forget about your weaknesses? What are the consequences of doing that?

Bryan Delph, *Exploration Geologist,* BPH Billiton, Houston, TX

At a symposium on intelligence, 24 psychologists offered 24 different views about the nature of intelligence."

However, we approach and include this information because many students have met with great success by identifying and molding their study environments and habits to reflect their learning style and personality type. If you have ever been in a class where you felt lost, inadequate, or simply out of place, it may have been because your professor was not teaching to your learning style. Conversely, if you are doing very well in a class, it may be because the information, professor, or class format matches the way you process information best.

By taking your time and carefully and honestly completing each assessment instrument, you will be able to better understand and identify your strongest traits and then tailor your individual study process to better understand information that may have been difficult to understand in class.

> One learns by doing the thing; though you think you know it, you have not certainty until you try. —SOPHOCLES

TAKE THE MIS

The Multiple Intelligences Survey

Robert M. Sherfield, Ph.D., 1999, 2002, 2005

Directions: Read each statement carefully and thoroughly. After reading the statement, rate your response using the scale below. There are no right or wrong answers. This is not a timed survey. The MIS is based, in part, on *Frames of Mind* by Howard Gardner, 1983.

3 = Often Applies
2 = Sometimes Applies
1 = Never or Almost Never Applies

_____ 1. When someone gives me directions, I have to visualize them in my mind in order to understand them.

_____ 2. I enjoy crossword puzzles and word games like Scrabble.

_____ 3. I enjoy dancing and can keep up with the beat of music.

_____ 4. I have little or no trouble conceptualizing information or facts.

_____ 5. I like to repair things that are broken such as toasters, small engines, bicycles, and cars.

_____ 6. I enjoy leadership activities on campus and in the community.

_____ 7. I have the ability to get others to listen to me.

_____ 8. I enjoy working with nature, animals, and plants.

_____ 9. I know where everything is in my home such as supplies, gloves, flashlights, camera, and compact discs.

_____ 10. I am a good speller.

_____ 11. I often sing or hum to myself in the shower or car, or while walking or just sitting.

_____ 12. I am a very logical, orderly thinker.

_____ 13. I use a lot of gestures when I talk to people.

_____ 14. I can recognize and empathize with people's attitudes and emotions.

_____ 15. I prefer to study alone.

_____ 16. I can name many different things in the environment such as clouds, rocks, and plant types.

_____ 17. I like to draw pictures, graphs, or charts to better understand information.

_____ 18. I have a good memory for names and dates.

_____ 19. When I hear music, I "get into it" by moving, humming, tapping, or even singing.

_____ 20. I learn better by asking a lot of questions.

Multiple Intelligences, Learning Styles, and Personality Typing   **179**

_____ 21. I enjoy playing competitive sports.

_____ 22. I communicate very well with other people.

_____ 23. I know what I want and I set goals to accomplish it.

_____ 24. I have some interest in herbal remedies and natural medicine.

_____ 25. I enjoy working puzzles or mazes.

_____ 26. I am a good storyteller.

_____ 27. I can easily remember the words and melodies of songs.

_____ 28. I enjoy solving problems in math and chemistry and working with computer programming problems.

_____ 29. I usually touch people or pat them on the back when I talk to them.

_____ 30. I understand my family and friends better than most other people do.

_____ 31. I don't always talk about my accomplishments with others.

_____ 32. I would rather work outside around nature than inside around people and equipment.

_____ 33. I enjoy and learn more when seeing movies, slides, or videos in class.

_____ 34. I am a very good listener and I enjoy listening to others' stories.

_____ 35. I need to study with music.

_____ 36. I enjoy games like Clue, Battleship, chess, and Rubik's Cube.

_____ 37. I enjoy physical activities such as bicycling, jogging, dancing, snowboarding, skateboarding, or swimming.

_____ 38. I am good at solving people's problems and conflicts.

_____ 39. I have to have time alone to think about new information in order to remember it.

_____ 40. I enjoy sorting and organizing information, objects, and collectibles.

Refer to your score on each individual question. Place that score beside the appropriate question number below. Then, tally each line at the side.

SCORE					TOTAL ACROSS	CODE
1 ___	9 ___	17 ___	25 ___	33 ___	_____	Visual/Spatial
2 ___	10 ___	18 ___	26 ___	34 ___	_____	Verbal/Linguistic
3 ___	11 ___	19 ___	27 ___	35 ___	_____	Musical/Rhythm
4 ___	12 ___	20 ___	28 ___	36 ___	_____	Logic/Math
5 ___	13 ___	21 ___	29 ___	37 ___	_____	Body/Kinesthetic
6 ___	14 ___	22 ___	30 ___	38 ___	_____	Interpersonal
7 ___	15 ___	23 ___	31 ___	39 ___	_____	Intrapersonal
8 ___	16 ___	24 ___	32 ___	40 ___	_____	Naturalistic

MIS TALLY

Multiple Intelligences

Look at the scores on the MIS. What are your top three scores? Write them in the space below.

Top Score	_____	Code	_____
Second Score	_____	Code	_____
Third Score	_____	Code	_____

This tally can help you understand where some of your strengths may be. Again, this is not a measure of your worth or capacities, nor is it an indicator of your future successes. Read the following section to better understand multiple intelligences.

A New Way of Looking at Yourself

UNDERSTANDING MULTIPLE INTELLIGENCES

In 1983, Howard Gardner, a Harvard University professor, developed a theory called Multiple Intelligences. In his book *Frames of Mind,* he outlines seven intelligences that he feels are possessed by everyone: visual/spatial, verbal/linguistic, musical/rhythm, logic/math, body/kinesthetic, interpersonal, and intrapersonal. In 1996, he added an eighth intelligence: naturalistic. In short, if you have ever done things that came easily for you, you are probably drawing on one of your intelligences that is well developed. On the other hand, if you have tried to do things that are very difficult to master or understand, you may be dealing with material that calls on one of your less developed intelligences. If playing the piano by ear comes easily to you, your musical/rhythm intelligence may be very strong. If you have trouble writing or understanding poetry, your verbal/linguistic intelligence may not be as well developed. This does not mean that you will never be able to write poetry; it simply means that you have not fully developed your skills in this area.

THE EIGHT INTELLIGENCES

The "Smart" descriptors were adapted from Thomas Armstrong (1994).

Visual/Spatial *(Picture Smart).* Thinks in pictures; knows where things are in the house; loves to create images and work with graphs, charts, pictures, and maps.

Verbal/Linguistic *(Word Smart).* Communicates well through language, likes to write, is good at spelling, great at telling stories, loves to read books.

Musical/Rhythm *(Music Smart).* Loves to sing, hum, and whistle; comprehends music; responds to music immediately; performs music.

Logic/Math *(Number Smart).* Can easily conceptualize and reason, uses logic, has good problem-solving skills, enjoys math and science.

Body/Kinesthetic *(Body Smart).* Learns through body sensation, moves around a lot, enjoys work involving the hands, is graced with some athletic ability.

Interpersonal *(People Smart).* Loves to communicate with other people, possesses great leadership skills, has lots of friends, is involved in extracurricular activities.

Intrapersonal *(Self-Smart).* Has a deep awareness of own feelings, is very reflective, requires time to be alone, does not get involved with group activities.

Naturalistic *(Environment Smart).* Has interest in the environment and in nature; can easily recognize plants, animals, rocks, and cloud formations; may like hiking, camping, and fishing.

> Education is learning what you didn't even know you didn't know. —DANIEL BOORSTIN

Making It Work for You

USING MULTIPLE INTELLIGENCES TO ENHANCE STUDYING AND LEARNING

Below, you will find some helpful tips to assist you in creating a study environment and study habits using your multiple intelligences.

VISUAL/SPATIAL

- Use visuals in your notes such as timelines, charts, graphs, and geometric shapes.
- Work to create a mental or visual picture of the information at hand.
- Use colored markers to make associations or to group items together.
- Use mapping or webbing so that your main points are easily recognized.
- When taking notes, draw pictures in the margins to illustrate the main points.
- Visualize the information in your mind.

Some people express themselves outwardly, while others are more reflective. How would you describe yourself? Are there certain situations that cause you to be more or less extroverted than you are normally?

VERBAL/LINGUISTIC
- Establish study groups so that you will have the opportunity to talk about the information.
- Using the information you studied, create a story or a skit.
- Read as much information about related areas as possible.
- As you read chapters, outline them in your own words.
- Summarize and recite your notes aloud.

MUSICAL/RHYTHM
- Listen to music while studying (if it does not distract you).
- Write a song or rap about the chapter or information.
- Take short breaks from studying to listen to music.
- Commit the information being studied to the music from your favorite song.

LOGIC/MATH
- Strive to make connections between subjects.
- Don't just memorize the facts; apply them to real-life situations.
- As you study the information, think of problems in society and how this information could solve those problems.
- Create analyzing charts. Draw a line down the center of the page, put the information at hand in the left column and analyze, discuss, relate, and synthesize it in the right column.
- Allow yourself some time to reflect after studying.

BODY/KINESTHETIC
- Don't confine your study area to a desk or chair; move around, explore, go outside.
- Act out the information.
- Study in a group of people and change groups often.
- Use charts, posters, flash cards, and chalkboards to study.
- When appropriate or possible, build models using the information studied.
- Verbalize the information to others.
- Use games such as chess, Monopoly, Twister, or Clue when studying.
- Trace words as you study them.
- Use repetition to learn facts; write them many times.
- Make study sheets.

INTERPERSONAL
- Study in groups.
- Share the information with other people.
- Teach the information to others.

- Interview outside sources to learn more about the material at hand.
- Have a debate with others about the information.

INTRAPERSONAL
- Study in a quiet area.
- Study by yourself.
- Allow time for reflection and meditation about the subject matter.
- Study in short time blocks and then spend some time absorbing the information.
- Work at your own pace.

NATURALISTIC
- Study outside whenever possible.
- Relate the information to the effect on the environment whenever possible.
- When given the opportunity to choose your own topics or research projects, choose something related to nature.
- Collect your own study data and resources.
- Organize and label your information.
- Keep separate notebooks on individual topics so that you can add new information to each topic as it becomes available to you.

Understanding Learning Styles Theory

Rita Dunn defines learning styles as, "the way in which each learner begins to concentrate on, process, and retain new and difficult information." We must note that there is a difference between a learning *style* and a learning *strategy*. A learning strategy is how you might choose to learn or study, such as by using note cards, flip charts, color slides, or cooperative learning groups. Flip charts and slides are strategies. Learning styles are more sensory. They involve seeing, hearing, and touching.

TAKE THE LEAD

The Learning Evaluation and Assessment Directory

Robert M. Sherfield, Ph.D., 1999, 2002, 2005

Directions: Read each statement carefully and thoroughly. After reading the statement, rate your response using the scale below. There are no right or wrong answers. This is not a timed survey. The LEAD is based, in part, on research conducted by Rita Dunn.

3 = Often Applies
2 = Sometimes Applies
1 = Never or Almost Never Applies

_____ 1. I remember information better if I write it down or draw a picture of it.

_____ 2. I remember things better when I hear them instead of just reading or seeing them.

_____ 3. When I get something that has to be assembled, I just start doing it. I don't read the directions.

_____ 4. If I am taking a test, I can "see" the page of the text or lecture notes where the answer is located.

_____ 5. I would rather the professor explain a graph, chart, or diagram than just show it to me.

_____ 6. When learning new things, I want to "do it" rather than hear about it.

_____ 7. I would rather the instructor write the information on the board or overhead instead of just lecturing.

_____ 8. I would rather listen to a book on tape than read it.

_____ 9. I enjoy making things, putting things together, and working with my hands.

_____ 10. I am able to quickly conceptualize and visualize information.

_____ 11. I learn best by hearing words.

_____ 12. I have been called hyperactive by my parents, spouse, partner, or professor.

_____ 13. I have no trouble reading maps, charts, or diagrams.

_____ 14. I can usually pick up on small sounds like bells, crickets, or frogs, or distant sounds like train whistles.

_____ 15. I use my hands and gesture a lot when I speak to others.

Refer to your score on each individual question. Place that score beside the appropriate question number below. Then, tally each line at the side.

SCORE					TOTAL ACROSS	CODE
1 ___	4 ___	7 ___	10 ___	13 ___	_____	Visual
2 ___	5 ___	8 ___	11 ___	14 ___	_____	Auditory
3 ___	6 ___	9 ___	12 ___	15 ___	_____	Tactile

LEAD SCORES

Learning Styles

Look at the scores on the LEAD. What is your top score?

Top Score _____ Code _____

If you learn best by *seeing* information, you have a more dominant *visual* learning style. If you learn best by *hearing* information, you have a more dominant *auditory* learning style. If you learn best by *touching or doing,* you have a more dominant *tactile* learning style. You may also hear the tactile learning style referred to as kinesthetic or hands-on.

Some of the most successful students have learned to use all three styles. If you were learning how to skateboard, you might learn best by hearing someone talk about the different styles or techniques. Others might learn best by watching a video where someone demonstrates the techniques. Still others would learn best by actually getting on the board and trying it. However, the student who involved all of his or her senses might gain the most. She might listen to the instructor tell about skateboarding, watch the video, and then go do it. Therefore, she would have involved all of her learning styles: visual, auditory, and tactile. Here are brief descriptions of the three styles.

Visual (*Eye Smart*). Thinks in pictures. Enjoys visual instructions, demonstrations, and descriptions; would rather read a text than listen to a lecture; avid note-taker; needs visual references; enjoys using charts, graphs, and pictures.

Auditory (*Ear Smart*). Prefers verbal instructions; would rather listen than read; often tapes lectures and listens to them in the car or at home; recites information out loud; enjoys talking, discussing issues, and verbal stimuli; talks out problems.

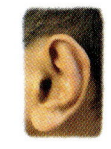

Tactile (*Action Smart*). Prefers hands-on approaches to learning; likes to take notes and uses a great deal of scratch paper; learns best by doing something, by touching it, or manipulating it; learns best while moving or while in action; often does not concentrate well when sitting and reading.

THE SIMILARITIES AND DIFFERENCES BETWEEN MULTIPLE INTELLIGENCES THEORY AND LEARNING STYLES THEORY

As you read over the components of MI theory and LS theory, you begin to see several common elements. Both theories deal with the visual, auditory, and tactile (or kinesthetic). Behind the surface, there are also similarities. According to Silver, Strong, and Perini (1997), "Both, in fact, combine insights from biology, anthropology, psychology, medical case studies, and an examination of art and culture." While several components and some background research of MI theory overlap LS theory, there are vast differences. "Learning styles emphasize the different ways people think and feel as they solve problems, create products, and interact. The theory of multiple intelligence is an effort to understand how cultures and disciplines shape human potential. Learning style models tend to concern themselves with the process of learning: how individuals absorb information, think about information, and evaluate the results" (1997).

MI theory, on the other hand, examines and "shows different levels of aptitude in various content areas. In all cases, we know that no individual is universally intelligent; certain fields of knowledge engage or elude everyone" (1997).

Simply stated, you can be a visual learner (this is a learning style) and yet not have visual/spatial (this is one of the multiple intelligences) be your dominant intelligence. How can this be possible? It may be that you learn best by watching someone paint a picture—watching their brush strokes, their method of mixing paints, and their spatial layout—but it may be that you will not be as engaged or as talented at painting as the person you watched. Your painting may lack feeling, depth, and expression. This is an example of how your visual learning style can be strong but your visual/spatial intelligence may not be your dominant intelligence.

On the other hand, your learning style may be visual and your dominant intelligence may be verbal/linguistic. If that is the case, you would learn how to paint by watching someone go through the process. Then, using your verbal/linguistic intelligence, you would be masterful at describing how to paint and talking about the process you observed.

What Can You Learn About Personality?

To begin, take the PAP assessment below.

TAKE THE PAP

The Personality Assessment Profile

Robert M. Sherfield, Ph.D., 1999, 2002, 2005

Directions: Read each statement carefully and thoroughly. After reading the statement, rate your response using the scale below. There are no right or wrong answers. This is not a timed survey. The PAP is based, in part, on the Myers-Briggs Type Indicator® (MBTI) by Katharine Briggs and Isabel Briggs-Myers.

3 = Often Applies
2 = Sometimes Applies
1 = Never or Almost Never Applies

_____ 1a. I am a very talkative person.

_____ 1b. I am a more reflective person than a verbal person.

_____ 2a. I am a very factual and literal person.

_____ 2b. I look to the future and I can see possibilities.

_____ 3a. I value truth and justice over tact and emotion.

_____ 3b. I find it easy to empathize with other people.

_____ 4a. I am very ordered and efficient.

_____ 4b. I enjoy having freedom from control.

_____ 5a. I am a very friendly and social person.

_____ 5b. I enjoy listening to others more than talking.

Multiple Intelligences, Learning Styles, and Personality Typing **187**

_____ 6a. I enjoy being around and working with people who have a great deal of common sense.

_____ 6b. I enjoy being around and working with people who are dreamers and have a great deal of imagination.

_____ 7a. One of my motivating forces is to do a job very well.

_____ 7b. I like to be recognized for, and I am motivated by, my accomplishments and awards.

_____ 8a. I like to plan out my day before I go to bed.

_____ 8b. When I get up on a non-school or non-work day, I just like to let the day "plan itself."

_____ 9a. I like to express my feelings and thoughts.

_____ 9b. I enjoy a great deal of tranquility and quiet time to myself.

_____ 10a. I am a very pragmatic and realistic person.

_____ 10b. I like to create new ideas, methods, or ways of doing things.

_____ 11a. I make decisions with my brain.

_____ 11b. I make decisions with my heart.

_____ 12a. I am a very disciplined and orderly person.

_____ 12b. I don't make a lot of plans.

_____ 13a. I like to work with a group of people.

_____ 13b. I would rather work independently.

_____ 14a. I learn best if I can see it, touch it, smell it, taste it, or hear it.

_____ 14b. I learn best by relying on my gut feelings or intuition.

_____ 15a. I am quick to criticize others.

_____ 15b. I compliment others very easily and quickly.

_____ 16a. My life is systematic and organized.

_____ 16b. I don't really pay attention to deadlines.

_____ 17a. I can be myself when I am around others.

_____ 17b. I can be myself when I am alone.

_____ 18a. I live in the here and now, in the present.

_____ 18b. I live in the future, planning and dreaming.

_____ 19a. I think that if someone breaks the rules, the person should be punished.

_____ 19b I think that if someone breaks the rules, we should look at the person who broke the rules, examine the rules, and look at the situation at hand before a decision is made.

_____ 20a. I do my work, then I play.

_____ 20b. I play, then do my work.

Refer to your score on each individual question. Place that score beside the appropriate question number below. Then, tally each line at the side.

SCORE					TOTAL ACROSS	CODE
1a____	5a____	9a____	13a____	17a____	_____	**E** Extrovert
1b____	5b____	9b____	13b____	17b____	_____	**I** Introvert
2a____	6a____	10a____	14a____	18a____	_____	**S** Sensing
2b____	6b____	10b____	14b____	18b____	_____	**N** iNtuition
3a____	7a____	11a____	15a____	19a____	_____	**T** Thinking
3b____	7b____	11b____	15b____	19b____	_____	**F** Feeling
4a____	8a____	12a____	16a____	20a____	_____	**J** Judging
4b____	8b____	12b____	16b____	20b____	_____	**P** Perceiving

PAP SCORES

Personality Indicator

Look at the scores on your PAP. Is your score higher in the E or I line? Is your score higher in the S or N line? Is your score higher in the T or F line? Is your score higher in the J or P line? Write the code to the side of each section below.

Is your higher score	E or I	Code _____
Is your higher score	S or N	Code _____
Is your higher score	T or F	Code _____
Is your higher score	J or P	Code _____

UNDERSTANDING PERSONALITY TYPING (TYPOLOGY)

The questions on the PAP helped you discover whether you are extroverted or introverted (E or I), sensing or intuitive (S or N), thinking or feeling (T or F), and judging or perceiving (J or P). These questions were based, in part, on work done by Carl Jung, Katharine Briggs, and Isabel Briggs-Myers.

In 1921, Swiss psychologist Carl Jung (1875–1961) published his work *Psychological Types*. In this book, Jung suggested that human behavior is not random. He felt that behavior follows patterns, and these patterns are caused by differences in the way people use their minds. In 1942, Isabel Briggs-Myers and her mother, Katharine Briggs, began to put Jung's theory into practice. They developed the Myers-Briggs Type Indicator®, which after more than 50 years of research and refinement has become the most widely used instrument for identifying and studying personality.

As indicated throughout this chapter, we must stress the fact that no part of this assessment measures your worth, your success factors, or your value as a human being. The questions on the PAP assisted you in identifying your type, but neither the PAP nor your authors want you to assume that one personality type is better or worse, more valuable or less valuable, or more likely to be successful. What personality typing can do is to "help us discover what best motivates and energizes each of us as individuals" (Tieger and Tieger, 2001).

Why Personality Matters

FUNCTIONS OF TYPOLOGY

When all of the combinations of E/I, S/N, T/F, and J/P are combined, there are 16 personality types. Everyone will fit into one of the following categories:

ISTJ	ISFJ	INFJ	INTJ
ISTP	ISFP	INFP	INTP
ESTP	ESFP	ENFP	ENTP
ESTJ	ESFJ	ENFJ	ENTJ

Let's take a look at the four major categories of typing. Notice that the stronger your score in one area, the stronger your personality type is for that area. For instance, if you scored 15 on the E (extroversion) questions, this means that you are a strong extrovert. If you scored 15 on the I (introversion) questions, this means that you are a strong introvert. However, if you scored 7 on the E questions and 8 on the I questions, your score indicates that you possess almost the same amount of extroverted and introverted qualities. The same is true for every category on the PAP.

E VERSUS I (EXTROVERSION/INTROVERSION)

This category deals with the way we *interact with others and the world around us*.

Extroverts prefer to live in the outside world, drawing their strength from other people. They are outgoing and love interaction. They usually make decisions with others in mind. They enjoy being the center of attention. There are usually few secrets about extroverts.

Introverts draw their strength from the inner world. They need to spend time alone to think and ponder. They are usually quiet and reflective. They usually make decisions by themselves. They do not like being the center of attention. They are private.

S VERSUS N (SENSING/INTUITION)

This category deals with the way we *learn and deal with information*.

Sensing types gather information through their five senses. They have a hard time believing something if it cannot be seen, touched, smelled, tasted, or heard. They like concrete facts and details. They do not rely on intuition or gut feelings. They usually have a great deal of common sense.

Intuitive types are not very detail-oriented. They can see possibilities, and they rely on their gut feelings. Usually, they are very innovative people. They tend to live in the future and often get bored once they have mastered a task.

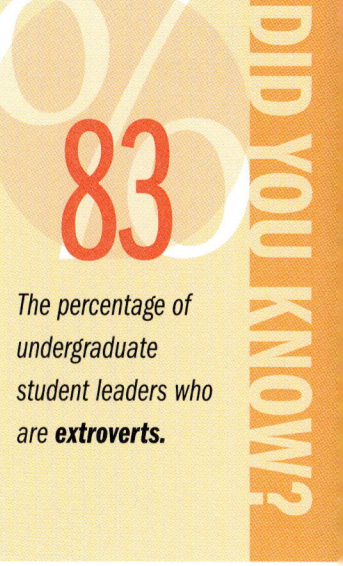

DID YOU KNOW?

83%

The percentage of undergraduate student leaders who are **extroverts**.

Source: Brightman, H. Georgia State University Master Teacher Program: On Learning Styles, www.gsu.edu/~dschjb/wwwmbti.html.

T VERSUS F (THINKING/FEELING)

This category deals with the way we *make decisions*.

Thinkers are very logical people. They do not make decisions based on feelings or emotion. They are analytical and sometimes do not take others' values into consideration when making decisions. They can easily identify the flaws of others. They can be seen as insensitive and lacking compassion.

Feelers make decisions based on what they feel is right and just. They like to have harmony, and they value others' opinions and feelings. They are usually very tactful people who like to please others. They are very warm people.

J VERSUS P (JUDGING/PERCEIVING)

This category deals with the way we *live*.

Judgers are very orderly people. They must have a great deal of structure in their lives. They are good at setting goals and sticking to their goals. They are the type of people who would seldom, if ever, play before their work was completed.

Perceivers are just the opposite. They are less structured and more spontaneous. They do not like timelines. Unlike the judger, they will play before their work is done. They will take every chance to delay a decision or judgment. Sometimes, they can become involved in too many things at one time.

After you have studied the charts on the following pages and other information in the chapter regarding your personality type, you can make some decisions about your study habits and even your career choices. For instance, if you scored very strong in the extroversion section, it may not serve you well to pursue a career where you would be forced to work alone. It would probably be unwise to try to spend all of your time studying alone. If you are a strong extrovert, you would want to work and study around people.

STRATEGIES FOR BUILDING ON YOUR BEST

Consider the following strategies for making the most of your learning styles, personality type, and dominant intelligence:

- Understand that everyone has a strength and aptitude for some skill or task.
- Improve your weaker learning styles by incorporating at least one aspect of those learning styles into your daily study plans.
- If your personality type clashes with your professor's personality type, try to make adjustments that enable you to get through the class successfully.
- Strengthen your less dominant intelligences by involving yourself in activities that cause you to use them.
- Adjust your learning style to match your professor's teaching style if possible.
- Understand that your primary intelligence can help you decide on your life's vocation.

Making Your Personality Work for You

ENHANCING YOUR LEARNING

Having identified your personality type, use the following suggestions to enhance studying using your present personality type, while improving your study skills using your less dominant type.

TYPE	CURRENT SUGGESTIONS	IMPROVEMENT
Extrovert	Study with groups of people in cooperative learning teams. Seek help from others. Discuss topics with friends. Establish debate or discussion groups. Vary your study habits; meet in different places with different people. Discuss new ideas and plans with your friends.	Work on listening skills. Be sure to let others contribute to the group. Force yourself to develop solutions and answers before you go to the group. Spend some time reflecting. Let others speak before you share your ideas and suggestions. Work to be more patient. Think before acting or speaking.
Introvert	Study in a quiet place, undisturbed by others. When reading and studying, take time for reflection. Use your time alone to read and study support and auxiliary materials. Set aside large blocks of time for study and reflection.	Get involved in a study group from time to time. Allow others inside your world to offer advice and opinions. Share your opinions and advice with others more often. Seek advice from others. Use mnemonics to increase your memory power. Instead of writing responses or questions, speak aloud to friends and peers.
Sensor	Observe the world around you. Experience the information to the fullest degree; feel it and touch it. Explain to your study group or partner the information in complete detail. Apply the information to something in your life that is currently happening. Create a study schedule and stick to it. If your old study habits are not working, stop and invent new ways of studying. Explore what others are doing.	Try to think about the information in an abstract form. Think "What would happen if . . . " Let your imagination run wild. Think about the information in the future tense. Let your gut feelings take over from time to time. Take more chances with the unknown. Trust your feelings and inspirations. Think beyond reality. Don't oversimplify.
Intuitive	After studying the information or data, let your imagination apply this to something abstract. Describe how the information could be used today, right now, in your life at the moment. Describe how this information could help others. View new information as a challenge. Vary your study habits; don't do the same thing all the time. Rely on your gut feelings.	Work on becoming more detail-oriented. Look at information through the senses. Verify your facts. Think in simple terms. Think about the information in a logical and analytical way. Try to explain new information in relation to the senses.

(continued)

TYPE	CURRENT SUGGESTIONS	IMPROVEMENT
Thinker	Make logical connections between new information and what is already known. Remain focused. Explain the information in detailed terms to a study group. Put things in order. Study with people who do their part for the group.	Try to see information and data in more abstract terms. Look for the "big picture." Develop a passion for acquiring new information. Think before you speak. Strive to be more objective and open.
Feeler	Establish a supportive and open study group. Teach others the information. Continue to be passionate about learning and exploring. Explain the information in a cause/effect scenario. Focus on the "people" factor.	Strive to look at things more logically. Work to stay focused. Praise yourself when others do not. Try to be more organized. Work to stick to policies, rules, and guidelines. Don't give in to opposition just for the sake of harmony. Don't get caught up in the here and now; look ahead.
Judger	Set a schedule and stick to it. Strive to complete projects. Keep your study supplies in one place so that you can locate them easily. Prioritize tasks that need to be completed. Create lists and agendas.	Take your time in making decisions. Complete all tasks. Look at the entire situation before making a judgment. Don't act or make judgments too quickly. Don't beat yourself up if you miss a deadline.
Perceiver	Study in different places with different people. Since you see all sides of issues, share those with your study group for discussion. Obtain as much information as possible so that you can make solid decisions. Create fun and exciting study groups with snacks and maybe music. Be the leader of the study team. Allow yourself a great deal of time for study so that you can take well-deserved breaks.	Become more decisive. Finish one project before you begin another. Don't put off the harder subjects until later; study them first. Learn to set deadlines. Create lists and agendas to help you stay on target. Do your work; then play.

A Closer Look at Your Personality Type

ISTJ 7–10% OF AMERICA	**ISFJ 7–10% OF AMERICA**	**INFJ 2–3% OF AMERICA**	**INTJ 2–3% OF AMERICA**
Have great power of concentration; very serious; dependable; logical and realistic; take responsibility for their own actions; they are not easily distracted.	Hard workers; detail-oriented; considerate of others' feelings; friendly and warm to others; very conscientious; they are down-to-earth and like to be around the same.	Enjoy an atmosphere where all get along; they do what is needed of them; they have strong beliefs and principles; enjoy helping others achieve their goals.	They are very independent; enjoy challenges; inventors; can be skeptical; they are perfectionists; they believe in their own work, sometimes to a fault.
ISTP 4–7% OF AMERICA	**ISFP 5–7% OF AMERICA**	**INFP 3–4% OF AMERICA**	**INTP 3–4% OF AMERICA**
Very reserved; good at making things clear to others; interested in how and why things work; like to work with their hands; can sometimes be misunderstood as idle.	Very sensitive and modest; adapt easily to change; they are respectful of others' feelings and values; take criticism personally; don't enjoy leadership roles.	They work well alone; must know others well to interact; faithful to others and their jobs; excellent at communication; open-minded; dreamers; tend to do too much.	Extremely logical; very analytical; good at planning; love to learn; excellent problem solvers; they don't enjoy needless conversation; hard to understand at times.
ESTP 6–8% OF AMERICA	**ESFP 8–10% OF AMERICA**	**ENFP 6–7% OF AMERICA**	**ENTP 4–6% OF AMERICA**
They are usually very happy; they don't let trivial things upset them; they have very good memories; very good at working with things and taking them apart.	Very good at sports and active exercises; good common sense; easygoing; good at communication; can be impulsive; do not enjoy working alone; have fun and enjoy living and life.	Creative and industrious; can easily find success in activities and projects that interest them; good at motivating others; organized; do not like routine.	Great problem solvers; love to argue either side; can do almost anything; good at speaking/motivating; love challenges; very creative; do not like routine; overconfident.
ESTJ 12–15% OF AMERICA	**ESFJ 11–14% OF AMERICA**	**ENFJ 3–5% OF AMERICA**	**ENTJ 3–5% OF AMERICA**
They are "take charge" people; they like to get things done; focus on results; very good at organizing; good at seeing what will not work; responsible; realists.	Enjoy many friendly relationships; popular; love to help others; do not take criticism very well; need praise; need to work with people; organized; talkative; active.	Very concerned about others' feelings; respect others; good leaders; usually popular; good at public speaking; can make decisions too quickly; trust easily.	Excellent leaders; speak very well; hard-working; may be workaholics; may not give enough praise; like to learn; great planners; enjoy helping others reach their goals.

All percentages taken from Tieger and Tieger, *Do What You Are,* 3rd ed., 2001.

BLUEPRINTS FOR CHANGE

NAME

DATE

REFLECTION

The most important thing to remember about learning styles, multiple intelligences, and personality typology is that, unlike an IQ test, they do not pretend to determine if you are "smart" or not. They simply allow you to look more closely at how you learn, what strengths you have in your innate personality, and what dominant intelligence you have.

Discovering your learning style can greatly enhance your classroom performance. For example, finally understanding that your **learning style** is visual and that your professor's **teaching style** is totally verbal can answer many questions about why you may have performed poorly in the past. Now, you have the knowledge and the tools to make your learning style work for you, not against you.

GET REAL

Below are a few questions to help you think about learning styles. Study each question carefully and respond accurately.

How can your personality affect your relationships with others?

How does understanding your strengths affect your self-esteem?

If your professor's teaching style is verbal and your learning style is visual, what techniques can you use to help you overcome this difference?

What is your primary intelligence (refer to the MIS on page 178)?_____ How can this intelligence help you decide on a vocation?

What is your *least dominant learning style* (refer to the LEAD on page 183)? _____ How can you strengthen this learning style in an English class?

What is your *most dominant learning style* (refer to the LEAD on page 183)? _____ How can you strengthen this learning style in a Biology class?

195

Case Study

NAME: LaDondo Johnson
SCHOOL: Houston Community College, Houston, TX
MAJOR: Early Childhood Education   **AGE:** 53

Below is a real-life situation faced by LaDondo. Read the brief case and respond to the questions.

Returning to college at 53 was not an easy decision, but I knew that I wanted to reach my goal of being a kindergarten teacher. It has been a dream of mine for many years. I found that my biggest problem in returning to the classroom was learning to listen to the professor. I continued to wonder why this was such a problem for me, and then I took a Learning Styles Inventory and discovered that my primary learning style is Visual. It made perfect sense to me then—my learning style was not matching my professor's teaching style.

I knew that my professor was not going to change teaching styles, so I had to learn to adapt and adjust. I began going home after each class and converting my notes onto note cards. By doing this, I was able to make the lecture visual. I would write questions on one side and answers on the other, sometimes drawing examples or using color to help me absorb the information better.

I found that by making the lecture visual, I understood what was being taught and could study the information more effectively. I also discovered that the more I looked at my cards, the more I retained. I discovered that repetition is as important to my learning process as visualization. Discovering both of these has helped me greatly.

Toward the end of the semester, I noticed another thing. I performed in class much better when I was able to interact and be a part of a group. I have always had an outgoing personality, but again, I never thought this would play a part in my college education. I found that because of my personality, I love to participate and share and draw from others. I guess my dominant intelligence is Interpersonal.

By discovering these things about my learning abilities, I am certain that I will be able to complete this degree and reach one of the most important goals in my life.

If LaDondo has a very outgoing personality, what is most likely her personality type according to this chapter? Why did you choose this type?

With LaDondo's outgoing personality, how could she be successful in a class that offered NO interaction or group work?

What role does personality play in academic success?

_____
_____
_____

If LaDondo takes a class that is totally verbal (the professor does only lecture), what other tips would you offer her to succeed in that type of classroom setting?

_____
_____
_____

How can any student successfully complete a class that centers on his or her LEAST dominant intelligence (for example, how can Jane succeed in math when math is her least dominant intelligence)?

_____
_____
_____

Where can you go on your campus to learn more about learning styles, personality typing, or multiple intelligences?

_____
_____
_____

at this moment journal

Refer to page 175 of this chapter. Having read and reflected upon the information in the chapter, consider how you might revise your goal to make it more:

REASONABLE

BELIEVABLE

MEASURABLE

ADAPTABLE

CONTROLLABLE

DESIRABLE

ONLINE JOURNAL

To complete an online journal entry, log onto the Companion Website at **www.prenhall.com/sherfield.** Go to Chapter 6 and click on the link to the Online Journal. You can respond to the questions provided or to questions assigned by your professor, or you may journal about your own experiences.

ADVICE TO GO

CORNERSTONES

for learning styles

Get involved in a *variety* of learning and social situations.

Use your less dominant areas more often to *strengthen* them.

Read more about personality typing and learning styles.

Answer inventories and surveys *thoughtfully*.

Learning styles *do not* measure your worth.

Work to *improve* your less dominant areas.

Surround yourself with people who are very different from you.

Try *different ways* of learning and studying.

LEARN

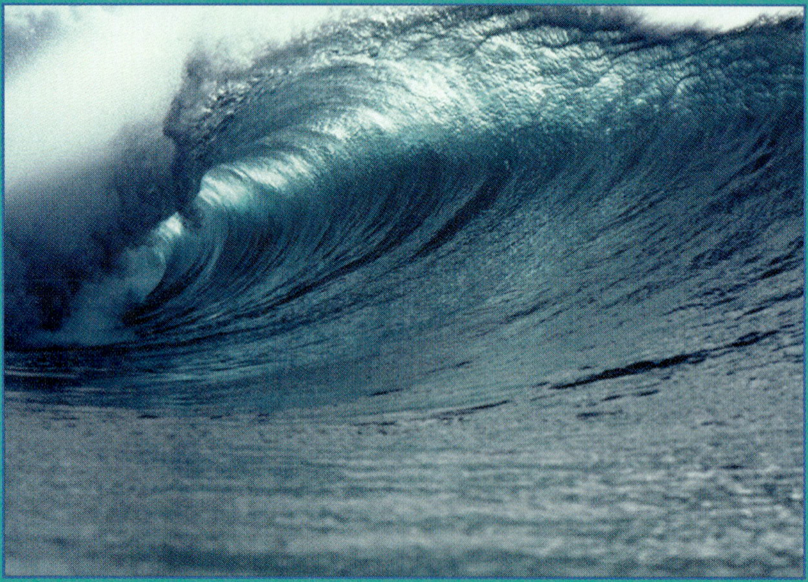

7 Listen

Know how to listen, and you will profit even from those who say nothing.

Plutarch

CHAPTER 7
LISTEN

LaTonya had been through a *rough evening.* She had received a phone call from home to say that *her grandmother was very ill and had been taken to the hospital.* As she sat in math class the next morning, her mind was flooded with images of home. She had lived with her grandmother most of her life. *In her mind's eye, she saw a house filled with people, and she could smell the bread baking in the oven.* She saw her grandmother calling her down to eat before the arrival of the school bus. Her daydream was so vivid that for a moment, LaTonya could feel the *gentle kiss of her grandmother on her forehead.*

LaTonya was filled with anxiety, *wondering whether her grandmother would be all right.* Her mind was a million miles away when a deep voice rang through her daydream. *"Do you agree with the solution to this problem, Ms. Griffin?"* LaTonya knew the voice was speaking to her, but *it took her a few seconds to focus on it.* Again the instructor asked, *"Do you agree with the solution to this problem, Ms. Griffin?"* LaTonya had no idea whether she agreed or not. *She had not heard the problem or the solution.* She looked at the instructor and out of embarrassment and intimidation, she answered, "Yes, I do."

Ability is what you are capable of doing. Motivation determines what you do. Attitude determines how well you do it.   —LOU HOLTZ

The Art of Active Listening

> LaTonya had no idea whether she agreed or not. She had not heard the problem or the solution.

The situation took a turn for the worse. "Why do you think this is the proper way to solve this problem, Ms. Griffin?" *LaTonya sat, bewildered, at her desk.* She looked down at her notes for help, but she had written only the date and the topic for the day on her notepad. The tension grew as the entire class waited for her answer. "I don't know, Dr. Huggins, I don't know."

QUESTIONS FOR REFLECTION

Consider responding to these questions online in the Questions for Reflection module of the Companion Website.

1. What role does concentration play in the listening process?

2. Compare LaTonya's situation to a listening situation you have encountered in class.

3. What role does listening play in the note-taking process?

Where are you... AT THIS MOMENT

Before reading this chapter, take a moment and respond to the following 10 questions. Consider each one carefully before answering, and then respond by circling the number in the appropriate box. When you have answered the questions, add your points and find your total score on the feedback chart below.

STATEMENT	STRONGLY DISAGREE	DISAGREE	DON'T KNOW	AGREE	STRONGLY AGREE	SCORE
1. What a speaker says is more important than how it is said.	5	4	3	2	1	
2. A sign of a good listener is to constantly try to guess what will be said next.	5	4	3	2	1	
3. I am a good listener even when I pay only partial attention to what is being said.	5	4	3	2	1	
4. I know how to listen for key words or phrases while taking notes.	1	2	3	4	5	
5. Really listening to others takes a good amount of effort and energy.	1	2	3	4	5	
6. Listening and hearing mean the exact same thing to me.	5	4	3	2	1	
7. Good listening is a passive process, not an active process.	5	4	3	2	1	
8. I ask questions about what I've listened to in an effort to make sure I've understood it correctly.	1	2	3	4	5	
9. I know how to listen for important verbal and nonverbal information and clues.	1	2	3	4	5	
10. When listening, it is important to try to relate what I'm hearing to something I already know.	1	2	3	4	5	
TOTAL VALUE						

SUMMARY

10–17   Your listening skills are very limited. You don't seem to know much about how pick out the main or important ideas in what you listen to. Further, you have difficulty paying attention when listening. You have to develop these skills to be an effective student in the classroom.

18–25   You have below average listening skills. You may be able to remember what you've heard for short periods of time, but you likely have difficulty understanding the meaning of what you've heard. Improving your listening skills will benefit your studies.

26–34   Your listening skills are average. You can usually pick out the key ideas in what you hear and can understand them. Refining your listening skills will benefit you in terms of your comprehension and ability to remember and apply what you've heard.

35–42   You are above average in your listening skills. You likely have few difficulties knowing what the important ideas are when listening, and you spend time and energy making sure you have heard accurately. You relate what you've heard to ideas and concepts you already know.

43–50   You are exceptional in your ability to focus, process, and understand when you listen. You put effort into comprehending what you listen to and realize that good listeners must actively try to incorporate what they hear into their existing knowledge base.

Goals... FOR CHANGE

Based on your total points, what is one goal you would like to achieve related to becoming a better listener?

Goal _____
_____

List three actions you can take that might help you move closer to realizing this goal.

1. _____
2. _____
3. _____

Questions FOR BUILDING ON YOUR BEST

As you read this chapter, consider the following questions. At the end of the chapter, you should be able to answer all of them. You are encouraged to ask a few questions of your own. Consider asking your classmates or professors to assist you.

1. What is the difference between listening and hearing?
2. How do the Chinese view listening? How does this differ from my current listening style?
3. What are the major obstacles to listening? How can I overcome them?
4. What phrases might a professor use to indicate that important information is coming?
5. What role do my emotions play in the listening process?

What additional questions might you have about listening in college and life?

1. _____
2. _____
3. _____

The Importance of Listening

Listening is one of the most important and useful skills human beings possess. For all animals, listening is a survival skill needed for hunting and obtaining food; for humans, listening is necessary for establishing relationships, growth, survival, knowledge, entertainment, and even health. It is one of our most widely used tools. How much time do you think you spend listening every day? Research suggests that we spend almost 70 percent of our waking time communicating, and 53 percent of that time is spent in listening situations (Adler, Rosenfeld, and Towne, 2001). Effective listening skills can mean the difference between success or failure, A's or F's, relationships or loneliness.

For students, good listening skills are critical. Over the next two to four years, you will be given a lot of information in lectures. Cultivating and improving your active listening skills will help you to understand the lecture material, take accurate notes, participate in class discussions, and communicate with your peers.

College classes demand active critical listening skills.

The Difference Between Listening and Hearing

We usually do not think much about listening until a misunderstanding occurs. You've no doubt been misunderstood or misunderstood someone yourself. Misunderstandings arise because we tend to view listening as an automatic response when it is instead a learned, voluntary activity, like driving a car, painting a picture, or playing the piano. Having ears does not make you a good listener.

After all, having hands does not mean you are capable of painting the Mona Lisa. You may be able to paint the Mona Lisa, but only with practice and guidance. Listening, too, takes practice and guidance. Becoming an active listener requires practice, time, mistakes, guidance, and active participation.

Hearing, however, is not learned; it is automatic and involuntary. If you are within range of a sound you will probably hear it although you may not be listening to it. Hearing a sound does not guarantee that you know what it is or what made it. Listening actively, though, means making a conscious effort to focus on the sound and to determine what it is.

Objective listening can be a difficult skill to learn. Have you encountered people with radically different views than your own? How did you respond?

ROAR

Listening is a four-step cycle, represented by the mnemonic **ROAR** (see Figure 7.1).

FIGURE 7.1 *ROAR.*

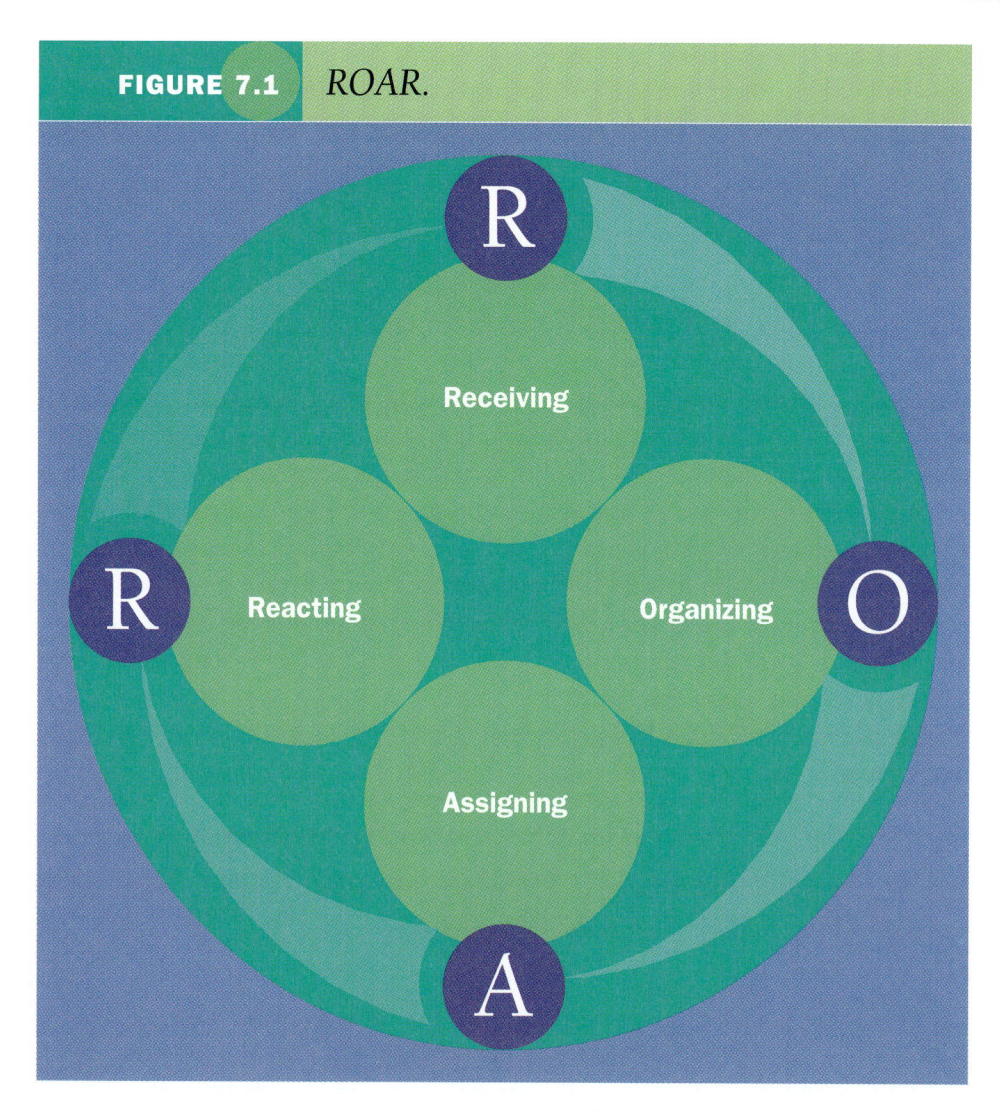

R—Receiving the information
O—Organizing the sounds heard and focusing on them
A—Assigning meaning
R—Reacting

Receiving. Receiving means that you were within the range of the sound when it was made. Receiving a sound is not the same as listening. To become an active listener, when receiving information make an effort to:

1. Tune out distractions other than the conversation at hand.
2. Avoid interrupting the speaker.
3. Pay close attention to nonverbal communication, such as gestures, facial expressions, and movements.
4. Concentrate on what is being said at the moment, not on what will be said next.
5. Listen for what is not said. Are important facts omitted?

Organizing. Organizing and focusing means choosing to listen actively to the sound, to pay attention to its origin, direction, and intention. To become an active listener, when organizing and focusing on information make an effort to:

1. Sit up straight or stand near the person speaking, so that you involve your entire body.
2. Make eye contact with the speaker; listen with your eyes and ears.
3. Try to create a visual picture of what is being said.

Assigning. Assigning refers to mentally assigning a name or meaning to what you have been listening to. Sometimes, you may have to pay special attention to sounds in order to assign the correct name or meaning to them. Have you ever been sitting inside and heard a crash? You might have had to hear it again before you could identify the sound as dishes falling, books dropping, or cars colliding. Your brain tries to create a relationship between what you hear and what you have heard before; it tries to associate one piece of information with another. Once the association is made, you will be able to identify the new sound by remembering the old sound.

To become an active listener, when assigning meaning to information make an effort to:

1. Relate the information to something that you already know.
2. Ask questions to ensure that there are no misunderstandings.
3. Identify the main ideas of what is being said.
4. Try to summarize the information into small "files" in your memory.
5. Repeat the information to yourself (or out loud if appropriate).

When you are actively listening in class, you will be able to relate new information to information you have heard previously. For instance, if you hear about *Oedipus Rex* in theater class, you might immediately relate it to the Oedipus complex you learned about in psychology class. If you hear about Einstein in history, you will probably make the connection from science. Active listening allows you to make associations that help create learning patterns for your long-term memory. Simply hearing information does not allow you to make these associations.

Reacting. Reacting is nothing more than making a response to the sound you hear. If you hear a crash, you might jump; if you hear a baby cry, you might pick the baby up; if you hear a voice, you might turn to see who is speaking. Reacting can be a barrier to active listening. Tuning out because you are bored or do not agree with the speaker's point of view is a way of reacting to information.

To become an active listener, when reacting to information make an effort to:

1. Leave your emotions behind; do not prejudge.
2. Avoid overreacting.
3. Avoid jumping to conclusions.
4. Ask yourself, "How can this information help me?"

FIGURE 7.2 *The Chinese pictograph for "listen."*

聽

- Ear
- Eyes
- Undivided attention
- Heart

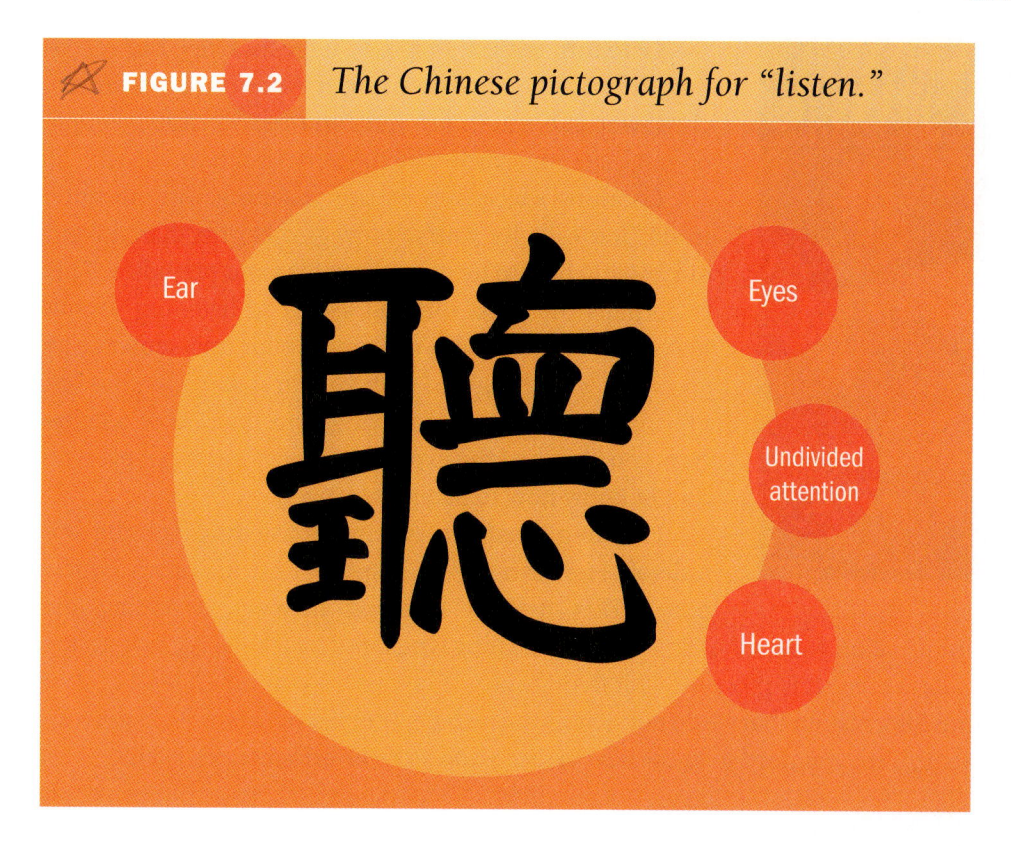

LISTENING DEFINED

According to Ronald Adler (Adler, Rosenfeld, and Towne, 2001), the drawing of the Chinese verb "to listen" (see Figure 7.2) provides a comprehensive and practical definition of listening. To the Chinese, listening involves the ears, the eyes, undivided attention, and the heart. Do you make it a habit to listen with more than your ears? The Chinese view listening as a whole-body experience. People from Western cultures seem to have lost the ability to involve their whole body in the listening process. We tend to use only our ears, and sometimes we don't even use them—remember LaTonya at the beginning of the chapter.

At its core, listening is "the ability to hear, understand, analyze, respect, and appropriately respond to the meaning of another person's spoken and nonverbal messages" (Daly and Engleberg, 2002). Although this definition involves the word "hear," listening goes far beyond just the physical ability to catch sound waves.

The first step in listening *is* hearing, but true listening involves one's full attention and the ability to filter out distractions, emotional barriers, cultural differences, and religious biases. Listening means that you are making a conscious decision to understand and show reverence for the other person's communication efforts.

Listening needs to be personalized and internalized. To understand listening as a whole-body experience, we can define it on three levels:

1. Listening with a purpose
2. Listening objectively
3. Listening constructively

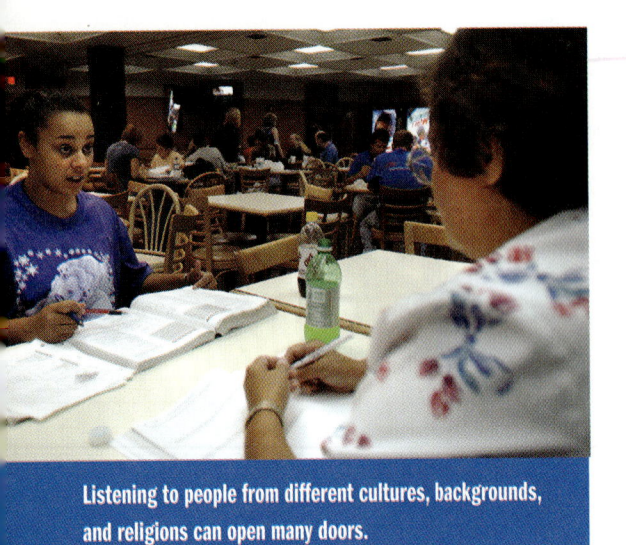

Listening to people from different cultures, backgrounds, and religions can open many doors.

Listening with a purpose suggests a need to recognize different types of listening situations—for example, class, worship, entertainment, and relationships. People do not listen the same way in every situation.

Listening objectively means listening with an open mind. You will give yourself few greater gifts than the gift of knowing how to listen without bias and prejudice. This is perhaps the most difficult aspect of listening. If you have been cut off in mid-conversation or mid-sentence by someone who disagreed with you, or if someone has left the room while you were giving your opinion of a situation, you have had the experience of talking to people who do not know how to listen objectively.

Listening constructively means listening with the attitude of "How can this be helpful to my life or my education?" This type of listening involves evaluating the information you are hearing and determining whether it has meaning to your life. Sound easy? It is more difficult than it sounds because, again, we all tend to shut out information that we do not view as immediately helpful or useful. To listen constructively, you need to know how to listen and store information for later.

What Did You Say?

OBSTACLES TO LISTENING

Several major obstacles stand in the way of becoming an effective listener. To begin building active listening skills, you first have to remove some barriers.

OBSTACLE ONE: PREJUDGING

Prejudging means that you automatically shut out what is being said; it is one of the biggest obstacles to active listening. You may prejudge because of the content; the person communicating; or your environment, culture, social status, or attitude.

Do You Prejudge Information or Its Source?

Answer yes or no to the following questions:

1. I tune out when something is boring.   YES   NO
2. I tune out when I do not agree with the information.   YES   NO
3. I argue mentally with the speaker about information.   YES   NO
4. I do not listen to people I do not like.   YES   NO
5. I make decisions about information before I understand all of its implications or consequences.   YES   NO

If you answered yes to two or more of these questions, you tend to prejudge in a listening situation.

Tips for Overcoming Prejudging

1. Listen for information that may be valuable to you as a student. Some material may not be pleasant to hear but may be useful to you later on.

2. Listen to the message, not the messenger. If you do not like the speaker, try to go beyond personality and listen to what is being said, without regard to the person saying it. Conversely, you may like the speaker so much that you automatically accept the material or answers without listening objectively to what is being said.

3. Try to remove cultural, racial, gender, social, and environmental barriers. Just because a person is different from you or holds a different point of view does not make that person wrong; and just because a person is like you and holds a similar point of view does not make that person right. Sometimes, you have to cross cultural and environmental barriers to learn new material and see with brighter eyes.

WORLD OF WORK

The ability to listen actively is a critical component to being successful in the world of work. As a cast member with Disneyland Resorts, I spend a great deal of my day listening to guests and other cast members. My capacity to completely focus on what the individual is saying is key to my ability to provide outstanding service to all those I work with. My position requires that I do a significant amount of entertaining, and learning to listen in the various environments in which I work has been quite a challenge. I've had to learn how to really hear what people are saying and then translate it into information that can be disseminated to the individuals who must act on the information.

One of the most important things that I learned in college was the importance of actively listening. I noticed in your textbook that the authors use the Chinese character to describe what active listening really involves. I've found that I must give the individual with whom I am speaking my undivided attention and utilize not only my ears but also my eyes and heart to truly understand what they are saying. College helped me to hone my listening skills, but I must constantly strive to become a better listener.

Another thing that I have come to realize is that listening is critical to my relationships with others. Call it pixie dust, call it magic, or call it a miracle, but your ability to interact and communicate with other people will get you further than almost any other skill that you have. Take every opportunity to learn social skills and graces, learn to communicate with others, and learn the fine art of give and take. Teamwork is the key to success.

Life is about learning, both through higher education and through daily lessons from living. You never know where life is going to lead you. Be open, think beyond the moment, and all your dreams may come true.

QUESTIONS FOR REFLECTION

Consider responding to these questions online in the Questions for Reflection module of the Companion Website.

1. When was there a time in your life when your livelihood depended on your listening abilities like Mrs. Rudisill?

2. Why is listening with the eyes, heart, and undivided attention so important to Mrs. Rudisill's profession?

3. Why does Mrs. Rudisill see teamwork and communication as essential in the workplace?

Maritza E. Rudisill, CMP, Catering and Convention Services Assistant Director, Disneyland Parks and Resorts, Anaheim, CA

OBSTACLE TWO: TALKING

Not even the best listener in the world can listen while he or she is talking. The next time you are in a conversation with a friend, try speaking while your friend is speaking—then see if you know what your friend said. To become an effective listener, you need to learn the power of silence. Silence gives you the opportunity to think about what is being said before you respond.

Are You a Talker Rather than a Listener?

Answer yes or no to the following questions:

1. I often interrupt the speaker so that I can say what I want. YES NO
2. I am thinking of my next statement while others are talking. YES NO
3. My mind wanders when others talk. YES NO
4. I answer my own questions. YES NO
5. I answer questions that are asked of other people. YES NO

If you answered yes to two or more questions, you tend to talk too much in a listening situation.

Tips for Overcoming the Urge to Talk Too Much

1. Force yourself to be silent at parties, family gatherings, and friendly get-togethers. We're not saying you should be unsociable, but force yourself to be silent for 10 minutes. You'll be surprised at what you hear. You may also be surprised how hard it is to do this. Test yourself.
2. Ask someone a question and then allow that person to answer the question.

Too often we ask questions and answer them ourselves. Force yourself to wait until the person has formulated a response. If you ask questions and wait for answers, you will force yourself to listen.

OBSTACLE THREE: BRINGING YOUR EMOTIONS TO THE TABLE

Emotions can form a strong barrier to active listening. Worries, problems, fears, and anger can keep you from listening to the greatest advantage. Have you ever sat in a lecture, and before you knew what was happening your mind was a million miles away because you were angry or worried about something, like LaTonya in the opening story? If you have, you know what it's like to bring your emotions to the table.

Do You Bring Your Emotions to the Listening Situation?

Answer yes or no to the following questions:

1. I get angry before I hear the whole story.   YES NO
2. I look for underlying or hidden messages in information.   YES NO
3. Sometimes, I begin listening on a negative note.   YES NO
4. I base my opinions of information on what others are saying or doing.   YES NO
5. I readily accept information as correct from people whom I like or respect.   YES NO

If you answered yes to two or more of these questions, you tend to bring your emotions to a listening situation.

Tips for Overcoming Emotions

1. Know how you feel before you begin the listening experience. Take stock of your emotions and feelings ahead of time.
2. Focus on the message; determine how to use the information.
3. Create a positive image about the message you are hearing.

Listening for Key Words, Phrases, and Hints

Learning how to listen for key words, phrases, and hints can help you become an active listener and an effective note taker. For example, if your English professor begins a lecture saying, "There are ten basic elements to writing poetry," jot down the number 10 under the heading "Poetry" or number your notebook page 1 through 10, leaving space for notes. If at the end of class you listed six elements to writing poetry, you know that you missed a part of the lecture. At this point, you need to ask the professor some questions.

Here are some key phrases and words to listen for:

- in addition
- most important
- you'll see this again
- for example
- in contrast
- the characteristics of
- on the other hand
- another way
- such as
- therefore
- to illustrate
- in comparison
- the main issue is
- as a result of
- above all
- specifically
- finally
- as stated earlier
- nevertheless
- moreover
- because

Picking up on transition words will help you filter out less important information and thus listen more carefully to what is most important. There are other indicators of important information, too. You will want to listen carefully when the professor:

Writes something on the board

Uses an overhead

Uses computer-aided graphics

Speaks in a louder tone or changes vocal patterns

Uses gestures more than usual

Draws on a flip chart

Once you have learned how to listen actively, you will reap several key benefits as a student, as an employee, and as a citizen.

Listening When English Is Your Second Language

SUGGESTIONS FOR ESL STUDENTS

For students whose first language is not English, the college classroom can present some uniquely challenging situations. One of the most pressing and important challenges is the ability to listen, translate, understand, and capture the message on paper in a quick and continuous manner. According to Lynn Forkos, Professor and Coordinator of the Conversation Center for International Students at the Community College of Southern Nevada, the following tips can be beneficial:

- Don't be afraid to **stop the professor** to ask for clarification. Asking questions allows you to take an active part in the listening process. If the professor doesn't answer your questions sufficiently, be certain to make an appointment to speak with him or her during his or her office hours.
- If you are in a situation where the professor can't stop or you're watching a movie or video in class, listen for words that you do understand and try to **figure out unfamiliar words in the context** of the sentence.
- **Enhance your vocabulary** by watching and listening to TV programs such as *Dateline, 20/20, Primetime Live, 60 Minutes,* and the evening news. You might also try listening to radio stations such as National Public Radio as you walk or drive.
- Be certain that you **write down everything** that the professor puts on the board, overhead, or PowerPoint. You may not need every piece of this information, but this technique gives you (and hopefully your study group) the ability to sift through the information outside of class. It give you a visual history of what the professor said.

- Finally, if there is a conversation group or club that meets on campus, take the opportunity to join. **By practicing language**, you become more attuned to common words and phrases. If a conversation group is not available, consider starting one of your own.

How Do I Get Others to Listen to Me?

TIPS FOR CREATIVE COMMUNICATING

As a college student, an employee, community leader, spouse, or caregiver, there will be times when you want people to listen to your views and opinions. There will be times when you want to speak out at a club meeting, a civic group meeting, or the PTA, and you want people to hear what you are saying. Below, you will find several tips that you can use to help other people listen to you.

Repetition. Make an effort to state your main ideas or points more than once when you're speaking. We need to hear things as many as 14 times to have them placed in our long-term memory. Repetition helps.

Movement. When you are speaking, use some degree of movement with your body, such as gestures and facial expressions. If you are standing in front of a group of people, you might want to move from one side of the room to the other. However, it is important to remember not to pace restlessly.

Energy. When you are speaking and trying to get others to listen to you, be energetic and lively with your words. It is hard to listen to someone who speaks in the same tone all the time. Be excited about what you are saying and people will listen to you more attentively. This is perhaps the single most important way to get people to listen to your views.

Creativity. This simply means that you need to have something to say when you are speaking, and you need to say it in a way that is creative, fresh, and new. You know how hard it is to listen to people who never actually say anything. They talk all the time, but seldom say anything important. When you speak, make sure that you are making a contribution to the topic.

STRATEGIES FOR BUILDING ON YOUR BEST

Consider the following strategies for improving listening in the classroom:

- Sit near the front of the room.
- Establish eye contact with the professor.
- Read the text or handout beforehand. Listening is aided greatly when you have advance knowledge of the subject.
- Memorize the *key words* listed previously to help you identify when important information is coming.
- Don't give up—even if the information is difficult and the professor is hard to understand.
- Enter class with a mind-set of learning. Remember, listening purposefully requires that you know the type of listening situation in which you will be involved and then prepare for that situation.

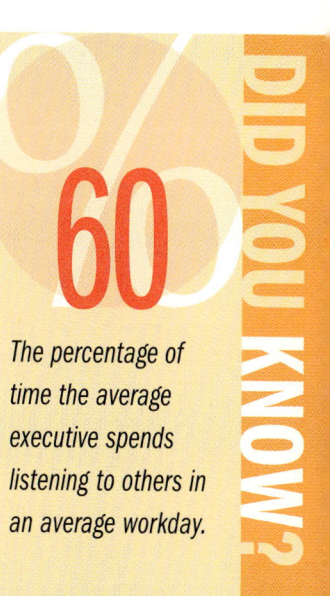

DID YOU KNOW?

60%

The percentage of time the average executive spends listening to others in an average workday.

Source: Daly, J., and Engleberg, I. *Presentations in Everyday Life: Strategies for Effective Speaking.* Boston: Houghton Mifflin, 2002.

Clarity. When making a point, try to arrange your thoughts and statements in a logical, reasonable fashion. It is much easier for people to listen to a clear message than one that is jumbled and disorganized.

Credibility. Few things are more important when trying to get others to listen to you than your past record of accuracy. Avoid fabricating or embellishing the truth. Know the facts before you speak. Your opinion is great, but when conversing with friends or speaking to a group, you should let people know whether you are speaking from opinion or fact.

Cultural thoughtfulness. The great thing about America is that you can say what you want to say. Freedom of speech is one of our Constitutional rights. However, one should also realize that for every statement made, consequences follow. When speaking to peers, colleagues, or members of a group, show respect for your audience. This does not mean that you have to agree or that you can't have controversial opinions. It is to say, however, that the quickest way to turn others off is to be rude, insensitive to differences, and arrogant in a belief that your own opinions are the only ones that matter. Think before you speak and others will listen actively.

In many situations, like cooperative learning teams, other people rely on your information to be accurate, timely, and useful.

Top 10 Reasons for Listening Actively

1. You will be exposed to more information and knowledge about the world, your peers, and yourself.
2. You will be able to help others if you listen to their problems and fears, and you will gain a greater sense of empathy.
3. You will avoid problems at school or work that result from not listening.
4. You will be able to participate in life more fully because you will have a keener sense of what is going on in the world around you.
5. You will gain friends and healthy relationships because people are drawn to those to whom they can talk and who they feel listen sincerely.
6. You will be able to ask more questions and to gain a deeper understanding about subjects that interest you or ideas you wish to explore.
7. You will be a more effective leader. People follow people who they feel listen to their ideas and give their views a chance.
8. You will be able to understand more about different cultures from around the world.
9. You will be able to make more logical decisions regarding pressing and difficult issues in your life and studies.
10. You will feel better about yourself because you will know in your heart and mind that you gave the situation your best.

BLUEPRINTS FOR CHANGE

NAME

DATE

REFLECTION

Yes, listening is a learned skill, but it is more than that. It is a gift that you give to yourself. It is a gift that promotes knowledge, understanding, stronger relationships, and open-mindedness. It is a gift that, when properly used, can help you personally and professionally throughout your life.

Listening is more than a physical skill possessed by many people—it is an attribute of the heart. Good listening skills can help you manage conflict, avoid misunderstandings, and establish trusting relationships. Perhaps most importantly at this point in your life, listening can help you become a more successful student. Once you learn how to listen with your whole body and mind, you will begin to see how your grades, your attitude, your relationships, and the world around you changes.

GET REAL

Below are a few questions to help you think about listening in college and in life. Study each question carefully and respond.

Before answering any of the questions, select a song from your *least* favorite genre. If you love rock, you might choose rap. If you love rap, you might choose country/western. Listen to that song at least three times, then answer the following questions.

What is the song's title and the genre?

What emotional response did you have to the music the first time you heard it? Why?

Did your feelings change the more times you heard the song? Why or why not?

What was the artist's message in the song?

While listening to the music, did your level of appreciation increase or decrease as a result? Why or why not?

Without re-listening to the song, list at least five facts, statements, comments, or quotes from the song.

Case Study

NAME: Melpo Kardon
SCHOOL: Central Missouri State University, Warrensburg, MO
MAJOR: Commercial Art   **AGE:** 20

Below is a real-life situation faced by Melpo. Read the brief case and respond to the questions.

Listening is not an easy task. It is especially hard to listen to boring information or things that we don't consider important to us. It is also quite difficult to listen to people with whom we don't agree or messages that go against our own beliefs.

Over the years, I have watched some of my classmates become very angry and offended by topics, questions, and suggestions that were not in line with their learned and traditional beliefs. Discussions about religion, politics, and ethics seemed to be especially frustrating for many classmates from more rural areas of the country. I even found myself troubled by some of the views of my professors and peers and had to struggle with my own listening abilities. I was surprised to find that, at times, I was closed-minded too.

If education has taught me one thing, it is this—open-mindedness is as important as any trait we'll ever learn. Without the ability to listen with an open mind, we stop growing. I find it interesting that, as I sat in classes with professors who lectured on topics that were controversial or troubling, there have been times, through active listening, I actually discovered another side or point I would have never considered. This led me to change my way of thinking on several issues.

Without active listening, this growth would never have come to me, and I would have suffered because of it.

Why is it important to your education to listen to varying viewpoints?

_____
_____
_____
_____

Why do you think it is difficult for people, like some of Melpo's classmates, to accept views or opinions counter to their own?

_____
_____
_____
_____

Who is the hardest person to whom you have ever had to listen? Why?

_____
_____
_____

How can listening help your study skills (such as note taking and test taking)?

_____
_____
_____

How can listening help your personal relationships?

_____
_____
_____

How can listening help you at work and with your colleagues?

_____
_____
_____

How can you begin to control your emotions when someone voices an opinion that is vastly different from your own?

_____
_____
_____

at this moment Journal

Refer to page 205 of this chapter. Having read and reflected upon the information in the chapter, consider how you might revise your goal to make it more:

REASONABLE

BELIEVABLE

MEASURABLE

ADAPTABLE

CONTROLLABLE

DESIRABLE

ONLINE JOURNAL

To complete an online journal entry, log onto the Companion Website at www.prenhall.com/sherfield. Go to Chapter 7 and click on the link to the Online Journal. You can respond to the questions provided or to questions assigned by your professor, or you may journal about your own experiences.

ADVICE TO GO
CORNERSTONES
for listening

Evaluate the *content*, not the delivery.

Leave your emotions at the door.

Listening requires an *open mind*.

Listen for *how* something is said.

Listen to the *whole* story.

Eliminate *distractions*.

Listen for what is *not* said.

Listening is *voluntary*.

Listen for *major* ideas.

Listen for *key* words.

Stop talking.

LISTEN

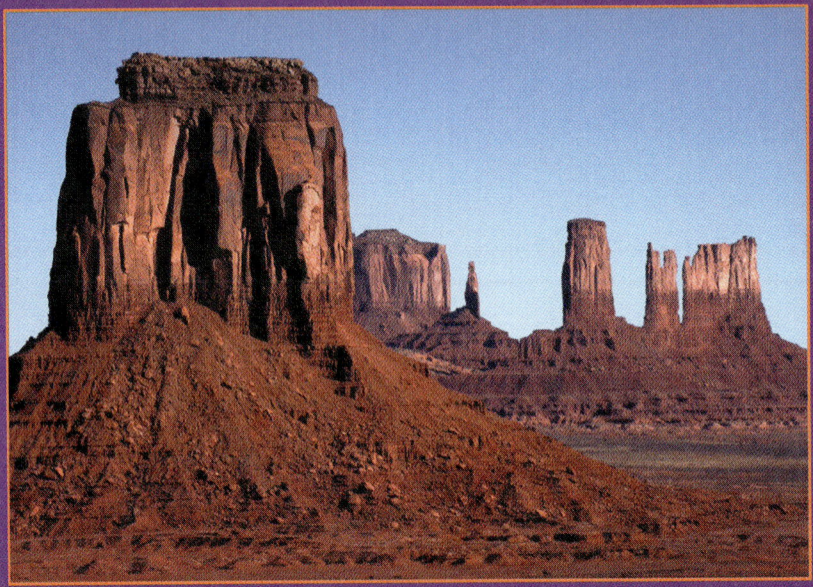

8 Record

Whoso neglects learning in youth, loses the past and is dead for the future.

Euripides

CHAPTER 8
RECORD

William loved to play pool. *Pool was his passion,* his hobby, his job, and his *first* love. *Few things ever got in the way of William's pool game.* On more than one occasion, *William cut class to go to the pool hall* with his buddies. "I'll just get the notes from Wanda," he would say. "She's always in class."

When class met on Monday morning, *William asked Wanda for her notes.* She told him that her handwriting was not very good and that *she took notes in her own shorthand.* "Oh, that's all right," William said. "I'll be able to get what I need from them." *Wanda agreed to make a copy of her notes* and to bring them to William on Wednesday.

> On more than one occasion, William cut class to go to the pool hall with his buddies.

Wanda kept her promise and brought a copy of her notes. William put them into his backpack just before class began. The notes stayed in his backpack until the night before the midterm exam. He had not taken them out to look at them or to ask Wanda any questions about them. When he unfolded the notes, *he was shocked at what he found.*

The notes read:

Psy started as a sci. disc. from Phi and Physio. Wihelm Wundt/GERM and Will James/US= fndrs. in lt. 19th cent.
APA est. by Stanely Hall in US.
5 mjr Pers in PSY=
    Biopsy. Per
    Psychodym. Per
    Humanistic. Per
    Cog. Per.
    Beh. Per.
Psy wk in 2 mjr. areas:
1. Acad.
2. Practicing

The only place success comes before work is in the dictionary. —DONALD KENDALL

Note-Taking Systems that Work

William was in trouble. He could not understand Wanda's shorthand, and it was too late to ask her to translate her notes. To add insult to injury, he had lost his textbook a few weeks earlier. After trying unsuccessfully to make sense of the notes, he gave up and went to the pool hall to relax and have fun before the test.

The following day, William failed his midterm. Not long after that, he quit the class, having wasted his time and money.

QUESTIONS FOR REFLECTION

Consider responding to these questions online in the Questions for Reflection module of the Companion Website.

1. When you miss a class, how do you go about getting the notes and materials from that class? Has this action helped you in the past? Why or why not?

2. How can translating your notes soon after the class has ended help you retain information?

3. How can shorthand help you and hurt you in the note-taking process?

Where are you... AT THIS MOMENT

Before reading this chapter, take a moment and respond to the following 10 questions. Consider each one carefully before answering, and then respond by circling the number in the appropriate box. When you have answered the questions, add your points and find your total score on the feedback chart below.

STATEMENT	STRONGLY DISAGREE	DISAGREE	DON'T KNOW	AGREE	STRONGLY AGREE	SCORE
1. I find it difficult to take notes and listen to my teacher at the same time.	5	4	3	2	1	
2. I usually bring my textbook with me to class.	1	2	3	4	5	
3. I can tell when what I'm seeing or hearing is important to include when taking notes.	1	2	3	4	5	
4. Rewriting and adding to my notes is something that I never do.	5	4	3	2	1	
5. When I review my notes, I'm often unsure about the meaning of what I've written.	5	4	3	2	1	
6. I keep notes from different classes together in the same notebook.	5	4	3	2	1	
7. When I get lost or behind in taking notes, I ask the teacher to repeat what I've missed.	1	2	3	4	5	
8. I make it a habit to connect with another student to compare notes, or to get notes that I've missed.	1	2	3	4	5	
9. I find that I try to write down too much or too little in my notes.	5	4	3	2	1	
10. I know how to use abbreviations and symbols when taking notes.	1	2	3	4	5	
TOTAL VALUE						

SUMMARY

10–17 Your note-taking skills are limited. You can't determine what to write down or how to effectively write it. Further, the notes you do take are likely useless to you as a learning tool. You must develop strategies and techniques to get better at this to be a successful student.

18–25 You have below average note-taking skills. You need to learn how to figure out what to write down and how to get it written efficiently. You would also benefit from networking with classmates who are good note takers to compare and improve your own notes.

26–34 You are average in your note-taking skills. You manage to get the important information written down in a format that you can later understand. You would likely benefit from using your notes as a study tool by rewriting, expanding, and reorganizing them between classes.

35–42 You are above average in your note-taking skills. Your notes are likely complete and a beneficial aid in studying. You probably spend time reviewing and improving your notes outside of class and know how to get ideas down on paper in an efficient manner.

43–50 You are exceptional in your note-taking skills. You likely possess a well-developed system for taking notes, including the use of symbols and abbreviations. You spend time reviewing your notes, and probably incorporate lecture notes with textbook and other materials.

Goals... FOR CHANGE

Based on your total points, what is one goal you would like to achieve related to note taking?

Goal _____
_____

List three actions you can take that might help you move closer to realizing this goal.

1. _____
2. _____
3. _____

Questions FOR BUILDING ON YOUR BEST

As you read this chapter, consider the following questions. At the end of the chapter, you should be able to answer all of them. You are encouraged to ask a few questions of your own. Consider asking your classmates or professors to assist you.

1. Why is it important to know and use several note-taking systems?
2. How can the L-STAR system help me take better notes?
3. Which class is best suited for the Cornell Note-Taking System?
4. Why is it best to use a 3-hole notebook for note taking?
5. Does rewriting my notes over at the end of class really help?

What additional questions might you have about note taking in and out of class?

1. _____
2. _____
3. _____

Good note-taking skills help you do more than simply record what you're taught in class or read in a book so that you can recall it. These skills can also help to reinforce that information so that you actually know it.

Why Take Notes?

Sometimes it all seems like a big, crazy chore, doesn't it? Go to class, listen, and write it down. Is note taking really important? Actually, knowing how to take useful, accurate notes can dramatically improve your life as a student. If you are an effective listener and note taker, you have two of the most valuable skills any student could ever use. There are several reasons why it is important to take notes:

- You become an active part of the listening process.
- You create a history of your course content when you take notes.
- You have written criteria to follow when studying.
- You create a visual aid for your material.
- Studying becomes much easier.

Writing It Right
TIPS FOR EFFECTIVE NOTE TAKING

You have already learned several skills you will need to take notes: *First,* you need to cultivate and build your active listening skills. *Second,* you need to overcome obstacles to effective listening, such as prejudging, talking during a discussion, and bringing emotions to the table. *Third,* you should be familiar with key phrases used by professors. *Fourth,* you need to understand the importance of note taking. *Fifth,* you need to prepare yourself to take effective notes. *Finally,* you must scan, read, and use your textbook to understand the materials presented. Following are a few more important tips for taking notes.

- **Attend class.** This may sound like stating the obvious, but it is surprising how many college students feel they do not need to go to class. "Oh, I'll just get the notes from Wanda," said William in the opening story. The only trouble with getting the notes from Wanda is that they are Wanda's notes. You may be able to copy her words, but you may very well miss the meaning behind them. If she has developed her own note-taking style, you may not be able to read many of her notes. She may have written something like this:

G/Oke lvd in C/SC for 1 yr ely 20c.

Can you decode this? How would you ever know that these notes mean "Georgia O'Keeffe lived in Columbia, South Carolina, for one year in the early part of the twentieth century"? To be an effective note taker, class attendance is crucial; there is no substitute for it.

- **Come to class prepared.** Do you read your assignments nightly? College professors are amazed at the number of students who come to class and

WORLD OF WORK

Good written communication skills are necessary for success in any business organization. Good note-taking skills lay the groundwork for effective written communication skills. Your college experiences will help you develop the ability to be a good listener and to take good notes.

As a college student, you are required to attend classes, listen intently, organize lecture materials, and convert that information into meaningful text for future use. Tomorrow, as a professional in your chosen field, you will be asked to attend meetings, seminars, and conferences; listen intently and analyze the information being disseminated; and then write reports for your organization. Throughout my career as a technical support/training professional, I was called upon to attend meetings with client/user groups, vendors, suppliers, and coworkers and to report to management the outcome of these meetings. The note-taking skills I developed in college enabled me to listen effectively, discern which information is most important, and convert my notes into meaningful reports and summaries.

Today, I am a university instructor and I'm still using the listening and writing skills I developed in college. Not only must I take accurate notes at faculty and committee meetings, but also I must take good notes when listening to students' reports and presentations to fairly assess their progress and learning. I must often meet with community and business leaders concerning various aspects of the Administrative Information Management program at USC and must keep track of who is willing to participate in which program, who will be speaking on which date, etc. This is achieved by taking good notes.

QUESTIONS FOR REFLECTION

Consider responding to these questions online in the World of Work module of the Companion Website.

1. How did Professor Tate's college note-taking skills help her in her chosen field?
2. How can learning to listen and take good notes help you in your chosen field?
3. Has a lack of note-taking skills ever caused you problems in your classes or at work? Why?

Garcia Mills Tate, Professor, College of Hospitality, Retail, Sport Management, The University of South Carolina, Columbia, SC

---

then decide they should have read their homework. Doing your homework—reading your text, handouts, or workbooks or listening to tapes—is one of the most effective ways to become a better note taker. It is always easier to take notes when you have a preliminary understanding of what is being said. As a student, you will find fewer tasks more difficult than trying to take notes on material that you have never seen or heard before. Coming to class prepared means doing your homework and coming to class ready to listen.

Coming to class prepared also means bringing the proper materials for taking notes: your textbook or lab manual, at least two pens, enough sharpened pencils to make it through the lecture, a notebook, and a highlighter. Some students also use a tape recorder. If you choose to use a tape recorder, be sure to get permission from the instructor before recording.

- **Bring your textbook to class.** Although many students think they do not need to bring their textbook to class if they have read the homework, you will find that many professors repeatedly refer to the text while lecturing. Always bring your textbook to class with you. The professor may ask you to highlight, underline, or refer to the text in class, and following along in the text as the professor lectures may also help you organize your notes.

- **Ask questions and participate in class.** Two of the most critical actions you can perform in class are to ask questions and to participate in the class discussion. If you do not understand a concept or theory, ask questions. Don't leave class without understanding what has happened and assume you'll pick it up on your own. Many professors use students' questions as a way of teaching and reviewing materials. Your questions and participation will definitely help you, but they could also help others who did not understand something!

You'll Be Seeing Stars
THE L–STAR SYSTEM

One of the most effective ways to take notes begins with the **L-STAR** system.

- **L** Listening
- **S** Setting It Down
- **T** Translating
- **A** Analyzing
- **R** Remembering

This five-step program will enable you to compile complete, accurate, and visual notes for future reference. Along with improving your note-taking skills, using this system will enhance your ability to participate in class, help other students, study more effectively, and perform well on exams and quizzes.

L—LISTENING

One of the best ways to become an effective note taker is to become an active listener. A concrete step you can take toward becoming an active listener in class is to sit near the front of the room where you can hear the professor and see the board and overheads. Choose a spot that allows you to see the professor's mouth and facial expressions. If you see that the professor's face has become animated or expressive, you can bet that you are hearing important information. Write it down. If you sit in the back of the room, you may miss out on these important clues. Listening was discussed in Chapter 7.

S—SETTING IT DOWN

The actual writing of notes can be a difficult task. Some professors are organized in their delivery of information; others are not. Your listening skills, once

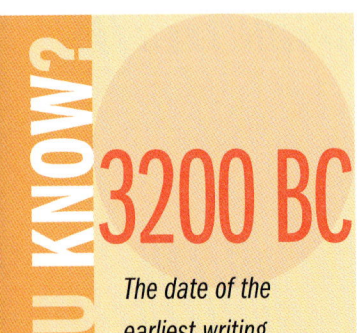

DID YOU KNOW?

3200 BC

The date of the earliest writing system known to man.

Source: Daniels, P., and Bright, W. *The World's Writing Systems.* England: Oxford University Press, 1996.

again, are going to play an important role in determining what needs to be written down. In most cases, you will not have time to take notes verbatim. You will have to be selective about the information you choose to set down. One of the best ways to keep up with the information being presented is to develop a shorthand system of your own. Many of the symbols you use will be universal, but you may use some symbols, pictures, and markings that are uniquely your own. Some of the more common symbols are:

w/	with	w/o	without
=	equals	≠	does not equal
<	less than	>	greater than
%	percentage	#	number
&	and	^	increase
+	plus or addition	−	minus or subtraction
*	important	etc	and so on
eg	for example	vs	against
esp	especially	"	quote
?	question	...	and so on

These symbols can save you valuable time when taking notes. Because you will use them frequently, it might be a good idea to memorize them. As you become more adept at note taking, you will quickly learn how to abbreviate words, phrases, and names.

Using the symbols listed and your own shorthand system, practice reducing the following statements. Be sure that you do not reduce them so much that you will be unable to understand them later.

1. *It is important to remember that a greater percentage of money invested does not necessarily equal greater profits.*

Reduce:

_____

_____

_____

2. *She was quoted as saying, "Money equals success." Without exception, the audience disagreed with her logic.*

Reduce:

_____

_____

_____

T—TRANSLATING

One of the most valuable activities you can undertake as a student is to translate your notes immediately after each class. Doing so can save you hours of work when you begin to prepare for exams. Many students feel that this step is not important, or too time-consuming, and leave it out. Don't. Often, students take notes so quickly that they make mistakes or use abbreviations that they may not be able to decipher later. This was a major problem for William in the opening story. He was working from untranslated notes.

After each class, go to the library or some other quiet place and review your notes. You don't have to do this immediately after class, but before the end of the day, you will need to rewrite and translate your classroom notes. This process gives you the opportunity to put the notes in your own words and to incorporate your text notes into your classroom notes. You can correct spelling, reword key phrases, write out abbreviations, and prepare questions for the next class. Sounds like a lot of work, doesn't it? It is a great deal of work, but if you try this technique for one week, you should see a vast improvement in your comprehension of material. Eventually, you should see an improvement in your grades.

Translating your notes helps you to make connections among previous material discussed, your own personal experiences, readings, and new material presented. Translating aids in recalling and applying new information. Few things are more difficult than trying to reconstruct your notes the night before a test, especially when they were made several weeks earlier. Translating your notes daily will prove a valuable gift to yourself when exam time comes.

A—ANALYZING

This step takes place while you translate your notes from class. When you analyze your notes, you are asking two basic questions: (1) What does this mean? and (2) Why is it important? If you can answer these two questions about your material, you have almost mastered the information. Though some instructors will want you to spit back the exact same information you were given, others will ask you for a more detailed understanding and a synthesis of the material. When you are translating your notes, begin to answer these two questions using your notes, textbook, supplemental materials, and information gathered from outside research. Once again, this process is not simple or quick, but testing your understanding of the material is important. Remember that many lectures are built on past lectures. If you do not understand what happened in class on September 17, you may not be able to understand what happens on September 19. Analyzing your notes while translating them will give you a more complete understanding of the material.

Sometimes two heads are better than one. A note-taking partner can help you translate and analyze your notes after each class.

R—REMEMBERING

Once you have listened to the lecture, set your notes on paper, and translated and analyzed the material, it is time to study, or remember, the information. Some effective ways to remember information include creating a visual picture, speaking the notes out loud, using mnemonic devices, and finding a study partner. Chapter 9 will help you with these techniques and other study aids.

Something for Everyone
THREE COMMON NOTE-TAKING SYSTEMS

There are three common note-taking systems: (1) the outline technique; (2) the Cornell, or split-page technique (also called the T system); and (3) the mapping technique.

> ## STRATEGIES FOR BUILDING ON YOUR BEST
>
> Consider the following strategies for note taking:
> - Always date your notes and use a meaningful heading.
> - Keep notes from each class separate by using dividers or separate notebooks.
> - Use 8 1/2 × 11 inch paper with a 3-hole punch.
> - Copy any information that is written on the board; used on an overhead; or presented in PowerPoint, charts, or graphs.
> - Organize and review your notes the same day you take them.
> - Do not doodle while taking notes.
> - Attach (or store) related handouts to appropriate notes.

It's as Simple as A, B, C—1, 2, 3
THE OUTLINE TECHNIQUE

The outline system uses a series of major headings and multiple subheadings formatted in hierarchical order (see Figure 8.1). The outline technique is one of the most commonly used note-taking systems, yet it is also one of the most misused systems. It can be difficult to outline notes in class, especially if your professor does not follow an outline while lecturing.

When using the outline system, it is best to get all the information from the lecture and afterward to combine your lecture notes and text notes to create an outline. Most professors would advise against using the outline system of note taking in class, although you may be able to use a modified version. The most important thing to remember is not to get bogged down in a system during class; what is critical is getting the ideas down on paper. You can always go back after class and rearrange your notes as needed.

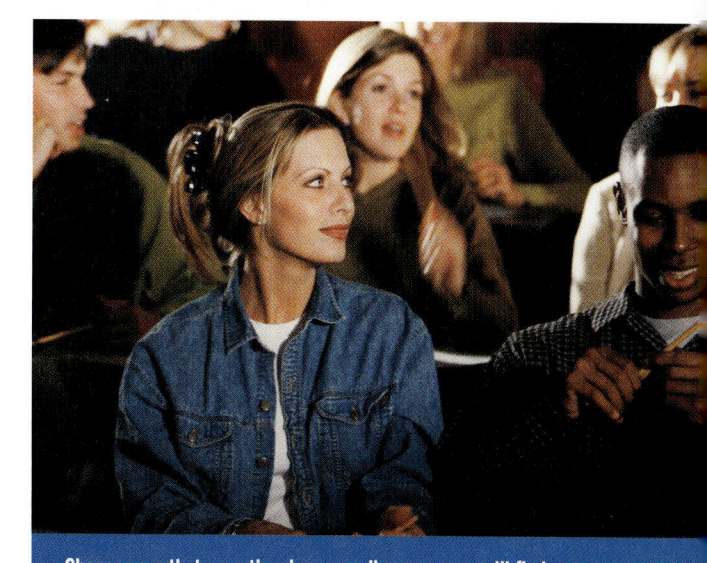

Chances are that sometime in your college career you'll find yourself in a large lecture hall class where it can be difficult to ask questions or seek clarification.

FIGURE 8.1 *The outline technique.*

```
Study Skills 101                                Oct. 17
                                                Wednesday
Topic: Listening
   I. The Process of Listening (ROAR)
       A. R = Receiving
           1. W/in range of sound
           2. Hearing the information
       B. O = Organizing & focusing
           1. Choose to listen actively
           2. Observe the origin, direction & intent
       C. A = Assignment
           1. You assign a meaning
           2. May have to hear it more than once
       D. R = Reacting
           1. Our response to what we heard
           2. Reaction can be anything
   II. Definitions of Listening (POC)
       A. P = Listening w/ a purpose
       B. O = Listening w/ objectivity
       C. C = Listening constructively
```

If you are going to use a modified or informal outline while taking notes in class, you may want to consider grouping information together under a heading as a means of outlining. It is easier to remember information that is logically grouped than to remember information that is scattered across several pages. If your study skills lecture is on listening, you might outline your notes using the headings "The Process of Listening" and "Definitions of Listening."

After you have rewritten your notes using class lecture information and material from your textbook, your notes may look like those in Figure 8.1.

It's a Split Decision

THE CORNELL (MODIFIED CORNELL, SPLIT PAGE, OR T) SYSTEM

The basic principle of the Cornell system, developed by Dr. Walter Pauk of Cornell University, is to split the page into two sections, each section to be used for different information (see Figure 8.2). Section A is used for questions that summarize information found in Section B; Section B is used for the actual notes from class. The blank note-taking page should be divided as shown.

FIGURE 8.2 *A blank Cornell frame.*

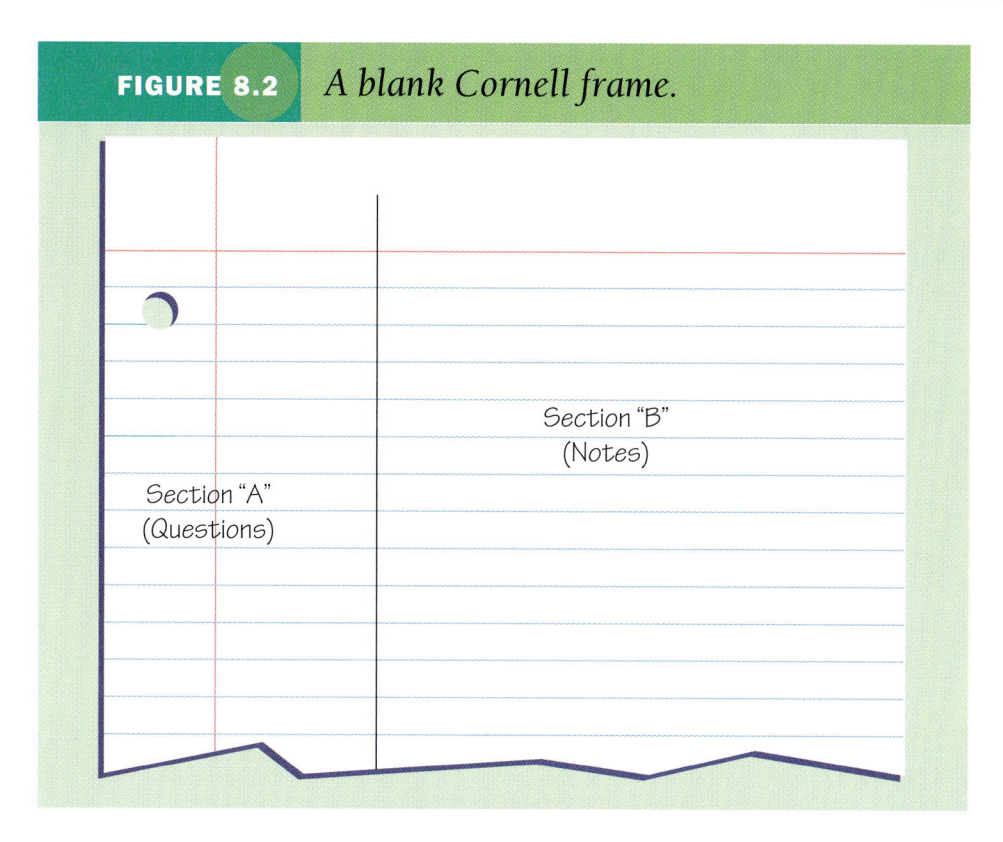

Section "A"
(Questions)

Section "B"
(Notes)

As shown in Figures 8.3 and 8.5, sometimes the basic Cornell layout is modified to include a third section at the bottom of the page for additional or summary comments. In such cases the layout is referred to as a "T system" for its resemblance to an upside-down T. To implement the Cornell system, you will want to choose the technique that is most comfortable and beneficial for you; you might use mapping (discussed below) or outlining on a Cornell page. An example of notes outlined using the Cornell system appears in Figure 8.3.

Going Around in Circles
THE MAPPING SYSTEM

If you are a visual learner, this system may be especially useful for you. The mapping system of note taking generates a picture of information (see Figures 8.4 and 8.5). The mapping system creates a map, or web, of information that allows you to see the relationships among facts or ideas. A mapping system might look something like the notes in Figure 8.4.

The most important thing to remember about each note-taking system is that it must work for you. Do not use a system because your friends use it or because you feel that you should use it. Experiment with each system or combination to determine which is best for you.

Always remember to keep your notes organized, dated, and neat. Notes that cannot be read are no good to you or to anyone else.

FIGURE 8.3 *Outline using a Cornell frame.*

```
Study Skills 101                                    Oct. 19
Topic: Listening                                    Friday
```

What is the listening process? (ROAR)	*The Listening Process (ROAR)
	   A= Receiving
	      1. Within range of sound
	      2. Hearing the information
	   B = Organizing
	      1. Choose to listen actively
	      2. Observe origin

Definition of Listening (POC)	*Listening Defined
	   A. Listening w/ a purpose
	   B. Listening objectively
	   C. Listening constructively

Obstacles (PET)	*What interferes w/ listening
	   A. Prejudging
	   B. Emotions
	   C. Talking

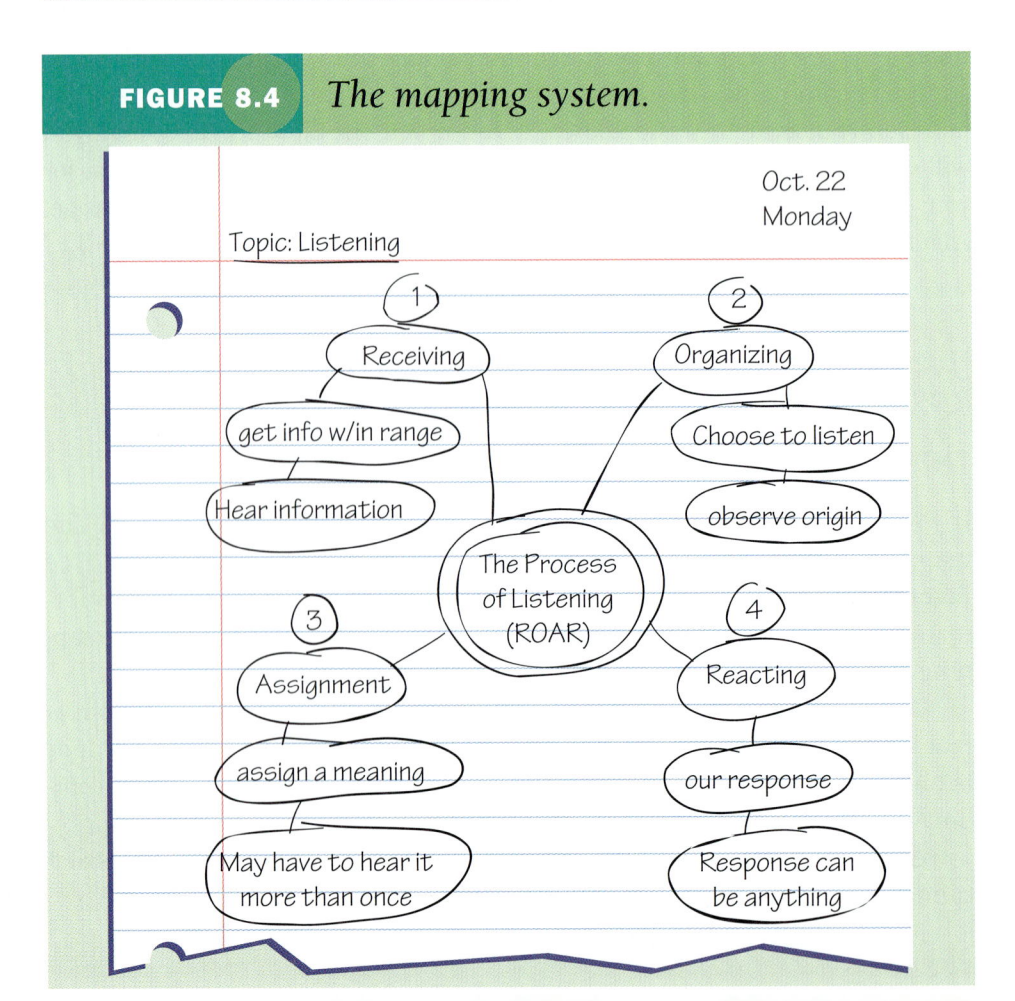

The listening process involves Receiving, Organizing, Assigning & Reacting - Talking, Prejudging & Emotions are obstacles.

FIGURE 8.4 *The mapping system.*

```
Topic: Listening                                    Oct. 22
                                                    Monday
```

①　Receiving
- get info w/in range
- Hear information

②　Organizing
- Choose to listen
- observe origin

The Process of Listening (ROAR)

③　Assignment
- assign a meaning
- May have to hear it more than once

④　Reacting
- our response
- Response can be anything

FIGURE 8.5 *Mapping using a Cornell frame.*

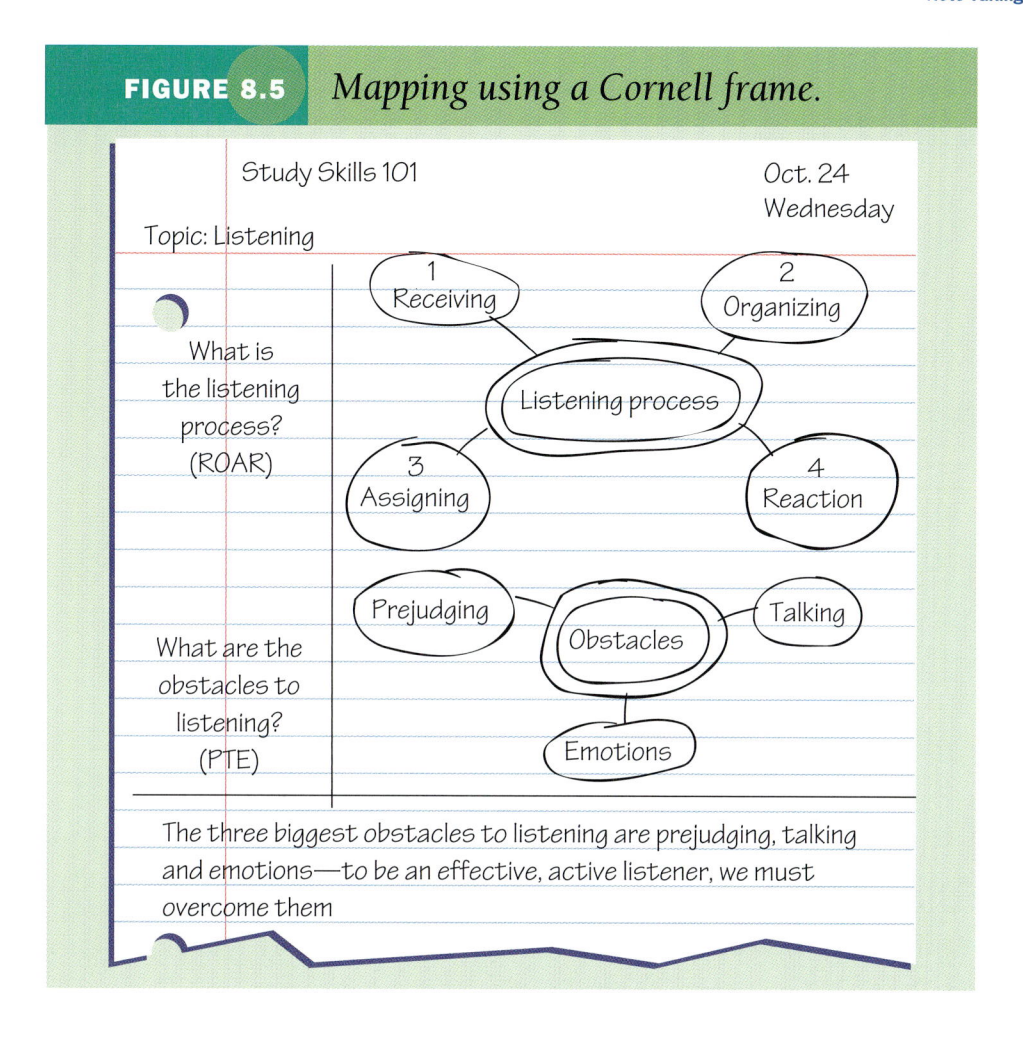

```
Study Skills 101                              Oct. 24
                                              Wednesday
Topic: Listening

                    ( 1 Receiving )      ( 2 Organizing )
What is
the listening            ( Listening process )
process?
(ROAR)              ( 3 Assigning )       ( 4 Reaction )


                    ( Prejudging )          ( Talking )
What are the              ( Obstacles )
obstacles to
listening?
(PTE)                      ( Emotions )

The three biggest obstacles to listening are prejudging, talking
and emotions—to be an effective, active listener, we must
overcome them
```

What to Do When You Get Lost

Have you ever been in a classroom trying to take notes and the professor is speaking so rapidly that you cannot possibly get all of the information? Just when you think you're caught up, you realize that he or she has made an important statement and you missed it. What do you do? How can you handle, or avoid, this difficult note-taking situation? Here are several hints:

- Raise your hand and ask the professor to repeat the information.
- Ask your professor to slow down.
- If he or she will do neither, leave a blank space with a question mark at the side margin (see Figure 8.6). You can get this information after class. This can be a difficult task to master. The key is to focus on the information at hand. Focus on what is being said at the exact moment.
- Meet with your professor immediately after class or at the earliest time convenient for both of you.
- Form a note-taking group that meets after each class. This serves two purposes: (1) you can discuss and review the lecture, and (2) you will be able to get the notes from one of your note-taking buddies.

> **FIGURE 8.6** *What to do when you get lost.*
>
> Public Speaking   Oct. 7
> Lecture: Types of Research for Speeches
>
> | *Periodicals | - Magazines, trade & professional |
> | *Newspapers | Local, state & national (some international as well) |
> | *Reference materials | Specialized... (?) |
> | *Government documents | - Maps, reports, federal proceedings |
>
> } If you missed it, leave it blank

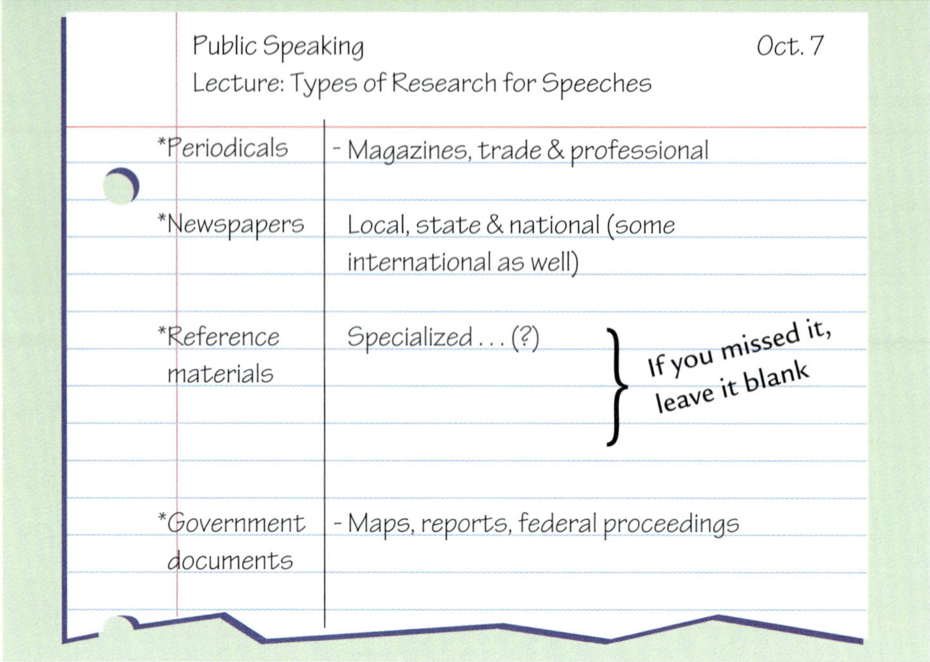

- Never lean over and ask questions of another student during the lecture. This will cause them to lose the information as well.
- Rehearse your note-taking skills at home by taking notes from TV news magazines or channels like the History Channel.
- As a last resort, you can ask the professor's permission to use a tape recorder during the lecture. Do not record a lecture without permission. We suggest that you try to use other avenues, such as the ones listed above, instead of taping your notes. It is a time-consuming task to listen to the lecture for a second time. However, if this system works for you, use it.

Using Your Laptop Computer for Note Taking

In this age of high technology, some students prefer to take notes or transfer their notes onto their computers. Some students bring laptops to class while others immediately type and reorganize their notes after class. If you choose to use a computer for note taking, use the following tips:

IN CLASS
- Come to class early to set up your computer. Don't disturb others by arriving late.

- Try to sit where you can see the professor and overhead, but also be respectful of other students. Tapping on the keyboard can disturb others' concentration.
- Don't worry too much about spelling or grammar. You can run the spelling and grammar checker after class while cleaning up your notes.
- Set your tabs before you begin. You can set them to use an outline format or the Cornell format.

OUT OF CLASS

- If you are going to type your notes into the computer, do so as quickly after class as possible. The information obtained in class needs to be fresh in your mind. Try to reorganize your notes within 24 hours.
- Combine your textbook notes and lecture notes together. This will help you access the big picture of the information.

GENERAL HINTS

- Save your notes on both a disk and your hard drive.
- Always print your notes after each entry. It can be catastrophic if all of your notes are on one disk or one hard drive and the computer crashes or the disk is lost.
- After you have printed your notes, use a 3-hole punch and place your notes in a 3-ring binder. Arrange computer notes with related handouts.

A last note about copying your notes by hand or into a computer: this technique, while valuable to some students, does not constitute studying. Dr. Walter Pauk (2001), creator of the Cornell note-taking system, suggests that "contrary to what most people think, almost no learning takes place during the keyboarding of scribbled notes." Finally, don't be threatened by those who decide to use the computer in class or those who come to class with typewritten, printed notes. *Cornerstone* in general, and this chapter specifically, is about choices. You have to find and use a system that is convenient, easy, and useful to you.

If you remember the concepts of the L-STAR system (listening, setting it down, translating, analyzing, and remembering) and use this system as a study pattern, and if you find a note-taking system that is comfortable and useful for you, then you will begin to see significant improvement in your ability as a note taker and in your performance as a student.

BLUEPRINTS FOR CHANGE

NAME

DATE

REFLECTION

Note taking is a survival skill. There may be classes in which you do not need to take many notes, but those classes will be few. The ability to take notes—and take them quickly, accurately, and effectively—can mean the difference between an "A" and an "F"

Taking notes in a college classroom can be very simple in some classes and nearly impossible in others. Your note-taking ability can be helped or hampered by your shorthand method, the system you use, the professor's speed and willingness to help you along, and your preparation.

Becoming adept at listening and developing your own note-taking system are two of the greatest talents that you can polish when working toward success as a college student. Additionally, being prepared for class by reading the text and reviewing previous notes will help you be mentally ready for new information.

GET REAL

Below are a few questions to help you think about the note-taking process. Study each question carefully and respond accurately.

What role does your ability to listen objectively play in note taking?

How can you practice note-taking skills at home with no professor present?

In which of your current classes would the Cornell note-taking system best be used? Why?

If you have problems taking notes, translating your notes, or understanding which note-taking system to use, where could you go on your campus for assistance?

Phone # _____

Review the notes from your most difficult class. Using those notes, predict at least four essay questions that might appear on your next test.

1. _____
_____
2. _____
_____
3. _____
_____
4. _____
_____

Case Study

NAME: Rebekah Bicknell
SCHOOL: Roane State University, Lenoir City, TN
MAJOR: Marketing/Business   **AGE:** 18

Below is a real-life situation faced by Rebekah. Read the brief case and respond to the questions.

In high school, I was always a great note taker. My listening skills helped me greatly with my note-taking abilities. I learned that if I missed just one thing or changed a few words around, the entire meaning may be altered in the process.

In college, I have found that my biggest problem is that I write down too much. I write almost every word that professors say. It is a gift on one end and a curse on the other. I find myself writing down things that don't really matter—the fluff of the course, as well as things that are very important. Sometimes, I miss the core of what was being said because I'm too busy getting down every word.

This has helped me and hurt me. When studying in a crunch, I have many, many notes to go through and this takes a lot of time. My main points are not pulled out and I can't reference the core quickly. On the other hand, when I have time to study over the course of a few days, I have a great transcript of almost the entire class. If someone has missed a fine point in the lecture, I usually have it.

I'm trying to find the balance between too much and too litte.

What advice would you give Rebekah in finding the balance between too many notes and too few notes?

Could listening for "key words" help Rebekah refine her note-taking skills? Why or why not?

Where could she turn for help if she were a student on your campus?

What note-taking style could Rebekah adopt to help her organize her notes in a more "user-friendly" way? Why?

Based on what you have experienced so far, what advice would you give to a first-year student who is not good at note taking during class?

What advice would you give a first-year student about note-taking while reading a text?

at this moment Journal

Refer to page 227 of this chapter. Having read and reflected upon the information in the chapter, consider how you might revise your goal to make it more:

REASONABLE

BELIEVABLE

MEASURABLE

ADAPTABLE

CONTROLLABLE

DESIRABLE

ONLINE JOURNAL

To complete an online journal entry, log onto the Companion Website at **www.prenhall.com/sherfield.** Go to Chapter 8 and click on the link to the Online Journal. You can respond to the questions provided or to questions assigned by your professor, or you may journal about your own experiences.

ADVICE TO GO

CORNERSTONES

for effective note taking

If it's on the board or on an overhead, *write it down.*

Keep the notes for each course *separate.*

Use *abbreviations* and special notes.

Recopy your notes after each class.

Attend and *participate* in class.

Sit where you can *see* and *hear.*

Develop your listening abilities.

Keep your notes *neat* and clear.

Use loose-leaf paper.

Be *prepared.*

Ask questions.

RECORD

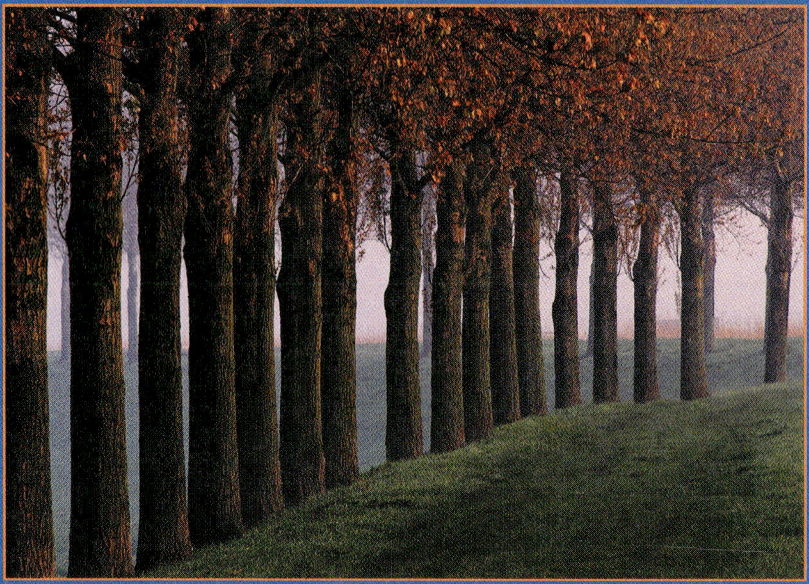

9 Remember

If you have knowledge, let others light their fire by it. — M. Fuller

CHAPTER 9
REMEMBER

Tyrone walked into class beaming. *He was happy, joking, and smiling,* and he spoke to everyone on the way to his seat. He was always a delightful student, *but today he seemed even happier than usual.* Several classmates asked how he could possibly be so up. They could not understand his jovial attitude because *today was test day.* How could he be happy today of all days? *How could anyone be happy on test day?*

Tyrone told his classmates *that he was happy because he was prepared.* "I'm ready for the world," he said. *"I studied all week and I know this stuff."* Most of his classmates ribbed him and laughed. In the final moments before the test began, all the other students were deeply involved in questioning each other and looking over their notes. Tyrone stood by the window finishing his soda until time was called.

After all was said and done, *Tyrone scored the highest on the exam of all his peers—a 98.* Several students asked him how he did so well. Intrigued by their curiosity, I asked Tyrone to share his secret to successful test taking.

Live as if you were to die tomorrow. Learn as if you were to live forever. —M. K. GANDHI

Empowering Your Memory

I found his answer extremely useful, *especially in light of his active life:* Tyrone was on the basketball team, held a part-time job, cared for his elderly grandmother, dated, and worked on the college newspaper.

"You have to do it in steps," Tyrone said. *"You can't wait until the night before, even if you have all evening and night."* He explained that he incorporated study time into his schedule several weeks before the test.

> **How could he be happy today of all days? How could anyone be happy on test day?**

If the test was to cover four chapters, he would review two chapters the first week and two chapters the second week. "I have a study room at the library because my house is so full of people. I make an outline of my notes, review my text, answer sample questions in the book, and many times I find someone to quiz me on the material."

QUESTIONS FOR REFLECTION

Consider responding to these questions online in the Questions for Reflection module of the Companion Website.

1. How do you usually feel on the day of a test? Why?

2. How can studying in chunks of time benefit you?

3. How can developing test questions as you read, then answering them and studying the answers help you learn the material?

Where are you... AT THIS MOMENT

Before reading this chapter, take a moment and respond to the following ten questions. Consider each one carefully before answering, and then respond by circling the number in the appropriate box. When you have answered the questions, add your points and find your total score on the feedback chart below.

STATEMENT	STRONGLY DISAGREE	DISAGREE	DON'T KNOW	AGREE	STRONGLY AGREE	SCORE
1. I know which environments are best for me when I'm studying.	1	2	3	4	5	
2. My mind often wanders when I'm trying to study.	5	4	3	2	1	
3. I often try to visualize or picture what I'm trying to memorize.	1	2	3	4	5	
4. When I study, I try to think of examples to illustrate the material.	1	2	3	4	5	
5. I rarely think about how what I'm studying relates to my world or other information that I know.	5	4	3	2	1	
6. I tend to review information over and over in moderate doses over time rather than "cramming" all at once.	5	4	3	2	1	
7. I usually only go over my study materials once or twice at most.	5	4	3	2	1	
8. I try to approach my study times with a positive, upbeat attitude.	1	2	3	4	5	
9. Memorizing information and understanding it are practically the same thing.	5	4	3	2	1	
10. I use mnemonics or memory tricks and techniques to help me remember information.	1	2	3	4	5	
TOTAL VALUE						

SUMMARY

10–17 Your strategies for getting information into your memory are limited. You likely focus on cramming information into your memory at the last minute and haven't thought much about the factors that help or hurt you in your efforts to memorize material. Significant improvements will need to be made to aid you in your college career.

18–25 You have below average skills in knowing how to get information into your memory. You may be minimally aware of when and where to study and probably think that being able to recall information is all that is necessary. You will need to develop strategies to help you remember materials so that you can also understand them.

26–34 Your skills in being able to remember course information are average. You are somewhat aware of how to study materials so that you can later remember them. You may benefit from learning additional memorization strategies and connecting memorization and comprehension of information.

35–42 You are above average in being able to remember information you've studied. You probably tend to study materials several times and know that a key to remembering is understanding. You probably also have some memory tricks up your sleeve, but might benefit from learning a few more.

43–50 You are exceptional in your ability to store and retrieve information. You likely tend to review materials repeatedly, and know that remembering is easier when you can relate materials to things you already know. Your satisfaction at mastering materials further motivates you.

Goals... FOR CHANGE

Based on your total points, what is one goal you would like to achieve related to studying and memory development?

Goal _____
_____

List three actions you can take that might help you move closer to realizing this goal.

1. _____
2. _____
3. _____

Questions FOR BUILDING ON YOUR BEST

As you read this chapter, consider the following questions. At the end of the chapter, you should be able to answer all of them. You are encouraged to ask a few questions of your own. Consider asking your classmates or professors to assist you.

1. How can I study smarter instead of harder?
2. What difference can my study environment really make?
3. What techniques can I use to help my memory develop?
4. Why is it important to make a commitment to understanding the material instead of just memorizing it?
5. How can I transfer information to long-term memory?

What additional questions might you have about studying and memory development?

1. _____
2. _____
3. _____

Why Study? I Can Fake It

You may choose a nontraditional study environment, but be sure that you are able to study effectively in it.

"I didn't have to study very hard in high school; why should I do it now?" This thought may have crossed your mind by this point in the semester. Many students feel that there is no real reason to study. They believe that they can glance at their notes a few moments before a test and fake it. Quite truthfully, some students are able to do this. Some tests and professors lend themselves to this type of studying technique. More than you may imagine, however, this is not the case. College professors are notorious for thorough exams, lengthy essay questions, tricky true–false statements, and multiple choices that would confuse Einstein. If you want to succeed in your classes in college, you will need to make studying a way of life.

Effective studying requires a great deal of commitment, but learning how to get organized, taking effective notes, reading a textbook, listening in class, developing personalized study skills, and building memory techniques will serve you well in becoming a successful graduate. Faking it is now a thing of the past.

The Importance of Your Study Environment

You may wonder why your study place is important. The study environment can determine how well your study time passes. If the room is too hot, too noisy, too dark, or too crowded, your study time may not be productive. In a room that is too hot and dimly lit, you may have a tendency to fall asleep. In a room that is too cold, you may spend time trying to warm yourself. Choose a location that is comfortable for you.

Different students need different study environments. You may need to have a degree of noise in the background, or you may need complete quiet. You have to make this decision. If you always have music in the background while you are studying, try studying in a quiet place one time to see if there is a difference. If you always try to study where it is quiet, try putting soft music in the background to see if it helps you. You may have to try several environments before you find the one that is right for you.

DID YOU KNOW?

20%

The percentage of students who report spending fewer than 5 hours a week preparing for class.

Source: Young, J. "Homework? What homework?" *The Chronicle of Higher Education*, December 6, 2003.

I Forgot to Remember!

UNDERSTANDING MEMORY

There may be times when you feel that your mind is just full. *"I can't remember another thing,"* you might say. That is a total myth. Many researchers and memory experts suggest that we do not come even close to using all of our memory's

WORLD OF WORK

As an inner-city Chicago kid, I was always driven for success. I came from a family of five children and parents with limited education. Although we were far from wealthy, there was an expectation that the children would have two characteristics: *integrity and striving to be our best.*

Because of our financial situation, the opportunity for a college education was always a desire for me, but not a certainty. I was fortunate enough to receive an entry scholarship to Loyola University of Chicago. Frankly, I did not take very good advantage of this opportunity early on in my college career. My performance was not up to expectation. My professors were pretty candid about this, and I knew I needed to refocus. It was at this point that I determined the approach that has influenced the rest of my career:

EDUCATION IS AN OPPORTUNITY AND A PRIVILEGE.

From that time, I attacked every class with interest, curiosity, and a desire to maximize my learning. Upon graduation, this attitude and approach carried over into my work life—no job was too trivial, and every person was one from whom I could learn. As I reflect on those college years, I realize that they were among my most formative ones.

The importance of preparing and "doing one's homework" became very clear to me. Without sounding too "preachy," I would offer the following suggestions on preparation:

- **Be clear on what you want your outcome to be.** It may be getting an "A" on an exam, mastering a particular subject, or proving to the professor that you could survive the semester!
- **Determine what you will need to prepare.** Do not wait until you are in the study mode to determine that one of the texts and the two pieces of research that you need are not available. Get the most out of your study time by anticipating what will be needed.
- **Plan your time.** Always begin with scheduling your time. The enemy of preparation is time. The word "cramming" was probably invented for or by a college student. You are always better served if you can prepare for an exam or write a research paper over time. This allows for review, improvement, and final preparation.
- **Work hard.** It is important to know that there are not any real shortcuts in life. Things earned do come from the sweat of our brow. When you receive those grade reports at the end of the semester, usually you will get what you deserve!
- **Celebrate.** When you have achieved what you set out to do, celebrate. If only for a short time, allow yourself the luxury of having succeeded at a goal.

QUESTIONS FOR REFLECTION

Consider responding to these questions online in the World of Work module of the Companion Website.

1. How have the expectations of others affected your decisions about college?
2. Have you ever learned from those with whom you work like Mr. Peterson did? Who was the person and what did you learn?
3. Why is it important to celebrate your successes?

Coleman Peterson, *Executive Vice President—People Division,* Wal-Mart Stores, Inc., Bentonville, AR

Choosing the best study environment can be challenging. The best study place may depend on the different accommodations available to you and may vary with the kinds of studying required. What kind of study environment has worked best for you?

potential. One study in the 1970s concluded that if our brains were fed 10 new items of information every second for the rest of our lives, we would never fill even *half* of our memory's capacity (Texas A&M University).

It may feel like you've lost your mind when you are in the middle of a speech, or when you read that test question that takes your breath away, or at other times during the semester—but no, you haven't lost your mind and you haven't lost your memory. As a matter of fact, it would be pretty hard to lose your memory (short of a medical issue or accident). Some researchers suggest that we never forget anything—that the material is simply "covered up" by other material, but it is still in our brain. The reason we can't recall that information is that it was not important enough, not stored properly, or not used enough to keep it from being covered up.

So, why is it so hard to remember the dates of the Civil War or who flew with Amelia Earhart or how to calculate the liquidation value of stocks or the six factors in the communication process? The primary problem is that we never properly filed or stored this information.

What would happen if you typed your English research paper into the computer and did not give it a file name? When you needed to retrieve that paper, you would not know how to find it. You would have to search through every file until you came across the information you needed. Memory works in much the same way. We have to store it properly if we are to retrieve it easily at a later time.

This section will detail how memory works and why it is important to your studying efforts. Below, you will find some basic facts about memory.

- Everyone remembers some information and forgets other information.
- Your senses help you take in information.
- With very little effort, you can remember some information.
- With rehearsal (study), you can remember a great deal of information.
- Without rehearsal or use, information is forgotten.
- Incoming information needs to be filed in the brain if you are to retain it.
- Information stored, or filed, in the brain must have a retrieval method.
- Mnemonic devices, repetition, association, and rehearsal can help you store and retrieve information.

> Clear your mind of can't.
> —SAMUEL JOHNSON

Psychologists have determined that there are three types of memory: sensory memory; short-term, or working, memory; and long-term memory.

Sensory memory stores information gathered from the five senses: taste, touch, smell, hearing, and sight. Sensory memory is usually temporary, lasting about one to three seconds, unless you decide that the information is of ultimate importance to you and make an effort to transfer it to long-term memory. Although your sensory memory bank is *very large,* sensory information does not stay with you very long (Woolfolk, 2001). Sensory memory allows countless stimuli to come into your brain, which can be a problem when you are trying to concentrate on your professor's lecture. You need to make a conscious effort to remain focused on the words being spoken and not on competing noise. When you make an effort to concentrate on the professor's information, you are then committing this information to short-term memory.

Short-term, or working, memory holds information for a short amount of time. Your working memory bank can hold a limited amount of information, usually about five to nine separate new facts or pieces of information at once (Woolfolk, 2001). Although it is sometimes frustrating to forget information, it is also useful and necessary to do so. If you never forgot anything, you would not be able to function. Educational psychologist Anita Woolfolk suggests that most of us can hear a new phone number, walk across the room, and dial it without much trouble, but if we heard two or three new numbers, we would not be able to dial them correctly. This is more information than our working memory can handle. If you were asked to give a person's name immediately after being introduced, you would probably be able to do so. If you had met several other new people in the meantime, unless you used some device to transfer the name into long-term memory, you would probably not be able to recall it.

Short-Term Memory Assessment

Theo, Gene, and Suzanne were on their way home from class. As they drove down Highway 415 toward the Greengate subdivision, they saw a 1994 Honda Civic pull out in front of a 1998 Nissan Maxima. There was a crash as the two cars collided. Theo stopped the car. Gene and Suzanne jumped from the car to see if they could help. Suzanne yelled for someone to call 911; Robertina, a bystander, ran to the pay phone at the corner of Mason and Long streets. Within 10 minutes, an ambulance arrived and took Margaret, the driver of the Maxima, to St. Mary's Hospital. Tim, the driver of the Honda, was not badly injured.

Cover this scenario with a piece of paper and answer the following questions.

1. Who was driving the Honda? _____
2. What highway were they driving on? _____
3. Who called 911? _____
4. What hospital was used? _____
5. What year was the Maxima? _____

How many questions did you answer correctly? If you answered four or five questions correctly, your working memory is strong. If you answered only one or two questions correctly, you will need to discover ways to commit more information to your short-term, or working, memory. Some techniques for doing this are discussed later in this chapter.

Some people do not become thinkers because their memories are too good. —NIETZSCHE

As a student, you would never be able to remember all that your professor said during a 50-minute lecture. You have to take steps to help you to remember information. Taking notes, making associations, drawing pictures, and visualizing information are all techniques that can help you to commit information to your long-term memory bank.

Long-term memory stores a lot of information. It is almost like a computer disk. You have to make an effort to put something in your long-term memory, but with effort and memory techniques, such as rehearsal and practice, you can store anything you want to remember there. Long-term memory consists of information that you have heard often, information that you use often, information that you might see often, and information that you have determined necessary. Just as you name a file on a computer disk, you name the files in your long-term memory. Sometimes, you have to wait a moment for the information to come to you. While you are waiting, your brain disk is spinning; if the information you seek is in long-term memory, your brain will eventually find it. You may have to assist your brain in locating the information by using mnemonics and other memory devices.

Long-Term Memory Assessment

Without using any reference materials, quickly answer the following questions using your long-term memory.

1. What is your mother's maiden name? _____
2. Who was the first U.S. president? _____
3. What is the capital of California? _____
4. Who wrote A Christmas Carol? _____
5. What shape is a stop sign? _____
6. What is your Social Security number? _____
7. Name one of the tallest buildings in America. _____
8. What is the title of Dr. Martin Luther King's most famous speech? _____
9. What does the "A" stand for in the L-STAR method? _____
10. What does the acronym "IBM" stand for? _____

Did the answers come to you quickly? If you review your answers, you will probably find that you responded quickly to those questions whose content you deal with fairly frequently, such as your Social Security number. Although you were probably able to answer all the questions, in some instances your brain had to search longer and harder to find the answer. This is how long-term memory works.

Empowering Your Memory **257**

> **A**ll things are filled full of signs, and it is a wise person who can learn about one thing from another. —PLOTINUS

This Isn't Your Daddy's VCR
USING VCR3 TO INCREASE MEMORY POWER

Countless pieces of information are stored in your long-term memory. Some of it is triggered by necessity, some may be triggered by the five senses, and some may be triggered by experiences. The best way to commit information to long-term memory and retrieve it when needed can be expressed by:

V Visualizing
C Concentrating
R Relating
R Repeating
R Reviewing

$$VCR^3$$

Consider the following story.

As Katherine walked back to the dorm room after her evening class, she heard someone behind her. She turned to see two students holding hands walking about 20 feet behind her. She was relieved. This was the first night that she had walked back to the residence hall alone.

Katherine pulled her book bag closer to her as she increased her pace along the dimly lit sidewalk between the Salk Biology Building and the Horn Center for the Arts. "I can't believe that Shana didn't call me," she thought to herself. "She knows I hate to leave class alone."

As Katherine turned the corner onto Suddith Street, she heard someone else behind her. She turned but did not see anyone. As she continued to walk toward the residence hall, she heard the sound again. Turning to see if anyone was there, she saw a shadow disappear into the grove of hedges along the sidewalk.

Startled and frightened, Katherine crossed the street to walk beneath the streetlights and sped up to get closer to a group of students about 30 feet in front of her. She turned once more to see if anyone was behind her. Thankfully, she did not see anyone.

By this time, she was only one block from her residence hall. The lighting was better and other students were around. She felt better, but vowed never again to leave class alone at night.

To **visualize** information, try to create word pictures in your mind as you hear the information. If you are being told about a Revolutionary War battle, try to see the soldiers and the battlefield, or try to paint a mind picture that will help you to remember the information. You may also want to create visual aids as you read or study information.

As you read Katherine's story, were you able to visualize her journey? Could you see her walking along the sidewalk? Did you see the two buildings? What did they look like? Could you see the darkness of her path? Could you see that shadow disappearing into the bushes? Could you see her increasing her pace to catch up to the other students? What was she wearing?

If you did this, then you are using your visual skills—your mind's eye. This is one of the most effective ways to commit information to long-term memory. See it, live it, feel it, and touch it as you read it and study it, and it will become yours.

Concentrating on the information given will help you commit it to long-term memory. Don't let your mind wander. Stay focused. If you find yourself having trouble concentrating, take a small break (two to five minutes).

As you read the story about Katherine, did your mind wander? Were you able to concentrate only on the story at hand? Why or why not? Is it easier to read a "story" than to read a textbook? Is it easier to concentrate on material that is entertaining than material that is bland? You probably answered yes to both questions.

As you read your next assignment in a text, try to turn that assignment into a visual story such as Katherine's. It will be harder in some classes, but many texts lend themselves to "story format." If you approach the chapter knowing what you want to get from it, it is easier to concentrate on it.

Relating the information to something that you already know or understand will assist you in filing or storing the information for easy retrieval. Relating the appearance of the African zebra to the American horse can help you remember what the zebra looks like.

Could you relate Katherine's story to a similar experience in your life or the life of one of your friends? If so, it will be even easier to commit this story to long-term memory. Have you ever walked alone at night and heard something? When? What happened? All of these relationships help increase retention.

Repeating the information out loud to yourself or to a study partner facilitates its transfer to long-term memory. Some people have to hear information many times before they can commit it to long-term memory.

Can you go back and tell the story of Katherine to a friend of yours? Can you tell the details? Can you name the buildings? Can you remember the sequence of events? If not, use your concentration skills for a moment and repeat the story in your own mind. If the details are sketchy, then reread the story. Memory experts agree that repetition is one of the STRONGEST tools to increase the retention of material.

Reviewing the information is another means of repetition. The more you see and use the information, the easier it will be to remember it when the time comes. As you review, try to remember the main points of the information.

Walter Pauk, educator and inventor of the Cornell note-taking method, found in a study that people reading a textbook chapter forgot 81 percent of what they had read after 28 days (Pauk, 2001).

With this in mind, it may behoove you to review Katherine's story (and other material in your texts) on a regular basis. Reviewing is a method of repetition and of keeping information fresh.

REMEMBERING KATHERINE

Without looking back, answer the following questions about Katherine. Use your visualization and concentration skills to recall the information.

1. What was the name of the biology building?_____

2. Did she see the shadow before or after she saw the two people behind her?_____

3. What were the two people behind her doing?_____

4. What was the name of the arts building?_____

5. Why did she cross the street?_____

6. How far ahead of her was the group of students?_____

7. When she saw the group of students in front of her, how far was she from her residence?_____

8. What was Katherine's friend's name?_____

What Helps? What Hurts?
ATTENDING TO YOUR MEMORY

For any part of the body, there are things that help you and hurt you. Your memory is no different. Just as your body will begin to fail you without proper attention, exercise, and nutrition, if neglected or mistreated, your memory will do the same. Consider the following things that can help or hinder your memory.

MEMORY HELPERS
- Proper sleep
- Proper nutrition/diet
- Exercise
- Mental exercises such as crossword puzzles, brain teasers, name games
- A positive mind-set
- The proper environment
- Scheduled study breaks
- Repetition and visualization

MEMORY HINDRANCES
- Internal and external distractions
- Alcohol
- Drugs
- Stress
- Closed-mindedness (tuning out things you don't like)
- Inability to distinguish important facts from unimportant facts

With these in mind, try to develop habits that incorporate the "memory helpers" into your life. Eat properly, get enough rest, take study breaks if you feel yourself drifting or getting tired, find the proper place to read and study, keep your mind sharp by reading for pleasure or doing crossword puzzles, and above all, approach your studying with a positive attitude.

KNOWING VERSUS MEMORIZING

Why don't you forget your name? Why don't you forget your address? The answer is that you KNOW that information. You OWN it. It belongs to you. You've used it often enough and repeated it often enough that it is highly unlikely that you will ever forget it. Conversely, why can't you remember the details of Erickson's Stages of Development or Maslow's Hierarchy of Basic Needs or Darwin's Theory of Evolution? Most likely because you memorized it and never "owned" it.

If you think back to what you can and can't remember, memorization plays a great role. Rote memory is when you literally memorize something and days later it is gone. You memorized it because you needed it for something like a test or a discussion, but it was not important enough to you to know it for life.

Knowing something means that you have made a personal commitment to make this information a part of your life. For example, if you needed to remember the name Stephen and his phone number of 925-6813, the likelihood of your remembering this depends on *attitude*. Do you need to recall this information because he is in your study group and you might need to call him, or because he is the caregiver for your infant daughter while you are in class? How badly you need that name and number will determine the commitment level that you make to just *memorizing* it (and maybe forgetting it) or *knowing* it (and making it a part of your life).

Think about your study habits for a moment. When you are reading your chapter, listening in class, or studying at home, what is your **commitment level?** How much energy, brainpower, zeal, and fervor do you put into it? Again, it will depend on how you perceive the value of that information.

The difference between **rote memory** and **knowing** (understanding) can literally make a dramatic and permanent change in every area of your life, certainly in your role as a college student. Rote memory is a task of repeating until you have memorized. Knowing is making a commitment to understanding relationships, making associations, comparing and contrasting, classifying, demonstrating, describing, and applying what you have learned.

These terms may sound familiar. They should. You covered them in Chapter 5. They belong to Bloom's Taxonomy. If you remember, this is the technique used to help you understand and apply what you have read. This same

Sometimes success is due less to ability and more to zeal. The winner is the person who gives him or herself to his or her work, body and soul. —CHARLES BUXTON

theory can help you increase your memory power and retention abilities. To review Bloom's Taxonomy, refer to page 160 of Chapter 5.

To OWN knowledge, you have to work from many angles, and Bloom's theory can help you do that. After you have read a chapter, visualized the information, related it to something you already know, and reviewed it for accuracy, ask yourself a few questions. These questions can help you KNOW the information, thus helping you transfer it to long-term memory and *life-long ownership*.

Questions such as these can help you move from simple memorization to ownership of the material:

- Can I relate x to y?
- Can I illustrate how x does y?
- Can I compare and contrast x to y?
- Can I apply x to y in the real world?
- Can I distinguish x from y?
- Can I define, identify, name, and describe x?
- Can I solve the problem of x?
- Can I modify or rearrange x to make it work with y?
- Can I support the theory of x and y?
- Can I defend my knowledge of x or y?

By asking questions from Bloom's Taxonomy, you can begin to own that information.

Consider the following picture. Study it carefully and completely. Look at everything in the picture from top to bottom, left to right.

Look at the picture again with the areas marked.

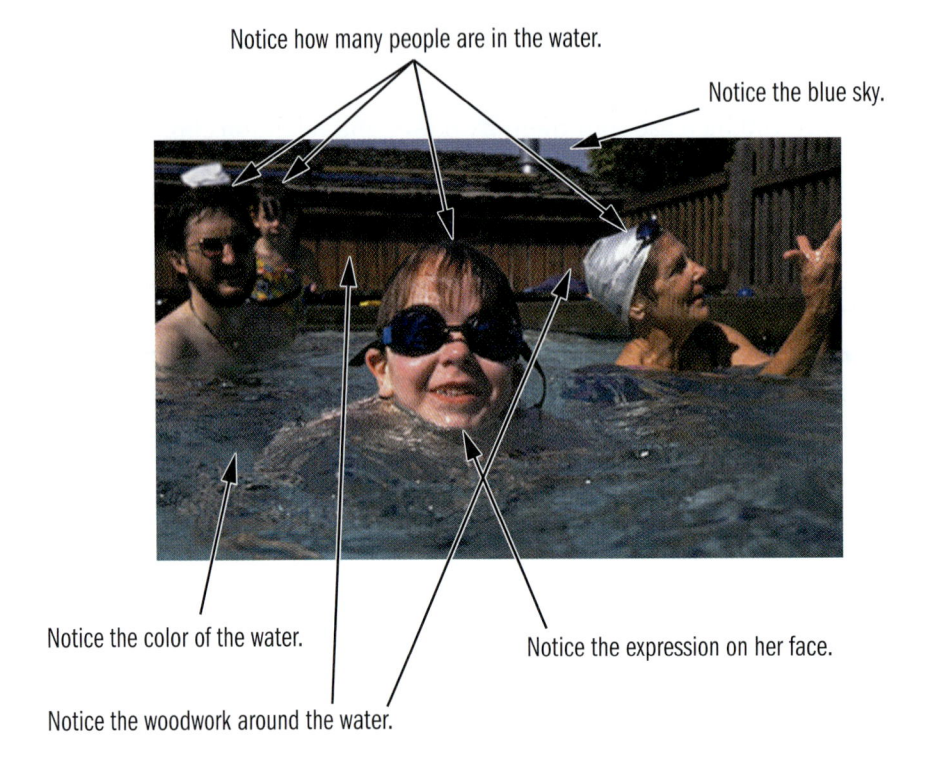

Notice how many people are in the water.

Notice the blue sky.

Notice the color of the water.

Notice the expression on her face.

Notice the woodwork around the water.

Now, **cover this picture** and answer the following questions:

1. How many people are in the water? _____

2. What color is the water? _____

3. Is the sky clear or cloudy? _____

4. Is the child happy or sad? _____

5. Is the woodwork a fence or a house? _____

6. What is the relationship between the man and the woman in the water?
   _____

7. Who is older? _____

8. How many people are wearing goggles? _____

9. How many people are wearing bathing caps? _____

10. What colors are in the bathing suit of the child standing in the rear? _____
    _____

11. Is the man or woman wearing a necklace? _____

12. Is there any foliage in the picture? _____

13. What is the general mood of the people in the water? _____

Could you answer them all without looking? The purpose of this exercise is to help you understand the real difference between casually looking at something and REALLY looking at something. To truly know something, you have to go beyond what is given. You have to look and examine more than you are told or more than what is pointed out for you. To know and own something, you have to be totally committed to examining every detail, every inch, and every angle of that information. You will need to practice and master the technique of "going beyond."

Ready, Set, Go!
MEMORY AND STUDYING

In Chapter 4 you got organized and prioritized your tasks. In Chapters 7 and 8 you actively listened and developed a note-taking system. So far in this chapter, you've found the appropriate study environment. Now it's time to study. That's exciting, isn't it? No? Well, it can be. All it takes is a positive attitude and an open mind. Next, you'll learn about three methods of studying that you can use to put yourself in charge of the material. The box on the following page provides a brief summary of these methods, which are discussed in more detail beginning below. After you've reviewed these methods, you may want to use some combination of them, or you may prefer to use one method exclusively. The only rule for choosing a study plan is that the plan must work for you. You may have to spend a few weeks experimenting with several plans and methods to determine the one with which you are most comfortable. Don't get discouraged if it takes you a while to find what is right for you.

THE SQ3R METHOD

You were introduced to this method in Chapter 5. This method can help you commit material to memory. As a quick review, to use SQ3R, you would:

- **Survey** the chapter: headings, photos, quotes, indentions, bolded words, etc.
- Write **Questions** from headings: use *who, what, when, where, why, how*.
- **Read** the chapter: look up unfamiliar words, highlight important sections, take notes while reading, paraphrase the information.
- **Recite** the information: close the text and determine if you can "tell the story" of the chapter.
- **Review** the chapter: return to the chapter often and look over the information.

Three Studying Strategies

SQ3R METHOD	MNEMONICS	COOPERATIVE LEARNING
Best used for surveying and reading textbooks	Can be used when studying lecture or text notes	Can be used when studying in groups for tests, projects, note sharing, and analysis
Survey	Jingles/Rhymes	Questioning
Question	Sentences	Comparing
Read	Words	Drilling
Recite	Story lines	Brainstorming
Review	Acronyms	Sharing
	Pegs	Mapping

Using SQ3R as a study method can help you increase your understanding of the material and commit the information to long-term memory.

MNEMONIC DEVICES

Mnemonic, pronounced (ni-mŏn-ik), devices are memory tricks or techniques that assist you in putting information into your long-term memory and pulling it out when you need it. I recently gave a test on the basic principles of public speaking. A student asked if she had to know the parts of the communication process in order. When I replied that she should be able to recall them in order, she became nervous and said that she had not learned them in order. Another student overheard the conversation and said, "Some men can read backward fast." The first student asked, "What do you mean by that?" I laughed and said that the mnemonic was great! The student had created a sentence to remember *source, message, channel, receiver, barriers,* and *feedback*. The relationship worked like this:

Some	=	Source
Men	=	Message
Can	=	Channel
Read	=	Receiver
Backward	=	Barriers
Fast	=	Feedback

The first student caught on fast; she could not believe how easy it was to remember the steps in order using this sentence. This is a perfect example of how using memory tricks can help you retrieve information easily.

The following types of mnemonic devices may help you with your long-term memory.

> **For the things we have to learn, we learn by doing them.** —ARISTOTLE

✓ **Jingles/Rhymes.** You can make up rhymes, songs, poems, or sayings to assist you in remembering information; for example, "Columbus sailed the ocean blue in fourteen hundred and ninety-two."

As a child, you learned many things through jingles and rhymes. You probably learned your ABC's through a song pattern, as well as your numbers. If you think about it, you can still sing your ABC's, and maybe your numbers through the "Ten Little Indians" song. You could probably sing every word to the opening of *The Brady Bunch* or *Gilligan's Island* because of the continual re-runs on TV. Jingles and rhymes have a strong and lasting impact on our memory—especially when repetition is involved.

✓ **Sentences.** You can make up sentences such as "Some men can read backward fast," to help you remember information. Another example is "Please excuse my dear Aunt Sally," which corresponds to the mathematical operations: **p**arentheses, **e**xponents, **m**ultiplication, **d**ivision, **a**ddition, and **s**ubtraction.

Other sentences in academic areas include:

1. **M**y **V**ery **E**lderly **M**other **J**ust **S**aved **U**s **N**ine **P**ennies. This is a sentence mnemonic for the nine planets in order from the sun: Mercury, Venus, Earth, Mars, Jupiter, Saturn, Uranus, Neptune, Pluto.

2. **E**very **G**ood **B**ird **D**oes **F**ly is a sentence mnemonic for the line notes in the treble clef in music.

3. **S**ome **M**en **H**elp **E**ach **O**ther is a sentence mnemonic for the Great Lakes from west to east: Superior, Michigan, Huron, Erie, Ontario.

✓ **Words.** You can create words. For example, Roy G. Biv may help you to remember the colors of the rainbow: **r**ed, **o**range, **y**ellow, **g**reen, **b**lue, **i**ndigo, and **v**iolet.

Other word mnemonics include:

1. **HOMES** is a word for the Great Lakes in no particular order: Huron, Ontario, Michigan, Erie, Superior.

2. **FACE** is a word mnemonic for the space notes in the treble clef.

Story lines. If you find it easier to remember stories than raw information, you may want to process the information into a story that you can easily tell. Weave the data and facts into a creative story that can be easily retrieved from your long-term memory. This technique can be especially beneficial if your professor gives essay exams, because the "story" that you remember can be what was actually told in class.

Acronyms. An acronym is a word that is formed from the first letters of other words. You may see re-runs for the famed TV show *M*A*S*H*. This is an acronym for **M**obile **A**rmy **S**urgical **H**ospital. If you scuba dive, you know that *SCUBA* is an acronym for **S**elf-**C**ontained **U**nderwater **B**reathing **A**pparatus. Other common acronyms include:

NASA (**N**ational **A**eronautic **S**pace **A**dministration)

NASCAR (**N**ational **A**ssociation of **S**tock **C**ar **A**uto **R**acing)

NASDAQ (**N**ational **A**ssociation of **S**ecurities **D**ealers **A**utomated **Q**uotation)

NATO (**N**orth **A**tlantic **T**reaty **O**rganization)

BART (**B**ay **A**rea **R**apid **T**ransit)

Pegging. The peg system uses association, visualization, and attachment for remembering. With this system, you "attach" what you want to remember to something that is already familiar to you. This is a visual means to remember lists, sequences, and even categories of information.

Most peg systems use numbers and rhyming words to correspond such as:

1 = sun   6 = sticks
2 = shoe   7 = heaven
3 = bee   8 = gate
4 = shore   9 = fine
5 = alive   10 = pen

To attach information to the number, you visually attach a word (such as sun, shoe, bee, shore) to the word you want to remember. For example, if you wanted to remember a shopping list that included ice cream, rice, Ajax, milk, water, and cookies, this might be your plan:

You see **ice cream** melting in the **sun**.

You see **rice** filling a **shoe**.

You see **Ajax** sprinkled on a **bee**.

You see **milk** rushing to the **shore**.

You see **water** keeping you **alive** on a deserted island.

You see **cookies** being offered to you on a **stick** (like a s'more).

You can also "attach" information to a thing or a place. For example, you might place information in the following places: kitchen, hall, bedroom, living room, bathroom, or dining room.

Again, you visually "attach" the information you want to remember to a part of the house (and you should use *your* house, beginning with the door in which you enter). For example, if you were giving a speech on the death penalty, you might put the **introduction in the kitchen**, the **transition statement in the hallway**, the **first point in the bedroom**, and the **second point in the living room**. This helps you keep your information organized.

You could "attach" information to parts of a car, such as the steering wheel, the tires, the trunk, the roof, the back seat, the driver's seat, the passenger seat.

For example, if you wanted to remember the planets, you could put **Mercury** as the **steering wheel**, **Venus** as the **tire**, **Earth** in the **trunk**, **Mars** on the **roof**, **Jupiter** in the **back seat**, etc.

Now that you have your peg system, you can begin to "attach" information to those places and use your visual skills for recall.

COOPERATIVE LEARNING

There is strength in numbers. Many times, groups of people can accomplish what a single individual cannot. This is the idea behind cooperative learning. We form and use groups in our daily lives in situations like work, worship, and hobbies, and we even group our friends together. We develop groups for inspiration, excitement, and reflection, to advance social causes and to grow. Studying in groups can have the same effect. Cooperative learning can benefit you because you have pulled together a group of people who have the same interests and goals as you: to pass the course. Studying and working in groups can help you in ways such as drilling exercises, brainstorming, group sharing, and mapping.

STRATEGIES FOR BUILDING ON YOUR BEST

Consider the following strategies for making the most of your study time and memory development:

- Choose a study environment that is right for YOU.
- Study in blocks of time and don't wait until the last minute to begin studying.
- Make a commitment to KNOW rather than memorize.
- Take short breaks when studying to fight fatigue.
- Use repetition to commit information to long-term memory.
- VISUALIZE the information so that your mind's eye can help you remember it.
- Test your memory and understanding by using Bloom's Taxonomy.

Before we talk about those specific details, we should discuss how to form a study group. The most effective study group will include people with different strengths and weaknesses. It would do little good to involve yourself in an accounting study group with people who are all failing accounting. Here are some tips for forming a cooperative study group:

- Limit the group size to five to seven people.
- Search for students who participate in class.
- Include people who take notes in class.
- Include people who ask questions in class.
- Include people who will work diligently.
- Include people who do their share for the group.
- Invite people who are doing well in a specific area; they may not attend every meeting, but they may be of assistance periodically.

Appoint members of your team to be responsible for the following jobs:

Timekeeper	This person will let the group know when it is time to move on to another topic.
Note Taker	This person will keep the notes for the team and will usually assist in getting them copied for everyone in the group.
Facilitator	This person will lead the group and keep the group on task during the meeting.

When the group is formed, you can engage in several different activities to learn, share, and reinforce information.

- **Questioning.** With this technique, group members bring several questions to the next session. These may be predicted exam questions, questions about methods or formulas, or questions that the member was not able to answer individually.
- **Comparing.** The study group is a good place to compare notes taken in class or from the text. If you are having problems understanding a concept in your notes, maybe someone in the group can assist you. It is also a good time to compare your notes for accuracy and missing lecture information.
- **Drilling.** This technique assists you with long-term memory development. Repetition is an important step in transferring information to long-term memory. Have a group member drill the other members on facts, details, solutions, and dates. A verbal review of the information will help you and other members retain the information.
- **Brainstorming.** During each session, members can use this technique (discussed in detail in the chapter on critical thinking) to predict exam questions, review information, and develop topic ideas for research, projects, future study sessions, and papers.

> Have you ever studied with a group of people? What were some of the benefits that you experienced? What are some advantages over studying alone?

- **Sharing.** The study group is a time when you can give and receive. At the beginning or end of each session, students in the group can share the most important aspect of the lecture or readings. This will assist other members in identifying main points and issues pertaining to the lecture.
- **Mapping.** This technique can be used in a variety of ways. It is similar to the mapping system discussed in the note-taking chapter. On a board or large sheet of paper, let one member write a word, idea, or concept in the center. The next student will add information, thus creating a map or diagram of information and related facts. This can help the group make connections and associations and assist members in identifying where gaps in knowledge exist.

Using groups can benefit your study efforts tremendously. If you are asked to participate in a group, take advantage of the opportunity. If you feel that a group could help you master the information, take steps to form a cooperative learning group on your campus.

Studying with Small Children in the House

For many college students, finding a place or time to study is the hardest part of studying. Some students live at home with younger siblings; some students have children of their own. If you have young children in the home, you may find the following hints helpful when it comes time to study.

Study at school. Your schedule may have you running from work to school directly to home. Try to squeeze in even as little as half an hour at school for studying, perhaps immediately before or after class. A half hour of pure study time can prove more valuable than five hours at home with constant interruptions.

Create crafts and hobbies. Your children need to be occupied while you study. It may help if you have crafts and hobbies available that they can do while you are involved with studying. Choose projects your children can do by themselves, without your help. Depending on their ages, children could make masks from paper plates, color, do pipe cleaner art or papier-mâché, use modeling clay or dough, or build a block city. Explain to your children that you are studying and that they can use this time to be creative; when everyone is finished, you'll share what you've done with each other.

Study with your children. One of the best ways to instill the value of education in your children is to let them see you participating in your own education. Set aside one or two hours per night when you and your children study. You may

If you view your studying responsibilities positively, your children will too. Try to separate the time you spend with your family from the time you need to spend on your school work.

be able to study in one place, or you may have separate study areas. If your children know that you are studying and you have explained to them how you value your education, you are killing two birds with one stone: you are able to study, and you are providing a positive role model as your children study with you and watch you.

Rent movies or let your children watch TV. Research has shown that viewing a limited amount of educational television, such as *Sesame Street, Reading Rainbow,* or *Barney and Friends,* can be beneficial for children. If you do not like what is on television, you might consider renting or purchasing age-appropriate educational videos for your children. This could keep them busy while you study, and it could help them learn as well.

Invite your children's friends over. What?! That's right. A child who has a friend to play or study with may create less of a distraction for you. Chances are your children would rather be occupied with someone their own age, and you will gain valuable study time.

Hire a sitter or exchange sitting services with another student. Arrange to have a sitter come to your house a couple of times a week. If you have a classmate who also has children at home, you might take turns watching the children for each other. You could each take the children for one day a week, or devise any schedule that suits you both best. Or you could study together, and let your children play together while you study, alternating homes.

Ask if your college has an on-site daycare center such as the Boys and Girls Club. Some colleges provide daycare facilities at a reduced cost, and some provide daycare at no charge. It is certainly worth checking out.

Talk to the financial aid office on your campus. In some instances, there will be grants or aid to assist you in finding affordable daycare for your child.

Studying at any time is hard work. It is even harder when you have to attend to a partner, children, family responsibilities, work, and a social life as well. You will have to be creative in order to complete your degree. You are going to have to do things and make sacrifices that you never thought possible. But if you explore the options, plan ahead, and ask questions of other students with children and with responsibilities outside the classroom, you can and will succeed.

What Do You Mean the Test Is Tomorrow?

STUDYING IN A CRUNCH

Let's be straight upfront. No study skills textbook will ever advise you to cram. It is simply a dangerous and often futile exercise in desperation. You'll never read the words, *"Don't waste your party time studying, CRAM the night before."* Cramming is just the opposite of what this whole chapter is about—*knowing* versus memorizing. Cramming will never help you know; it can only help you memorize a few things for storage in short-term memory. You may spend several hours cramming, and shortly after the test, the information is gone, evaporated, vanished!

But, let's be straight about something else. We know that you may have obligations that take enormous hours from your week. This is simply a matter of fact in the 21st century. So, there may be times when time runs out and the only option is to cram. If you find yourself in this spot, consider the following tips and suggestions for cramming. These probably won't get you an "A," but they may help you with a few questions.

Depressurize. Just tell yourself up front what you are doing. Don't pretend that cramming is going to save you. Let yourself realize that you are memorizing material for short-term gain and that you won't be able to keep it all. With this admission, your stress will diminish.

Ditch the blame game. You know you're at fault, so accept that and move on. Sitting around bemoaning your fate will not help. Just tell yourself, "I messed up this time; I won't let it happen again."

Know what. When cramming, it is important to know what you're cramming for. If you're cramming for a multiple-choice test, you'll need different types of information than for an essay test. Know what type of test it is for which you are studying.

Read it quick. Think about **H2 FLIB**. This is a mnemonic for: read the **headings, highlight** the important words, read the **first sentence** of every paragraph, read the **last sentence** of every paragraph, read the **indented** and **boxed** material. This can help you get through the chapter when pinched for time.

Make connections. As you are reading, quickly determine if any of the information has a connection with something else you know. Is there a comparison or contrast? Is there a relationship of any kind? Is there a cause and effect in motion? Can you pinpoint an example to clarify the information? These questions can help you with retention.

Use your syllabus or study guide. If your professor lists questions that you should know (mastery questions) in the syllabus, or if he or she gave you a study sheet, this is the place to start. Answer those questions. If you don't have either, look to see if the text gives study questions at the end of the chapter. Try to answer the questions using the text *and* your lecture notes.

See it. Visualizing the information through mapping, diagrams, photos, drawings, and outlines can help you commit this information to short-term memory.

Repeat! repeat! repeat! Repetition is the key to committing information to memory. After you read information from the text or lecture notes, repeat it time and time again. When you think you've got it, write it down, then repeat it again.

Choose wisely. If you're cramming, you can't do it all. Make wise choices about which material you plan to study. This can be driven by your study sheet, your lecture notes, or questions in your syllabus (if they are listed).

One of the most important things about cramming is that this information is going to leave you. Don't rely on it for the next test or the final. You will need to go back and re-learn (truly understand) this information to commit it to long-term memory. Good luck!

BLUEPRINTS FOR CHANGE

NAME

DATE

REFLECTION

Just as reading is a learned skill, so is memory development. You can improve your memory, but it will take practice, patience, and persistence. By making the decision that "this information is important to me and my life," you've won the battle; for when you make that decision, your studying becomes easier.

Making a commitment to truly understand and know the material instead of just memorizing it can help you establish a knowledge base that you never imagined. It can help you retain information that otherwise would have been lost. It can help you amass a powerful vocabulary, and it can help you pull information from one class to another for papers, speeches, reports, and discussions.

Your memory needs constant care and attention. If you provide the proper rest, nutrition, and exercise, it will carry you through your degree (and beyond) with flying colors.

GET REAL

Below are a few questions to help you think about studying and memory development. Study each question carefully and respond accurately.

How can a positive mind-set about studying and memory help you be successful beyond college?

How can choosing to "know" the material (instead of just memorizing it) affect your ability to discriminate and make rational choices?

Describe your study environment, detailing why you think it is the perfect environment.

What concrete steps do you plan to take to increase your memory power?

Describe three techniques that you plan to use to commit information to your long-term memory.

If you are having trouble studying and remembering information, where could you go to find assistance on your campus?

Phone # _____

Case Study

NAME: Martin Zavala
SCHOOL: Southwest Texas State University, San Marcos, TX
MAJOR: Urban Planning   AGE: 28

Below, is a real-life situation faced by Martin. Read the brief case and respond to the questions.

I entered college 10 years ago right out of high school. I was a very good high school student, graduating in the top 25th of my class. College turned out to be a different story. For the first time in my life, I was out of my parents' home and had the freedom to do what I wanted to do. Finally.

During my first semester, I made the decision that socializing was much more important than studying for my classes. I had to make new friends, right? I decided to make friends with people who knew how to party and *wanted* to party!

So, I began to stay out very late. In the mornings, I did not feel like going to classes, so I cut them. When I partied instead of studying and doing the homework, I cut classes because I did not have the assignments. Between the parties, the drugs, and the hangovers, my brain just stopped working.

I was not interested in school for academic reasons. I was not interested in studying. I wanted to have a good time. That first semester was a blast. The second semester *was not a blast* because I did not make it to midterms. I left college and have been gone for 10 years. Today, I'm back as a first-year student.

How can your social life affect your academic life?

_____
_____
_____

Can you have both a successful academic life and a fun social life? How?

_____
_____
_____

In your opinion, what was Martin's biggest problem? Why?

_____
_____
_____

How can "freedom" affect your personal and academic life?

_____
_____
_____
_____

How would dropping out of college for 10 years affect your personal plans?

_____
_____
_____
_____

How would dropping out of college for 10 years affect your financial dreams?

_____
_____
_____
_____

What role might alcohol and drugs play in your memory development?

_____
_____
_____
_____

at this moment Journal

Refer to page 251 of this chapter. Having read and reflected upon the information in the chapter, consider how you might revise your goal to make it more:

REASONABLE

BELIEVABLE

MEASURABLE

ADAPTABLE

CONTROLLABLE

DESIRABLE

ONLINE JOURNAL

To complete an online journal entry, log onto the Companion Website at www.prenhall.com/sherfield. Go to Chapter 9 and click on the link to the Online Journal. You can respond to the questions provided or to questions assigned by your professor, or you may journal about your own experiences.

ADVICE TO GO

CORNERSTONES

for effective studying

Review your classroom and textbook notes.

Use the *SQ3R* method when studying texts.

Study your *hardest* material *first*.

Take breaks every half hour.

Study in a *brightly lit* area.

Have a *healthy snack*.

Use *mnemonic* devices.

Overlearn the material.

Set *rules* for studying.

Turn the *heat down*.

REMEMBER

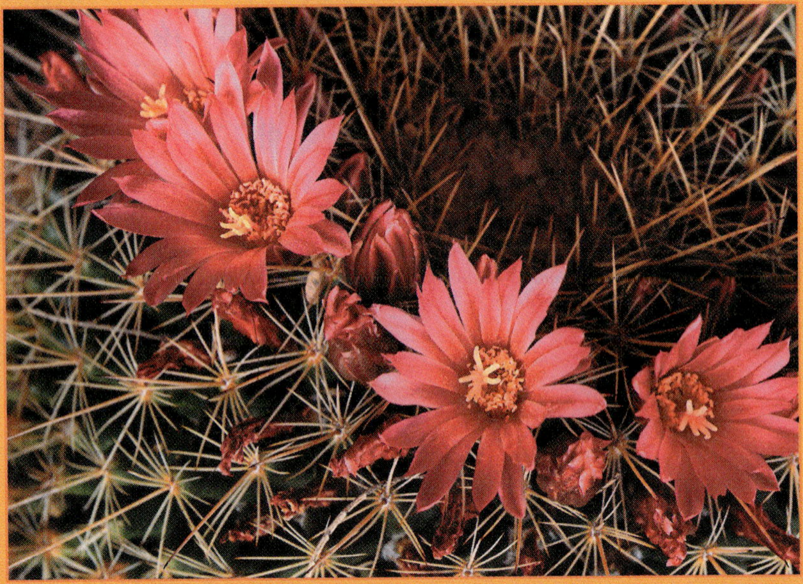

10 Assess

Learning is not attained by chance; it must be attained by diligence.

Abigail Adams

CHAPTER 10
ASSESS

Marchia could tell that something was wrong with her roommate, Ellen. Ellen had been quiet and distant for the past two days. That evening, while walking to the dining hall, Marchia asked Ellen if there was something bothering her. Ellen confided that the first test in her nursing class was in one week and that if she failed the test, *she would be asked to leave the nursing program.*

Marchia tried to tell Ellen that she had plenty of time to study the material and prepare for the test. Ellen replied that she was not worried so much about knowing the material, *but that she was worried because she was a poor test taker.* "I can know it from beginning to end," Ellen said, "but when she puts that test in front of me, *I can't even remember my name!* What am I going to do? *This test is going to determine the rest of my life.*"

Marchia explained to Ellen that she suffered through the same type of anxiety and fear in high school until her math teacher taught the class how to take a test and how to reduce test anxiety. *"It's just a skill, Ellen, like driving a car or typing a research paper. You can learn how to take tests if you're really serious."* Ellen asked if Marchia could give her some hints about test taking.

As they finished eating, Marchia told Ellen that they could begin working for an hour every morning and an hour every evening to learn how to take exams and to reduce anxiety.

The week of the test rolled around, and *Ellen was confident that she knew the material that she was to be tested on.* She still had a degree of anxiety, *but she had learned how to be in control of her emotions during a test.* She had also learned how to prepare herself physically for the exam. She went to bed early the night before the exam. On exam day, she got up early, ate a healthy breakfast,

The splendid achievements of the intellect, like the soul, are everlasting. —UNKNOWN

Strategies for Test Taking

had a brief review session, packed all the supplies needed for the exam, and *headed to class early so that she could relax a little* before the instructor arrived.

When the exam was passed out, *Ellen could feel herself getting somewhat anxious,* but she quickly

> ... when she puts that test in front of me, I can't even remember my name.

put things into perspective. She sat back and took several deep breaths, listened carefully to the professor's instructions, read all the test instructions before beginning, *told herself silently that she was going to ace the exam,* and started.

After one hour and five minutes, time was called. Ellen put her pencil down, leaned back in her chair, took a deep breath, rubbed her aching finger, and cracked the biggest smile of her life. Marchia had been right. The strategies worked. *Ellen was going to be a nurse.*

QUESTIONS FOR REFLECTION

Consider responding to these questions online in the Questions for Reflection module of the Companion Website.

1. What role do you think your attitude (positive or negative) plays in your preparation and execution of exams?

2. What can you do to better prepare physically for an exam?

3. What can you do to better prepare mentally for an exam?

Where are you... AT THIS MOMENT

Before reading this chapter, take a moment and respond to the following ten questions. Consider each one carefully before answering, and then respond by circling the number in the appropriate box. When you have answered the questions, add your points and find your total score on the feedback chart below.

STATEMENT	STRONGLY DISAGREE	DISAGREE	DON'T KNOW	AGREE	STRONGLY AGREE	SCORE
1. I get anxious when taking a test.	5	4	3	2	1	
2. My mind often blanks out during tests.	5	4	3	2	1	
3. I remember the information I've studied after finishing a test.	1	2	3	4	5	
4. I feel a lack of confidence when taking a test.	5	4	3	2	1	
5. I know how to physically prepare myself to take a test.	1	2	3	4	5	
6. I know test-taking strategies for different kinds of test questions (such as multiple choice vs. essay questions).	1	2	3	4	5	
7. I usually have very little idea about what will be on a test before I take it.	5	4	3	2	1	
8. I skip past the directions on the tests that I take.	5	4	3	2	1	
9. I am often tempted not to come to school on days when tests are scheduled.	5	4	3	2	1	
10. When taking a test, it is best to answer the questions you know first and come back to the others later.	1	2	3	4	5	
TOTAL VALUE						

SUMMARY

10–17 Your skills in preparing for and taking tests are very limited. You likely have very little idea of what to expect on the tests that you take and don't know how to study for different types of test questions. Further, your test anxieties are likely preventing you from doing your best. Significant improvements have to be made to help you be a successful test taker.

18–25 You have below average skills in preparing for and taking tests. Your level of test anxiety is likely making matters worse. You need to learn how to anticipate what your tests may look like and how to prepare for them effectively.

26–34 Your skills in preparing for and taking tests are average. You are somewhat aware of how to study for different types of tests, and your test anxieties are manageable. You would benefit from improvement in test preparation strategies to be able to really show what you know.

35–42 You are above average in preparing for and performing on tests. You likely have a good idea about what information will be on the tests and how to approach different types of questions. Adjustments in your strategies might help you perform even better on tests.

43–50 You are exceptional in your test preparation and test-taking skills. You know how to prepare yourself mentally and physically for a test, and have a sense of confidence about your test-taking performances. You likely get satisfaction at being able to rise to the challenge of tests.

Goals... FOR CHANGE

Based on your total points, what is one goal you would like to achieve related to test taking?

Goal _____
_____

List three actions you can take that might help you move closer to realizing this goal.

1. _____
2. _____
3. _____

Questions FOR BUILDING ON YOUR BEST

As you read this chapter, consider the following questions. At the end of the chapter, you should be able to answer all of them. You are encouraged to ask a few questions of your own. Consider asking your classmates or professors to assist you.

1. How can I recognize symptoms of extreme test anxiety?
2. How can I determine my personal test-anxiety level?
3. How can I develop strategies for controlling my test anxiety?
4. Which strategies can I apply to taking true–false tests?
5. Which strategies can I use for taking multiple-choice tests?

What additional questions do you have about testing and test anxiety?

1. _____
2. _____
3. _____

How do you really feel about tests? Some students (most, to be honest) view tests as punishment and cruel treatment by professors. Some students believe that testing is not necessary and that it is a tool of coercion. Successful students, however, realize that testing is necessary and even useful, that it has several positive purposes. Testing provides motivation for learning, offers feedback to the student and to the professor, and determines mastery of material.

Successful people accept testing as a fact of life. You have to be tested to drive a car; to continue in school; to join the armed services; to become a teacher, a lawyer, a doctor, or a nurse; and often to be promoted at work. To pretend that testing is not always going to be a part of your life is to deny yourself many opportunities. Testing now prepares you for the world of work.

You may dread tests for a variety of reasons and may be afraid of the test itself and the questions it may pose. Test anxiety can be overcome, however, and this chapter will present several ways you can become a more confident test taker and get started on the path to success.

Controlling Test Anxiety

A student jokes with a professor, "I have five thousand dollars in my savings account and it is yours if you don't make us take the test!" Well, this may be a bit extreme, but many students would do almost anything to get out of taking exams and tests. Some students have physical reactions to testing, including nausea, headaches, and blackouts. Such physical reactions may be a result of being underprepared or not knowing how to take an exam.

Why do you experience test anxiety?

_____
_____
_____
_____
_____

Your answer to this question is more than likely negative. You may approach tests thinking:

I'm going to fail.
I knew I couldn't do this.
There is no way I can do well; the teacher hates me.
I should never have taken this class.

These types of attitudes can cause you to be unsuccessful in testing, but with an attitude adjustment and some basic preparation, you can overcome a good deal of your anxiety about tests. You can reduce anxiety when you are in control of the situation, and you can gain control by convincing yourself that you can and will be successful. If you can honestly tell yourself that you have done everything possible to prepare for a test, then the results are going to be positive.

It is important to realize that a test is not an indication of who you are as a person or a mark of your worth as a human being. Not everyone can be good at all things. You will have areas of strength and of weakness. You will spare yourself a great deal of anxiety and frustration if you understand from the start that you may not score 100 on every test. If you expect absolute perfection on everything, you are setting yourself up to fail. Think positively, prepare well, and do your best, but also be prepared to receive less than a perfect score on occasion.

Complete the checklist below. If you check off more than five items on this list, you experience test anxiety. If you check off 10 or more, you have severe test anxiety.

PREDICTING EXAM QUESTIONS

You can also reduce test anxiety by trying to predict what types of test questions the professor will give. Professors frequently give clues ahead of time about what they will be asking and what types of questions will be given.

Several classes before the test is scheduled, find out from your professor what type of test you can expect. This information can help you study more effectively. Some questions you might ask are:

1. What type of questions will be on the test?
2. How long is the test?
3. Is there a time limit on the test?
4. Will there be any special instructions, such as use pen only or use a number 2 pencil?

Most test anxiety can be reduced by studying, predicting questions, reviewing, and relaxing.

Test-Anxiety Scale

Check the items that apply to you when preparing for a test.

- ○ I do not sleep well the night before a test.
- ○ I get sick if I eat anything before a test.
- ○ I am irritable and hard to be around before a test.
- ○ I see the test as a measure of my worth as a student.
- ○ I blank out during the test and am unable to recall information.
- ○ I worry when other students are still testing and I am finished.
- ○ I worry when others finish and I am still testing.
- ○ I am always afraid that I will run out of time.
- ○ I get frustrated during the test.
- ○ I have a negative attitude about testing.
- ○ I think about not taking the test.
- ○ I always average my grades before a test.
- ○ My body reacts negatively to testing (sweats, nervousness, butterflies).

5. Is there a study sheet?
6. Will there be a review session?
7. What is the grade value of the test?

Asking these simple questions will help you know what type of test will be administered, how you should prepare for it, and what supplies you will need.

You will want to begin predicting questions early. Listen to the professor intently. Professors use cue phrases, such as, "You will see this again," and "If I were to ask you this question on the test." Pay close attention to what is written on the board, what questions are asked in class, and what areas the professor seems to be concentrating on more than others. You will begin to get a feel for what types of questions the professor might ask on the test.

It may also be beneficial for you to keep a running page of test questions that you have predicted. As you read through a chapter, ask yourself many questions at the end of each section. When it is time to study for the test, you may have already predicted many of the questions your professor will ask.

Save all quizzes and exams that your professor lets you keep (some professors take the exams back after students have had a chance to review them).

Helpful Reminders for Reducing Test Anxiety

- Approach the test with an "I can" attitude.
- Prepare yourself emotionally for the test, control your self-talk, and be positive.
- Remind yourself that you studied and that you know the material.
- Overlearn the material—you can't study too much.
- Chew gum or eat hard candy during the test if allowed; it may help you relax.
- Go to bed early. Do not pull an all-nighter before the test.
- Eat a healthy meal before the test.
- Arrive early for the test (at least 15 minutes early).
- Sit back, relax, breathe, and clear your mind if you become nervous.
- Come to the test with everything you need: pencils, calculator, and other supplies.
- Read over the entire test first; read all the directions; highlight the directions.
- Listen to the professor before the test begins.
- Keep an eye on the clock.
- Answer what you know first, the questions that are easiest for you.
- Check your answers, but remember, your first response is usually correct.
- Find out about the test before it is given; ask the professor what types of questions will be on the test.
- Find out exactly what the test will cover ahead of time.
- Ask the professor for a study sheet; you may not get one, but it does not hurt to ask!
- Know the rules of the test and of the professor.
- Attend the review session if one is offered.
- Know what grade value the test holds.
- Ask about extra credit or bonus questions on the test.
- When you get the test, jot down any mnemonic you might have developed on the back or at the top of a page.
- Never look at another student's test or let anyone see your test.

These are a wonderful resource for studying for the next exam or for predicting questions for the course final.

Take a moment to try to predict two essay test questions from Chapter 9.

Question 1.
_____
_____

Why do you think this question will be asked?
_____
_____

Question 2.
_____
_____

Why do you think this question will be asked?
_____
_____

Three Types of Responses to Test Questions

Almost every test question will elicit one of three types of responses from you as the test taker:

- Quick-time response
- Lag-time response
- No response

Your response is a *quick-time response* when you read a question and know the answer immediately. You may need to read only one key word in the test question to know the correct response. Even if you have a quick-time response, however, always read the entire question before answering. The question may be worded in such a way that the correct response is not what you originally expected. By reading the entire question before answering, you can avoid losing points to careless error.

You have a *lag-time response* when you read a question and the answer does not come to you immediately. You may have to read the question several times or even move on to another question before you think of the correct response. Information in another question will sometimes trigger the response you need. Don't get nervous if you have a lag-time response. Once you've begun to answer other questions, you usually begin to remember more, and the response may come to you. You do not have to answer questions in order on most tests.

No response is the least desirable situation when you are taking a test. You may read a question two or three times and still have no response. At this point, you should move on to another question to try to find some related information. When this happens, you have some options:

1. Leave this question until the very end of the test.
2. Make an intelligent guess.
3. Try to eliminate all unreasonable answers by association.
4. Watch for modifiers within the question.

It is very difficult to use intelligent guessing with essay or fill-in-the-blank questions. Remember these important tips about the three types of responses:

1. Don't be overly anxious if your response is quick; read the entire question and be careful so that you don't make a mistake.
2. Don't get nervous if you have a lag-time response; the answer may come to you later, so just relax and move on.
3. Don't put down just anything if you have no response; take the remaining time and use intelligent guessing.

Test-Taking Strategies and Hints for Success

Wouldn't it be just great if every professor gave the same type of test? Then, you would have to worry about content only, and not about the test itself. Unfortunately, this is not going to happen. Professors will continue to test differently and to have their own style of writing tests. Successful students have to know the differences among testing techniques and know what to look for when dealing with each type of test question. You may have a preference for one type of question over another. You may prefer multiple-choice to essay questions, whereas someone else may prefer essay to true–false questions. Whatever your preference, you are going to encounter all types of questions. To be successful, you will need to know the techniques for answering each type.

The most common types of questions are:

- Matching
- True–false
- Multiple-choice
- Short answer
- Essay

Before you read about the strategies for answering these different types of questions, think about this: There is no substitute for studying! You can know all the tips, ways to reduce anxiety, mnemonics, and strategies on earth, but if you have not studied, they will be of little help to you.

What's Sleep Got To Do With It?

You've heard the old saying, "You are what you eat." This may be true, but many sleep experts would say, "You are how you sleep." Sleep deprivation is one of the leading causes of poor productivity and academic performance, workplace and auto accidents, lack of concentration, diminished immune systems, decreased metabolism, cardiovascular problems, and even poor communication efforts.

The National Traffic Safety Administration estimates that 100,000 crashes each year are the result of sleepy drivers. These crashes cause nearly 1600 deaths, 71,000 injuries, and $12.5 billion in property loss and diminished activity (*Hidden Menace*, 2003).

Mark Rosekind, Ph. D., an expert on fatigue and performance issues and a member of the board of directors for the National Sleep Foundation, states, "Without sufficient sleep it is more difficult to concentrate, make careful decisions, and follow instructions; we are more likely to make mistakes or errors, and are more prone to being impatient and lethargic. Our attention, memory, and reaction time are all affected" (Cardinal, 2003).

According to the National Sleep Foundation, the following symptoms can signal inadequate sleep:

- Dozing off while engaged in an activity such as reading, watching TV, sitting in meetings, or sitting in traffic.
- Slowed thinking and reacting.
- Difficulty listening to what is said or understanding directions.
- Difficulty remembering or retaining information.
- Frequent errors or mistakes.
- Narrowing of attention, missing important changes in a situation.
- Depression or negative mood.
- Impatience or being quick to anger.
- Frequent blinking, difficulty focusing eyes, or heavy eyelids.

Indeed, lack of sleep can decrease your ability to study, recall information, and perform well on tests and assignments. This can be especially true during midterm and final exam periods. Those late or all-night cram sessions can actually be more detrimental to your academic success than helpful. By including your study sessions in your time-management plan, you can avoid having to spend your sleep time studying.

Different people need different amounts of sleep within a 24-hour period. Some people absolutely need 8–10 hours of sleep, while others can function well on 4–6 hours. If you are not sleeping enough to rest and revive your body, you will experience sleep deprivation.

Researchers suggest that missing as little as 2 hours of sleep for *one* night can take as long as 6 days to recover—if it is recovered at all (Mass, 1990). It is generally estimated that 8–9 hours of *good, solid, restful* sleep per night can decrease your chances of sleep deprivation.

Below, you will find some helpful hints for getting a good night's rest:

- Avoid alcohol and caffeine (yes, alcohol is a depressant, but it interrupts both REM and slow-wave sleep, and caffeine can stay in your system for as long as 12 hours).
- Exercise during the day (but not within four hours of your sleep time).
- Regulate the temperature in your bedroom to a comfortable setting for you.
- Wind down before trying to sleep. Complete all tasks at least one hour prior to your bedtime. This gives you time to relax and prepare for rest.
- Avoid taking naps during the day.
- Have a set bedtime and try to stick to it.
- Take a warm bath before bedtime.
- Go to bed only when you are tired. If you are not asleep within 15–30 minutes, get up and do something restful like reading or listening to soft music.
- Use relaxation techniques such as visualization and mind travel.
- Avoid taking sleeping aids. This can cause more long-term problems than sleep deprivation.

STRATEGIES FOR MATCHING QUESTIONS

Matching questions frequently involve knowledge of people, dates, places, or vocabulary. When answering matching questions, you should:

- Read the directions carefully.
- Read each column before you answer.
- Determine whether there is an equal number of items in each column.
- Match what you know first.
- Cross off information that is already used.
- Use the process of elimination for answers you might not know.
- Look for logical clues.
- Use the longer statement as a question; use the shorter statement as an answer.

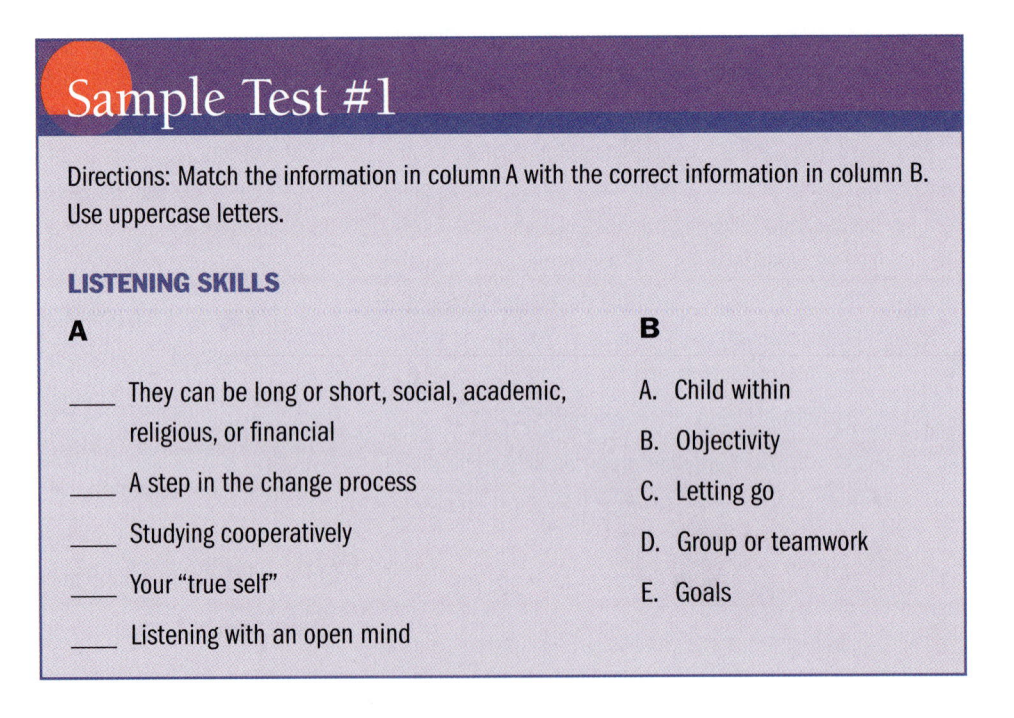

Sample Test #1

Directions: Match the information in column A with the correct information in column B. Use uppercase letters.

LISTENING SKILLS

A

____ They can be long or short, social, academic, religious, or financial

____ A step in the change process

____ Studying cooperatively

____ Your "true self"

____ Listening with an open mind

B

A. Child within

B. Objectivity

C. Letting go

D. Group or teamwork

E. Goals

STRATEGIES FOR TRUE–FALSE QUESTIONS

True–false tests ask if a statement is true or not. True–false questions can be some of the trickiest questions ever developed. Some students like them; some hate them. There is a 50/50 chance of answering correctly, but you can use the following strategies to increase your odds on true–false tests:

- Read each statement carefully.
- Watch for key words in each statement, for example, negatives.

There is no substitute for studying!

- Read each statement for double negatives, such as "not untruthful."
- Pay attention to words that may indicate that a statement is true, such as "some," "few," "many," and "often."
- Pay attention to words that may indicate that a statement is false, such as "never," "all," "every," and "only."
- Remember that if any part of a statement is false, the entire statement is false.
- Answer every question unless there is a penalty for guessing.

Sample Test #2

Place "T" for true or "F" for false beside each statement.

NOTE-TAKING SKILLS

1. _____ Note taking creates a history of your course content.
2. _____ "Most importantly" is not a key phrase.
3. _____ You should always write down everything the professor says.
4. _____ You should never ask questions in class.
5. _____ The L-STAR system is a way of studying.
6. _____ W/O is not a piece of shorthand.
7. _____ You should use 4-by-6-inch paper to take classroom notes.
8. _____ The outline technique is best used with lecture notes.
9. _____ The Cornell method should never be used with textbook notes.
10. _____ The mapping system is done with a series of circles.

STRATEGIES FOR MULTIPLE-CHOICE QUESTIONS

Many college professors give multiple-choice tests because they are easy to grade and provide quick, precise responses. A multiple-choice question asks you to choose from among usually two to five answers to complete a sentence. Some strategies for increasing your success in answering multiple-choice questions are the following:

- Read the question and try to answer it before you read the answers provided.
- Look for similar answers; one of them is usually the correct response.
- Recognize that answers containing extreme modifiers, such as *always*, *every*, and *never*, are usually wrong.
- Cross off answers that you know are incorrect.

- Read all the options before selecting your answer. Even if you believe that A is the correct response, read them all.
- Recognize that when the answers are all numbers, the highest and lowest numbers are usually incorrect.
- Recognize that a joke is usually wrong.
- Understand that the most inclusive answer is often correct.
- Understand that the longest answer is often correct.
- If you cannot answer a question, move on to the next one and continue through the test; another question may trigger the answer you missed.
- Make an educated guess if you must.
- Answer every question unless there is a penalty for guessing.

Sample Test #3

Directions: Read each statement and select the best response from the answers given below.

STUDY SKILLS

1. Which statement is true according to the 2000 Census?
   A. Men earn more than women.
   B. Women earn more than men.
   C. People with a doctorate earn the most money of any education level.
   D. Males and females earn just about the same amount of money.

2. To calculate a GPA, you would:
   A. divide quality points by the number of semester hours.
   B. multiply total points by quality points.
   C. divide total points by the number of semester hours.
   D. multiply the quality points by the total points.

3. To be an effective priority manager, you have to:
   A. be very structured and organized.
   B. be very unstructured and disorganized.
   C. be mildly structured and organized.
   D. be sometimes a little of both.
   E. know what type of person you are and work from that point.

4. The listening process involves:
   A. receiving, organizing, assigning, and reacting.
   B. receiving, assigning, transferring, and encoding.
   C. encoding, assigning, organizing, and reacting.
   D. encoding, decoding, organizing, and assigning.

WORLD OF WORK

I believe that the primary focus for higher education is to provide society with an intelligent and highly productive workforce. Not only did higher education prepare me for my profession, but I know that I have applied the skills learned as a college student to schedule my work and leisure time more reasonably and logically, to make my work time more fruitful and still leave me time for my friends, family, and hobbies.

In my role as a college professor who teaches hospitality accounting and finance, my college experience prepared me to use materials, resources, and technology in the wisest way by focusing on relevant, important, and reliable information sources and disregarding irrelevant, unimportant, and unreliable information.

Of course, the information I share in my courses is reinforced through the use of tests. I know students are particularly frightened of quantitative courses, and therefore the tests I give create a great deal of stress for my students. I give tests because I believe that they prepare students for the world of work in two ways. They help strengthen the basic knowledge students have learned in or out of class, and they sharpen their ability to think logically or reason through the analyzing of data. Without tests, students would have no reason to pull everything together so that they can see the whole picture. Tests, stressful as they may be, encourage students to really get into the material and analyze it so that they can synthesize new information in meaningful ways.

QUESTIONS FOR REFLECTION

Consider responding to these questions online in the World of Work module of the Companion Website.

1. How can you apply Dr. Gu's suggestion of focusing on relevant, important, and reliable information sources to the courses you are currently taking?

2. How could you implement Dr. Gu's suggestions about test taking to your own testing strategies?

3. Have you ever prepared for a test and then used those same strategies in some way to aid you in your career? Why or why not? How?

Zheng Gu, *College Professor,* The University of Nevada, Las Vegas, NV

STRATEGIES FOR SHORT-ANSWER QUESTIONS

Short-answer questions, also called fill-in-the-blanks, ask you to supply the answer yourself, not to select it from a list. Although "short answer" sounds easy, these questions are often very difficult. Short-answer questions require you to draw from your long-term memory. The following hints can help you answer this type of question successfully:

- Read each question and be sure that you know what is being asked.
- Be brief in your response.
- Give the same number of answers as there are blanks; for example, _____ and _____ would require two answers.
- Never assume that the length of the blank has anything to do with the length of the answer.

- Remember that your initial response is usually correct.
- Pay close attention to the word immediately preceding the blank; if the word is "an," give a response that begins with a vowel (a, e, i, o, u).
- Look for key words in the sentence that may trigger a response.

Sample Test #4

Directions: Fill in the blanks with the correct response. Write clearly.

LISTENING SKILLS

1. Listening is a _____ act. We choose to do it.
2. The listening process involves receiving, organizing, _____, and reacting.
3. _____ is the same as listening with an open mind.
4. Prejudging is an _____ to listening.
5. Leaning forward, giving eye contact, being patient, and leaving your emotions at home are characteristics of _____ listeners.

STRATEGIES FOR ESSAY QUESTIONS

Most students look at essay questions with dismay because they take more time. Yet essay tests can be one of the easiest tests to take because they give you a chance to show what you really know. An essay question requires you to supply the information. If you have studied, you will find that once you begin to answer an essay question, your answer will flow easily. Some tips for answering essay questions are the following:

- More is not always better; sometimes more is just more. Try to be as concise and informative as possible. A professor would rather see one page of excellent material than five pages of fluff.
- Pay close attention to the action word used in the question and respond with the appropriate type of answer. Key words used in questions include the following:

discuss	illustrate	enumerate	describe
compare	define	relate	list
contrast	summarize	analyze	explain
trace	evaluate	critique	interpret
diagram	argue	justify	prove

- Write a thesis statement for each answer.

- Outline your thoughts before you begin to write.
- Watch your spelling, grammar, and punctuation.
- Use details, such as times, dates, places, and proper names, where appropriate.
- Be sure to answer all parts of the question; some discussion questions have more than one part.
- Summarize your main ideas toward the end of your answer.
- Write neatly.
- Proofread your answer.

Learning how to take a test and learning how to reduce your anxiety are two of the most important gifts you can give yourself as a student. Although tips and hints may help you, don't forget that there is no substitute for studying and knowing the material.

Using proper study techniques and remembering testing tips can increase your chances of success on most tests.

Sample Test #5

Directions: Answer each question completely. Use a separate paper if you wish.

STUDY SKILLS

1. Give two examples of mnemonics.

2. Discuss why it is important to use the SQ3R method.

3. Justify your chosen notebook system.

4. Compare an effective study environment with an ineffective study environment.

STRATEGIES
FOR BUILDING ON YOUR BEST

Consider the following strategies for taking tests and relieving test anxiety:

- Prepare carefully, thoroughly, and continuously in order to prevent test anxiety.
- Pay close attention to the professor in order to predict the types of questions that may be included on an exam.
- If the professor offers study sessions, attend and ask questions if you do not understand any part of the review.
- Use the suggestions in this chapter to respond to a variety of test questions.
- Review your institution's student handbook and become familiar with the code of ethics that has been endorsed by your faculty, students, and administrators.
- Be sure you understand exactly what constitutes plagiarism, including using information found on the Internet.
- Establish an exemplary code of personal ethics and academic integrity so that, above all else, you can respect yourself and earn the respect of others.

Academic and Personal Integrity

MAKING THE RIGHT DECISIONS

As a college student, you will be faced with temptations that require you to make hard choices. You have probably already been forced to make decisions based on ethics. Do I cheat and make a higher grade so I can compete with top students? Will cheating help me earn higher grades so I get a better job? Do I copy this paper from the Internet? Who will know? No one said specifically that copying from the Internet is wrong. Why shouldn't I do this if everybody else is copying? Why shouldn't I buy one of the term papers that is floating around my fraternity? What if I lose my scholarship? What if I just copy someone's homework and not cheat on a test? What if I lie to the instructor and say I was sick so I can get more time for a test for which I am not prepared? What if I let someone look on my paper during a test; I'm not cheating, am I? These are all ethical questions that require you to use your personal integrity to make the right decision.

Integrity is purely and simply doing what you think is right. It's about understanding who you are as a person and making decisions about what is right and wrong according to your personal code of ethics. What will you do when nobody knows but you? It is also making decisions about what is right and wrong according to your institution's standards. As a college student, you will see many people do things that you think are not right. You have to decide what is right for you and follow your values no matter what others may be doing. Just because "everyone is doing it" doesn't make it right, and certainly it doesn't make it right for you.

Your college years should refine your character and hopefully help you assess and evaluate your value system. You will no doubt find some of your views and values changing over the next few years. One of your challenges is to ensure that you are improving your character rather than compromising who you are and hope to become. You are building yourself today for the long haul—not for a few short years!

Change occurs, progress is made, and difficulties resolved if people merely do the right thing, and rarely do people *not know* what the right thing is. —FATHER HESSBURG

LISTEN TO YOUR CONSCIENCE

What does your conscience tell you? If it nags at you about an action you are about to take, don't do it! Making ethical decisions can be as simple as listening to your conscience. If you have a nagging, recurring feeling that what you are doing is not right, it probably isn't. If you can't sleep at night because you have done something that you cannot respect, chances are you need to reflect on your decisions. Real integrity is doing the right thing when nobody knows but you, or refraining when you could probably get away with copying a test question or committing an infraction of the rules. Your personal code of ethics is based on your value system, the standards and ideals that you use to make tough decisions.

Even if you cheat and don't get caught, you lose. You lose respect for yourself, your self-esteem is likely to decline, and you cheat yourself of the knowledge for which you are paying. You also lose because you damage your character and the person you hope to become. Cheating can cause you to feel guilty and stressed because you are afraid that someone might find out.

Eventually, cheating will become a crutch that you lean on in order to pass and make good grades, and it will become easy to decide to cheat instead of working and earning your grades. The habit of cheating is likely to carry over into the workplace if you have embraced it as a way of life in college. Gradually, day by day, you are building the person you want to become. Ultimately, the person who is harmed the most by cheating is the one who does it. In some shape or fashion, cheating will always come back to haunt you. You, personally, will pay the price.

Academic integrity says a lot about who you are and what you believe in. Following a code of ethics is important for another reason as well. If you are honest, work hard, and do your own work, you will most likely get a good education. Your future depends on what you are learning today!

> *You are fast becoming what you are going to be.*
> —ANONYMOUS

WHAT DO YOU NEED TO KNOW ABOUT ACADEMIC MISCONDUCT?

It is important to know what constitutes dishonesty in an academic setting. Following is a list of offenses that most colleges consider academic misconduct.

- Looking on another person's test paper for answers.
- Giving another student answers on tests, homework, or lab projects.
- Using any kind of "cheat sheets" on a test or project.
- Using a computer, calculator, dictionary, or notes when not approved.
- Discussing exam questions with students who are taking the same class at another time.
- Plagiarism or using the words or works of others without giving proper credit. This includes the Internet!
- Stealing another student's class notes.

DID YOU KNOW?

15%

The percentage of 4,471 U.S. high school students surveyed in a recent study who admitted that they had turned in papers copied entirely from the Internet.

Source: Jerome, R., and Grout, P. "Cheat wave." *People Magazine,* June 17, 2002, p. 84.

- Using an annotated instructor's edition of a text.
- Having tutors do your homework for you.
- Submitting the same paper for more than one class during any semester.
- Copying files from a lab computer or borrowing someone else's disk with the work on it.
- Bribing a student for answers or academic work such as papers or projects.
- Buying or acquiring papers from individuals or the Internet.
- Assisting others with dishonest acts.
- Lying about reasons you missed a test or a class.

David Letterman, comedian and late night talk show host, often uses "top 10" lists to evoke laughter. The top 10 questions below are designed to make you think BEFORE you make a bad decision regarding personal and academic ethics.

Top 10 Questions to Ask About Academic Ethics

10. If other people found out about your actions, could you defend what you did?
9. Is the action you are taking worth the risk and the stress?
8. Is it worth failing the course if the professor learns you cheated?
7. How would you feel about being expelled from school for this action?
6. Is your decision fair to all people concerned?
5. Does your decision make you proud of who you are as a person?
4. Have you made a carefully thought out, responsible, mature decision regardless of what everyone else is doing?
3. Is it the right thing to do?
2. If this action were to appear in the headlines of the newspaper tomorrow morning, would you feel proud?
1. If your family knew about your decision, would they be proud of you?

BLUEPRINTS FOR CHANGE

NAME   DATE

REFLECTION

Learning to deal with test anxiety and to get your fears under control early in your college years can lead to greater success as you move through your college career. With the right kinds of practice, you can become much more adept at test taking and can greatly reduce your stress.

Another important part of this chapter dealt with academic and personal integrity. You can't control anyone's behavior other than your own. Your challenge is to focus on developing excellent test-taking abilities and study habits while earning the best grades you can. When you have done this, you can look in the mirror and be proud of the person you see without having to be ashamed of your character or having to worry about being caught cheating. You are building your character for the long haul—not just a few short years.

GET REAL

Below are a few questions to help you think about academic integrity, test anxiety, and methods to help you relieve stress. Study each question and respond honestly.

Discuss one experience you have already had this semester that caused you to have extreme test anxiety.

How can you apply at least one of the tips for controlling test anxiety during your next exam?

How can you prepare mentally and physically for taking tests more successfully?

How can you use the information in this chapter, as well as Ellen's opening story, to improve your test-taking ability?

How can you apply what you have learned in this chapter in the workplace in either a full- or part-time job?

How can you use the character building suggestions related to academic integrity to grow in stature and become the kind of person you want to be while you are in college?

Case Study

NAME: Oscar Bowser, Jr.
SCHOOL: Midlands Technical College, Columbia, SC
MAJOR: Nursing   AGE: 52

Below is a real-life situation faced by Oscar. Read the brief case and respond to the questions.

I am a former Marine, an ex-New York state public safety officer, an ex-correctional officer, and a certified rescue scuba diver. Over the course of my life, there have been very few things that I have feared and not conquered. It may seem strange, but I was afraid of math.

My goal is to become a professional registered nurse, and math is a major part of that curriculum. When I began college, I would avoid registering for any math course or I would register and withdraw at some point during the course to avoid my anxiety of math. Numerous times, I've taken math exams without having read or studied the chapter; therefore, I could not comprehend the directions.

Finally, it dawned on me that the cause of my math anxiety, or any anxiety in general, is simply this: "the lack of knowing." You don't have anxiety when driving a car because you know how by repetition. You don't have anxiety walking through your home at night without lights on because you have familiarized yourself with the environment. Due to this discovery, I have eliminated my anxiety. To study for my math exams, I use the following techniques: reading, writing, reciting, repeating, and memorizing.

In addition, I have learned that to conquer anything in life you must practice self-motivation, self-determination, and self-discipline. This semester, my grades in math thus far are 95, 105, 89, and 100! Nursing Degree, here I come!

How can a positive attitude like Oscar's affect your classroom performance?

Do you think Oscar is correct in his explanation of what causes anxiety? Why or why not?

What role does self-discipline play in reducing test anxiety?

How can reducing test anxiety help you perform better?

_____
_____
_____

What concrete methods do you plan to employ to reduce your testing anxiety?

_____
_____
_____

How do you plan to improve your self-discipline and self-determination to help with your test-taking strategies?

_____
_____
_____

Where can you go on your campus to learn more about controlling test anxiety, learning to take tests more effectively, and studying for tests in general?

_____
_____
_____

at this moment Journal

Refer to page 283 of this chapter. Having read and reflected on the information in the chapter, consider how you might revise your goal to make it more:

REASONABLE

BELIEVABLE

MEASURABLE

ADAPTABLE

CONTROLLABLE

DESIRABLE

ONLINE JOURNAL

To complete an online journal entry, log onto the Companion Website at www.prenhall.com/sherfield. Go to Chapter 10 and click on the link to the Online Journal. You can respond to the questions provided or to questions assigned by your professor, or you may journal about your own experiences.

ADVICE TO GO
CORNERSTONES
for test taking

Maintain your personal *integrity*.

Never use drugs or alcohol to get through a test.

Read over the entire test *before* beginning.

Check punctuation, spelling, and grammar.

Write your *name* on every test page.

Ignore the pace of your classmates.

Ask questions of the professor.

Answer *all* questions.

Watch *time* limits.

Think *positively*.

Write *clearly*.

ASSESS

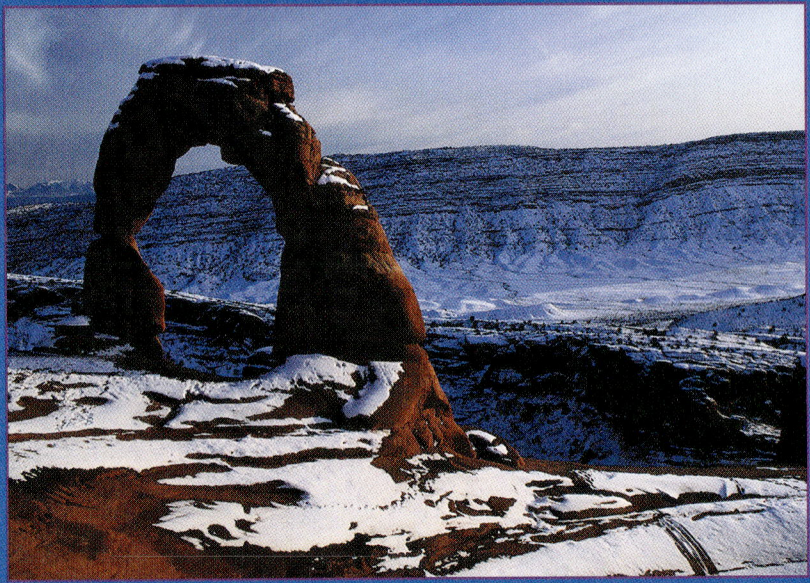

11 Think

The road to success is often off the beaten path.

F. Tyger

CHAPTER 11

THINK

Josh and Martha quickly volunteered to be the two students in their interpersonal communication class to debate the topic of the death penalty. Josh and Martha both seemed to have an unbridled passion for this discussion.

Both students worked exceedingly hard to prepare for the debate. Each one was resolved to "win." Both Josh and Martha interviewed people, conducted research on the Internet, read articles from journals, and reviewed up-to-date information in newspapers and magazines on their topic. They were prepared. They were determined.

As class began, the professor laid the groundwork for the debate, reviewed the procedures, and reminded everyone of the rules and time limits. Josh and Martha were somewhat nervous, but both knew that they were prepared and psyched about the event. Martha began.

> There is no greater repayment to the victim or victim's family than the execution of the person who committed the violent act. In the words of David Anderson, a death penalty supporter and author of the Death Penalty—A Defense, "The execution is the only means by which we are 100% certain that that perpetrator will never commit another crime."
>
> The death penalty has been associated with racism. This is a fallacy. The Bureau of Justice reports that the majority of those executed since 1976 have been white. According to Thomas Eddlem, whites still comprise the majority on death row. In 2000, 49 out of 85 people put to death were white.
>
> Liberals argue that the legal system and indeed the death penalty are laden with mistakes and innocent people are put to death. It is true that a few people have died by error, but with the introduction of DNA evidence, the case for the death penalty is even stronger, for DNA can conclusively identify the proper perpetrators. With DNA evidence, there will be no mistakes in the future.
>
> Further, if DNA evidence did not exist, our Constitution, as explained by Franklin Zimring, provides for an "exhaustion of remedies" before an execution can take place.
>
> Many argue that the cost of putting a person to death is unreasonably high. The only argument that can be made here is a statement by Eddlem, "Justice isn't up for sale to the lowest bidder."
>
> Lastly, I will quote David Anderson again as he makes his argument for the death penalty. He states, "The death penalty defends human dignity. The death penalty expresses society's compassion to the victim. The death penalty gives peace of mind to the victims. The death penalty creates a safer society, and the death penalty is the only way to show that our society is serious about crime." Thank you for your attention.

After Martha's argument, Josh approached the lectern with the same energy and passion for his side of the story. He took a deep breath, waited for the timekeeper to signal, and began.

Critical- and Creative-Thinking Skills

There is no greater barbaric act on earth than the murder of another person. To quote Amnesty International, "The death penalty is the ultimate cruel, inhumane, and degrading punishment. It violates the right to life. It is irrevocable and can be inflicted on the innocent. It has never been shown to deter crime more effectively than other punishments."

The death penalty is a racist, economic tactic that seeks to destroy a segment of our population. According to Roger Clegg, over a five-year period, death penalty cases were brought against 973 defendants. Of these 973 defendants, only 166 were white (17%). Seven hundred and fifty-eight (78%) were either Hispanic or African American, making them over-represented on death row compared to their makeup in the general population.

The death penalty is exceedingly expensive for society. According to the website, TheElectricChair.com, Florida spends 3.2 million dollars on a death row inmate compared to only $535,000 for a 40-year prison sentence. The average cost for a death penalty trial is almost $300,000.

The death penalty has cost many innocent people their lives. Over a 25-year period, over 100 people on death row were released after being found innocent. How many were not found in time?

The United States remains one of the last industrialized nations to carry out the death penalty. We hold this rank with only China, the Congo, and Iran. To date, over 106 nations and 30 countries have abolished this cruel and inhumane punishment.

In an article, Michael Radelet states that since 1982 over 30 executions have been botched and resulted in horrendous inhumane treatment. From executionees catching fire, to misplaced syringes in collapsed veins, to allergic reactions, to six-inch flames spewing from a man's head due to equipment failure, the list continues with case after case of inhumane treatment.

Finally, it has never been determined that the death penalty is a deterrent to crime. According to Amnesty International, "Scientific studies have consistently failed to find convincing evidence." Thank you for listening to me.

Questions for Reflection

Consider responding to these questions online in the Questions for Reflection module of the Companion Website.

1. Which argument is more convincing? Why?

2. If you were debating this topic, how would you research your material?

3. Which argument do you trust more? Why?

Where are you... AT THIS MOMENT

Before reading this chapter, take a moment and respond to the following ten questions. Consider each one carefully before answering, and then respond by circling the number in the appropriate box. When you have answered the questions, add your points and find your total score on the feedback chart below.

STATEMENT	STRONGLY DISAGREE	DISAGREE	DON'T KNOW	AGREE	STRONGLY AGREE	SCORE
1. I tend to trust the information I get from the mass media without analyzing it.	5	4	3	2	1	
2. It is difficult for me to approach a topic with an open mind once I have already come to a conclusion about it.	5	4	3	2	1	
3. I question and scrutinize the "facts" that I get from others.	1	2	3	4	5	
4. I am easily persuaded by information that sounds rational.	5	4	3	2	1	
5. The ability to think critically is really only of use in school.	5	4	3	2	1	
6. When I'm trying to understand another person's point of view, my emotions or opinions get in the way.	5	4	3	2	1	
7. Information I get from TV, magazines, or newspapers doesn't need to be questioned or challenged.	5	4	3	2	1	
8. When I'm trying to solve a problem, I rely on the "try something and see" approach, rather than devising a plan.	5	4	3	2	1	
9. I possess the courage and tolerance for the risk taking it takes to be creative in problem solving and thinking.	1	2	3	4	5	
10. I know how to tell if a statement is a fact or an opinion.	1	2	3	4	5	
TOTAL VALUE						

SUMMARY

10–17 Your critical-thinking skills are limited. You have difficulty keeping an open mind, are easily influenced by opinions, and need to sharpen your ability to separate facts from things that sound like facts. You must explore these issues to be successful in school and the outside world.

18–25 You have below average skills in critically analyzing information. You need to learn how to better separate fact from propaganda. You likely also need to improve your ability to eliminate your emotional reactions to information while analyzing it.

26–34 You are average in your critical-thinking and reasoning skills. You are likely able to distinguish fact from opinion and sometimes stop to question the information that you've been exposed to. You would benefit from refined critical-thinking strategies.

35–42 You have above average critical-thinking skills. You know that it is important to distinguish real facts from statements that just sound like facts. You are also probably good at analyzing information from an open-minded, neutral perspective.

43–50 You have exceptional critical-thinking skills. You likely make it a habit to question and analyze most information that you come across. You probably incorporate creative and flexible thinking in your analyses.

Goals... FOR CHANGE

Based on your total points, what is one goal you would like to achieve related to critical and creative thinking?

Goal _____
_____

List three actions you can take that might help you move closer to realizing this goal.

1. _____
2. _____
3. _____

Questions FOR BUILDING ON YOUR BEST

As you read this chapter, consider the following questions. At the end of the chapter, you should be able to answer all of them. You are encouraged to ask a few questions of your own. Consider asking your classmates or professors to assist you.

1. Why is critical thinking important to my life?
2. How can critical thinking help me become a better student?
3. What steps can I take to become a more critical and creative thinker?
4. Why is problem solving important to my life?
5. When will I ever need to use critical thinking in the "real world"?

What additional questions might you have about thinking more critically and creatively?

1. _____
2. _____
3. _____

Thinking About Thinking

Take a moment to evaluate the two sides presented by Martha and Josh. Having just read the opening remarks, how do you feel about the issue? Did you learn anything new? Did you approach the argument with an open mind? Did your emotions cloud your thoughts? Is there a right or wrong side to the death penalty? What are you thinking right now? More importantly, why are you thinking the way you are right now? What is causing you to believe, feel, or think one way or the other about those two questions? What are the facts and/or opinions that have led you to your conclusion?

At this moment, are you basing your thoughts about this issue on emotions or facts, fallacies or truths, data or opinions, interviews or hearsay, reason or misjudgment, fear or empathy?

Understanding why and how we formulate thoughts and ideas is the main objective of this chapter. This chapter is about believing and disbelieving, seeking, uncovering, debunking myths, proving the impossible possible. It is about proof, logic, evidence, and developing ideas and opinions based on hard-core facts or credible research. This chapter is about seeking truth and expanding your mind to unimaginable limits. This chapter is about the fundamental aspect of becoming an educated citizen; it is about human thought and reasoning.

Almost any profession you choose to go into will require the ability to think through problems, make decisions, and apply other critical thinking skills.

What Is It Anyway?
A WORKING DEFINITION OF CRITICAL THINKING

All right, it is your turn. Suppose your best friend asked you why you favored (or did not favor) the death penalty. What would your answer be? If you are FOR the death penalty, would you say that it is justified, warranted, necessary, or reasonable? If you are AGAINST the death penalty, would you say that it is murder, inhumane, cruel, unjustifiable, unneeded, reprehensible, or vindictive?

For those of you who are *for* the death penalty, let's say that you hold the death penalty as *justified*. For those of you who are *against* the death penalty, let's say that you hold the death penalty as *vindictive*.

Before you go any further, explain to your friend just what *justified* (or *vindictive*) means. Make him or her understand it. Make him or her understand your reason for using that word. Can you do it? You know what you mean, but can you make your friend understand your position? Can you explain in great detail what the word is and how it applies to capital punishment? Can you define the word? Can you explain what it implies? Can you give examples of the word as related to the death penalty?

This technique, as explained by Peter Facione (1998), is the best way to define critical thinking. Critical thinking is what you are doing with that word *right now.* It is searching, plotting, making associations, explaining, analyzing, probing for multiple angles, justifying, scrutinizing, making decisions, solving problems, and investigating. *It is literally thinking about something from many angles.*

Another way to define critical thinking is to consider people who use critical thinking in their daily lives:

- The lawyer who found the loophole to free his client.
- The doctor who searched deeply enough, ordered the correct tests, and found the cancer that was missed by three other physicians.
- The computer repair technician who found the one tiny circuit problem in your computer.
- The auto repair person who found the faulty wiring in your car.
- The nurse who sensed something was wrong and noticed the error in the medication chart.
- The teacher who finally found a way to teach Johnny to read with pictures.
- The homemaker who discovered a way to reduce the household debt each month.
- The marketing expert who developed the winning campaign for Mountain Dew.
- The student who discovered that reading the material before class made listening easier.

These people and their discoveries define critical thinking better than any definition we could provide here.

Critical thinking is about making informed, enlightened, educated, open-minded decisions in college, in relationships, in finances, and in life in general.

When Will I Ever Use It?
THE IMPORTANCE OF CRITICAL THINKING

Have you ever made a decision that turned out to be a mistake? Have you ever said to yourself, "If only I could go back . . . "? Have you ever regretted actions you took toward a person or situation? Have you ever planned an event or function that went off flawlessly? Have you ever had to make a hard, painful decision that turned out to be "the best decision of your life"? If the answer to any of these questions is yes, you might be able to trace the consequences back to your thought process at the time of the decision. Let's face it, sometimes good and bad things happen out of luck. More often than not, however, the events in our lives are driven by the thought processes involved when we made the initial decision.

Critical thinking can serve us in many areas as students and citizens in society. As a student, critical thinking can help you focus on issues; gather

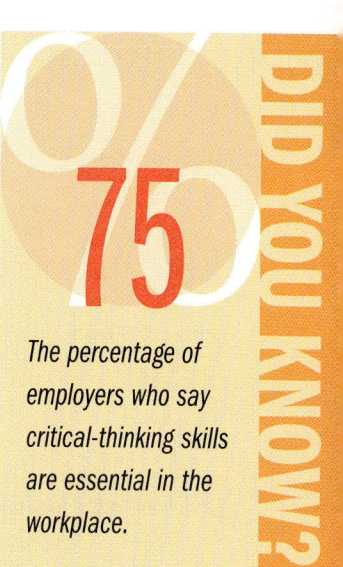

DID YOU KNOW?

75%

The percentage of employers who say critical-thinking skills are essential in the workplace.

Source: Hickman, R., and Quinley, J. *A Synthesis of Local, State, and National Studies in Workforce Education and Training.* Washington, DC: The American Association of Community Colleges, 1997.

relevant, accurate information; remember facts; organize thoughts logically; analyze questions and problems; and manage your priorities. It can assist in your problem-solving skills and help you control your emotions so that you can make rational judgments. It can help you produce new knowledge through research and analysis and help you determine the accuracy of printed and spoken words. It can help you detect bias and determine the relevance of arguments and persuasion.

How Critical Thinking Can Help You Beyond the Classroom

THE SITUATION	CRITICAL THINKING CAN HELP YOU DECIDE...
Relationships	• Whom to date. • Whom to trust. • In whom you can confide. • How seriously involved you should get.
Goal Setting	• If the goal is realistic. • How to develop a plan of action. • What resources you need and how to get them.
Finances	• How to develop a realistic budget. • If you should charge or lay away. • How much you have to save to pay tuition and fees. • How to search for scholarships.
Decision Making	• How to approach a difficult decision. • How to analyze your options. • How the decision will affect your life. • If the decision is a solid one.
Problem Solving	• How to identify the real problem. • How to solicit assistance. • How serious the problem really is. • When to implement the solution.
Environmental Issues	• Whether to buy an SUV or "green" car. • How recycling helps the earth. • How your personal behaviors contribute to the warming effect.
Civic Duties	• For whom to cast your vote. • How to get involved in your community. • For which organization to volunteer. • To which organization to donate money.

A Plan for Critical Thinking

MAKING IT WORK FOR YOU

As you begin to build and expand your critical-thinking skills, consider the steps involved. Critical-thinking skill development involves

- Restraining emotions
- Looking at things differently
- Analyzing information
- Asking questions
- Solving problems
- Distinguishing fact from opinion
- Seeking truth in argument and persuasion

The remainder of this chapter will detail, through explanation, exploration, and exercises, how to build a critical-thinking plan for your academic and personal success.

STEP ONE: RESTRAINING EMOTIONS

Did James Earl Ray really kill Martin Luther King, Jr.? Is there life on other planets? Should Eminem's music be banned from music stores? Should the drinking age be lowered to 18? Should 16-year-olds be allowed to drive a car? Should hate crime laws be abolished? What emotions are you feeling right now? Did you immediately formulate answers to these questions in your mind? Are your emotions driving your thinking process?

Emotions play a vital role in our lives. They help us feel compassion, help others, and reach out in times of need, and they help us relate to others. Emotions, on the other hand, can cause some problems in your critical-thinking process. You do not have to eliminate emotions from your thoughts, but it is crucial that you know when your emotions are clouding an issue.

> What we need is not the will to believe, but the will to find out. —BERTRAND RUSSELL

Consider the following topics:

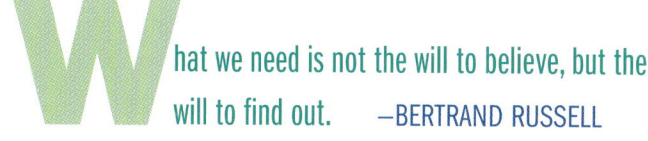

- Should drugs and prostitution be legalized?
- Can the theories of evolution and creationism coexist?
- Is affirmative action reverse discrimination?
- Should terminally ill patients have the right to state-assisted and/or privately-assisted suicide?

As you read these topics, did you immediately form an opinion? Did old arguments surface? Did you feel your emotions coming into play as you thought about the questions? If you had an immediate answer, it is likely that you allowed some past judgments, opinions, and emotions to enter the decision-making process, unless you have just done a comprehensive, unbiased study of one of

WORLD OF WORK

An old mentor suggested that "the quality of your life is based upon the questions you ask." Great questions come from increasingly better thinking involving a lot of creativity. I found my best questions were always intangible in nature. My ability to extract experiences and learning from my college life, which helped me build sharp new questions, was certainly one of the most important skills I took away from college. Frequently, these questions evolved into challenges or applications of things I had already learned. Here are some of my favorites:

- **Visualize.** Can I visualize what the answer of a problem is? What does success look like? Your ability to apply yourself creatively to tangibly or intangibly visualize the outcome is critical to success. The more you can visualize, the more likely you are to accomplish. If you can visualize it, you probably will create a new paradigm.

- **Use all efforts.** Am I doing everything I possibly can to succeed at this? (With emphasis on "everything.") Surprisingly, most people stop short of giving many efforts an all-out try. Swing for the fences. The last 5 percent of effort frequently makes a success or failure difference. Go for it!

- **Focus energy.** There is no substitute for bringing a laserlike focus and an extreme concentration of energy and passion to your undertaking. Demonstrate tremendous stamina and focus. College has taught all of us, in some way, not to give up. Add this to more concentrated levels of energy, and success will visit more frequently.

- **Speed and timing.** Some say "the fastest learner wins." If you think about it, this applies to many things in life. However, timing is also important, and having a strong sense of timing frequently makes all the difference in the world. This is an important skill that can be cultivated. Those who are able to supplement their priorities and speed of action with the creative gift of better timing (in their personal life, business, sports, family, etc.) find most things fall more easily into place.

- **Be outrageous.** Am I effectively being outrageous? The hard answers are frequently outside of the box and may require unconventional thinking to get there. Don't be afraid to be different. Don't be afraid to not stand in line like everyone else. Demonstrate mental agility and capacity in conceptual and abstract thinking. Go ahead, and if required, be outrageous.

QUESTIONS FOR REFLECTION

Consider responding to these questions online in the World of Work module of the Companion Website.

1. When have you had to be outrageous just to survive?
2. Can you visualize answers before you know them? Why or why not?
3. Have you ever had an opportunity for greatness and your energy level would not allow you to seize it?

Glenn E. Montgomery *President,* Montgomery Consultants, Denver, CO

these issues. As you discussed these in class or with your friends, how did you feel? Did you get angry? Did you find yourself groping for words? Did you find it hard to explain why you held the opinion that you voiced? If so, these are warning signs that you are allowing your emotions to drive your decisions. If we allow our emotions to run rampant (not using restraint) and fail to use research, logic, and evidence (expansive thinking), we will not be able to examine the issues critically or have a logical discussion regarding the statements.

If you feel that your emotions caused you to be less than objective, you might consider the following tips when you are faced with an emotional decision:

- Listen to all sides of the argument or statement before you make a decision or form an opinion.
- Make a conscious effort to identify which emotions are causing you to lose objectivity.
- Do not let your emotions withdraw you or turn you off from the situation.
- Don't let yourself become engaged in "I'm right, you're wrong" situations.
- Work to understand why others feel their side is valid.
- Physiological reactions to emotions, such as increased heart rate and blood pressure and an increase in adrenaline flow, should be recognized as an emotional checklist. If you begin to experience these reactions, relax, take a deep breath, and concentrate on being open-minded.
- Control your negative self-talk or inner voice toward the other person(s) or situation.
- Determine whether your emotions are irrational.

In the space provided below, develop a step-by-step plan to evaluate one of the controversial topics listed previously. You do not have to answer the question; your task is to devise a plan to address the topic critically without emotional interference. For example: Do violent TV programs and movies cause violent crime? Before you answer yes or no, your first step might be to define violent TV/movies. A second step might be to define violent crime. A third step might be to research the connection between the two. A fourth step might be to evaluate the research objectively, asking the following questions: (1) From where does the research originate: the TV or movie industry, a parental guidance group, or a completely independent agency? (2) How old is the research? (3) For how long a period was the research conducted? This type of questioning does not allow your emotions to rule the outcome.

Candid discussions, and sometimes brutal honesty, are useful and necessary when you are addressing complex or difficult issues. However, be careful not to let emotions take over your objectivity.

Select one of the topics from those listed on page 313, or develop your own statement, and devise a plan for critical analysis.

Statement

Step 1.

Step 2.

Step 3.

Step 4.

Step 5.

STEP TWO: LOOKING AT THINGS DIFFERENTLY

Critical thinking involves looking at an issue from many different angles. It encourages you to dig deeper than you have before; get below the surface; struggle, experiment, and expand. It asks you to look at something from an entirely different angle so that you might develop new insights and understand more about the problem, situation, or question. Thinking on a higher level involves looking at something that you may have never seen before or something that you may have seen many times, and trying to think about it more critically than before.

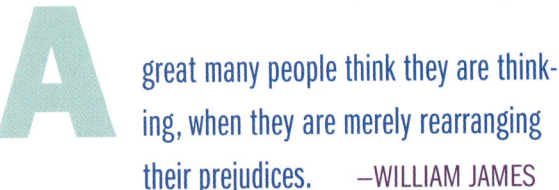

A great many people think they are thinking, when they are merely rearranging their prejudices. —WILLIAM JAMES

As you begin to look "with different eyes," take a moment to complete the activities below. They are provided to encourage you to look at simple, common situations in a new light. Remember, these exercises do not measure intelligence.

Review the following example of a "brain teaser" and solve the remaining teasers. You will need to break down a few barriers in thought and look at them from a new angle to get them all.

BRAIN TEASERS

Examples: 4 W on a C   4 Wheels on a Car
              13 O C   13 Original Colonies

1. SW and the 7 D
2. I H a D by MLK
3. 2 P's in a P
4. HDD (TMRUTC)
5. 3 S to a T
6. 100 P in a D
7. T no PLH
8. 4 Q in a G
9. I a SWAA
10. 50 S in TU

How did you do? Was it hard to look at the situation backward? Most of us are not used to that. As you continue to build your critical-thinking skills, look at the design at the right. You will find nine dots. Your mission is to connect all nine dots with four straight lines without removing your pencil or pen from the paper. Do not retrace your lines. Can you do it?

Finally, as you begin to think beyond the obvious, examine the penny below. You will see the front and back sides of the penny. Pretend that the world has ended and all traces of civilization are gone. Someone from another planet, who speaks our language, has come to earth and the only thing left from our civilization is one penny. Below, list the things that could be assumed about our civilization from this one small penny. You should find at least 10.

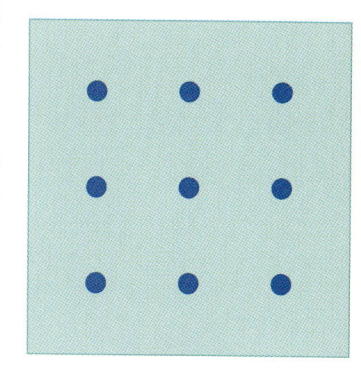

1. _____
2. _____
3. _____
4. _____
5. _____
6. _____
7. _____
8. _____
9. _____
10. _____

While these activities may seem somewhat trivial, they are provided to help you begin to think about and consider information from a different angle. This is a major step in becoming a critical thinker: looking beyond the obvious, thinking outside the box, examining details, and exploring possibilities.

STEP THREE: ANALYZING INFORMATION

Critical thinking goes further than thinking on a different or higher level or using emotional restraint; it also involves analyzing information. To analyze, you break a topic, statement, or problem into parts to understand it more clearly. This is a simple, yet crucial, step in critical thinking. An easy way to analyze is to create a chart of the information using right- and left-hand columns. Consider the example on the following page that examines the death penalty from the opening debate.

As you can see, a question properly analyzed prevents you from simply answering the question with a bland and poor answer such as, "It's good," or "It's bad." It can also prevent you from becoming too emotional since you must rely on facts to support your answer. An analysis forces you to ask *why* it is good or bad, right or wrong, proper or improper.

Nothing in life is to be feared, it is to be understood. —MARIE CURIE

> ## Example
>
> Why should the death penalty be abolished?
>
> **It is barbaric.** The United States is the last industrialized nation in the world to use capital punishment. We are in the company of the Congo, Iran, and China.
>
> **It is racist.** More African Americans and Hispanics are put to death than Caucasians. The proportion of African American and Hispanic inmates on death row is greater than their porportion of the general population.
>
> **It is expensive.** It costs over $3 million to put a person to death, while it costs slightly more than $500,000 to imprison him or her for 40 years.

Now, it's your turn. Analyze the following question: *How can an undeclared student take steps to decide on a career?* Hint: The answer can be found in Chapter 15 of *Cornerstone*.

Column A (Answer)   *Column B (Explanation)*

_____   _____

_____   _____

_____   _____

_____   _____

_____   _____

_____   _____

_____   _____

_____   _____

_____   _____

_____   _____

_____   _____

_____   _____

_____   _____

_____   _____

This method can also be used to formulate new information on a subject. If you read a chapter or an article, hear a conversation, or are faced with a problem, you can analyze it by creating questions that need to be answered in Column A and providing the answer in Column B. You may have to use more than one source of information to answer the questions you posed in Column A.

STEP FOUR: ASKING QUESTIONS

You've asked questions all of your life. As a child, you asked your parents, "What's that?" a million times. You probably asked them, "Why do I have to do this?" In later years, you've asked questions of your friends, teachers, strangers, store clerks, and significant others. Questioning is not new to you, but it may be a new technique for exploring, developing, and acquiring new knowledge. Curiosity may have killed the cat, but it was a smart cat when it died! Your curiosity is one of the most important traits you possess. It helps you grow and learn, and it may sometimes cause you to be uncomfortable. That's OK. This section is provided to assist you in learning how to ask questions to promote knowledge, solve problems, foster strong relationships, and critically analyze difficult situations.

Let's start with a simple questioning exercise. If you could meet anyone on earth and ask five questions, who would you meet, why would you meet that person, and what questions would you ask?

I'd like to meet _____

Because _____

I'd ask the person:

1. _____
2. _____
3. _____
4. _____
5. _____

Sometimes you want to ask questions of experts or those whose opinions you value to aid your own thinking. Are there questions you have for any of these people?

Asking questions can be fun in many situations. They help us gain insight where we may have limited knowledge. They can also challenge us to look at issues from many different angles. Answering properly posed questions can help us expand our knowledge base.

If you were Josh or Martha and about to embark on writing a college paper dealing with the death penalty in the United States, what questions would you want to have answered at the end of the paper? Take some time to think about the issue. Write down at least five questions.

My five questions are:

1. _____
2. _____
3. _____
4. _____
5. _____

Questioning also involves going beyond the obvious. Examine the following advertisement. The car dealership has provided some information, but it is

YOUR CHOICE $149 PER MO.

New ZX2

Over 75 ZX2s to choose from!

New Ranger

Over 50 Rangers to choose from!

Quality + Safety + Economy + Performance = Super Value

not enough to make an educated decision. What other questions would you ask to make sure that you are getting a good deal?

1. _____
_____
2. _____
_____
_____
3. _____
_____
4. _____
_____
5. _____

STEP FIVE: SOLVING PROBLEMS

You face problems every day; some are larger and more difficult than others. You may have transportation problems. You may have child care problems. You may have academic problems or interpersonal problems. Many people don't know how to solve problems at school, home, or work. They simply let the problem go unaddressed until it is too late to reach an amiable solution. There are many ways to address and solve problems. In this section, we will discuss how to identify and narrow the problem, research and develop alternatives, evaluate the alternatives, and solve the problem.

> **N**ot everything that is faced can be solved. Nothing can be solved until it is faced. —JAMES BALDWIN

It is important to remember that every problem does have a solution, but the solution may not be what we wanted. It is also imperative to remember the words of Mary Hatwood Futrell, President of the NEA. She states that "finding the right answer is important, of course. But more important is developing the ability to see that problems have multiple solutions, that getting from X to Y demands basic skills and mental agility, imagination, persistence, patience."

Identify and narrow the problem. Put your problem in writing. When doing this, be sure to jot down all aspects of the problem, such as why it is a problem, whom it affects, and what type of problem it is. Examine the following situation: You have just failed two tests this week and you are dreadfully behind on an English paper. Now, that's a problem . . . or is it? If you examine and reflect on the problem, you begin to realize that because of your nighttime job, you always get to class late, you are tired and irritable when you get there, and you never have time to study. So, the real problem is not that you can't do the work; the problem is that your job is interfering with your study time. Now that you have identified and narrowed the problem, you can begin to work toward a solution.

Research and develop alternatives. A valuable method of gathering ideas, formulating questions, and solving problems is brainstorming. To brainstorm, gather a group of people and ask them to let ideas flow. A brainstorming session allows all thoughts to be heard without any fear of ridicule. You can brainstorm any matter, almost anywhere. You may want to set some guidelines for your sessions to make them more productive.

- Identify the topic, problem, or statement to be discussed.
- Set a time limit for the entire brainstorming session.
- Write all ideas on a board or flip chart.
- Let everyone speak.
- Don't criticize people for their remarks.
- Concentrate on the issue; let all of your ideas flow.
- Suspend judgment until all ideas are produced or the time is up.
- If you're using the session to generate questions rather than solutions, each participant should pose questions rather than make statements.

Using the problem identified on the previous page (my nighttime job is causing me to not have enough time for sleep or study), jot down the first few alternatives that come to mind. Don't worry about content, clarity, or quality. Just let your mind flow. Verbalize these ideas when the class brainstorms this problem.

IDEAS _____

_____

_____

_____

Evaluate the alternatives. Some of your ideas or your classmates' ideas may not be logical in solving the problem. After careful study and deliberation, without emotional interference, analyze the ideas and determine if they are appropriate or inappropriate for the solution. To analyze, create Columns A and B. Write the idea in Column A and a comment in Column B. Example:

A (IDEA)	B (COMMENTS)
Quit the job.	Very hard to do. I need the money for tuition and car.
Cut my hours at work.	Will ask my boss.
Find a new job.	Hard to do because of the job market—but will look into it.
Get a student loan.	Visit financial aid office tomorrow.
Quit school.	No—it is my only chance for a promotion.

With your comments in Column B, you can now begin to eliminate some of the alternatives that are inappropriate at this time.

Solve the problem. Now that you have a few strong alternatives, you have some work to do. You will need to talk to your boss, go to the financial aid office, and possibly begin to search for a new job with flexible hours. After you have researched each alternative, you will be able to make a decision based on solid information and facts.

YOUR TURN

Pretend that your best friend, Nathan, has just come to you with a problem. He tells you that his parents are really coming down hard on him for going to college. It is a strange problem. They believe that Nathan should be working full time and that he is just wasting his time and money, since he did not do well in high school. They have threatened to take away his car and kick him out of the house if he does not find a full-time job. Nathan is doing well and does not want to leave college.

When solving a problem, it is helpful to look at all possible alternatives and decide on the best one. Sometimes there is one right answer, but often you'll have to settle for the best answer.

In the space provided below, formulate a plan with multiple alternatives to help Nathan solve this problem.

_____
_____
_____
_____
_____
_____

STEP SIX: DISTINGUISHING FACT FROM OPINION

One of the most important aspects of critical thinking is the ability to distinguish fact from opinion. In many situations—real life, TV, radio, friendly conversations, and the professional arena—opinions surface more often than facts.

One can't believe impossible things.

Reread the previous sentence. This is an example of an opinion cloaked as a fact. There is no research supporting this opinion. It sounds as if it could be true, but without evidence and proof, it is just an opinion.

A fact is something that can be proven, something that can be objectively verified. An opinion is a statement that is held to be true, but one that has no objective proof. *Statements that cannot be proved should always be treated as opinion.* Statements that offer valid proof and verification from credible, reliable sources can be treated as factual.

When trying to distinguish between fact and opinion, you should take the following guidelines into consideration:

- If you are in doubt, ask questions and listen for solid proof and documentation to support the statement.

- Listen for what is not said in a statement.
- Don't be led astray by those you assume are trustworthy and loyal.
- Don't be turned off by those you fear or consider untruthful.
- Do your own homework on the issue. Read, research, and question.
- If you are unsure about the credibility of the source or information, treat the statement as opinion.

Examine the following statements. Before you glance at the answer below, try to determine if you think the statement is a fact or an opinion. Circle one.

Gone With the Wind is a movie.	Fact	Opinion
Gone With the Wind is a movie made in 1939.	Fact	Opinion
Gone With the Wind is the best movie ever made.	Fact	Opinion
Tom Hanks is an actor.	Fact	Opinion
There is a "heaven" and a "hell."	Fact	Opinion
Some people believe in a "heaven" and a "hell."	Fact	Opinion
Lincoln was the best president to ever head the U.S.	Fact	Opinion

STATEMENT	ANSWER	EVIDENCE
Gone With the Wind is a movie.	Fact	This can be proven by watching the movie and by reading movie reviews.
Gone With the Wind is a movie made in 1939.	Fact	This can be verified by many movie sources and by the Motion Picture Association of America.
Gone With the Wind is the best movie ever made.	Opinion	This is only the opinion of some critics and could never be proven.
Tom Hanks is an actor.	Fact	This can be proven by viewing his movies and verifying his two Academy Awards® for acting.
There is a "heaven" and a "hell."	Opinion	As controversial as this answer is, the exsistence of heaven and hell has never been scientifically proven. Both are opinions of various religions.
Some people believe in a "heaven" and a "hell."	Fact	This can be verified by many books and articles and by simply taking a poll of people you know.
Lincoln was the best president to ever head the United States.	Opinion	This is only an opinion that can be disputed by many people. This cannot be proven.

STEP SEVEN: SEEKING TRUTH IN ARGUMENTS AND PERSUASION

Whether or not you realize it, arguments and persuasive efforts are around you daily—hourly, for that matter. They are in newspaper and TV ads, editorials, news commentaries, talk shows, TV magazine shows, political statements, and religious services. It seems at times that almost everyone is trying to persuade us through argument or advice. This section is included to assist you in recognizing faulty arguments and implausible or deceptive persuasion.

There is nothing so powerful as truth, and often nothing so strange. —DANIEL WEBSTER

First, let's start with a list of terms used to describe faulty arguments and deceptive persuasion. As you read through the list, try to identify situations in which you have heard arguments that fit these descriptions.

Terminology For Fallacious Arguments

Ad baculum	Ad baculum is an argument that tries to persuade based on force. Threats of alienation, disapproval, or even violence may accompany this type of argument.
Ad hominem	Ad hominem is when someone initiates a personal attack on a person rather than listening to and rationally debating his or her ideas. This is also referred to as slander.
Ad populum	An ad populum argument is based on the opinions of the majority of people. It assumes that because the majority says X is right, then Y is not. It uses little logic.
Ad verecundiam	This argument uses quotes and phrases from people in authority or popular people to support one's own views.
Bandwagon	The bandwagon approach tries to convince you to do something just because everyone else is doing it. It is also referred to as "peer pressure."
Scare tactic	A scare tactic is used as a desperate measure to put fear in your life. If you don't do X, then Y is going to happen to you.
Straw argument	The straw argument attacks the opponent's argument to make one's own argument stronger. It does not necessarily make argument A stronger; it simply discounts argument B.
Appeal to tradition	This argument looks only at the past and suggests that we have always done it "this way" and we should continue to do it "this way."
Plain folks	This type of persuasion is used to make you feel that the people making the argument are just like you. Usually, they are not; they are only using this appeal to connect with your sense of space and time.
Patriotism	This form of persuasion asks you to ignore reason and logic and support what is right for state A or city B or nation C.
Glittering generalities	This type of persuasion or argumentation is an appeal to generalities (Bosak, 1976). It suggests that a person or candidate or professional is for all the "right" things: justice, low taxes, no inflation, rebates, full employment, low crime, free tuition, progress, privacy, and truth.

IDENTIFYING FALLACIOUS ARGUMENTS

Below, you will find statements intended to persuade you or argue for a cause. Beside each statement, identify which type of faulty persuasion is used.

AB	Ad baculum	SA	Straw argument
AH	Ad hominem	AT	Appeal to tradition
AP	Ad populum	PF	Plain folks
AV	Ad verecundiam	PM	Patriotism
BW	Bandwagon	GG	Glittering generalities
ST	Scare tactic		

_____ 1. This country has never faltered in the face of adversity. Our strong, united military has seen us through many troubled times, and it will see us through our current situation. This is your country; support your military.

_____ 2. If I am elected to office, I will personally lobby for lower taxes, a new comprehensive crime bill, a $2500 tax cut on every new home, and better education, and I will personally work to lower the unemployment rate.

_____ 3. This is the best college in the region. All of your friends will be attending this fall. You don't want to be left out; you should join us, too.

_____ 4. If you really listen to Governor Wise's proposal on health care, you will see that there is no way that we can have a national system. You will not be able to select your doctor, you will not be able to go to the hospital of your choice, and you will not be able to get immediate attention. His proposal is not as comprehensive as our proposal.

_____ 5. My father went to Honors College, I went to Honors College, and you will go to Honors College. It is the way things have been for the people in this family. There is no need to break with tradition now.

_____ 6. The witness's testimony is useless. He is an alcoholic; he is dishonest and corrupt. To make matters worse, he was a member of the Leftist Party.

_____ 7. The gentleman on the witness stand is your neighbor, he is your friend, he is just like you. Sure, he may have more money and drive a Mercedes, but his heart never left the Elm Community.

_____ 8. John F. Kennedy once said, "Ask not what your country can do for you; ask what you can do for your country." This is the time to act, my fellow citizens. You can give $200 to our cause and you will be fulfilling the wish of President Kennedy.

_____ 9. Out of the 7000 people polled, 72 percent believed that there is life beyond our planet. Therefore, there must be life beyond Earth.

_____ 10. Without this new medication, you will die.

_____ 11. I don't care what anyone says. If you don't come around to our way of thinking, you'd better start watching your back.

As you develop your critical-thinking skills, you will begin to recognize the illogical nature of thoughts, the falsehoods of statements, the deception in some advertisements, and the irrational fears used to persuade. You will also begin to understand the depths to which you should delve to achieve objectivity, the thought and care that should be given to your own decisions and statements, and the methods by which you can build logical, truthful arguments.

Creative Thinking
FROM RIDICULOUS TO POSSIBLE

Creative thinking is much like critical thinking in that you are producing something that is uniquely yours. You are introducing something to the world that is new, innovative, and useful. Creative thinking does not mean that you have to be an artist, a musician, or a writer. Creative thinking means that you have examined a situation and developed a new way of explaining information, delivering a product, or using an item. It can be as simple as discovering that you can use a small rolling suitcase to carry your books around campus instead of the traditional backpack. Creative thinking means that you have opened your mind to possibilities!

> Why should we use our creative power? Because there is nothing that makes people so generous, joyful, lively, bold and compassionate. —BRENDA UELAND

Creative thinking and critical thinking both require that you "loosen up" your brain and be more flexible in your approaches and tactics. In her book *The Artist's Way: A Spiritual Path to Higher Creativity* (1992), Julia Cameron suggests that there are basic principles of creativity, including the following:

- Creativity is the natural order of life.
- There is an underlying, indwelling creative force infusing all of life.
- We are, ourselves, creations. And we, in turn, are meant to create ourselves.
- The refusal to be creative is counter to our true nature.

So, how do we become more creative in our thought process? It may be easier than you think. Your individual creativity can be revealed if you make a daily effort to hone and use your creative skills. Consider the tips in the box at left.

As you explore your own creativity, you may find yourself struggling and even at odds with your own opinions. That is perfectly OK. Remember, if everything is easy and smooth,

STRATEGIES
FOR BUILDING ON YOUR BEST

Consider the following strategies for creative thinking:

- Understand that the creative process is not an organized process. It can be chaotic and disorderly—downright crazy at times.
- Never be afraid to ask ANY question, even those you think may be silly.
- Jot your weirdest and funkiest ideas down; you may need them later.
- Take risks! Greatness has never been achieved by playing it safe. Dream, and dream big.
- Hone your sense of adventure and exploration by playing and thinking like a child.
- Force yourself to develop at least five creative solutions to any problem you face.
- Force yourself to do something old in a new way.

Creative Thinking Involves...

Compassion	Creative thinkers have a zest for life and genuinely care for the spirit of others.	**Example:** More than 40 years ago, community members who wanted to feed the elderly created Meals on Wheels, now a national organization feeding the elderly.
Courage	Creative thinkers are unafraid to try new things, to implement new thoughts and actions.	**Example:** An NBC executive moves the *Today Show* out of a closed studio onto the streets of New York, creating the number one morning news show in America.
Truth	Creative thinkers search for the true meaning of things.	**Example:** The astronomer and scientist Copernicus sought to prove that Earth was *not* the center of the universe—an unpopular view at the time.
Dreams	Creative thinkers allow themselves time to dream and ponder the unknown. They can see what is possible, not just what is actual.	**Example:** John F. Kennedy dreamed that space exploration was possible. His dream became reality.
Risk Taking	Creative thinkers take positive risks every day. They are not afraid to go against popular opinion.	**Example:** WWF wrestler Jesse "The Body" Ventura took a risk and ran for mayor in a small Minnesota town, never having had any experience in politics. Later, he became governor of the state.
Innovation	Creative thinkers find new ways to do old things.	**Example:** Instead of continuing to fill the earth with waste such as aluminum, plastic, metal, and old cars, means were developed to recycle these materials for future productive use.
Competition	Creative thinkers strive to be better, to think bolder thoughts, to do what is good and to be the best at any task.	**Example:** Andre Agassi had a several-year slump in tennis. Most people thought he was a "has-been." He came back to win tournament after tournament because he knew that he could.
Individuality	Creative thinkers are not carbon copies of other people. They strive to be true to themselves.	**Example:** A young man decides to take tap dancing instead of playing baseball. He excels and wins a fine arts dancing scholarship to college.

(continued)

Creative Thinking Involves..., *continued.*

Thinking	Creative thinkers are always thinking about the world, people, and new ideas.	**Example:** A scientist is not afraid to take time to sit alone with his or her data to study and ponder the results, make connections, and develop ways to use the information.
Curiosity	Creative thinkers are interested in all things; they want to know much about many things.	**Example:** A 65-year-old retired college professor goes back to college to learn more about music appreciation and computer programming to expand her possibilities.
Perseverance	Creative thinkers do not give up. They stick to a project to its logical and reasonable end.	**Example:** Dr. Martin Luther King, Jr., did not give up on his dream in the face of adversity, danger, and death threats.

it only means that you are not challenging and stretching yourself. Thinking creatively and critically is NOT easy for everyone, but can benefit you greatly.

To begin the creative process, consider the items in the "Creative Thinking Involves..." chart. These are some of the characteristics that creative thinkers have in common.

Using your imaginative and innovative juices, think about how you would *creatively* solve this problem. Write down at least five possibilities. Come on, make it count!

THE PROBLEM

Jennifer is a first-year student who does not have enough money to pay her tuition, buy her books, and purchase a few new outfits and shoes to wear to class and her work-study job on campus.

What should she do? Should she pay her tuition and purchase her books, or pay her tuition and buy new clothes and shoes to wear to class and work? What creative ideas (solutions) can you give Jennifer?

MY CREATIVE SOLUTIONS:

1. _____
2. _____
3. _____
4. _____
5. _____

BLUEPRINTS FOR CHANGE

NAME

DATE

REFLECTION

Both critical and creative thinking require a great deal of commitment on your part. Just as Martha and Josh had to work tirelessly to present their best arguments, you will too. Critical and creative thinking are not easy for everyone, but with practice, dedication, and an understanding of the need, everyone can achieve both.

Critical and creative thinking can affect the way you live your life, from relationships to purchasing a new car, from solving family problems to investing money, from taking the appropriate classes for graduation to getting a promotion at work.

Creative and critical thinking are truly the hallmarks of an educated person. They are hallmarks of character and integrity, and they are hallmarks of successful students. Let them be yours.

GET REAL

Below are a few questions to help you think about critical and creative thinking in college and in life. Study each question carefully and respond accurately.

How can critical thinking affect your college success?

How can critical thinking affect the way you look at TV advertising?

How can open-mindedness affect your decision-making abilities?

If you did not understand the methods or types of persuasion, how could this affect your life?

In which of your current classes is critical thinking most important? Why?

Why is the question sometimes more important than the answer?

Case Study

NAME: Deepa Bhalla
SCHOOL: New York Institute of Technology, Central Islip, NY
MAJOR: Elementary Education   AGE: 22

Below is a real-life situation faced by Deepa. Read the brief case and respond to the questions.

During my first semester, I ran into a serious problem with my English composition class. My first few papers were not well received by the professor, and I could not figure out why.

I would begin the paper the night before class and turn in a paper that discussed the topic and met the length requirement. I just could not figure out why I was not getting good grades on my papers.

I heard a few other students saying that they had worked on their papers for days and had researched and planned their approach. I knew that I had not taken the time to plan out the paper or critically think about the content or the research. I knew that I had just rushed and put my ideas down on paper to have something to turn in without critically or creatively evaluating what I was doing.

I never imagined that time management and critical thinking had anything to do with each other, let alone an English paper. Who knew?

What was Deepa's first problem?

What is the relationship between time management and critical thinking?

What role does critical thinking play in your college classes?

How can critical thinking play a role in writing a paper or speech?

How can time management play a role in writing a paper or speech?

What role might critical thinking play in your current job or future profession?

What role does critical thinking play in your finances?

at this moment Journal

Refer to page 309 of this chapter. Having read and reflected upon the information in the chapter, consider how you might revise your goal to make it more:

REASONABLE

BELIEVABLE

MEASURABLE

ADAPTABLE

CONTROLLABLE

DESIRABLE

ONLINE JOURNAL

To complete an online journal entry, log onto the Companion Website at **www.prenhall.com/sherfield.** Go to Chapter 11 and click on the link to the Online Journal. You can respond to the questions provided or to questions assigned by your professor, or you may journal about your own experiences.

ADVICE TO GO
CORNERSTONES
for critical thinking

Use only *credible* and *reliable* sources.

Distinguish *fact* from *opinion*.

Be *flexible* in your thinking.

Use emotional *restraint*.

Avoid generalizations.

Avoid *stereotyping*

Strive for *objectivity*.

Reserve judgment.

Do *not* assume.

Ask questions.

Seek *truth*.

THINK

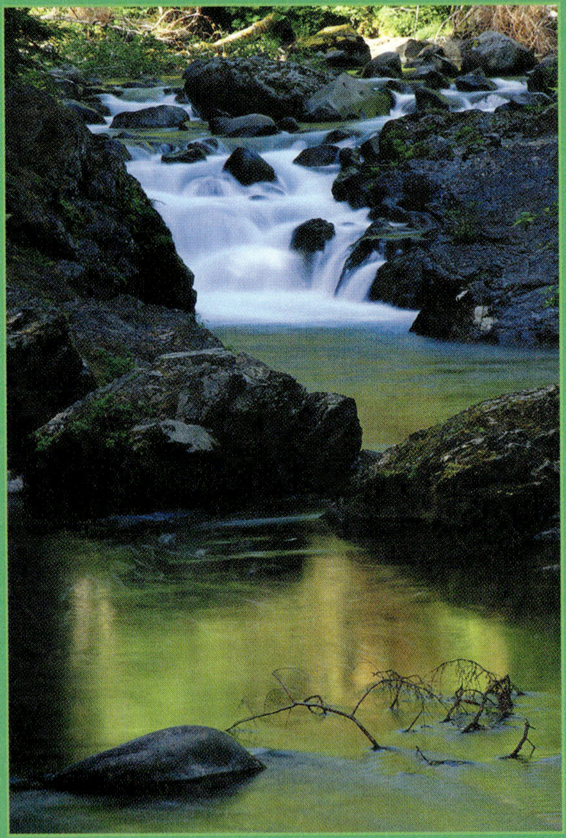

12 Communicate

Let thy speech be better than silence, or be silent.

— Dionysius

CHAPTER 12

COMMUNICATE

I had been teaching public speaking for almost 5 years. I had performed in over 30 plays and spoken to groups of business and education leaders numbering in the thousands. I even *majored in public speaking* in college. When the phone call came on a Monday morning in December, it should have been a "piece of cake" to accept the opportunity to deliver yet another speech. *It wasn't.* The phone call held a double punch. A wonderful friend had died from cancer, and her husband was calling to ask if I would deliver a part of her eulogy. *It wasn't a piece of cake!*

I agreed to speak at Doris' funeral *not realizing how life-altering the event would be.* For the remainder of that day, I reminisced about our time together. I remembered the joy of sharing an office space with her. I remembered *the daily jokes, the sharing of dreams, and the bond we had.* I remembered the time that we took a group of students to Washington, D.C. I remembered that it *was her hand I held as we watched the news of the space shuttle Challenger.*

I honestly believe that *I remembered every moment that we shared together.* So, I spent the day jotting down memories that I wanted to share. The hardest part still lay ahead.

After careful consideration and meticulously choosing my words, the speech was ready. That is to say, the written word was ready—*surprisingly, I was not.* On the morning of the funeral, I had never been more nervous, and for the first time in my public speaking career, *I was about to deliver a speech that I had never gotten through without becoming emotionally overwhelmed.*

I arrived early so that I could stand behind the lectern, get a feel for the auditorium, and make any last-minute adjustments to my speech. *After all, this is what I would have told any student to do.* I think I really got there early to see if there were any miracles floating around. As I sat on the podium at the front of the auditorium, I watched over 200 people enter the room. I was getting more nervous by the second. *My palms were sweating, my throat was dry, my heart was beating out of my chest, and if I had had a mirror, I know that I could have seen the horror reflected on my own face.*

In the final moments before I was to stand, I remember thinking desperately to myself, "What

Wisdom is the one treasure that no thief can touch. —JAPANESE PROVERB

336

Practical Steps for Writing and Speaking

would you tell a student to do? What?!" My mind ran through my public speaking teaching notes that I used on a daily basis. The miracle that I had hoped for happened. In an instant, "it" came to me. *I saw it on the page as clear as crystal.* "This is your moment in the sun." It sounds so simple, so trivial, but the statement I used with my students every semester came to me, and the cloud lifted. *How could I have missed it? How could I not have known that this was the key? The miracle?*

> **It should have been a piece of cake . . . to deliver another speech. It wasn't.**

I walked to the lectern, opened my outlined notes, took a breath, and began *to tell the audience how Doris had changed my life.* I was even able to smile as I shared some of the wonderful memories.

You may be asking yourself, "What does 'this is your moment in the sun' mean?" *For me, it meant that this would be the only time in the history of the world that I would ever have the opportunity to tell over 200 people how I felt about Doris.* It would be the last time in my life that I would ever have this moment. The voice inside my head said, "Shine!" From that day forward, I have approached every speech with that philosophy.

Whether I'm speaking about leadership, change, Generation X, study skills, or camping, I look at the opportunity and say to myself, *"This is my moment and I don't know if it will ever come again . . . so, make the most of it!"*

QUESTIONS FOR REFLECTION

Consider responding to these questions online in the Questions for Reflection module of the Companion Website.

1. Why is speaking in front of a group so difficult for most people?

2. Why do you think the teacher of public speaking arrived early to assess the environment?

3. Can you think of a situation in class or at work where you can use the teacher's tips for overcoming nervousness?

Where are you... AT THIS MOMENT

Before reading this chapter, take a moment and respond to the following ten questions. Consider each one carefully before answering, and then respond by circling the number in the appropriate box. When you have answered the questions, add your points and find your total score on the feedback chart below.

STATEMENT	STRONGLY DISAGREE	DISAGREE	DON'T KNOW	AGREE	STRONGLY AGREE	SCORE
1. I am confident about speaking in front of a group of people.	1	2	3	4	5	
2. I have no difficulty clearly explaining my thoughts to others.	1	2	3	4	5	
3. The ability to make my points clearly to others will have no real impact in my future career.	5	4	3	2	1	
4. I know how to select a topic for a paper or presentation in class.	1	2	3	4	5	
5. When preparing a paper or presentation, it doesn't really matter who the audience will be.	5	4	3	2	1	
6. I know how to access necessary research materials at the library.	1	2	3	4	5	
7. When organizing materials for a paper or presentation, I never use an outline.	5	4	3	2	1	
8. I don't usually bother with documenting the source of the facts I use for papers and projects.	5	4	3	2	1	
9. The use of visual aids during speeches is important.	1	2	3	4	5	
10. My GPA will be more important in getting a job than my speaking skills.	5	4	3	2	1	
TOTAL VALUE						

SUMMARY

10–17 Your communication skills are poor, and you have little understanding of how to prepare papers, projects, and presentations. Significant learning and development in these areas is needed to help you be successful in college.

18–25 Your communication skills are somewhat low, and your ability to prepare papers and presentations is limited. Improvement in these areas will be necessary for success in school.

26–34 You are average in your ability to communicate in verbal and written formats. You are aware of the basic processes in preparing papers and projects for school, and likely have had some success in these tasks, although some improvement would be helpful to you.

35–42 Your skills in communicating with others in both written and oral formats are above average. You are probably skilled in organizing materials and presenting them clearly to others.

43–50 You are exceptional in your ability to communicate with others. You are skilled in finding, organizing, and presenting materials in a clear and meaningful manner, regardless of the format for presentation.

Goals... FOR CHANGE

Based on your total points, what is one goal you would like to achieve related to speaking or writing?

Goal _____
_____

List three actions you can take that might help you move closer to realizing this goal.

1. _____
2. _____
3. _____

Questions FOR BUILDING ON YOUR BEST

As you read this chapter, consider the following questions. At the end of the chapter, you should be able to answer all of them. You are encouraged to ask a few questions of your own. Consider asking your classmates or professors to assist you.

1. How do I select a topic and theme for an oral or written presentation?
2. What do I need to know about the audience before I deliver a speech or write a paper?
3. What methods of research can I use to develop a presentation or a paper?
4. How are writing well and speaking well connected?
5. How can I use technology and audiovisuals to complement my presentation?

What additional questions do you have about oral and written communications?

1. _____
2. _____
3. _____

Your Chance to Shine

"Writing! Research! Public speaking! If I wanted to write papers or speak in front of people, I would have taken a writing class or a public speaking course," you might be saying at this moment. Relax. You are not alone in your anxiety about writing papers or speaking publicly. In fact, according to *The Book of Lists*, 3000 Americans surveyed listed public speaking as their *number one* fear. Public speaking came in ahead of sickness, insects, financial troubles, deep water, and even *death!*

> The language of the heart, which comes from the heart and goes to the heart, is always simple, graceful, and full of power. —BOVEE

So, why do we include a chapter on writing and public speaking in a first-year orientation text? You probably won't like the answer, but the simple truth is that you are going to be asked to write and speak in many of your classes; from history to chemistry, from engineering to computer programming, writing and speaking are a way of life for today's college students. The more you know about writing papers and speeches and delivering speeches, the more confident you are going to feel in every class.

The Power of Words

The benefits and value of written and oral communication cannot be measured. The power of words has changed nations, built civilizations, preserved traditions, freed masses, and prevented destruction. Think of the words written or spoken by Dr. Martin Luther King, Jr., Lorraine Hansbury, Maya Angelou, Booker T. Washington, Franklin Roosevelt, Frederick Douglass, Spike Lee, Ann Richards, Steven Spielberg, and Princess Diana. Good or bad, right or wrong, appropriate or inappropriate, their words have changed many lives.

The ability to write and speak with confidence and credibility is empowering. According to Beebe and Beebe (2002), learning to speak well will give you an edge that people with less skills lack. Even if someone else has superior knowledge, skills, and experience, if you can speak better, you may come across better. The ability to speak and write positions you to move to the next level. A survey of top executives who earned more than $250,000 per year was conducted by a large executive search firm. The survey found that these executives believe their communication skills were the number one factor that carried them to the top (Advanced Public Speaking Institute, 2003).

A report entitled "What Students Must Know to Succeed in the 21st Century" (1996) states, "Clear communication is critical to success. In the marketplace of ideas, the person who communicates clearly is also the person who is

> If all my talents and powers were to be taken from me, and I had the choice of keeping but one, I would unhesitatingly ask to be allowed to keep the power of speaking, for through it, I would quickly recover the rest. —DANIEL WEBSTER

WORLD OF WORK

Speaking and writing are two of the most important skills you can develop while in college. Corporations consistently rank these two skills at the top of the list of abilities that are most important when interviewing college graduates. You have a long list of attributes that you must develop and polish while in college—none will ever be more important to you than communication skills.

In my job as Senior Vice President, Global Sales and Customer Advocate for Marriott International, I constantly use speaking and writing. My job is to maintain and improve the excellent customer service reputation for which Marriott is known. Not only do I personally need to be able to speak and write well, but all of our associates need these skills as well. The job of greeting guests, interacting with them, taking care of them, and making them feel welcome and comfortable is all about communication. We pride ourselves on greeting every guest with a big smile, a helping hand, and words that make them understand how much we appreciate their business. One of the best ways to move up the corporate ladder at Marriott is to be excellent at taking care of guests by interacting positively with every person. When we interview people, our top criterion is to find people who are excellent communicators and leaders. If two candidates for a job have virtually the same skills, we will **always** select the best communicator.

Not only are face-to-face communications important, the ability to write thoughtful notes to guests is a necessity. Marriott employees constantly e-mail messages to their colleagues and clients. It is imperative that the corporate image is represented well in every communication, whether it is a formal letter or an informal e-mail. Every day, we have executive directors and convention managers as guests in our hotel while they decide if they want to bring a large meeting to our facility. Of course, we roll out the red carpet for these people who impact our business so heavily. Thoughtful notes delivered with a bottle of wine and a basket of fruit and an appreciative follow-up letter to each person are all part of the Marriott package of taking care of customers. But what we really want is for all of our associates to provide every guest with the red carpet treatment, and the secret to that is excellent communications training for every employee. In addition, we want our associates to be thoughtful and respectful of each other. I frequently encourage our associates to write congratulatory notes to their colleagues and employees, as well as other letters of recognition for a job well done. Excellent communications includes providing the red carpet treatment to every person you meet, including both your internal and external customers.

Over the years, I have been asked to speak at many functions. Today, I frequently keynote large conventions and share the Marriott customer advocacy message. The ability to make formal presentations has been one of the primary reasons that I have become a corporate executive for Marriott. Today, I like nothing better than to have the opportunity to address 5000 people at a national convention. The training ground for my ability to keynote a convention began in college when I was struggling to learn to speak in front of a class. You should know that almost everybody is afraid to speak in front of a group when they are learning. I am absolutely sure that communication skills have contributed greatly to my personal success in the business world.

I cannot overemphasize to you the importance of working very hard to become the best speaker and writer you possibly can! Take every opportunity to speak in front of groups; work to improve your vocabulary; practice extemporaneous speaking by voluntarily responding to professors' questions; become a leader when given team and group assignments. Work on your body language and your

continued

facial expressions to be sure that you are communicating the fact that you are an enthusiastic, friendly, interesting person. When speaking to any group, tailor your message specifically for that group. Think about this question as you write your speech: "What is important to this particular audience?"

Finally, I would tell you to go out of your way to be exceptionally nice to people. Listen to them, encourage them, offer to help them. Everything you give to other people will come back to you. Open up your heart and mind to all kinds of people from all races, ethnic backgrounds, and geographic locations, and your life will be richly blessed.

QUESTIONS FOR REFLECTION

Consider answering these questions online in the World of Work module of the Companion Website.

1. What did you learn from Mr. Dow's article that can help you with relationships as you move through your next several years as a college student?

2. How can you use Mr. Dow's information about the "red carpet treatment" in college, in part-time jobs you may have, and in your career?

3. What tips did Mr. Dow give you that can assist you now in learning to become an effective public speaker?

Roger Dow, Senior Vice President, Global Sales and Customer Advocate, Marriott International, Bethesda, MD

---

seen as thinking clearly. Oral and written communication are not only job-securing, but job-holding skills." The ability to speak and write tops the list of skills that are sought after by corporations. Survey after survey reveals that the most important thing a college graduate can learn to do is speak and write well. The box below ranks the importance of preferred skills sought by employers.

Top Ten Personal Qualities Employers Seek

RANK	TYPE OF PREFERRED SKILL
1	Communication skills
2	Motivation/initiative
3	Teamwork skills
4	Leadership skills
5	Academic achievement/GPA
6	Interpersonal skills
7	Flexibility/adaptability
8	Technical skills
9	Honesty/integrity
10	Work experience

Source: *Job Outlook 2000*, a survey conducted by the National Association of College Employers.

Ten Steps to Communication Success

OVERVIEW OF SIMILARITIES AND DIFFERENCES BETWEEN WRITING AND SPEAKING

STEPS	WRITER	SPEAKER
Topic	Most likely assigned by the professor. Can be very broad to appeal to a mass audience. Can be narrative, informative, biographical, technical, analytical, etc.	May be assigned by the professor, most likely chosen by the student. Usually narrowed for a specific audience or class. Will usually be informative, demonstrative, or persuasive for classroom purposes
Audience Analysis	Usually written for the professor	Usually written and delivered for the class
Purpose Statement	Referred to as a thesis statement, it is usually at the beginning of the paragraph and introduces the topic	Referred to as a purpose or transition statement, it is usually at the end of the introduction and serves as a bridge to the body of the speech
Research Process	Research based on your topic and thesis statement	Research based on your topic and thesis statement
Organizational Process	May be assigned by the professor. May use a formal outline	Usually determined by the type of speech. Will probably use a less formal outline
Writing Process	Writer can create a draft and revise until polished. May be allowed a rewrite after a grade is assigned	Speaker can create a draft and rehearse until polished. Seldom allowed a second chance for another grade
Documentation	Written at the end of the paper as a bibliography or reference page, depending on documentation style	Research and sources usually documented verbally during speech and may be written at the end of the speech as required by the professor
Outlining Delivery Notes	Not required for a written paper	Speaker can use a variety of notes such as key word outlines, note cards, or overheads if allowed by the professor
Audiovisual	Not required for a written paper	Adds strength to the presentation. Increases audience attention and retention. Speaker must rehearse with the aids used
Rehearsal and Delivery	Not required for a written paper	Speaker must spend a great deal of time in rehearsal to deliver a polished presentation

Step 1: Topic Selection

Almost every writing and speaking expert will tell you to select a topic on which you are an expert, or a topic on which you have a keen interest and enough preparation time to become an expert. This does not mean that you cannot write or speak on topics that are new or unfamiliar to you, but if you choose such a topic, your preparation time will need to be extended. If you have a choice for your paper or speech, keep the following tips in mind.

Writing and speaking are two of the most important skills a person can possess at any time.

TIPS FOR TOPIC SELECTION

- Know what type of paper or speech you will be writing and/or delivering.
- What are your talents, interests, and experiences?
- Can you find sufficient material and information for your paper or speech?
- Is your topic appropriate to you and your audience?
- Can you adequately discuss the topic within the given time frame or page length?
- Can the topic be narrowed?

As you work your way through this chapter, you will be asked to build a paper or speech. Following your instructor's guidelines, begin to develop your paper or speech by identifying a topic or using the topic given to you in class.

The type of paper or speech for which I am preparing is:

_____
_____
_____

My topic is:

_____
_____
_____

Why have you chosen this topic?

_____
_____
_____
_____
_____

Step 2: Audience Analysis

Have you ever read a paper that was boring or listened to someone speak about a topic that was so technical that you understood very little of it? It could be because the paper or the speech was poorly written, but it may be that the boring paper or technical speech was inaccessible to you because it was written for a different audience. If you don't understand your audience, it is unlikely that you will be able to maintain their attention, inform or persuade them, or expect them to act on your advice. Although your immediate paper or speech will be written for your professor or class, there will be instances in the future when it will be advantageous to complete an analysis of your audience. This will assist you in learning more about the diversity or homogeneity of your audience. Figure 12.1 will assist you in developing a comprehensive audience analysis.

> **Y**ou compose your speech for an audience, and the audience is judge. —ARISTOTLE

An audience analysis might also consist of customized questions about your topic. If you were writing a paper or delivering a speech on genetic engineering, you might poll your audience to find out how many people believe that we should clone human beings.

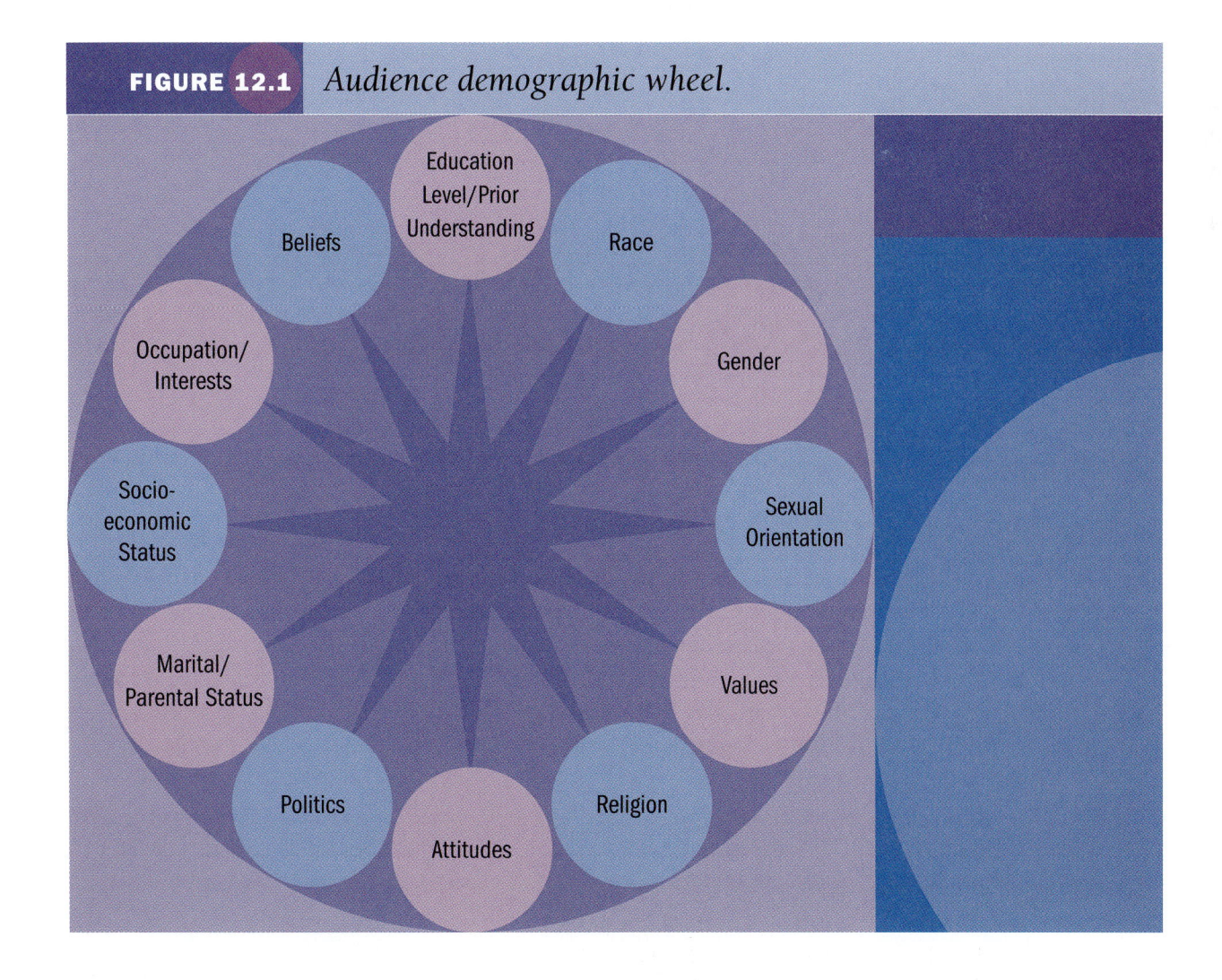

FIGURE 12.1 *Audience demographic wheel.*

- Education Level/Prior Understanding
- Beliefs
- Race
- Occupation/Interests
- Gender
- Socio-economic Status
- Sexual Orientation
- Marital/Parental Status
- Values
- Politics
- Religion
- Attitudes

As a writer or speaker, knowing your audience can create a positive rapport.

When you gather this information, you can use it to address the needs of your audience and write a paper or speech that "speaks" to them on a personal level. For instance, if you found out that a majority of your audience members were very concerned about their safety on campus, your paper or speech could detail ways to enhance personal safety. This paper or speech would then have a good chance to gain their attention.

Using your classroom setting as your audience, write a brief analysis of this audience. You may have to make some educated guesses based on observation and keen listening skills, but you may also have to interview them or issue a questionnaire. As a basis for your understanding, you will want to seek answers to the 12 factors in the demographic wheel. You may also need to answer questions such as: "What do I know about them?" "What do I need to find out?" "What do they expect?" and "What does my analysis mean to my paper or speech?"

Brief analysis of your classroom audience:

___

Step 3: Writing a Thesis Statement

Simply stated, what do you want to accomplish? Are you writing or speaking to entertain, to persuade, or to inform? What do you want your audience to do or feel when you are finished? Do you want them to change their minds, sign a petition, join a cause, give blood, practice safer sex, or enjoy a trip down memory lane? If you can answer this question, you are well on your way to writing an effective and engaging paper or speech.

Anyone who wishes to fulfill a mission in the world must have an overmastering purpose that guides and controls them.   —UNKNOWN

Your thesis statement is one sentence that tells your audience *exactly* what you hope to accomplish. Examples of some thesis statements are the following:

- You will understand the effects of domestic abuse, know how to look for warning signs, and know where to turn for assistance.
- Today, it is my intent to persuade you to complete the organ donor cards that I have brought with me.
- After you have had time to reflect on the research, interviews, and personal testimonials offered, you will stop smoking.

Traditionally, the thesis will come at the end of the first or second paragraph. Placing it earlier in the paper or speech does not serve as an attention-gaining device. More will be discussed about gaining attention in the section on writing an introduction.

Using the topic you selected earlier, write your thesis statement below.

_____

_____

_____

_____

Step 4: Researching Your Speech or Paper

Now that you have selected and narrowed your topic, analyzed your audience, and developed your purpose statement, you are ready to begin accumulating information to support your paper or speech. As you begin to consider resources, you will want to investigate and explore a variety of sources, including the following:

- Personal interviews with experts on your topic
- Electronic and print indexes, such as the *Reader's Guide* and *Humanities Index*
- Books
- Electronic card catalogs and computerized databases
- The Internet (start with Yahoo!, Infoseek, Alta Vista, and Netscape Navigator, for example)
- Periodicals such as *Newsweek, Vital Speeches,* and *American Psychologist*
- Newspapers such as *The New York Times, Chicago Sun Times,* and *Atlanta Constitution*

- Reference materials such as encyclopedias, dictionaries, directories, atlases, almanacs and yearbooks, books of quotations, and bibliographical directories
- Government documents

When collecting your research, you will find that information comes in a variety of forms such as case studies, surveys, polls, statistics, testimonials, and experiment results. You will need to do a variety of research to be able to write your paper or speech objectively. You should also have at least three or more sources supporting your claim or thesis. If you have only one research article supporting your view, you may not have gotten the entire picture.

The success of any argument, short or long, depends in large part on the quantity and quality of the support behind it. —ANNETTE ROTTENBERG

As you begin to collect your data, you may want to consider the following tips to keep your information orderly:

- Collect and keep copies of articles, pages of books, or chapters. You may want to copy them if the copyright laws permit.
- Always keep hard copies of your Internet research. Be sure to write the URL and the date you accessed it on each article.
- When taking notes from articles, chapters, pages, or the Internet, try to take them in an organized manner to save you time later in the writing process.

As a researcher, you should know the validity of the sources and research that you plan to use to write your papers and speeches. The credibility of your sources can mean the difference between having a valid argument or thesis and having unsubstantiated opinions. With the Internet becoming an increasingly popular source for information, it is of ultimate importance that you know the validity of your Internet resources.

To critically analyze any information sources, whether Internet or print, use the following guidelines by Ormondroyd, Engle, and Cosgrave (2001) from Cornell University Libraries:

- Who is the author and what are his or her credentials, educational background, past writings, or experience? Has your instructor mentioned the author? Is he or she cited in other works? Is the author associated with any organizations or institutes?
- When was the source published? If it is a webpage, the date is usually found on the last page or the home page. Is the source current or out of date for your topic?

Internet research can be helpful, quick, and timely. But you must watch for false or misleading information.

- What edition is the source? Second and third editions suggest that the source has been updated to reflect changes and new knowledge.
- Who is the publisher? If the source is published by a university press, it is likely to be a scholarly publication.
- What is the title of the source? This will help you determine if the source is popular, sensational, or scholarly and indicates the level of complexity:
  - Popular journals are resources such as *Time, Newsweek, Vogue, Ebony,* and *Reader's Digest.* They seldom cite their sources.
  - Sensational resources are often inflammatory and written on an elementary level. They usually have flashy headlines, and they cater to popular superstitions. Examples are *The Globe, The National Enquirer,* and *The Star.*
  - Scholarly resources are defined as having a solid base. They are substantial. They always cite their sources and are usually written by scholars in their fields. Usually, they report on original research.
- What is the intended audience of your source? Is the information too simple, too advanced, or too technical for your needs?
- Is the source factually objective, is it opinionated, or is it propaganda? Objective sources look at all angles and report on each one honestly. Sources of opinion give unfounded information. Propaganda is information that spreads the same message over and over until it is believed by the masses.
- Does the information appear to be valid and well researched or does it just gloss over the material? Is it supported by evidence? Usually, the more in-depth the source, the more substantial it is going to be to your research.

When using the Internet for resources, use extreme caution. Anyone can create a web page or present information on the Internet. This can be good, but it can also create a situation where you have little control over the validity of your resources. Laura Cohen (1996a) of the University of Albany Libraries suggests, "Internet sites change over time according to the commitment and inclination of the creator. Some sites demonstrate an expert's knowledge, while others are amateur efforts. Some may be updated daily, while others may be outdated."

To conduct research on the Internet, you can do several things: (1) join a Listserv® or Usenet newsgroup; (2) go directly to a site if you have the address; (3) browse the Internet using one of the search engines such as Google, Infoseek, Yahoo!, or AOL; or (4) navigate through a subject directory. When using the Internet, you will need to learn how to narrow your topic search. If your subject is *rape*, it may be too broad. You may have to narrow that search to *date rape*, or you could use the words *college-date-rape* if you wanted to see data pertaining only to rape on college campuses.

To evaluate Internet resources, Cohen (1996b) suggests the following:

- Consider the intended audience of the Internet piece.
- Bear in mind that many items on the Internet are peripheral or useless.

- Check to see if the piece has an author listed (with the author's address).
- To check the validity of the author, trace back the URL to determine where the document originates.
- Don't take the information presented at face value; conduct additional research using a variety of sources.
- Because websites are rarely monitored or reviewed like scholarly journals and books, look for point of view, bias, currency, and comprehensiveness.

As a final note, don't hesitate to ask your librarian for assistance. Librarians are trained professionals who devote much of their lives to helping people discover information.

Brainstorm for a moment and jot down what types of research you will need in order to write an informed, objective paper or speech. You may want to visit the library before completing this section.

Source # 1 _____

Source #2 _____

Source #3 _____

Step 5: Organizing Your Paper or Speech

Now that you have gathered enough information from a variety of resources, what are the most effective ways to present your findings and ideas? As you know, every good paper and speech will have an introduction, body, and conclusion. A complete discussion of introductions and conclusions will follow in the next section on writing.

Organizing the body of your paper or speech can be done using one of several proven methods.

SPATIAL ORGANIZATION is when you arrange information or items according to their direction or location.

Example: If you were describing the mall in Washington, DC, you could begin with the Lincoln Memorial and then move on to the reflecting pond, the Washington Monument, and the Smithsonian.

CAUSE–EFFECT ORGANIZATION is when you arrange your information in the cause-and-effect order. You would discuss the causes of a problem and then explore its effects.

Example: If you were speaking about high blood pressure, you would first examine the causes of high blood pressure such as diet, hereditary factors, and weight and then move on to the effects such as heart attack and stroke.

CHRONOLOGICAL ORGANIZATION is presenting information in the order in which it happened. Speeches that deal with historical facts and how-to speeches often use chronological organization.

> Order and simplification are the first steps toward mastery.
> —THOMAS MANN

Example: If you were giving a speech or writing a paper on the history of automobiles in America since 1950, you would begin with the 50s, move to the 60s, 70s, 80s, and 90s. If you were giving a how-to speech on refinishing a table, you would begin with the first process of stripping the old paint or varnish and move forward to the last step of applying a new coat of paint or varnish.

PROBLEM-SOLVING ORGANIZATION is often used in persuasive papers and speeches. Usually, you are trying to get your reader or audience to accept your proposal. You first begin by pointing out the major problem(s) and then move on to revealing the solutions, and the advantages of the solutions.

Example: If you were writing or speaking about crime on college campuses, you would begin by informing the reader or listener about the problems, the crime statistics, and the personal toll on students. You would then propose solutions and tell how the solutions would help all students.

TOPICAL/CATEGORICAL ORGANIZATION is when you group information into subdivisions or cluster information into categories. Some information naturally falls into specific categories, such as the different types of palm trees or the types of rollerblades available.

Example: If you were writing a speech or paper on taxes in the United States, you might categorize your information into local taxes, state taxes, federal taxes, luxury taxes, "sin" taxes, and special taxes.

COMPARE/CONTRAST ORGANIZATION is when you present your information in a fashion that shows its similarities to and differences from other information.

Example: You may be writing a paper or speech that compares the health care system in the United States to that of England or Canada.

IMPORTANCE/PRIORITY ORGANIZATION allows you to arrange information from the most important issue to the least or the least important to the most important. You can also arrange your information from the top priority to the lowest priority or vice versa.

Example: If you were writing a paper or delivering a speech to inform readers and listeners about buying diamonds, you might arrange your information so that you speak first about the most important aspects of diamond buying and later about less important factors.

Using the topic that you selected at the beginning of the chapter, and referring to the research that you have gathered, which type of organization do you feel would best suit your needs?

_____

_____

_____

Why?

_____
_____
_____

Step 6: Writing Your Paper or Speech

One Sunday morning, the congregation of a local church was surprised to find the following printed in their bulletins: *"Thursday at 5:00 pm, there will be a meeting of the Little Mother's Club. Anyone wishing to become a little mother should meet the minister in his study."* A letter to the San Antonio Veterans' Administration read, *"I am annoyed to find out that you have branded my child as illiterate. It is a dirty, rotten lie. I married his father one week before he was born."* And finally, a sign hanging in a hotel in Mexico reads, *"We are pleased to announce that the manager has personally passed all of the water served here."*

> The two most engaging powers of an author are to make new things familiar, and familiar things new. —SAMUEL JOHNSON

At some point in time, we have all made written or verbal blunders that caused us embarrassment or that even hurt someone. The power of words, as mentioned earlier, is phenomenal. They make us laugh and cry, feel pain and joy, understand and react. When writing your papers and speeches, it is important to remember that you have the power of words at your side. They can be used for good or bad, strengthening or weakening, building or tearing down, love or hatred. The choice is always up to you.

ETHICAL CONSIDERATIONS

As a writer and speaker, you have a personal responsibility to consider the ethics and consequences of your statements.

Gamble and Gamble, in their book *Public Speaking in the Age of Diversity* (1998), suggest that you follow these guidelines when considering the ethical dimensions of writing and speaking:

- Share only what you know to be true.
- Be fully prepared and informed.
- Consider the best interest of your receivers.
- Make it easy for your receivers to understand your message.
- Refrain from using words as weapons.
- Don't wrap information in a positive spin just to succeed.
- Respect the cultural diversity of your receivers.
- Remember: You are accountable for what you say.

DID YOU KNOW?

#1

The National Association of College Employers rank skill in COMMUNICATION as the number one quality employers seek.

Source: National Association of College Employers. "Top ten personal qualities employers seek." *Job Outlook 2000.* NACE, 2001.

USING LANGUAGE

As you begin to write your paper or speech, there are several factors that will assist you in building colorful, meaningful, and memorable work. When writing, consider the following:

- Use colorful, vivid language to evoke images and word pictures.

  Example: Instead of telling the reader or listener about a dog, tell about the six-week-old, black, playful Labrador Retriever. This helps your reader or listener "see" rather than imagine.

- Use unbiased, nonsexist, nonracist, nonageist language.

  Example: Instead of writing or saying, "Everyone should bring his lab kit to class tomorrow," the proper language would be, "Everyone should bring his or her lab kit to class tomorrow."

- Use simple, nontechnical, familiar, layperson terminology (the language should suit the audience).

  Example: Instead of writing or speaking about the absence of monocholorodifloromethane, simply say that the air conditioner was out of Freon. Your audience will appreciate it; so will your spellchecker.

- Use concrete language.

  Example: Instead of saying, "She drove a very expensive car," say, "She drove a Lexus." Instead of saying, "The building was crummy," say, "The building's foundation was crumbling, the walls were dirty, and the roof was in need of repair."

- Use similes and metaphors to enhance your language.

  Example: A simile compares by using the words "as" or "like": *"Life is like a box of chocolates."* A metaphor uses implied comparisons: *"The winter of our discontent."*

- Use repetition for understanding and memory.

  Example: If you introduce an idea in the introduction, explain it in detail in the body, and repeat it in the conclusion. Remember the old public speaking formula: "Tell 'em what you're gonna tell 'em. Tell 'em what you've gotta tell 'em. Then tell 'em what you've told 'em."

- Use parallelism for balance.

  Example: If you open by telling a story about the abuses suffered by Martha and her child, you can mention them in the body and end the story in the conclusion. Martin Luther King, Jr., used parallelism in his "I Have a Dream" speech by repeating throughout the speech, "I have a dream . . ."

SELECTING THE MAIN IDEAS AND ISSUES

At this point, you have carefully selected and narrowed your topic. You have taken a careful look at your audience; you have decided on the basic needs you plan to address; you have written a comprehensive thesis; and you have collected your research. Upon reviewing your research, you have decided on an organizational pattern, and finally, you have examined some interesting and creative ways to add variety and color to your paper or speech. Now, based on your research, you are ready to decide on the main issues and major details that you plan to share with your readers or audience.

The main issues are going to be derived from your research and your thesis statement. Main issues are the major divisions of your paper or speech. David Zarefsky, in his book *Public Speaking: Strategies for Success* (2001), suggests that you can identify main ideas and issues by asking the following questions:

- What does it mean?
- What are the facts?
- What are the reasons?
- How often does it occur?
- What is my view?
- What are the parts?
- What is the reasoning?
- What is the cause?
- How will it happen?
- Who is involved?
- What are some examples?
- What are some objections?
- What is the effect?
- What is preventing it?

ORGANIZING THE BODY

One of the most effective ways to begin composing your paper or speech is to create a rough outline of the points you would like to cover. As you begin to outline, remember that your organizational pattern should guide you through this phase. The following is an example of a generic outline:

I. **Point 1 or Major Issue 1**

Types of Evidence
    a. Who, what, when, where, and why?
    b. Statistics, polls, results
    c. Personal testimonials, case studies
    d. Causes
    e. Problems and solutions

II. **Point 2 or Major Issue 2**

Types of Evidence
    a. Who, what, when, where, and why?
    b. Statistics, polls, results
    c. Personal testimonials, case studies
    d. Causes
    e. Problems and solutions

III. **Point 3 or Major Issue 3**

Types of Evidence
    a. Who, what, when, where, and why?
    b. Statistics, polls, results
    c. Personal testimonials, case studies
    d. Causes
    e. Problems and solutions

Once you have developed your outline, you can begin to write your paper or speech. Using the topic you selected earlier, organize the body of your paper or speech by completing an outline of your resources. Use a separate sheet of paper for this exercise.

> Communication is simply mutual understanding. —STEVEN R. COVEY

INTRODUCTIONS

Throughout the day, you are bombarded with ideas, messages, and ads begging for your attention. How do you decide on the messages to which you will direct your attention? Is it the low-key, dull message or idea that grabs you? Is it the idea or message that you have heard countless times? No, it is the message that is vibrant, new, creative, and alive that catches your attention and holds you long enough to hear the information. You are now at the point where you will need to consider the introduction and conclusion to your paper or speech.

The introduction to your work will, in a very large part, determine how the reader or audience perceives you and your work, and it will determine if you are going to obtain and maintain their interest. While the introduction is a very small part of your overall piece, it should never be taken lightly. Oprah Winfrey, noted talk-show host and actress, once profiled a new book each month on her show. She has said that the first line of the book is the most important to her. If the first line does not grab her or sell her, it is hard for her to be drawn into the message. She gives the example of Toni Morrison's book *Paradise*. The opening line reads, "They shoot the white girl first." Winfrey said that she was lured in by that line. The very same rule can be applied to papers and speeches. It is the first few lines that will lure your audience to your message or turn them to thoughts of last night's supper. Attention spans are short, so you must use attention-getting devices.

An introduction serves multiple purposes:

- To gain the attention and interest of the reader or audience
- To indicate the direction of the speech or paper
- To prepare the reader or audience for the thoughts to come
- To establish your credibility and the relevance of your topic
- To reveal the subject matter of the paper or speech
- To build suspense and arouse curiosity

As you study the techniques of introducing that are detailed below, think about the topic you chose earlier. Determine which technique would best suit your individual writing and/or delivery style, which would most greatly appeal to your audience, and which technique you feel would best gain their attention. Introductions are not necessarily written first. Many writers and speakers write their introduction last. Keep this in mind as you begin to compose. Below, you will find a variety of techniques used to create effective introductions:

- Telling a story or creating a vivid, visual illustration
- Using startling facts or statistics

- Referring to an incident with which the audience or reader is familiar
- Asking rhetorical, yet pertinent questions
- Using novel ideas or striking statements
- Using quotations
- Using humor or humorous stories
- Showing a visual

The following is an example of an introduction using the technique of telling a story. Note the thesis statement at the end of the introduction:

It was a normal Friday, just like every other Friday for the past ten years. Jane had gone to the grocery store, driven home, pulled into her driveway, and started unloading the groceries from the car. Just as she opened the trunk, she heard a loud scream from inside the house. She threw the groceries back into the trunk and ran toward the house. The front door was slightly ajar. As she entered the front door, her greatest horror was realized. Her 6-year-old son Jeff was sitting in the middle of the floor with blood on the front of his shirt. He was holding his left arm, crying and screaming. Immediately, Jane thought, "Did he fall out of that treehouse again?" "Did he have another accident on his bicycle?" The answer came when she saw her husband coming down the hall with a Ping Pong paddle in his hand and blood on his shirt—drinking again.

What Jane began to realize at this moment was that two years ago when Jeff had a broken arm, he had not fallen out of the treehouse, and last month, when he suffered two cracked ribs, he had not fallen off his bicycle. What she began to realize was that Jeff was suffering from the same thing that she had suffered from for nine years—domestic abuse.

(Thesis or Purpose Statement) This paper will inform you about (or . . . Today, I am going to speak to you about) the causes, effects, and signs of domestic abuse. I will also provide information that will help you gain assistance if you are involved in an abusive relationship or know someone who is.

In the space provided below, choose one technique, or a combination of the techniques we've discussed, to construct an introduction to your topic.

Technique(s) used

_____

_____

Introduction

_____

_____

_____

_____

CONCLUSIONS

Without exception, the conclusion should be one of the most carefully crafted components of your paper or speech. Long after your reader has finished reading or your audience has finished listening, the last part of your work is more than likely going to be the part they remember the most. Some writers and speakers suggest that you write your conclusion *first,* so that your paper or speech is directed toward a specific end result. That decision, of course, is up to you. However, a great piece of advice from writing experts tells us that captivating writers always know how their stories will end long before they begin writing them.

If you have ever read a poor ending or heard a speaker try to deliver an unprepared conclusion, then you know the importance of a well-crafted closing. Don't make the mistake of telling your readers or audience that you are concluding your paper or remarks and then carry on for seven more pages or ten more minutes. One of the worst mistakes you can make is talking too long. A conclusion should be brief, powerful, creative, and memorable. It should refocus attention, reenergize audience members, and redirect the audience toward the desired goals.

The following are some techniques for concluding a paper or speech:

- Summarize and re-emphasize the main points.
- Make a final appeal for action or challenge.
- Refer to the introduction (story, quote, or joke); this is parallelism.
- Complete the opening story.
- Re-emphasize the impact of your topic.
- Use a vivid analogy or simile.
- End powerfully.

The following is an example of a conclusion using the technique of referring to the introduction (parallelism) and making an appeal for action.

> Jane had denied the abusive situation for so long that she could not see how it was affecting her son. Just as the men and women profiled in this speech (paper) feared retaliation and more violence if they left the relationship, we saw that there were a variety of resources available for assistance such as the Women's Program for Abuse, Sister Care, Americans for an Abuse Free Nation, and local police departments. I call on you today, if you are in an abusive relationship or know someone who is, to act deliberately and immediately. Tomorrow may be one day too late.

STRATEGIES FOR BUILDING ON YOUR BEST

Consider the following strategies for public speaking:

- Select topics that interest your audience.
- Analyze your audience and how you might best relate to them.
- Carefully research your papers and presentations.
- Document your resources carefully and attentively.
- Polish your presentation by practicing aloud many times.
- Face your fears about speaking by speaking in public as frequently as you possibly can.
- Keep in your mind the slogan from the opening story, "This is your moment in the sun." Use it wisely.

In the space provided below and using your topic from the beginning of the chapter, write a memorable, creative conclusion.

Technique(s) used

_____
_____

Conclusion

_____
_____
_____
_____
_____
_____

Step 7: Documenting Your Paper or Speech

When writing your paper or speech, and certainly once it has been written, you should take careful precautions to document all research and information that is not your own. If you have written a paper, you will need to document and cite all statistics, quotes, and excerpts from works that you referenced. The most common means of doing this is by quoting within the paper and then compiling a reference or bibliography sheet at the end. If you have written a speech, you can verbally document researched facts, statistics, quotes, and excerpts. The following is an example of verbal documentation:

> The telling of a falsehood is like the cut of a knife; though the wound may heal, the scar of it will remain. —SAADI

Jane and her son Jeff are not alone in their abusive situation. According to Ronald Cohen in his book *Psychology and Adjustment,* over 1.5 million cases of abuse occur in the United States every year.

This allows the listeners to focus on the research and lets them know where the facts, statistics, or excerpts came from.

When writers or speakers fail to give credit where credit is due, this is called plagiarism. "Plagiarism is presenting another person's words or ideas as if they are your own. By not acknowledging a source, you mislead readers into thinking that the material you are presenting is yours, when, in fact, it is the result of someone else's time and effort" (Kirszner & Mandell, 1995). The previous statement was taken from another book; thus, it is cited as not being an original passage written for *Cornerstone.*

According to Kirszner and Mandell, there are four types of unintentional plagiarism:

- Borrowed words not enclosed in quotation marks
- Paraphrasing too close to its source
- Statistics not attributed to a source
- Writer's words and ideas not differentiated from those in the source

Although the above words are borrowed and not in quotation marks, they are cited in the preceding sentence. Therefore, the reader knows that the list was not written by *Cornerstone* authors.

Kirszner and Mandell have also compiled a list of "What to Document":

- Direct quotations
- Opinions, judgments, and insights of others that you summarize or paraphrase
- Information that is not widely known
- Information that is open to dispute
- Information that is not commonly accepted
- Tables, charts, graphs, and statistics taken from a source

There are several popular documentation styles used today. They include, but are not limited to: *The Modern Language Association (MLA), The American Psychological Association (APA),* and *The Chicago Manual of Style (CMS).*

Using your topic, choose two of your research sources, choose a documentation style, and properly document them in the space below.

Style chosen:

Source #1

Source #2

Step 8: Outlining Your Notes for Delivery

The techniques for outlining a speech are exclusive to delivery only. If you have used this chapter as a guideline for writing papers, this section and the last two sections on audiovisual aids and rehearsal will not be relevant to you at this time.

If you have ever watched and heard a disorganized speaker, or had to endure a speaker *read* an entire presentation, then you know the value of well-designed speaking notes.

> Speeches cannot be made long enough for the speakers, nor short enough for the hearers. —PERRY

After your speech has been formally written, it is time to outline your speaking notes. It is the mark of an unprofessional, unprepared speaker to read verbatim from pages and pages of typed notes. Instead, with rehearsal and a comprehensive keyword outline, you can use surprisingly few notes.

An outline should be used to keep you organized and to assist you should you get lost or blank out during your presentation. It should not be used for reading your speech to the audience. Some speakers prefer to use note cards (3 × 5 or 5 × 7), while others prefer to use several sheets of paper in outline form. The choice is yours unless specified otherwise by your professor.

When outlining, you will want to choose the most important words, names, numbers, or dates to assist you in delivery. Don't waste space writing words like "a," "an," or "the" and don't use complete sentences. Again, these are written cues, not notes to be read verbatim. Examples of a note card and a note outline are provided in Figure 12.2.

In the space provided below, outline the introduction that you wrote earlier in the chapter. Remember, use only key words. Do not write it out verbatim.

FIGURE 12.2 *Outlined notes.*

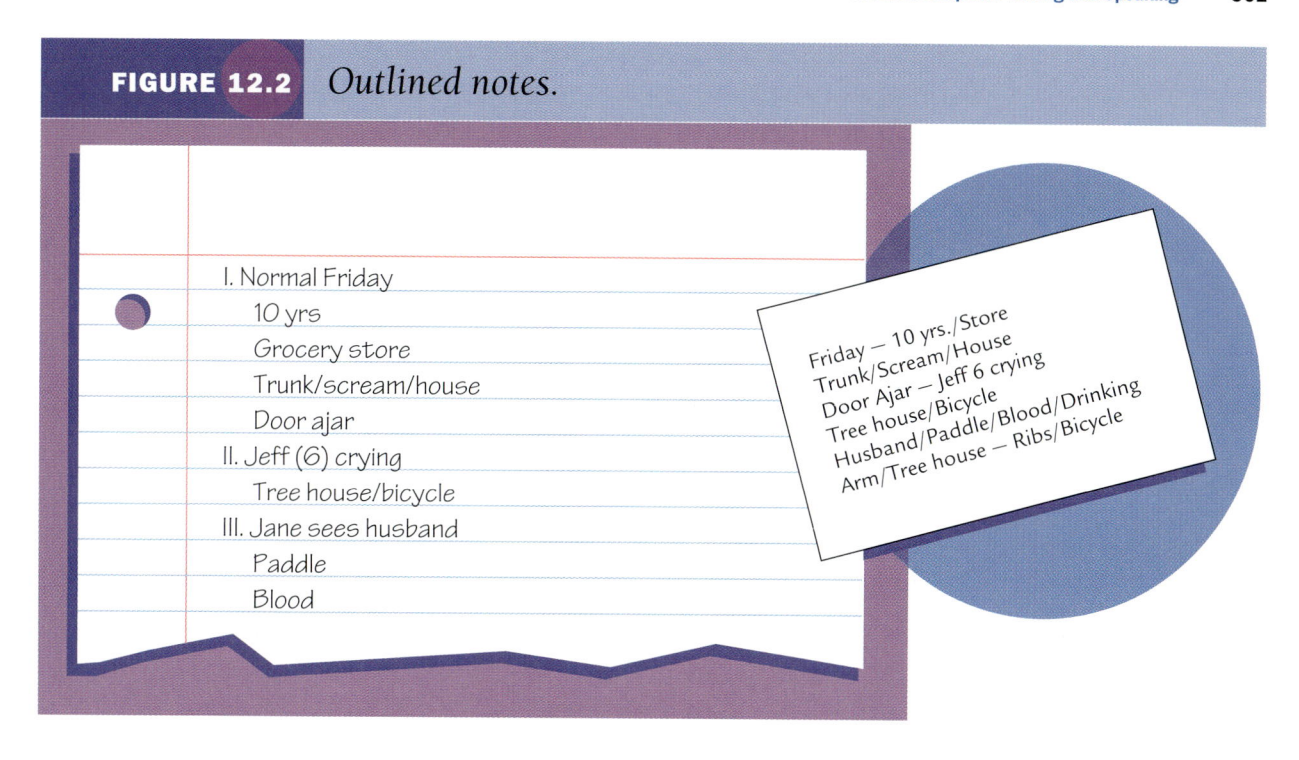

I. Normal Friday
   10 yrs
   Grocery store
   Trunk/scream/house
   Door ajar
II. Jeff (6) crying
   Tree house/bicycle
III. Jane sees husband
   Paddle
   Blood

Friday — 10 yrs./Store
Trunk/Scream/House
Door Ajar — Jeff 6 crying
Tree house/Bicycle
Husband/Paddle/Blood/Drinking
Arm/Tree house — Ribs/Bicycle

Step 9: Using Audiovisual Aids

You have heard it said, "A picture is worth a thousand words." Nowhere is that more true than in public speaking. Visual aids can assist your audience in retaining the information longer. If you simply tell an audience a fact, three days later, they will remember only 10 percent of what you said. If you tell them and show them, three days later, they will remember 65 percent of what you said (Gamble and Gamble, 1998).

Props and audiovisuals can be used to warm up an audience. When you become adept as a speaker, you can use slides and other visuals to replace notes, as long as you don't make them too detailed. They can help focus attention on the points you are trying to make, and they can, if used properly, add interest and variety to your presentation.

One speaker used hats to illustrate his points and to remind him of what to say. He wore a baseball cap backward when he talked about a company when it was young and getting started. He wore a top hat when he discussed the company's maturity. Then, he put on a safari hat to talk about searching for new business ventures. His audience probably remembered his key points because of the hats.

Several important factors should be considered when developing your visual aids. First, an audiovisual aid is a supplement to, not a substitute for, a presentation. Simply stated, even the most wonderfully creative visual aid will not support a poorly written and delivered speech. When choosing your aid, consider your audience, the location, and your time limits. You should also consider your comfort level with the aid that you have chosen. There are many types of aids available to you:

- Physical objects
- Models
- Drawings
- Maps
- Videotapes
- Audio recordings
- Real people
- Overhead transparencies
- Graphs, tables, and charts
- Photographs and slides
- Slick boards and chalkboards
- Yourself (probably the most important)
- Posters and flip charts
- Computer-generated presentations (such as PowerPoint slides) and CD-ROMs

Eighty percent of all information comes to us through sight.   —BEEBE AND BEEBE

For a smooth, clean, polished presentation, consider the following guidelines when using your visual aids:

- *Always* rehearse with your audiovisual (AV) aids.
- Make sure your AV is visible to all audience members.
- Make sure all equipment works before you begin your speech.
- Bring any item that you might need to make your AV work (such as extension cords, tape, push pins, and magic markers).
- Reveal each AV when you are ready to use it, not all at once.
- Explain each AV as it is revealed.
- Do not pass any AV around the room.
- Remove the AV when you have finished using it.
- Use any living AV with caution.
- Don't speak to the AV; speak to your audience.
- Use handouts with extreme caution. They should be issued only at the very end of your speech.

Consider the information and research that you plan to share. What type of audiovisual aid would best suit you, your presentation, and your audience?

Type of AV _____

Why? _____

_____

Step 10: Rehearsal and Delivery

The time has come! All of your hard work, creativity, and energy will culminate in this one moment in the sun. You have taken all of the necessary steps for a successful presentation. Now, you only need to consider a few more details before taking the lectern.

Public speaking is an unfair beast. If you study for an exam and do well or fail to study and do poorly, the results are known only to you and the professor. However, the results of your public speaking performance are known to all present. You are evaluated immediately. That is just an accepted fact in the art of speaking. In order to do your very best, consider the following anxiety-reducing and delivery tips.

> Speech is power: Speech is to persuade, to convert, to compel. —RALPH WALDO EMERSON

REDUCING ANXIETY

As we mentioned earlier in the chapter, the fear of public speaking is rated as the number one fear among Americans. According to Gamble and Gamble (1998), there are several reasons why we fear public speaking:

- Fear of failure
- Fear of the unknown
- Fear of evaluation
- Fear of being the center of attention
- Fear of difference
- Fear imposed by culture

These fears are real, but they are also manageable. When faced with anxiety over public speaking, keep the following tips in mind:

- A certain degree of anxiety is good for you. Use it to create energy.
- Choose a topic about which you know a great deal and one about which you care deeply.
- Prepare for your speech thoroughly!
- When rehearsing, try to re-create the speaking environment, or if possible, rehearse in the room where the speech will be delivered.
- Approach the speech with an "I can" attitude. The more confident you act, the more confident you will eventually become.
- After your first speech, jot down what happened to you physically; that is, did your heart beat faster, did you sweat, did your breathing become erratic? Keep a running list of these reactions so that you can recognize them and begin to control them.
- Realize that your small mistakes will not be seen and will rarely be heard by the audience; they are magnified in your own mind.
- Remember that listeners want you to succeed; most audiences are supportive.
- Instead of looking at the entire audience as a "room full of people," choose one person and look at him or her for a brief moment. Then, move on to the next person, and so on. This creates the feeling of speaking to only one person at a time.

- Don't try to be something that you are not. Just be yourself, use your own voice, your own gestures, and your own style.
- Don't concentrate on the evaluation. If you have prepared and do your best, you will be evaluated fairly.
- Visualize your success; the power of positive thinking is vastly underrated.

REHEARSAL AND DELIVERY

The moment is close at hand. Your topic is sterling, you have all of the information that you need to succeed, and you have prepared and rehearsed. To achieve a polished and professional touch, keep these final tips in mind:

- Always practice aloud so that you can practice your volume, tone, pace, and articulation.
- Rehearse from beginning to end without stopping.
- Rehearse at least once in front of a mirror so you can see your gestures, facial expressions, and body language.
- Rehearse using minimal notes.
- Rehearse using a tape recorder so that you may evaluate your own performance.
- When rehearsing, use a timer so that you can adjust your speech accordingly.
- Never, ever, under any circumstances, apologize for your speech or presentation.
- Watch your nonverbal communication (body language, facial expressions, and gestures).
- Remove temptations to fidget with things such as keys, change in your pocket, pens, and clips.
- Always maintain eye contact with your audience.
- The occasion should dictate your dress, so dress for the occasion.
- Don't stand in front of an audience and read; know your topic and simply talk to them.

The steps outlined in this chapter will assist you in writing and delivering a paper and public speech. However, without a positive "I can" attitude, much of your preparation will be fruitless. Public speaking is an exciting, rewarding experience that will assist you in almost every endeavor of your collegiate and professional life. The more you practice, the better you'll become! This is your moment in the sun—SHINE!

BLUEPRINTS FOR CHANGE

NAME   **DATE**

REFLECTION

Learning to speak and write well will greatly improve your success in college and will make a dramatic impact on your career. If you are nervous about speaking in front of a group, you are like most other people. Regardless of how calm your classmates might appear to you, they are probably just as nervous as you are.

The opening story discussed speaking as an opportunity for you to shine, and that's exactly what it is. The more you stand up and express yourself in front of a group, the better you will become and the more at ease you will be. You are encouraged to take every opportunity you get to write a speech or a paper and to deliver it in front of a group.

Speaking is like riding a bicycle. You will stumble a few times, but if you stick with it, you will gradually improve, and the rewards will be amazing both in and out of the classroom.

GET REAL

Below are a few questions to help you think about developing your communication skills. Study each question and respond honestly.

Describe one speaking experience you had that did not go well and left you with a fear of speaking in front of a group.

Discuss one positive experience you have had speaking in front of a group.

What was the primary difference between the two events?

How can you use the information in this chapter to help you in most of your courses?

How can you apply the information in this chapter to the workplace in either a part-time or full-time job?

If you improved your writing skills as a first-year student, how would this affect your entire college career?

Case Study

NAME: Lauren Stock
SCHOOL: Massasoit Community College, Brockton, MA
MAJOR: Physical Therapy   AGE: 19

Below is a real-life situation faced by Lauren. Read the brief case and respond to the questions.

I have often heard that the greatest fear faced by people is the fear of public speaking. It wasn't necessarily my number one fear, but I certainly had a great deal of apprehension about the course. I found that almost everyone in the room had fears and anxieties about speaking in front of a crowd. I found that my biggest fear was not really the speech, but what others would think of me.

I was lucky in that I had given several speeches in front of large groups, but no one had ever really shown me how to research and organize my speech. I did not know how to properly use an outline or improve my eye contact. I had been a heavy note user in the past, which always diminished my eye contact. My speech professor made it clear that she would grade on research, content, organization, and eye contact. That caused some anxiety as well.

My first speech this semester was on the Amish culture. I was very nervous, but I knew that I had researched my presentation thoroughly, organized it using one of the styles presented in class, practiced it aloud in front of the mirror, and satisfied the time limit set for us during my rehearsals. I was amazed and very happy that all of my preparation garnered me an A– on my first college speech. Without the research and oral preparation, I do not believe that I would have done as well.

Does public speaking cause you any anxiety? Why or why not?

___

Do you think that using Lauren's plan can help you? Why or why not?

___

How can you overcome the fear of what others think about you?

_____
_____
_____
_____

If you gained more confidence in yourself because of improved speaking skills, how would this impact your relationships?

_____
_____
_____
_____

If you overcame most of your fears regarding speaking in front of a group, how would it impact your college career?

_____
_____
_____
_____

If you gained more confidence in your ability to speak in public, how would this impact your current or future job?

_____
_____
_____
_____

at this moment Journal

Refer to page 339 of this chapter. Having read and reflected upon the information in the chapter, consider how you might revise your goal to make it more:

REASONABLE

BELIEVABLE

MEASURABLE

ADAPTABLE

CONTROLLABLE

DESIRABLE

ONLINE JOURNAL

To complete an online journal entry, log onto the Companion Website at **www.prenhall.com/sherfield.** Go to Chapter 12 and click on the link to the Online Journal. You can respond to the questions provided or to questions assigned by your professor, or you may journal about your own experiences.

ADVICE TO GO

CORNERSTONES

for research, writing, & speaking

Develop a *comprehensive* thesis statement.

Use *credible, documented* research.

Always rehearse *aloud.* Rehearse often.

Use a *logical* organizational pattern.

Use a *variety* of research sources.

This is your moment in the *sun!* SHINE!

Develop an *"I can"* attitude.

Speak on what you *know.*

Use a *keyword* outline.

Analyze the audience.

Use *vivid* language.

COMMUNICATE

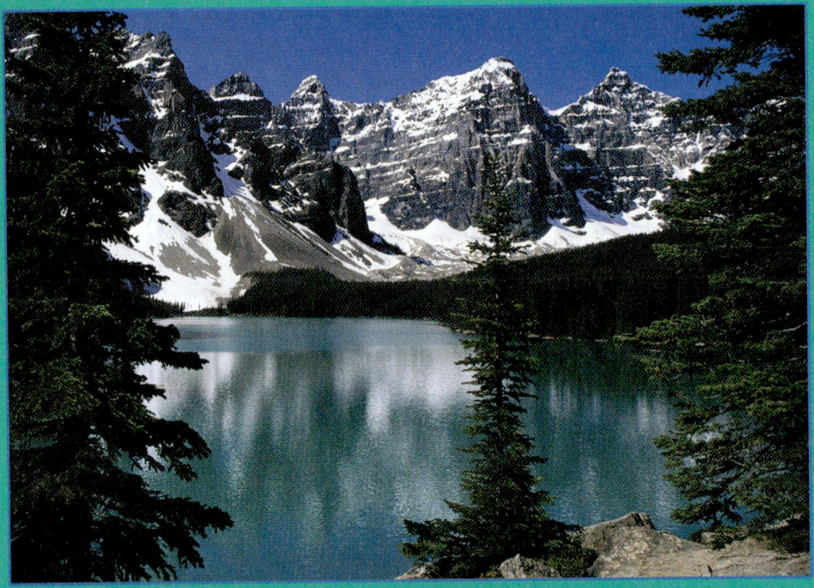

13 Relate

Friendship is the only cement that will ever hold the world together.

Woodrow Wilson

CHAPTER 13

RELATE

Bryan was born and raised in a small town. He went to school with the same group of friends since first grade and even had the same girlfriend since seventh grade. He chose to attend an urban university because of its excellent reputation in public health, the major he plans to study. There is some sense of security because his girlfriend, Harmony, has selected the same university.

Things go along smoothly for Bryan until Tuesday afternoon in biology class. His professor assigns new partners for each assignment. Today, Bryan arrives at his assigned station to find what he considers a strange looking young woman covered from head to toe in a *knumur*. Her dress is loose so as not to show the shape of her body, and the fabric is thick so the color of her skin is not shown. Only her face and hands are showing. Bryan knows nothing about the Muslim culture, and he is a little put off by her appearance.

He feels awkward at first, but as they work on their assignment, he discovers that Fareeha is very bright, and she already knows everything about this assignment. *As they work, he quizzes her about her background.* Fareeha reluctantly answers at first, but then she realizes that there is no malice in Bryan, just honest curiosity, and she begins to openly answer his questions.

He discovers that her family now lives in North Carolina, where her father owns a successful engineering firm. She and her brothers and sisters are all studying engineering. Her family's expectations of her and her siblings are very demanding. She has to make A's or suffer her father's wrath.

"So you must really love science and math?"

"Actually, I don't," said Fareeha, "but I really have no choice. My father will not allow me to study anything but engineering. I would love to study music."

Bryan is very interested in talking with Fareeha and walks with her outside after class. He notices that other students look at them, some with curiosity and some with open contempt. *He wonders if Fareeha faces this kind of behavior every day.*

Without realizing it, Bryan has become interested in this girl and her culture. "Would you like to get something to eat?" he asks her shyly.

"I can't," she replies nervously. "My brother is picking me up in a few minutes."

Bryan asks, "Could I meet him?"

"No," she says quickly and definitely, "I don't think that would be a good idea."

At that moment, her brother drives up, and Fareeha runs to the car and leaves. Bryan notices that her brother stares at him for a long time before driving off.

A Celebration of People, Cultures, and Self

That evening, Bryan can't seem to get this interesting and unusual young woman off his mind. He looks for Fareeha at his next biology class and goes to sit beside her. He tries to engage her in conversation, and she gradually begins to talk to him as the days go by. At every class period, Bryan seeks her out and sits with her. He notices the random rude stares and remarks, but he ignores them. *More and more, Bryan begins to look forward to seeing her and learning about her customs, culture, and religion.*

==Bryan begins to admire Fareeha's discipline and faith.== *He learns that her religion teaches patience, humility, charity, fasting, and praise for Allah.* He spends more and more time studying about her religion and culture. He attends her worship services and watches her family across the room. Bryan is confused and even a little frightened as he realizes he is moving further and further away from his fraternity, his family, and even his girlfriend as he becomes more attracted to Fareeha.

> **Without realizing it, Bryan has become interested in this girl and her culture.**

"What in the world will my family think?" he wonders. "They think people from New York are foreigners; they'll never understand this. Me—interested in a Muslim woman, how can I ever explain this?"

Later in the evening, his girlfriend, Harmony, calls him and reminds him that they are supposed to go to a movie that evening. "I don't think I can go," Bryan says apologetically. "Why not?" Harmony asks. "I'm just not feeling well tonight," he replies. "Come on, Bryan, this is the third time you've cancelled a date in the past two weeks. What's going on?"

QUESTIONS FOR REFLECTION

Consider responding to these questions online in the Questions for Reflection module of the Companion Website.

1. Have you ever had a negative reaction to someone who is from a different culture or religion from yours? Why or why not?

2. Do you believe you are strong enough to face the rude remarks, stares, and criticism of others to befriend or date someone from a different culture or religion?

3. What obstacles do you believe are ahead for Bryan and Fareeha? How do you think they can overcome them?

Where are you... AT THIS MOMENT

Before reading this chapter, take a moment and respond to the following ten questions. Consider each one carefully before answering, and then respond by circling the number in the appropriate box. When you have answered the questions, add your points and find your total score on the feedback chart below.

STATEMENT	STRONGLY DISAGREE	DISAGREE	DON'T KNOW	AGREE	STRONGLY AGREE	SCORE
1. I am aware of my prejudices and attitudes toward other people.	1	2	3	4	5	
2. I make an effort to learn about a person without judging them.	1	2	3	4	5	
3. Defensiveness and/or anger tend to get the best of me during conflicts.	5	4	3	2	1	
4. I am not very good at compromising when resolving conflicts.	5	4	3	2	1	
5. It is important to know and like yourself when trying to have a positive relationship with others.	1	2	3	4	5	
6. I have difficulty meeting new people and making new friends.	5	4	3	2	1	
7. I am not good at managing all the different relationships (friends, family, romantic, community) in my life.	5	4	3	2	1	
8. I see how my relationship with myself impacts all my other social relationships.	1	2	3	4	5	
9. I know where to turn for help if I feel I am a victim of prejudice or discrimination.	1	2	3	4	5	
10. I am impatient or intolerant of people who come from other cultures.	5	4	3	2	1	
TOTAL VALUE						

SUMMARY

10–17 Your skills in relating to others are limited. You need to increase your level of self-awareness, as well as your skills in resolving conflicts, in order to successfully navigate the social environments you'll encounter in college.

18–25 You have below average skills in relating to other people. Your awareness of your own attitudes is low, and you likely feel fear or anger toward those that are different from you. You need to improve your ability to communicate with others and resolve conflicts.

26–34 Your skills in being able to form relationships with others are average. You are somewhat aware of how your own attitudes and ideas impact your relationships with others and can usually get along with people who are different from yourself.

35–42 You are above average in being able to form relationships with others. You are likely aware of how your own self-concept and self-esteem affect the ways that you relate to others. You are also usually willing to get to know someone before making judgments about him or her.

43–50 You are exceptional in your ability to form relationships with others. You likely enjoy the diversity that you encounter in others and can find ways to get to know them. You are also aware of how your attitudes and experiences can color your perceptions.

Goal... FOR CHANGE

Based on your total points, what is one goal you would like to achieve related to relationships?

Goal _____
_____

List three actions you can take that might help you move closer to realizing this goal.

1. _____
2. _____
3. _____

Questions FOR BUILDING ON YOUR BEST

As you read this chapter, consider the following questions. At the end of the chapter, you should be able to answer all of them. You are encouraged to ask a few questions of your own. Consider asking your classmates or professors to assist you.

1. Why are relationships important?
2. What are the qualities of a "true" friend?
3. In what ways have I unknowingly demonstrated prejudice toward someone who is different from me?
4. How can I develop a healthy relationship with someone from another culture or background?
5. How can I improve my communication skills in relating to people from different cultures and backgrounds?

What additional questions might you have about relationships and diversity in college and life?

1. _____
2. _____
3. _____

Relationships

Life is about relationships. Relationships between people, between people and nature, and between people and the environment. The statement "No man is an island" is true. You would literally have to be shipwrecked on an island to be free of relationships with other humans, but you would still have relationships with nature, the animals, birds, and reptiles on the island. People do not live in a vacuum. We are the sum total of all of our relationships.

For many of you, the sum total of your relationships has been a rather homogenized sum. If you grew up in a metropolitan area, you may have been exposed to a wider variety of cultures, but you tend to "hang with your own tribe." Although this practice might bring comfort and peace, it usually does not lead to a great deal of growth because it is only when you step outside your comfort zone that you can truly learn about yourself and about the world around you.

For those of you who come from smaller communities, there might not have been as much opportunity to explore other cultures. Higher education is designed to give you the opportunity to meet, study with, befriend, and come to understand people who walk a different path than you—be it a different age, gender, race, religion, culture, sexual orientation, or physical challenge.

Why Are Relationships Important?

To function in a happy and healthy manner, human beings need one another. Everything we learn in this life comes through and from our relationships with others. We need each other to help us laugh, help us cry, help us learn, help us work, help us provide for the survival of the species, and help us die when the time comes.

Throughout our lives, we experience a myriad of relationships. We are someone's son or daughter, we may be someone's brother or sister, we probably will be someone's friend and someone's lover, as well as someone's helpmate through life. Each of these relationships has its own individual dynamics, but all successful relationships have some similarities.

College offers many opportunities for developing relationships with people from backgrounds different than your own.

Communities

Most, if not all, of our relationships take place within a community. Carolyn Shaffer and Kristin Amundsen, in their book *Creating Community Anywhere* (1994), define a community as a dynamic whole that emerges when a group of people:

- Participate in common practices.
- Depend on one another.
- Make decisions together.
- Identify themselves as part of something larger than the sum of their individual relationships.
- Commit themselves for the long term to their own, to one another's, and to the group's well-being.

You may find yourself involved in several separate communities: a home community, a school community, a work community. Communities may involve a group of diverse individuals. There is nothing wrong with this; to the contrary, it can be rewarding. You may also find that your communities overlap at times, adding more balance to your life.

What is your current community like? Your community has most likely changed recently because of your entry into higher education. In the past, your community may have been dictated by your physical surroundings, your parents and extended family, or the school you attended. Now you have many more choices in how your community looks and feels, and you also have more say about who will be a part of your community.

Types of Relationships

Within your personal community, your relationships will take many forms. You will have relationships with friends, family, professors, and peers, and you will most likely have relationships that involve romantic love. You will, however, first and foremost, need to understand and explore your relationship with yourself.

RELATIONSHIP WITH YOURSELF

It has been said that you can't love someone until you love yourself. You will remember from Chapter 2 a discussion on self-motivation and self-esteem and how improving yourself can help you establish healthier relationships with other people.

This is the time when you will reach deep within yourself and start to build the relationship within. This is when you will begin to learn who you are and what it is that you truly believe. As you begin this journey into higher education, take this time to ask yourself the big questions, and remember, you don't have to be satisfied with someone else's answers.

Consider the following ideas when trying to strengthen your personal character:

- Establish a value system that enables you to feel pride in yourself.
- Be honest with yourself about your strengths and shortcomings.
- Review your value system and make adjustments that will propel you toward the person you are building.

> The worst solitude is to be destitute of sincere friendship. —FRANCIS BACON

As you are working on the relationship with yourself, you will begin to understand that part of this relationship is learning to be alone. Being alone does not necessarily mean that you are lonely; however, there may be times when you do experience feelings of loneliness.

Loneliness is especially common among first-year college students. Here are some suggestions for how to get through the periods of loneliness you may experience:

1. Join a campus club or activity that involves one of your hobbies or interests.
2. Go to the new-student mixers that most colleges sponsor.
3. Volunteer in one of the organizations sponsored by your department or school, or get a part-time job in the field you are studying.
4. Ask one of your classmates to be a study partner. You could suggest meeting after each class to discuss the day's lecture, readings, and activities.
5. Offer to serve on one of your residence hall's committees.

If these activities don't seem to work for you, if your feelings of loneliness are intensifying and causing you to feel depressed, consider making an appointment with one of the counselors on campus. You can check the campus directory for names and numbers or ask the student health center to direct you to the appropriate person. These feelings are normal; the key is not to stay in this state of loneliness, but to be proactive and deal with the situation. Counselors are trained to help students do just that.

RELATIONSHIP WITH FRIENDS

It has been said that a very lucky person has three to four good friends at any given time in his or her life. True friends are hard to find, and even harder to keep! Many of us approach friendship as if it just happens, and, in some cases, it does. Think about your best friend. How did you meet? Probably by chance. Perhaps, fate brought you together. Sometimes, circumstances can cause you to drift apart.

Why is it important to build strong friendships? Friendships can bring you comfort, understanding from another person, and loyalty, and they give you someone to talk with about joys and sorrows. You can share your hopes and dreams and fears with good friends. Another reason for developing friendships is to have people with whom you share common interests and who allow you to have uninhibited fun. Really good friends bring joy into your life. Close and trusted friends are among the most important components of your personal community.

You may already have many friends, but have you ever thought about why they are your friends? The following exercise will ask you to build the "perfect" friend for your community. While no one is perfect, this activity reinforces and clarifies why certain friends (and qualities) in your life are important to you.

BUILDING A FRIEND...

Activity

Directions: Take a moment and think about the qualities that you would like to have in a true friend. As you begin to list these qualities, determine if they are related to the body, the mind, or the soul. Also, think about why these qualities are important to you.

Qualities of the Mind
_____
_____
_____
_____
_____
_____
_____

Qualities of the Soul
_____
_____
_____
_____
_____
_____
_____

Qualities of the Body
_____
_____
_____
_____
_____
_____
_____
_____

RELATIONSHIP WITH FAMILY

Everyone has a family in one form or another, be it a biological family, an adoptive family, or one pulled together from friends and loved ones. There is nothing that promises that any one of these families will be any more functional than the other. They can either help you succeed or help you fail. The power you give them to control your life is up to you. Regardless of what your choices might be, a family can be either your biggest fan or number one critic.

When dealing with your family (regardless of its makeup), here are a few pointers:

- Honesty is the best policy—all of us, at one time or another, have tried lying to our parents, friends, or loved ones and paid the price for it. Just remember the old saying, "Honesty without love is brutality."
- Talk things out; remember, you have two ears and one mouth. Use them in that proportion.
- Family is forever, whether it's the one you were born into or the one you have chosen. Your connections are powerful and should not be taken lightly or abused because of a whim or a passing bad mood.
- The words spoken cannot be unspoken. This is not to say you won't be forgiven, but forgiving is different from forgetting. The wounds your words cause may last a lifetime, so choose them carefully.

LOVE RELATIONSHIPS

There are many types and degrees of love relationships. The love between two old friends differs tremendously from the passion of two lovers. Love can be as relaxing and comfortable as an easy chair or as tumultuous and exhilarating as any rollercoaster ride. The way love is manifested in a relationship does not necessarily attest to the degree or intensity of the love.

Love is patient, love is kind. It does not envy, it does not boast, it is not proud. It is not rude, it is not self-seeking, it is not easily angered, it keeps no record of wrongs. Love does not delight in evil but rejoices with the truth. It always protects, always trusts, always hopes, and always perseveres.
—1 CORINTHIANS 13:4–7

Loving someone means caring about that person's happiness, trying to understand and to be understood by that person, and giving as well as receiving emotional support. Most love relationships involve intimacy to some degree. Intimacy is not synonymous with sex; it may or may not involve sexual relations. Intimacy refers to the emotional openness that usually develops over time between two people who love each other. Intimacy allows people to share hopes and dreams as well as pain and sorrows.

Some of you will meet and fall in love with your lifelong partner in college, and the ritual you will most likely use to become acquainted is dating. Keep the following tips in mind when you begin dating a person:

- Don't go out alone with a stranger; go out in a group until you are better acquainted with your date.
- Make sure someone knows with whom you are going out, where you are going, and the approximate time you'll return; call that person if your plans change.
- Have your own transportation so that you can leave if you are uncomfortable.
- Don't go to someone's home unless you know that person very well.
- Establish a friendship before you try a relationship.

When Relationships Go Sour

Every relationship, whether it is a friendship or love relationship, has its period of exhilaration when nothing the other person does is wrong. Everything in the world is brighter because this person is in your life. You also know that these feelings may taper off. After the newness of a relationship wears off, you discover whether or not it will continue to be part of your life. This is the ordinary cycle of a relationship. If a person is meant to be a part of your life, you begin to settle into a rhythm that works for both of you; if not, hopefully you part ways in a friendly manner that hurts no one.

Unfortunately, there are times when this is not possible, when one or both parties hang on to each other because they are not emotionally prepared to go it alone. Often, this leads to a very toxic situation. What does a toxic situation look like? You may have seen one or even participated in one. Here are some things to look for:

- One person's inability to function apart from the other.
- Blaming each other (or perhaps just one of you) for everything that is going wrong in your lives (life).
- Using abusive language and/or trying to control through intimidation.
- Using intimate knowledge of your weaknesses to hurt you or someone else.
- Using intimate knowledge to manipulate you or someone else.
- The use of physical violence or any controlling technique.

Another type of toxic relationship may be when sexual harassment is involved.

Sexual Harassment

Those of us in higher education would like to believe that we are immune to problems of sexual harassment, that we foster an atmosphere in which such behavior is not tolerated. But the cold, hard facts prove otherwise. On many campuses, sexual harassment takes place among students, between students and faculty, among faculty, and between faculty and administration.

Male and female professors have been accused and convicted of sexual harassment involving students. Most colleges have adopted strict policies on student–faculty relationships. No faculty member has a right to ask you to be personally involved. If you have been verbally harassed, threatened, or coerced into an unwanted sexual or personal situation, contact your department chair and/or the professor's department chair. He or she is required to act on this grievance. If the department chair does not act on your grievance, go to his or her dean.

The federal government defines sexual harassment as deliberate or repeated unsolicited verbal comments, gestures, or physical contact of a sexual nature that is considered to be unwelcome by the recipient, male *or* female. It includes:

- Verbal abuse or harassment
- Unwelcome sexual overtures or advances
- Pressure to engage in sexual activity
- Remarks about a person's body, clothing, or sexual activities
- Leering at, or ogling, somebody's body
- Telling unwanted dirty jokes
- Unnecessarily touching, patting, or pinching someone
- Unwanted letters, telephone calls, or written materials
- Pressure for dates
- Personal questions of a sexual nature
- Sexual innuendoes or stories
- Touching of any kind
- Referring to people as babes, hunks, dolls, honey, boy toy, and so forth

If you are faced with a situation that you believe is sexual harassment, you can take several steps to protect yourself.

1. Make a conscious effort to keep interactions between you and the person harassing you as impersonal as possible.
2. Avoid being alone with the person harassing you. If that person is your professor, bring a friend with you to meetings and arrange to meet in a classroom either right before or right after class.
3. Keep a record of the harassment in case you have to bring formal charges.
4. Tell the harasser that you believe he or she is harassing you and you want the behavior to stop. Be very specific, so that the person knows what you perceive as harassment.
5. Tell your academic advisor or a campus counselor about the events. Seek their counsel.
6. See a lawyer. Sexual harassment is against the law, and you may need to bring formal charges.

Rape

Rape is a cause of fear and concern among college students, and date, or acquaintance, rape has become as much a concern as rape by strangers. You can take steps to reduce the possibility of rape.

TO DECREASE THE CHANCES OF RAPE BY A STRANGER:

1. Know where campus security is located; keep emergency phone numbers handy.
2. Use campus transportation services.
3. Set up signals with other students in your residence hall to alert one another in case of a problem.
4. List only your first initials in the campus directory or on your mailbox.
5. Be aware of your surroundings and avoid unsafe places.
6. Vary your route and walk in groups whenever possible.
7. Stay on well-lighted paths, sidewalks, and streets.
8. If a car pulls up beside you, stay at least an arm's length away; never get into the car.
9. If you are afraid, yell "No!" or "Call 911."
10. Use dead-bolt locks on your doors and keep windows locked.
11. Have your keys ready when you approach your car door or home.
12. Drive with your doors locked.
13. Always check the identification of people such as utility workers, security officers, or salespeople who come to your door.
14. Check the back seat and under your car before getting in.
15. Do not park in garages at night if you are alone.

TO DECREASE THE CHANCES OF ACQUAINTANCE OR DATE RAPE:

1. Until you are very familiar with your date, avoid being alone together or going to secluded places.
2. Stay sober.
3. Be very clear about your sexual intentions.
4. Tell a friend whom you are out with, where you are going, and when you expect to return home.
5. Use your own transportation.
6. Learn the signs of date rape and "club" drugs.

College is an environment fraught with new experiences, new relationships, and new behaviors. It is our hope that this chapter will help you think about the situations you may find yourself in and prompt you to make responsible decisions.

In some worst-case scenarios, sexual harassment has led to acts of violence, stalking, and even rape. The following section provides advice on how to decrease the chances of being raped by an acquaintance or a stranger.

Relationships with Diverse Others

We have discussed the closest relationships you might form with family, friends, and lovers. The remainder of this chapter will focus on your relationships with people from different cultures, religions, ages, gender, or sexual orientations who may have beliefs and values different from your own. One of the biggest advantages of going to college is the fact that you live and study in an international community. If you approach diverse populations with an open mind and heart, you can benefit greatly from the exposure to people who are different from you.

THE POWER OF AN OPEN MIND

To experience other people and to receive the benefits of knowing someone, you need to enter all relationships with an open mind. If you have a derogatory mind-set toward a race, an ethnic group, a sexual orientation, or a religion, for example, you have internal barriers that can keep you from getting to know who a person really is.

Learning to interact with people from different cultures is a matter of keeping an open mind and looking at each person as an individual, not as a race, a class, or a religion. We cannot help but be influenced by what we have been taught and what we have experienced, but we can overcome prejudices and biases if we view people as individuals. If you intend to grow as an educated person and as a human being, you will need to expand your capacity to accept and understand people from different cultures within and outside your country.

YOU ARE A CULTURE OF ONE

During our formative years, each of us develops a unique set of values, beliefs, and customs. We are virtually programmed, based on who raises us, our race, our nationality, where we live, where we go to school, our religion or lack of religion, our friends, our relatives, and our experiences and opportunities. Like fingerprints, no two people with their beliefs, customs, and experiences are exactly alike. This amazing phenomenon is what makes human beings interesting and makes the differences we see in people from cultures other than our own especially interesting as well as personally educational.

Culture is learned. People are born into a culture, but their culture is not a physical trait, such as eye color or hair texture. You probably developed, or absorbed, most of your personal culture from your family. The process is almost like osmosis in plants; it is as though culture seeps gradually through your skin. Many of the beliefs and values you embrace have been passed from one generation to another.

In college, you are likely to find your values, beliefs, and actions changing as you meet new people and become

How can getting to know people from different backgrounds or cultures enhance your personal education?

involved in new situations and as your horizons broaden. Quite simply, your college experience enhances your understanding, and your cultural beliefs change as a result. This change is known as cultural adjustment. You can, and should, expect to have your beliefs greatly tested—and perhaps adjusted—before you graduate.

Cultural adjustment doesn't mean that you must abandon your family, church, basic values, and friends. It may mean, however, that you need to reevaluate why you feel the way you do about certain situations and certain groups. You may have been taught that people belonging to a certain group are not acceptable. As you learn and grow, you may find that they are not bad at all, just different from you. You may discover that this different culture is one to be celebrated.

The Ties That Bind
COMPONENTS OF CULTURE

Sometimes we can tell that people are from a different culture or ethnic group because of the way they look and dress or by the way they speak—dress and speech are two visible signs of culture. Other components of culture are not so visible. Sociologist David Popenoe (1993) identifies five components of culture:

- Symbols
- Language
- Values
- Norms
- Sanctions

Symbols are items that stand for something, such as the American flag. Most Americans respect the flag and know that it stands for honor, duty, patriotism, service, and freedom. People of other nationalities might not understand that the stars and stripes on the American flag are significant symbols in American culture. The key to relating to people from any culture is understanding. Some common symbols and what they stand for are as follows:

Purple signifies royalty in some cultures.

A *pineapple* is a sign of welcome and hospitality in the southern United States.

Red is associated with anger in some cultures.

An *octagon sign* indicates "Stop!" in several countries.

Name a symbol from your culture:

_____

_____

What does this symbol mean?

_____

_____

DID YOU KNOW?

69%

The percentage of lesbian, gay, bisexual, and transsexual youth who reported experiencing some form of harassment or violence in school.

Source: Posted from *Just the Facts*, http:msn.planetout.com/people/teens/features/2000/08/facts.html.

386 CHAPTER 13 RELATE

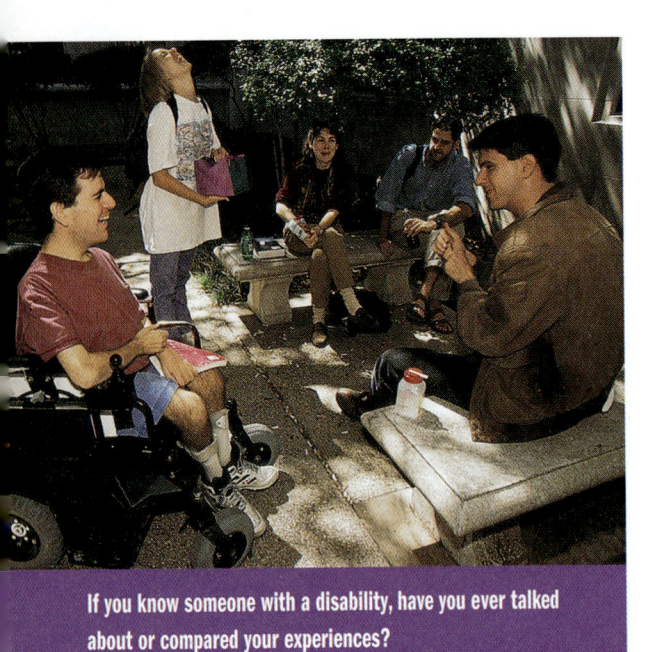

If you know someone with a disability, have you ever talked about or compared your experiences?

Language is another important component of culture; the meaning of a word can vary across cultures. For example, if you were to ask for a biscuit in England, you would get a cookie. How many different words can you think of for that nonalcoholic, carbonated beverage many of us like to drink? Pop? Soda? Soft drink? Coke?

The African American culture in the United States has given some words meanings that are specific to that culture. For example, a "shade and fade" haircut is typical of language used by African American college students. Other cultures within the United States have done the same.

What is a phrase specific to your culture?
_____
_____

What does it mean?
_____
_____

Values are typically based on family traditions and religious beliefs. What is unacceptable in one society may be acceptable in another. Most young people in the United States would be unwilling to allow their parents to choose their future spouse, yet in many countries this practice is still common. Some religious services are joyous celebrations; others are formal and solemn. The African American AME church is usually filled with soulful, joyous singing, while the Primitive Baptist Church may include songs not accompanied by musical instruments and may be more solemn—there is no one proper way to conduct a religious ceremony. Like so much else, what is correct depends on the culture.

Name a value of the culture in which you were raised.
_____
_____

Why is this value important to you?
_____
_____

Norms relate directly to the values of a culture or society—they are how we expect people to act based on those values. In an elegant restaurant, for example, you expect people to conduct themselves with more dignity than you might expect in a fast-food restaurant.

What is a norm in your culture?

_____

_____

Why do you think it is a norm? Why is it important?

_____

_____

Sanctions are the ways in which a society enforces its norms. When a society adopts a set of norms that are upheld as valuable, it typically seeks a way to enforce these norms through formal laws. In every society, there are people who do not abide by the rules, people who break the law. A person in the United States who breaks the law may be sent to jail or may be required to perform community service. In some cultures, punishment is much more severe. For example, the punishment for stealing in some Middle Eastern cultures may be to sever the thief's hand. In the United States, this punishment would not be acceptable, but elsewhere it is.

Give an example of a sanction in your culture.

_____

_____

Why do you think it is a sanction?

_____

_____

If you have a desire to understand and appreciate others, you can learn to celebrate diversity and gain valuable lessons from almost everyone you meet.

Who Are You?

In *Managing Diversity,* Gardenswartz and Rowe (1993) refer to "individuals as being like the proverbial onion with layer upon layer of cultural teaching." They suggest that cultural identity is shaped by the following factors:

- Ethnicity—the ethnic group with which a person identifies and the person's native language
- Race—the racial group or groups with which a person identifies
- Religion—the organized denomination or sect to which a person subscribes, if any
- Education—the level and type of learning a person receives
- Profession/field of work—the type of work a person is trained to do
- Organizations—groups or associations to which a person belongs or has belonged, such as the military, a scouting group, a labor union, or a fraternal organization

- Parents—the messages, verbal and nonverbal, given by a person's parents about ethnicity, religion, values, and cultural identity

In addition to these powerful cultural influences, gender, family, peers, and place of birth also significantly determine a person's cultural identity.

Because we are so very different on many levels, sometimes relationships with others "go bad." Call it human nature, call it pride, call it anger, or call it ignorance, few people, if any, go through life without some degree of conflict. If relationships with friends, family, lovers, and people of diverse backgrounds are important to you, you may want to learn how to recognize the signs of conflict and how to avoid unhealthy conflict when you can. When conflict can't be avoided, learning how to manage conflict can be beneficial to any relationship.

STRATEGIES FOR BUILDING ON YOUR BEST

Consider the following strategies when trying to resolve a conflict:

- Control yourself. Keep your words, actions, tone of voice, and body language respectful. Resist the urge to use name calling, hurtful words, and interruptions. Remember, you can't control or change anyone else.

- Establish an environment where people feel safe. This is not the time for intimidating body language, yelling, or obscenities. If you are going to resolve a conflict, you must keep your anger under control.

- Listen to what the other person has to say first. Let the other person know that you respect his or her opinions and rights.

- Avoid "gunnysacking," which is the practice of suppressing a long list of complaints and bringing them up all at one time. Sometimes, this suppressed hostility explodes and escalates.

- Try to reach some common ground. Focus your conversations on finding solutions instead of placing blame.

- Think of ways you can arrive at a "win-win" solution by first looking for common ground and things that you do agree on. Be sure you are considering the other person's needs as well as your own. Taking care of your needs and leaving the other person unhappy will only result in future conflicts that may be even worse.

Conflict Is Inevitable

HOW DO YOU DEAL WITH IT?

Many people intensely dislike conflict and will go to extreme measures to avoid it. On the other hand, some people seem to thrive on conflict and enjoy creating situations that put people at odds with each other. While in college, you certainly will not be sheltered from conflicts. In fact, on a college campus where a very diverse population lives and learns together, conflict is likely to arise on a regular basis. The simple truth is, conflict is pervasive throughout our culture, and you simply cannot avoid having some confrontations with other people. Therefore, you should not try to avoid conflict; rather, you can use it to create better relationships by exploring workable solutions.

You may experience conflict in a classroom when another student takes issue with your opinions and continues to harass you about your ideas after the class is over. You could be placed on a team where conflicts arise among the members. A major conflict could erupt in the parking lot if someone thoughtlessly pulls into a parking space that you have been waiting for. You could even experience conflict with a faculty member because you intensely disagree with the grade he or she assigned you on a project. Conflict can occur in any relationship, whether it is your parents, your girlfriend or boyfriend, your best friend, a roommate, a spouse or partner, your children, or a total stranger.

Before you go any further, take a moment and complete the Conflict Management Assessment.

CONFLICT MANAGEMENT ASSESSMENT — *Activity*

Read the following questions carefully and respond according to the key below. Take your time and be honest with yourself.

1 = NEVER typical of the way I address conflict
2 = SOMETIMES typical of the way I address conflict
3 = OFTEN typical of the way I address conflict
4 = ALMOST ALWAYS typical of the way I address conflict

1. When someone verbally attacks me, I can let it go and move on. 1 2 3 4
2. I would rather resolve an issue than have to "be right" about it. 1 2 3 4
3. I try to avoid arguments and verbal confrontations at all costs. 1 2 3 4
4. Once I've had a conflict with someone, I can forget it and get along with that person just fine. 1 2 3 4
5. I look at conflicts in my relationships as positive growth opportunities. 1 2 3 4
6. When I'm in a conflict, I will try many ways to resolve it. 1 2 3 4
7. When I'm in a conflict, I try not to verbally attack or abuse the other person. 1 2 3 4
8. When I'm in a conflict, I try never to blame the other person; rather, I look at every side. 1 2 3 4
9. When I'm in a conflict, I try not to avoid the other person. 1 2 3 4
10. When I'm in a conflict, I try to talk through the issue with the other person. 1 2 3 4
11. When I'm in a conflict, I often feel empathy for the other person. 1 2 3 4
12. When I'm in a conflict, I do not try to manipulate the other person. 1 2 3 4
13. When I'm in a conflict, I try never to withhold my love or affection for that person. 1 2 3 4
14. When I'm in a conflict, I try never to attack the person; I concentrate on their actions. 1 2 3 4
15. When I'm in a conflict, I try to never insult the other person. 1 2 3 4
16. I believe in give and take when trying to resolve a conflict. 1 2 3 4

CONTINUED

Activity

17. I understand AND USE the concept that kindness can solve more conflicts than cruelty. 1 2 3 4
18. I am able to control my defensive attitude when I'm in a conflict. 1 2 3 4
19. I keep my temper in check and do not yell and scream during conflicts. 1 2 3 4
20. I am able to accept "defeat" at the end of a conflict. 1 2 3 4

Total number of 1s _____

Total number of 2s _____

Total number of 3s _____

Total number of 4s _____

If you have more 1s, you do not handle conflict very well and have few tools for conflict management. You have a tendency to anger quickly and lose your temper during the conflict.

If you have more 2s, you have a tendency to want to work through conflict, but you lack the skills to carry this tendency through. You can hold your anger and temper for a while, but eventually, it gets the best of you.

If you have more 3s, you have some helpful skills in handling conflict. You tend to work very hard for a peaceful and mutually beneficial outcome for all parties.

If you have more 4s, you are very adept at handling conflict and do well with mediation, negotiation, and anger management. You are very approachable; people turn to you for advice about conflicts and their resolution.

The world is full of difficult people, but most of them can be dealt with if you keep a lid on your own hostility. The basic idea of resolving conflict is to get a handle on your own emotions. You need to remove threatening behaviors, words, and body language and be prepared to compromise so everyone leaves feeling like they won something. Think of conflict resolution as a way to gain a new friend instead of adding a new enemy.

The Golden Rule for Celebrating Diversity

At one time or another, most of us have been exposed to the Golden Rule: "Do unto others as you would have them do unto you." As you work to improve and expand your knowledge of cultural diversity, it may help you to look at this rule from a different angle. In considering the following scenarios, first by yourself and then with a group, see if you can apply a new version of the Golden Rule: "Do unto others as they would have you do unto them."

> **M**ulticulturalism appreciates everyone's "roots" and promotes equality of all cultures. —SHARON HANNA

I THINK I WOULD . . . AN EXERCISE IN CULTURAL UNDERSTANDING

Respond to each scenario in the space provided. Discuss how the situation makes you feel, how you would feel if you were the person in the cultural minority depicted, and what you might do or say to improve this situation for everyone involved.

Your class may be asked by the instructor to discuss your responses to these scenarios in an open discussion. If so, be aware that these scenarios contain information sensitive to some of your classmates, perhaps to you. While the purpose of the discussion will be to help everyone understand how their

> **Y**ou have to move to another level of thinking, which is true of me and everybody else. Everybody has to learn to think differently, think bigger, to be open to possibilities. —OPRAH WINFREY

classmates feel, each person in the class should be mindful of others' feelings. Think before you speak. Speak your mind openly, but carefully, to avoid damaging others' self-esteem. Remember, we all take in "messages" about ourselves from others. Be aware of your body language as well as your words.

You may find that some of your beliefs change slightly—or maybe even dramatically—as you work on these exercises. Growth that allows you to open up your mind, to move beyond biases and prejudices, and to seek to understand people who are different from you is positive growth.

SCENARIO 1

You and Jack, a friend from high school, are attending the same college. Jack has a physical disability that requires him to use a wheelchair. He was an outstanding basketball player and swimmer prior to a diving accident, which left him a paraplegic. Jack is an honor roll student. He is an avid basketball fan, attends all the games, and plays on a wheelchair team. He has a great sense of humor. He long ago dealt with his personal situation and now he even jokes about it. Jack is one of your favorite people.

Since you and Jack have been in class together, you have been noticing that people tend to treat him differently from others. Sometimes people talk loudly when talking to Jack, as if he can't hear. Because getting to and from classes is difficult, Jack has someone to help him maneuver around campus. One day you overhear a student talking to the person who is helping Jack as if Jack weren't there. "What happened to him?" "Can he use his arms?" Although Jack is handsome, friendly, and personable, he is usually left out of the many social activities in which other classmates participate. You know that your classmates would like and admire Jack if they got to know him.

How do you think Jack feels when people treat him as though he doesn't exist?

_____
_____
_____

Why do you think some people have difficulty relating to people who have physical disabilities?

_____
_____
_____

What could you say to classmates that might help them understand how to relate to Jack better and might make them and him feel more comfortable?

_____
_____
_____
_____

SCENARIO 2

Douglas met Andy on the first day of class. Douglas struck up a conversation with Andy because he saw a tennis racket in Andy's gym bag—a welcome sight. Douglas had not found anyone to play tennis with since his arrival on campus. The two decided to get together later in the afternoon to play a game. When the game was over, each knew that he had found a friend. They discovered that they lived in the same residence hall, had the same professor for English, only at different times, and both loved to play tennis. As the semester progressed, Douglas and Andy became very close friends; they studied history together, went to parties together, ate together when their schedules permitted, and double-dated once or twice.

> am a citizen, not of Athens or Greece, but of the world. —SOCRATES

Douglas and Andy enjoyed many of the same sports and movies and had similar tastes in music. Douglas felt that he had met a true soulmate, and Andy could not have been happier to have Douglas to talk to and hang around with. Andy knew, however, that things could soon change. He had made a serious decision; before the Christmas break, he would tell Douglas that he was gay.

Exams ended on Wednesday. Andy decided to break the news to Douglas on Tuesday night. They talked and laughed sitting on a bench outside the athletic center; then the conversation grew still, and Andy chose his words carefully. He told Douglas that he was gay and that he had been involved with someone at home for almost a year.

If you were Douglas, what would your reaction have been?

Should Andy have told Douglas about his sexual orientation? If so, should he have told him sooner? Why or why not?

Imagine that Douglas, a heterosexual, accepted Andy's orientation, but that Andy went on to say that he was interested in having a relationship with Douglas. How do you think Douglas would have reacted?

Does being gay carry a cultural or social stigma? Why or why not?

SCENARIO 3

Tonya was a first-year student at a major research university. She had an excellent academic background. She had always loved science and math and was seriously considering a major that would allow her to incorporate her love of these subjects into a career. In her second semester at the university, she enrolled in a calculus class taught by Dr. Ralph Bartlett. This class was especially important to Tonya for two reasons. First, Dr. Bartlett was the department chair for the program she was considering pursuing, and second, the course was her first college math course, so she wanted to start off strong.

On the first day of class, Dr. Bartlett made some disparaging jokes about women in the field of science. Although these comments made Tonya uncomfortable, she thought perhaps she was being oversensitive. As the semester progressed, so did Dr. Bartlett's derogatory asides about women. Nonetheless,

WORLD OF WORK

As college students who will soon be entering the real world of work, you need to know that many situations you will face will be vastly different from the college campus and college life, or from the place where your parents entered the workforce. Diversity is a frequently discussed issue and impacts every aspect of the workplace, from employment practices to promotion, from leadership and management styles to employee relations, from domestic relationships to global interaction, and from product creation to marketing. I can tell you without reservation that learning to celebrate and appreciate diversity is an absolute must for success in your careers.

As an African American with over 35 years experience in the automotive industry, I have experienced some "not too pleasant" people along the way; however, I have learned to stay focused on my career goals and to be absolutely sure that I am being fair and consistent in my own workplace habits where diversity is concerned. I am responsible for my actions. I can't do anything about other people's personal prejudices and biases whether based on race, religion, gender, national origin, or sexual orientation, but I can be sure that I give every person a fair chance and judge them on their character and performance.

As a corporate executive for the world's largest manufacturer, I have had unlimited opportunities to interact with people from diverse backgrounds—from the White House to a remote Habitat building site in Poland. I, therefore, had to adjust in order to form solid relationships with people who are different from me. My personal reward is accepting those differences and learning to appreciate people for who they are and for what they can contribute to the betterment of my job, my company, my country, and the world.

About 10 years ago, I was vice president for corporate communications at Saturn Corporation, a wholly owned subsidiary of General Motors, located in Spring Hill, Tennessee. My primary responsibility was to protect and enhance the image and reputation of the company. That meant taking into consideration many factors that might impact our diverse customer base, especially in Japan.

I have taken those **"best practices"** from Saturn to my current position at GMAC, one of the largest financial service organizations in the world. It is my responsibility to ensure that our advertising, promotion, communication, and public relation efforts send the right messages to our worldwide audience.

GMAC is part of an even larger organization, General Motors Corporation, with nearly 380,000 employees selling vehicles and services in 200 countries around the world. Working in such a global organization, I cannot and will not act in a manner that could have a negative impact on my career or the image and reputation of my company. I encourage you to open your minds and hearts. You will be richly rewarded in your career and in your personal development.

QUESTIONS FOR REFLECTION

Consider responding to these questions online in the World of Work module of the Companion Website.

1. Why do you think Mr. Farmer has been so successful in his career?
2. What kinds of prejudices do you think Mr. Farmer has experienced?
3. What can you learn from Mr. Farmer that you can apply to your own life and later at work?

James E. Farmer, Vice President, Merchandising, Advertising, and Communications, General Motors (GMAC), Detroit, MI

Tonya loved the course; she was earning A's and she felt that she had found her niche. She decided to major in this area. Tonya made an appointment to discuss possible career opportunities with Dr. Bartlett. Shortly into the appointment, Dr. Bartlett made it clear to Tonya that he didn't think she could cut it and suggested that she look for another program.

How would you feel if you were in Tonya's shoes?

_____
_____
_____

Should you allow one person's assessment of your abilities to dictate your course in life?

_____
_____
_____

How would you feel if you were a male in Tonya's class?

_____
_____
_____

Why do you think women face discrimination in higher education? In the workforce?

_____
_____
_____

SCENARIO 4

Rebecca is a nontraditional student who is 38 years old. She is a single parent and has two young children. Although she is not a college graduate, she has been promoted through the ranks to a responsible position at a major bank. Because she has now reached the highest level she can achieve without a college degree, she has returned to school. Rebecca has developed excellent computer skills from her on-the-job experience. Working full time, parenting two young children alone, and going back to school constitute a heavy load for Rebecca.

You notice that Rebecca comes into class at the last possible moment since she must rush to school from work and find a parking place. As soon as class is over, she makes a dash for her car so she can get back to work. Her classmates have very little time to get to know her and she tends to get left out of discussions.

You and Rebecca have been assigned to a team that has to work together to complete a group project. All of the team members except Rebecca are traditional students. At the first meeting, your group discusses times to meet, and most agree that 1:30 on Tuesday afternoons meets your schedules. When Rebecca tells the group that she can only meet at night because of her job and only on Wednesday nights when her mother can take care of her children, one of the team members makes the following hostile remark to Rebecca: "Well, perhaps you will have to find a way to meet when the rest of us want to since you are the only one causing a problem."

How can you use the conflict resolution techniques discussed earlier in this chapter to immediately ease the tension between team members?

_____
_____
_____

If Rebecca is unable to attend meetings held during her work hours, how can you help her catch up on what she needs to do to be an effective member of your team?

_____
_____
_____

What special skills and attributes can traditional students learn from a nontraditional student like Rebecca?

_____
_____
_____

SCENARIO 5

Jermale, an 18-year-old student of African American and Asian heritage, often feels left out because he doesn't seem to belong to either race. African Americans seem to feel that he is white and Asian Americans believe he is African American. Although he has friends of different races, he is sometimes the brunt of ignorant remarks. Jermale often feels lonely and fears that he might be the victim of a hate crime.

While returning to his residence hall one evening after a fraternity meeting, Jermale is frightened when a pickup truck slows to match his pace as he walks along the sidewalk. One of the two young men in the truck leans out the window and yells racial slurs at him and spits in his direction before the truck speeds away.

Upon reaching his residence hall, Jermale notices the same truck, now empty, parked outside the building. As he nears the front door, Jermale again hears loud racial slurs being yelled at him from a third-story window directly above the entrance to the dorm. Clearly, the students are very drunk and obnoxious, and they are waiting for him to arrive. As Jermale enters the door, the slurs become mixed with threats to urinate on him. He enters the residence hall just as drops of liquid fall around him. Angry and frightened, Jermale rushes to his room and locks the door.

How would you feel if you were Jermale?

_____
_____
_____

What action, if any, do you think Jermale should take?

_____
_____
_____

Do you think racial discrimination is a problem on college campuses?

_____
_____
_____

Slamming the Door on Hate

WHAT CAN YOU DO TO MAKE A DIFFERENCE?

Because we are a diverse population with people from all over the world making up our neighborhoods, our communities and individuals are often the victims of hate crimes. Hate crimes are vicious attacks on society in general and on communities and individuals specifically. The people who perpetrate hate crimes are usually misguided individuals who, nevertheless, cause great harm to many people. Hate mongers represent a very small minority of people on the fringes of society, yet they are serious stumbling blocks to racial harmony. Hate crimes can be directed at many diverse targets. They can be racially motivated or the result of religious intolerance. Sometimes, they are directed at people who have different sexual orientations. Intolerance of differences might be directed at gays and lesbians, Jews, African Americans, Native Americans, Hispanics, and others.

Regardless of the reason for the hate crime, the victims are left frightened, vulnerable, and feeling alone. According to the Southern Poverty Law Center (2000), "Somewhere in America, every hour someone commits a hate crime. Every day at least eight blacks, three whites, three gays, three Jews and one Latino become hate crime victims. Every week a cross is burned [in someone's yard]." Blacks are terrified of burning crosses because of the history of this evil act. A swastika is a symbol that brings back horrible images to Jews and tells them their lives are at risk. Hate crimes are aimed at entire groups of people, although they may directly impact only one person. Primarily the result of ignorance, lack of education, and inbred hatred passed from one generation to another, hate crimes hurt all of us. Because we are a diverse population, every American citizen needs to take a stand against all forms of hatred and intolerance.

GETTING INVOLVED AND MAKING A DIFFERENCE

Individuals and small groups of people can make a major difference in putting a stop to hate crimes. A list of things you can do to make a difference follows:

- Become knowledgeable about the kinds of hate crimes and how to combat each type.
- Learn the symbols and indicators used in hate crimes.
- Take a stand for decency. If you see someone being mistreated because he or she is different, stand up for the person. Get other people to join you. Make a phone call, organize a group to paint over hate graffiti, march with people who are standing up against hatred.
- Get the media involved. Get churches to join together with other civic organizations. Involve children so they learn to stand up against hatred and intolerance.
- Let the victims know they are not alone. Encourage neighbors to welcome racially diverse families.
- When a hate group does something vicious, organize something to counteract their actions. Paint a house in a minority neighborhood or organize a rally of decent people who are appalled at hate crimes.
- Speak up in positive ways and get community business leaders and politicians involved in taking a stand against intolerance.
- Teach tolerance to young children. Your group might be an elementary class, or you might teach your younger siblings and cousins.
- Talk to friends who demonstrate intolerance through their actions, words, or jokes. Tolerance can be learned; attitudes can be changed. You can be the catalyst.

Truth, kindness, and love by good, decent, caring people always wins out over hatred, intolerance, and bigotry. If you take a stand for what is right, you will have other good people step up and stand with you.

BLUEPRINTS FOR CHANGE

NAME

DATE

REFLECTION

As a college student, you can learn almost as much from the diverse population of students and peers as you can from the lessons you hear in the classroom. If you will open up your heart and mind to all kinds of possibilities, you will leave college a much more enlightened person than you were when you arrived.

College will provide you an opportunity to expand your horizons. Here you will have class with people from all over the world. They will not only speak and dress differently; they will most likely have different religions, beliefs, customs, values, and experiences. Rather than close out people who are different from you, embrace new and different cultures. While you don't have to be just like these new people, you are certain to learn to appreciate and benefit from the relationships.

GET REAL

Below are a few questions to help you think about change in college and in life. Study each question carefully and respond.

If you were unable to establish and maintain new relationships, how would that impact your experience in higher education?

Discuss one incident you have noticed this semester that could be categorized as intolerance or prejudice.

If you were to experience that same incident today, how might you react differently this time?

How will learning to be more tolerant of differences in people impact you in the world of work?

What is the relationship between education and tolerance?

Case Study

NAME: Forrest Evans
SCHOOL: University of Maryland—University College, Aldephi, MD
MAJOR: Legal Studies   AGE: 50

Below is a real-life situation faced by Forrest. Read the brief case and respond to the questions.

I can definitely relate to how people treat someone with a physical disability differently. I have only been disabled for seven years and I now understand this because I have been both "normal" and physically handicapped.

Since I've been disabled and wheelchair bound, a surprising number of people automatically assume that I am stupid. I have had people try to take advantage of me because of my disability, and I am constantly faced with the fact that so many people do not take me seriously. I've adjusted to people who yell at me because they think I'm deaf, step in front of me for rolling too slowly, ignore me or cut in front of me in customer service lines, and stare at me when I'm out in public with my wife.

I have an IQ of 132 and belong to the International High IQ Society. For several years after my stroke, I tried to return to my long-established job in the field of sales. Before my stroke, I was very much in demand because of my proven track record and my reputation for my ability to produce business. After becoming disabled, no one would seriously consider me for employment, and many would quietly snicker at me for asking about employment.

Perhaps the most devastating moment was while I was in training for a new position and the president of the company was coming to meet all of the new recruits. My boss told me to "take the day off" and did not tell me that the president was coming. I found this out later through colleagues who were able to meet the president of the company. I was considered an embarrassment to the company.

Why do you think people with disabilities are treated so differently?
_____
_____
_____
_____

Have you ever found yourself treating someone differently because of a handicap? _____
What happened?
_____
_____
_____
_____

What advice would you give to Forrest if he faced this type of employer again?

_____
_____
_____
_____

What advice would you give to a friend (or anyone) who has trouble accepting or dealing with people with disabilities?

_____
_____
_____
_____

What can you personally do to educate yourself about people with disabilities?

_____
_____
_____
_____

at this moment... Journal

Refer to page 375 of this chapter. Having read and reflected upon the information in the chapter, consider how you might revise your goal to make it more:

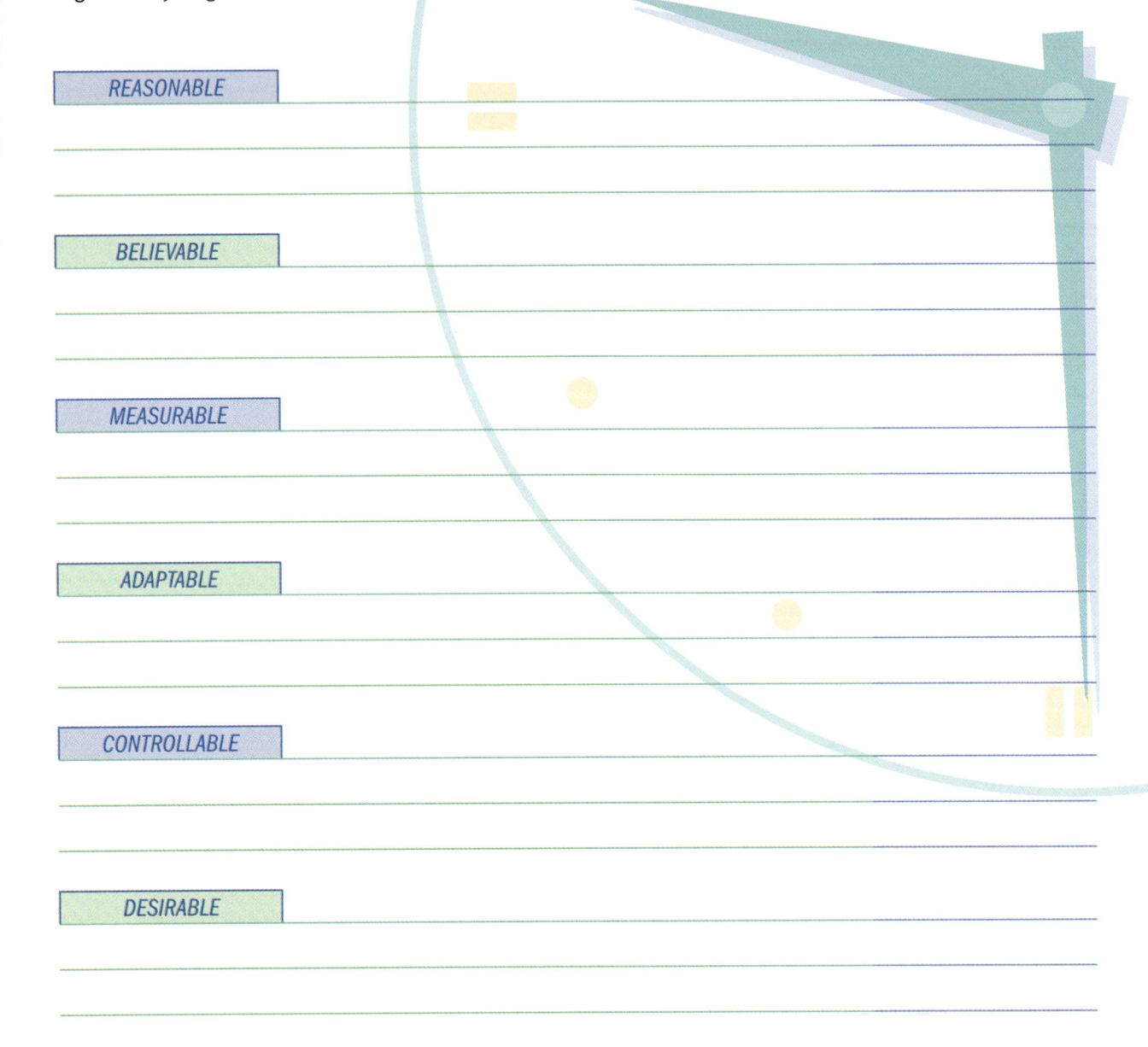

REASONABLE

BELIEVABLE

MEASURABLE

ADAPTABLE

CONTROLLABLE

DESIRABLE

ONLINE JOURNAL

To complete an online journal entry, log onto the Companion Website at **www.prenhall.com/sherfield**. Go to Chapter 13 and click on the link to the Online Journal. You can respond to the questions provided or to questions assigned by your professor, or you may journal about your own experiences.

ADVICE TO GO

CORNERSTONES

for relationships & personal responsibility

Examine your personal values and beliefs to determine if cultural *adjustments* are needed.

Listen to people and try to *understand* them.

Stand up against intolerance of any kind.

Help others understand the importance of *organizing* against hate crimes.

Develop relationships with people from a *variety* of backgrounds.

Develop important *relationships*.

Combat feelings of *loneliness*.

Learn to appreciate *differences*.

Maintain *close* friendships.

RELATE

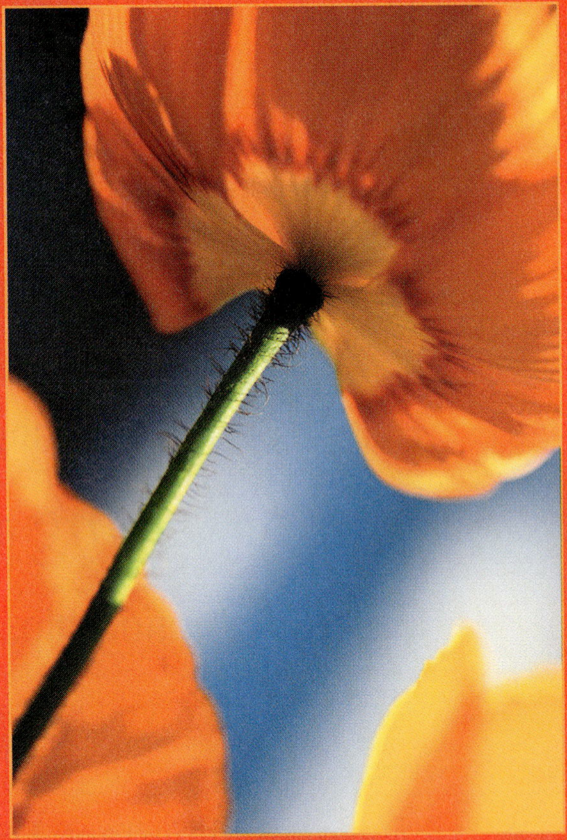

4 Live

The salvation of this human world lies nowhere else than in the human heart.

Vaclav Havel

CHAPTER 14
LIVE

Amanda was a first-generation college student who had overcome tremendous odds to go to college. A single mother *and the sole supporter of her three children,* she moved back home to live with her mother so that she could afford to go to school. Amanda's mother cared for the children while Amanda was in class or working. Amanda worked the night shift so that she could spend time with her children. She attended classes while they were in school, went home and took a nap, and then got up to do homework with the children and help her mother with chores around the house.

Amanda came to my office two weeks after the fall semester began to tell me *that she would not be in class because her mother had passed away.* We worked out a plan for her to make up her assignments and to take her test at a later date. She was unable to return as quickly as we had hoped because *she had trouble finding someone to help her care for her children.* Finally, she arranged for her sister to care for the children, and she returned to school.

Amanda made up her assignments and *scored one of the highest grades on the exam.* Several weeks later, she returned to my office in tears—*she*

The Serenity Prayer
God, grant me the serenity to accept the things I cannot change, the courage to change the things I can, and the wisdom to know the difference. —R. NIEBUHR

A Plan for Wellness, Stress Reduction, and Personal Responsibility

had just learned that her son was diagnosed with leukemia. She was devastated, but decided not to drop out of school because it was too late in the semester for her to be reimbursed for the tuition she had paid. She had to take her son to a medical center in another state. After her return, she worked diligently to keep her assignments current.

Amanda worked the night shift so that she could spend time with her children.

In spite of all this stress, Amanda completed the fall semester with very high grades. She preregistered for the spring semester and eventually completed her degree.

QUESTIONS FOR REFLECTION

Consider responding to these questions online in the Questions for Reflection module of the Companion Website.

1. What single event has caused you the most stress this semester? Why? How have you dealt with this stress?

2. Amanda made many sacrifices to attend college. What is the most important sacrifice you have made? Why was this an important thing to you?

3. Did sacrificing this "thing" cause you stress? Why or why not?

Where are you... AT THIS MOMENT

Before reading this chapter, take a moment and respond to the following ten questions. Consider each one carefully before answering, and then respond by circling the number in the appropriate box. When you have answered the questions, add your points and find your total score on the feedback chart below.

STATEMENT	STRONGLY DISAGREE	DISAGREE	DON'T KNOW	AGREE	STRONGLY AGREE	SCORE
1. My physical health is not that important to me.	1	2	3	4	5	
2. I am knowledgeable about the many types of STDs, including prevention and symptoms.	1	2	3	4	5	
3. I know how to make myself feel better when I'm feeling down.	1	2	3	4	5	
4. I frequently consume alcohol in large quantities (binge drinking).	5	4	3	2	1	
5. I don't know where to get help if I need it to become more mentally healthy.	5	4	3	2	1	
6. I am physically active, including involvement in a variety of activities.	1	2	3	4	5	
7. Good nutrition is not very important to me.	5	4	3	2	1	
8. I usually become overwhelmed by stress before I even notice it.	5	4	3	2	1	
9. I don't know how to control and reduce my stress.	5	4	3	2	1	
10. I know how legal and illegal drugs affect my mental and physical health.	1	2	3	4	5	
TOTAL VALUE						

SUMMARY

10–17 Your understanding of your own health is very limited. You seem unaware of how your mind and body function together. You likely take your health for granted, and don't know how or aren't willing to protect and improve it.

18–25 You have below average knowledge and skills related to your health. You are likely passive in regard to your health. You will need to improve your skills in managing your mental and physical health if you plan to be successful in college.

26–34 Your knowledge and skills related to your health are average. You are somewhat aware of how your mind and body function together. You probably understand the basics of managing your health, even if you don't always use what you know. You will likely benefit from becoming more aware of your mental and physical health levels.

35–42 You are above average in understanding your mental and physical health. You recognize the symptoms of mental and physical illness and usually know what to do about it. You might benefit from learning some additional strategies for getting and staying healthy.

43–50 You are exceptional in your understanding of your mental and bodily health. You know how the mind affects the body and vice versa. You take proactive steps toward safeguarding your health and know what to do when you're not feeling well.

Goals . . .   FOR CHANGE

Based on your total points, what is one goal you would like to achieve related to your overall wellness?

Goal _____
_____

List three actions you can take that might help you move closer to realizing this goal.

1. _____
2. _____
3. _____

Questions
FOR BUILDING ON YOUR BEST

As you read this chapter, consider the following questions. At the end of the chapter, you should be able to answer all of them. You are encouraged to ask a few questions of your own. Consider asking your classmates or professors to assist you.

1. What does it mean to be healthy?
2. Why is it important for me to strive for wellness in the mind, soul, and body?
3. How can peer pressure affect my decisions about sex, drugs, and other areas of personal responsibility?
4. How can I protect myself from pregnancy and/or sexually transmitted diseases?
5. What role does stress management play in my wellness plan?

What additional questions might you have about wellness, stress, and personal responsibility in college and life?

1. _____
2. _____
3. _____

What Does It Mean to Be Healthy?

Most people consider themselves healthy. They believe that if they are not sick, they are healthy. However, the absence of illness does not mean that you are healthy; it simply means that you are currently without illness.

The World Health Organization defines health as "not merely the absence of disease or infirmity, but a state of complete physical, mental, and social well-being." Realistically, health is a continuum: on one end you have death, and on the other you have excellent health. Most students are somewhere in the middle of the continuum, experiencing neither excellent health nor debilitating diseases. Often students slip slowly into a state of unhealthiness, which if ignored, could lead to serious health problems. Most of us take our health for granted. We place undue stress on ourselves and assume that our bodies will continue to take this abuse. This chapter will afford you the opportunity to review your own health status and to explore some issues that might help you to lead a healthier lifestyle.

The Mind, Soul, and Body
A HOLISTIC APPROACH TO WELLNESS

You cannot divide your approach to wellness into specific categories because all aspects of your health are interrelated. You cannot address your mental health without taking into account your physical well-being; you cannot talk about fitness without including nutrition in your discussion. If your body, mind, and soul are to function in a healthy manner, then your approach to wellness should be balanced. You need to explore and develop a holistic approach to wellness.

Ignoring your mental health can be dangerous. When was the last time you took a mental health break?

The Mind's Effect on Wellness

The mind is an incredibly complex organ. The health industry has not begun to tap the awesome power the mind has over a person's physical health. Very basic studies have shown that the mind is a vital link to physical health. For example, when patients were given placebos instead of medication, those who trusted their doctors and their prescribed treatments were more likely to report positive results from the placebos than were patients who did not trust their doctors or their prescribed treatment. There are thousands of anecdotal reports of people who have overcome tremendous physical illnesses through positive thinking and believing that they could overcome the illness. There is no question that the mind has power over the body, but just how and why are still a mystery.

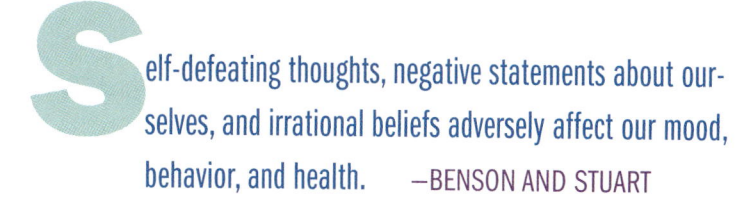

> Self-defeating thoughts, negative statements about ourselves, and irrational beliefs adversely affect our mood, behavior, and health. —BENSON AND STUART

Many of us tend to ignore mental health unless there is a serious problem. We are quick to visit a doctor if we have a broken bone, but we are much less willing to seek professional help if we are experiencing emotional distress. There is still a stigma attached to seeking professional counseling in regard to our mental well-being; yet mental health is often more important than physical health because of the important part it plays in maintaining physical well-being.

Mental health, like physical health, is not simply the absence of mental illness. People who are psychologically healthy:

- Have a positive sense of self-worth
- Are determined to make an effort to be healthy
- Can love and have meaningful relationships
- Understand reality and the limitations placed on them
- Have compassion for others
- Understand that the world does not revolve around them

Mental health, too, should be viewed as a continuum, ranging from excellent mental health, to suffering from minor mental illness, to life-threatening illnesses.

DEPRESSION

"Depression" is used to describe feelings ranging from feeling blue to utter hopelessness. The use of "I'm depressed" to mean "I'm sad" or "I'm down" is a far cry from the illness of clinical depression. Depression is a sickness that

> I must love this miserable state I'm in, because I've chosen to stay there since a quarter past ten. I know my mind can only think of one thing at a time so I keep focusing on making misery mine. But what if I choose to find a better space, could imagination find peace in a private place? —BARBARA GRAY

can creep up on an individual and render that person helplessly lost if it is not detected and properly treated. Signs of depression include the following (Donatelle and Davis, 2002):

- Lingering sadness
- Inability to find joy in pleasure-giving activities
- Loss of interest in work or school
- Unexplainable fatigue
- Sleep disorders, including insomnia or early-morning awakenings

Level of Dysfunction

Optimal mental health:	Normal coping devices and ego control
Level 1	Hyperreactions, anxiety, nervousness, minor physical symptoms
Level 2	Personality disorder, phobias
Level 3	Social offenses, open aggression, violent acts
Level 4	Severe depression and despondency, psychotic and bizarre behavior
Level 5	Severe psychological deterioration, loss of will to live

- Loss of sex drive
- Withdrawal from friends and family
- Feelings of hopelessness and worthlessness
- Desire to die

If you are feeling depressed, but your depression seems minor or situational, try some of these helpful hints for picking yourself up out of the blues:

1. Exercise. Getting physical exercise causes the release of endorphins, which help to stimulate you and give you a personal high.
2. Spend time talking with a good friend; share your thoughts and feelings.
3. Control your self-talk. If you're playing a negative tune, change to a positive song.
4. Do something special for yourself: Take a long walk in the park, watch a favorite movie, listen to a special CD, or eat a hot fudge sundae. It doesn't really matter what you do as long as it's something special.
5. Nurture yourself.
6. Don't be afraid or ashamed to seek professional assistance.

If you are depressed, where can you go or your campus (or in your community) for assistance? _____

Phone _____

The Soul's Effect on Wellness

The human being is an insatiably inquisitive creature. Our quest for the greater meaning of life is equaled only by our quest for eternal life. For some, these two quests become one in the search for spiritual meaning. Some people find the true meaning of life in the teachings of Jesus Christ; others study the Koran or the teachings of Buddha or worship the wonder of Nature. Whether they follow a formal religion or not, people have their own beliefs about the universe, hu-

Spirituality reduces stress, promotes healthy lifestyle choices, and increases a sense of belonging. Research also indicates that spiritual practices such as prayer, contemplation, and meditation have a measurable effect on the physiological process of the brain. —SEYMORE AND O'CONNELL

man nature, and the significance of life. How we approach our beliefs is related to our perception of our own spiritual nature, or the state of our soul.

Spirituality guides many aspects of our daily lives. From character development to ethics to personal responsibility to managing conflict, your spiritual nature helps determine how you act and how you treat others.

Spirituality is also about caring for yourself, appreciating your talents and natural gifts. It can also help reduce stress by bringing you a degree of peace and understanding. "Spirituality is concerned with self-determination and being able to face problems without going to pieces. It is about learning to solve problems and learning to come to conclusions that are positive for yourself, others, and the earth" (Sherfield, 2004).

If you are interested in expanding your spiritual nature, consider the following suggestions:

- Read books about different religions, spiritual journeys, and inspirational persons.
- Join a group on campus or in the community that explores different spiritual themes.
- Keep an open mind and listen to a variety of perspectives.
- Join a meditation group.
- Begin journaling (possibly in your online journal) about your feelings, desires, aspirations, and contributions you want to make to the world.

Medical research suggests that exercise fights depression. Is there a physical activity that you particularly enjoy? Do you have the access or opportunity to do it?

Your time in higher education provides an outstanding opportunity for you to explore the true meaning of life. Many campus organizations can help you in your quest for spirituality. Take this opportunity to explore your spirituality and to provide food for your soul. To ignore this aspect of yourself is to shut off a potentially rich and wonderful source of joy.

Make a list of the campus organizations that are designed to help students in their spiritual quest.

The Body's Effect on Wellness

What does it mean to be physically fit? Basically, physical fitness means being physically capable of meeting life's daily demands without impairing your health. Physical fitness, using this definition, is different for everyone.

Why is physical fitness important? The list of reasons for maintaining an activity level that will keep you physically fit is lengthy.

Among other benefits, physical fitness:

- Helps you have more energy
- Gives you increased confidence
- Helps you deal with stress
- Improves the health of your skin
- Helps prevent insomnia
- Reduces your risk of heart disease
- Helps control blood-serum cholesterol levels
- Helps control high blood pressure and diabetes
- Increases longevity of bone structure
- Helps maintain your quality of life

There is no universal fitness plan or program that fits everyone, but there are universal components of fitness. Cardiovascular fitness, flexibility, muscular strength, and muscular endurance are the four components of fitness.

Cardiovascular fitness is by far the most important component. Excellent cardiovascular fitness is ensured by maintaining a level of aerobic exercise that conditions your body to be able to carry larger amounts of oxygen to working muscles. Some aerobic activities are walking, jogging, biking, swimming, jumping rope, dancing, and cross-country skiing. The benefits of aerobic exercise include reducing the risk of heart disease, keeping blood pressure down, increasing the level of HDL (good cholesterol), and helping control weight.

Flexibility is the ability of joints to move through the full range of their motion. Good flexibility is believed to prevent pulls, tears, and other damage to your muscles and is particularly important in preventing back pain. The key to flexibility is stretching correctly. You should stretch in a slow relaxed movement.

Muscular strength is the muscles' ability to exert force in one motion, such as a jump or lift. **Muscular endurance** is the muscles' ability to perform repeated muscular contractions. These two components are interrelated in that most muscular contractions use some degree of muscular strength. You can increase both strength and endurance by doing exercises that involve resistance, usually weights. You gain strength by con-

Finding an exercise buddy can increase your motivation to exercise regularly.

ditioning your body to resist more and more weight; you improve endurance by increasing repetitions at the same weight.

Although an active lifestyle should include all four fitness components to some degree, the extent to which each is included is determined by your goals and the level of activity you wish to achieve in your life. If you would like to have a high level of activity so that you can work out or play a sport, here are some suggestions for getting started.

1. Start your program slowly.
2. If it hurts, stop!
3. Wear the proper gear.
4. Learn the proper form and technique.
5. Always warm up and cool down.

"I don't have time to join the gym," you might say. The following suggestions can help you be more active in your daily life.

1. Walk to class rather than drive or ride the bus.
2. Walk upstairs instead of taking the elevator.
3. Develop a hobby that involves physical activity, such as gardening or bowling.
4. Do volunteer work that involves physical activity.
5. Make a commitment to include some form of physical activity in your daily routine.

Almost everyone has at one time or another made a New Year's resolution or some other form of pledge to become more physically fit. Most people don't have trouble starting exercise programs; they only have trouble sticking with them.

Are You What You Eat?

THE BODY AND FOOD

Eating has become Americans' favorite hobby. Rather than eating to live, many of us live to eat. We socialize around food—dinner and a movie, pizza and a beer with friends, and so on. Virtually every holiday or celebration we observe has a food focus.

As you enter into this new stage of your life, balancing schedules, studying, and caring for others, you need to understand that your body will be undergoing tremendous biological stress. The hormonal changes that tend to coincide with the traditional college age,

When you're on the run it is easy to ignore your eating habits. How many times per day do you sit down to a balanced meal? Per week? Per month?

STRATEGIES
FOR BUILDING ON YOUR BEST

Consider the following strategies for healthy eating:

- Enjoy 2-4 servings of fruit, 3-5 servings of vegetables, and 3 servings of whole grains daily.
- Eat moderate portions such as 3 ounces of meat and a half cup of pasta or cereal.
- Balance your food choices so that you don't become tired of certain items.
- Try baking or broiling many food items instead of frying them. Such items include french fries, fish, and hamburger patties.
- Eat regularly. Many physicians suggest that you should have five moderate meals per day: Breakfast, mid-morning snack, lunch, mid-afternoon snack, and dinner.
- Plan to have healthy snacks. Instead of candy, try raisins. Instead of cookies or ice cream, try granola or yogurt.
- ALWAYS consult a physician before drastically changing your eating habits.

Research suggests that stress can trigger chemical releases in the body that might cause forgetfulness. Learning to relax, breathe properly, and maintain perspective can help reduce stress during tests.

18 to 22, may cause you to experience an alteration in your basal metabolic rate; you will no longer be able to eat like a horse and not gain a pound. At the same time, your lifestyle in college is likely to be more sedentary than was your lifestyle prior to college. As a result, you may well end up gaining the additional weight commonly referred to as the "freshman 15." To assist you with developing a healthy eating plan, many guides are available to help you make the correct choices of foods.

Stress and Wellness

Many things can affect our wellness and cause stress in our lives. Our mental and physical wellness and stress levels may be affected by our weight. Our weight may be affected by our mental state of depression or fear. Most people know what stress is when they "feel" it, but few understand the adverse ramifications of stress on the human body, mind, and soul.

WHAT IS STRESS?

The word *stress* is derived from the Latin word *strictus,* meaning "to draw tight." Stress is your body's response to people and events in your life; it is the mental and physical wear and tear on your body as a result of everyday life. Stress is inevitable, and it is not in itself bad. It is your response to stress that determines whether it is good stress (eustress) or bad stress (distress). The same event can provoke eustress or distress, depending on the person experiencing the event; just as "one person's trash is another's treasure" (or so you know if you shop at secondhand stores), so one person's eustress may be another person's distress.

The primary difference between eustress and distress is in your body's response. It is impossible to exist in a totally stress-free environment; in fact, some stress is important to your health and well-being. Only when the stress gets out of hand does your body become distressed. Some physical signs of distress are:

Headaches   Muscular tension and pain
Fatigue   Abdominal pain and diarrhea

WORLD OF WORK

In my job at Bank One, stress is an ever-present concern. However, somebody has to remain calm. I remember the first weeks of our bank conversion project, when we were managing 33 trainers at 7 sites; something that we had never done before. My insides were constantly torn up, but I had to remain calm on the outside. It is almost like the poised flight attendant when the plane is taking a nosedive. Someone has to be there, smiling and calm. I take a deep breath, think about the situation and ask myself, "Is this bad enough to make us shut down the project?" If the answer is no, then I can make it work. I have to put things into perspective and prioritize the tasks to be done. This is my way to control stress.

My job reminds me a lot of my college experience. In college, there are many requirements and some professor always needs something. You have only one semester to complete the tasks described in the syllabus, and they must be done on time. One must learn how to manage time to accomplish those things. The way I saw it, I had two choices. I had an entire semester to do it all. I could set priorities and work on projects and papers on a daily or weekly basis, or I could try to play catch-up at the very end. I chose to set priorities. This was a great choice for me, because it helps me maintain perspective on my job today. At work, it is like I almost make a syllabus for each major project I have to accomplish. This is a way that I can set goals, work toward completion, and control my stress level.

QUESTIONS FOR REFLECTION

Consider responding to these questions online in the World of Work module of the Companion Website.

1. Has your job ever caused you to "stress out"? If so, how did you deal with the stress?
2. What role does time management play in stress reduction in your life?
3. What role does maintaining a positive outlook, like Mr. Spearman, play in stress reduction?

Charles Steve Spearman, *Vice President & New Build Launch Manager for Branch Planning,* Bank One, Columbus

---

Dry mouth
Impotence
Coughs
Insomnia
Depression

Hypertension and chest pain
Heartburn and indigestion
Menstrual disorders
Loss of appetite
Suicidal tendencies

Stress can also have an effect on your memory. Tim Friend of *USA Today* (August 20, 1998) suggests that stressful events that cause the release of a hormone called cortisol can make you forget things you know you should know. "The findings could explain why the mind sometimes goes blank before a key business presentation, a test, or an acting debut." Therefore, learning to control stress and stressful events may be a key to better memory.

Other tips for reducing stress include:

- Adjust your attitude—try to look at problems, and life in general, through different eyes.
- Maintain a positive attitude.
- Use relaxation techniques such as visualization, listening to music, and practicing yoga.
- Let minor hassles and annoyances go. Ask yourself, "Is this situation worth a heart attack, stroke, or high blood pressure?"
- Don't be afraid to take a break. Managing your time can help you take more relaxation breaks.
- Practice "seat aerobics" such as inhaling and exhaling, stretching, and neck rolls.

If you remember Amanda from the opening story, her life was filled with stress caused by bereavement, illness, work, and parental responsibilities. By concentrating on stress reduction and actually practicing some of the techniques above, you, like Amanda, can effectively reduce the wear and tear that stress can have on your body, mind, and soul.

Three Types of Stressors

TYPE	CAUSES	REDUCTION
Situational	Change in physical environment	Change your residence or environment to suit your needs.
	Change in social environment	Find a quiet place to relax and study.
		Arrange your classes to suit your individual needs.
Psychological	Unrealistic expectations	Surround yourself with positive people.
	Homesickness	Surround yourself with people who support you.
	Fear	Talk to professors, counselors, family, and friends.
Biological	Hormonal changes	Develop a healthy eating plan.
	Weight loss/gain	Develop an exercise plan.
	Change in physical activities	Increase your daily activity.

STRESS TEST

To determine the level of distress you are currently experiencing in your life, check the items that reflect your behavior at home, work, or school, or in a social setting.

- ○ 1. Your stomach tightens when you think about your schoolwork and all that you have to do.

- ○ 2. You are not able to sleep at night.
- ○ 3. You race from place to place trying to get everything done that is required of you.
- ○ 4. Small things make you angry.
- ○ 5. At the end of the day, you are frustrated that you did not accomplish all that you needed to do.
- ○ 6. You get tired throughout the day.
- ○ 7. You need some type of drug, alcohol, or tobacco to get through the day.
- ○ 8. You often find it hard to be around people.
- ○ 9. You don't take care of yourself physically or mentally.
- ○ 10. You tend to keep everything inside.
- ○ 11. You overreact.
- ○ 12. You fail to find the humor in many situations others see as funny.
- ○ 13. You do not eat properly.
- ○ 14. Everything upsets you.
- ○ 15. You are impatient and get angry when you have to wait for things.
- ○ 16. You don't trust others.
- ○ 17. You feel that most people move too slowly for you.
- ○ 18. You feel guilty when you take time for yourself or your friends.
- ○ 19. You interrupt people so that you can tell them your side of the story.
- ○ 20. You experience memory loss.

TOTAL NUMBER OF CHECK MARKS

   0–5 = Low, manageable stress
   6–10 = Moderate stress
   11+ = High stress, could cause medical or emotional problems

What You Do Matters

PERSONAL RESPONSIBILITY AND WELLNESS

Cornerstone is about choices—plain and simple. You will find few places in this book where we say, "you *must*," or "you *have to*," or "you *should*." It is not our intention to tell you how to live your life or how to make life choices. Whether you are 18 or 58, we consider you an intelligent, rational adult and we have tried to address you accordingly.

The following section will not break tradition. We do not plan to tell you how you should live, whom you should see, what you should or should not drink or use, or with whom you should have intimate relations. These are your choices, and for us to tell you which ones to make would counter all the decision-making skills we have tried to provide you with throughout this book.

> I believe that there is an inner power that makes winners or losers. And the winners are the ones who really listen to the truth of their hearts. —SYLVESTER STALLONE

The following section will simply provide you with information that you can study and from there, make intelligent decisions about drinking, drug usage, smoking, and sexual behavior.

The only thing we ask is that you consider carefully this fact: Everything you put into your body and do with and to your body has a direct effect, either positively or negatively, on your overall wellness.

DRUGS AND ALCOHOL

First, let us state that alcohol IS a drug. It is legal for people over 21, but it is a drug just as cocaine and Ecstasy are drugs. Drugs can basically be divided into two categories—legal and illegal. It may sound strange, but drugs run the gamut from caffeine to crystal meth.

The decision to use a drug, legal or illegal, is yours and it is personal. However, every drug—from tobacco to roofies—has ramifications and health consequences. The following charts are provided to give you a better understanding of many legal and illegal drugs.

I Love the Night Life
IT'S ALL THE RAVE!

Several drugs on the chart below need to be discussed separately. Those drugs are more commonly called "cocktail drugs" or "club drugs." They are called such because they are most commonly found in dance clubs, raves, and other places where people are interacting and inhibitions are low.

It is important to note that they are extremely dangerous, even to the most casual user. The effects of club drugs (and many others) can range from elevated body temperatures to dehydration to increased blood pressure to adverse effects of serotonin in the brain. Those drugs are:

- Ecstasy
- Sextasy
- Destiny
- Roofies
- GHB

Sextasy is a mixture of Ecstasy and Viagra. Ecstasy increases one's senses, but can hinder sexual functioning. To increase sexual functioning, many people have begun taking Viagra, whose "real" purpose is to treat impotence and assist prostate cancer patients. The mixture can cause serious problems! "Doctors warn that combining the two drugs can cause heart problems or erections that don't subside for more than four hours, possibly leading to anatomical damage" (Leinwand, 2002).

Roofies and **GHB** are very common in the club scene and can be "slipped" into a drink (alcoholic or not) with little trouble. Because they are usually

DID YOU KNOW?

95%

The percentage of violent crimes on college campuses where alcohol was a factor!

Source: Manisses Communications Group: *Alcoholism & Drug Abuse Weekly*, 13(36), September 2001, p. 7.

Commonly Used Legal Drugs

NAME	USE	SOURCES	NEGATIVE EFFECTS	
Caffeine	Alertness Pleasure Energy Reduce fatigue	Coffee Tea Chocolate Some soft drinks Medications	A stimulant Increased anxiety Highly addictive Increased urination	Irregular heartbeat Indigestion
Alcohol	Relaxation Mood enhancer Overcome depression Overcome shyness Social acceptance Relieve tension Celebrate Bonding	Beer Wine Liquor Medications Some foods	Liver disease Memory loss Blackouts False euphoria Depression Hangovers	Birth defects Loss of balance Mental impairment Increased suicide rate Death
Tobacco	Stimulant Relaxation Social acceptance To curb appetite Alertness	Cigarettes Cigars Pipes Snuff Chewing tobacco	Highly addictive Increased heart and respiratory rate Increased blood pressure Decreased taste sensations Increased risk of cancer	Decreased hunger Lung disease Gum disease Birth defects Strokes Cardiovascular disease
Over-the-Counter Drugs	Weight loss Alertness Sleeping Body building Depression Pain relief	Laxatives Diet medications Sleep enhancers Stimulants Herbal medications Nasal sprays Cough medications Pain relievers	Addiction Organ damage Nausea Vomiting Reduced absorption of vitamins and minerals Liver damage	
Prescription Drugs	Weight loss Alertness Sleeping Depression Pain relief Mood enhancers Muscle relaxers	Found in many forms Prescribed by medical professionals from every area of medical science	Addiction Impaired judgment Loss of memory Weight loss/gain Blackouts Death	

Commonly Used Illegal Drugs

FROM THE NATIONAL INSTITUTE OF DRUG ABUSE

SUBSTANCE	STREET NAME	ADMINISTRATION	PERIOD OF DETECTION
MDMA	Ecstasy, E	Oral	1–2 days
MDMA+Viagra*	Sextasy	Oral	1–2 days
Synthetic Heroin	Destiny, D	Oral	1–2 days
Rohypnol	Roofies, Date Rape Drug	Oral and in drinks	3–5 days
Gamma Hydroxybutyrate	GHB	Oral and in drinks	3–5 days
Amphetamine	Black Beauties, Crosses, Hearts	Injected, oral, smoked, sniffed	1–2 days
Cocaine	Coke, Crack, Flake, Rocks, Snow	Injected, smoked, sniffed	1–4 days
Methamphetamine	Crank, Crystal, Glass, Ice, Speed	Injected, oral, smoked, sniffed	1–2 days
LSD	Acid, Microdot	Oral	8 hours
Phencyclidine & Analogs	PCP, Angel Dust, Boat, Hog, Love Boat	Injected, oral, smoked	2–8 days
Psilocybin	Magic Mushroom, Purple Passion, Shrooms	Oral	8 hours
Amphetamine Variants	Adam, STP	Oral	1–2 days
Marijuana	Blunt, Grass, Herb, Pot, Reefer, Sinsemilla, Smoke, Weed, Mary Jane	Oral, smoked	1 day–5 weeks
Hashish	Hash	Oral, smoked	1 day–5 weeks
Anabolic Steroids	Testosterone, Nandrolene	Oral, injected	Oral up to 3 weeks Injected up to 3 mo. Nandrolene up to 9 mo.
Heroin	Horse, Smack	Injected, smoked, sniffed	1–2 days
Opium	Dover's Powder	Oral, smoked	1–2 days
Barbiturates	Barbs	Injected, oral	2–10 days
Methaqualone	Quaalude, Ludes	Oral	2 weeks

*Viagra is not an illegal drug.

odorless and colorless and have a very quick effect on the body, they rapidly alter your alertness and ability to function.

PROTECTING YOURSELF

We mention these drugs specifically so that you can begin to pay more attention to your surroundings when at clubs, raves, or other gatherings where environments are crowded and dark. If you have children, you may want to consider sharing this information with your teenagers. It is never too early.

Consider the following tips when partaking of any beverage in public:

- Be suspicious of taking drinks from anyone you do not know or have not known and trusted for a long time.
- If you plan to drink anything, the best plan is to go to the service area and get it yourself or at least be close enough to see your drink being prepared or opened.
- Accept only *unopened* canned and/or bottled drinks when possible.
- Do not leave any beverage unattended while dancing or socializing. If you do, get another drink upon your return.
- Make it a habit to cover your drink with your hand while around a crowd of people. This can lessen the possibility of someone dropping a powder or liquid in your drink.
- Try to socialize with people you trust.

Out on a Binge
WHEN DRINKING GOES AWRY

Binge drinking is classified as having more than five drinks at one time. Many people say, "I only drink once a week." However, if that one drinking spell includes drink after drink after drink, it can be extremely detrimental to your liver, your memory, your digestive system, and your health in general.

Most college students report that they do not mean to binge drink, but it is caused by the situation such as a ballgame, a party, a campus event, or a special occasion. Researchers at Michigan State University found that only 5 percent of students surveyed say they party to "get drunk" (Warner, 2002).

In their breakthrough work, *Dying to Drink,* Harvard researcher Henry Wechsler and science writer Bernice Wuethrich explore the problem of binge drinking. They suggest, "two out of every five college students regularly binge drink resulting in approximately 1,400 student deaths, a distressing number of assaults and rapes, a shameful amount of vandalism, and countless cases of academic suicide" (Wechsler and Wuethrich, 2002).

CONTROLLING BINGE DRINKING

Trying to control your own binge drinking is a situation reminiscent of the old saying, "Letting the fox guard the hen house." After a few drinks, it is hard to "self-police," meaning that you may not be able to control your actions once the drinking starts. If you plan to drink, think about the following beforehand:

- Ask a friend to go with you so that you can "watch out" for each other.
- Drink two bottles of water for each alcoholic beverage you consume.
- Try to eat before, during, and after you drink.
- Consider NOT drinking and see how it goes.
- Give yourself a time limit for arriving and departing the event where alcohol is served.
- If you plan to have EVEN ONE DRINK, arrange for someone you know to take you home.
- Remember: A designated driver is NOT the person who has had the least amount to drink—it is the person who has had nothing to drink.

Goin' Out of My Head over You
THE RESIDUAL DAMAGE OF DRUGS AND ALCOHOL

Perhaps the greatest tragedy of drug and alcohol abuse is the residual damage of pregnancy, sexually transmitted diseases, traffic fatalities, and accidental death. You already know that drugs and alcohol lower your resistance and can cause you to do things that you would not normally do, such as drive drunk or have unprotected sex.

Surveys and research results suggest that students who participate in heavy episodic (HE) or binge drinking are more likely to participate in unprotected sex with multiple sex partners. One survey found that 61 percent of men who *do* binge drink participated in unprotected sex as compared to 23 percent of men who *did not* binge drink. The survey also found that 48 percent of women who *do* binge drink participated in unprotected sex as compared to only 8 percent of women who *did not* binge drink (Cooper, 2002).

These staggering statistics simply suggest one thing: alcohol and drug consumption can cause people to act in ways in which they may never have acted without alcohol—and those actions can result in personal damage from which recovery may be impossible.

Sexually Transmitted Diseases

Sexually transmitted diseases (STDs) are diseases that are generally transmitted through vaginal or anal intercourse or oral sex. Although they are most commonly spread through sexual contact, some can be transmitted through related nonsexual activities. (For example, human immunodeficiency virus, HIV, can be contracted by using contaminated needles, and crabs can be contracted through contact with contaminated bed linens or towels.)

It is estimated that one in every four Americans will contract an STD during his or her lifetime. The majority of these cases occur in people under the age of 25. Seven common STDs are described in the chart on the following page.

NEW WORRIES ABOUT HIV AND AIDS TRANSMISSION

There is good news and bad news. The good news, actually great news, is that there have been tremendous strides in the treatment of HIV and AIDS. In the past several years, a new generation of drugs called *protease inhibitors* have had a remarkable effect. They block reproduction of the HIV particles (Rathus, Nevid, and Fichner-Rathus, 1998). Used in connection with AZT and 3TC, these inhibitors have reduced HIV to below detectable levels in many people. The newest drug in trials, T-20, is called a fusion inhibitor. It blocks HIV from sticking to the blood cells that it attacks (Haney, 2003). For some, both HIV and AIDS have become more manageable illnesses.

This is the great news. *However,* the cocktail is not a cure. One of the most dangerous aspects of the new protease and fusion inhibitors is that people begin to think that HIV and AIDS are cured and that there is no longer a need to think about safe sex. **Nothing could be further from the truth!** While fantastic results have been shown in many people with HIV and AIDS, the cocktail is very expensive, and some people's bodies cannot tolerate the mixture.

Another worry comes from a study conducted at the University of California, San Diego. The results, reported in *The New England Journal of Medicine,* suggest that *ONE in FIVE new HIV cases is a drug-resistant strain* (Lieberman, 2002). This means that the virus has mutated to a state where current drugs on the market take longer to work or do not work at all.

David Kirby, in his article. "The Worst Is Yet to Come" (*The Advocate,* January 19, 1999), states: "Since the introduction of better AIDS treatments, researchers have been worried that safer-sex messages would lose their urgency. This year, those fears came true. One study after another, with depressing consistence, showed . . . alarming spikes in rates of HIV infection and ominously, of other sexually transmitted diseases as well."

Therefore, it is imperative that you know that HIV and AIDS have not been cured, and without considering your conduct and personal responsibility, you are as much at risk as you ever have been.

STDS AND BIRTH CONTROL

The following charts are provided to give you information about other serious sexually transmitted diseases and the most common birth control methods.

Seven Sexually Transmitted Diseases

STD	TRANSMISSION	SYMPTOMS	DIAGNOSIS	CONSEQUENCES
AIDS/HIV	Sexual contact (vaginal, oral, and anal) Infusion with contaminated blood (sharing needles, etc.) From mother to fetus Breast feeding	People may go years without symptoms. When symptoms appear they may include flu-like symptoms, fever, weight loss, fatigue, diarrhea, and cancer.	Bodily fluids such as blood, urine, or saliva reveal HIV antibodies. Two tests include the Western Blot and the ELISA.	Transmission to sexual partners Rapid progression if undiagnosed or untreated Cancer Pneumonia Death
CHLAMYDIA	Sexual contact (vaginal, oral, and anal) By touching one's eye after touching infected genitals From mother to child	Women: Sometimes no symptoms; painful urination, occasional vaginal discharge, bleeding between periods Men: Discharge from penis, painful urination	A cervical smear for women Extract of fluid from the penis for men	Transmission to sexual partners Various inflammations Possible sterility in men and women
GONORRHEA	Sexual contact (vaginal, oral, and anal) From mother to child	Women: Vaginal discharge, painful urination, bleeding between periods Men: Discharge from penis, painful urination	Medical examination from discharge or culture	Transmission to sexual partners Pelvic inflammatory disease Sterility in men and women
GENITAL WARTS	Sexual contact (vaginal, oral, and anal) Other types of contact such as infected towels or clothing	Women: Single or multiple soft, fleshy growths around anus, vulva, vagina, or urethra; itching or burning sensation around sexual organs Men: Burning around sexual organs; single or multiple soft, fleshy growths around anus or penis	Medical examination	Transmission to sexual and non-sexual partners Precancerous conditions Cannot be cured

Seven Sexually Transmitted Diseases, *continued*

STD	TRANSMISSION	SYMPTOMS	DIAGNOSIS	CONSEQUENCES
HERPES (Simplex Virus Types I and II)	Sexual contact (vaginal, oral, and anal) Touching Kissing Sharing towels, toilet seats	Women and Men: Single or multiple blisters or sores on genitals; generally painful, but disappears without scarring, reappears	Medical examination Culture and fluid inspections	Transmission to sexual and non-sexual partners Cannot be cured
HEPATITIS (Viral A, B, C, and D types)	Sexual contact, especially involving the anus Contact with infected fecal matter Transfusion of contaminated blood Severe alcoholism Exposure to toxic materials	Women and Men: Can be asymptomatic; mild flu-like symptoms, fever, abdominal pain, vomiting, and yellowish skin or eyes; loss of appetite; whitish bowel movements; brown urine	Medical examination of blood for herpes antibody; liver biopsy	Transmission to sexual and non-sexual partners Severe liver problems or failure Cancer of the liver Death
SYPHILIS	Sexual contact (vaginal, oral, and anal) Touching an infected chancre	Women and Men: Four stages: (1) painless red spots later forming a sore; (2) skin rash or mucous patches; (3) latent stage, no symptoms; (4) complications leading to possible death	Primary stages by medical examination of fluid from a chancre Secondary stage by blood test, VDRL	Transmission to sexual and non-sexual partners Death (although seldom advances this far today)

Adapted from: *Sex on Your Terms* by Elizabeth Powell, Allyn and Bacon, 1996, and *Access to Health,* 7th ed. by Rebecca J. Donatelle and Lorraine G. Davis, Allyn and Bacon, 2002.

Birth Control

TYPE	USAGE	PREVENTION OF STDS		
		YES*	NO	NOT NECESSARILY
Abstinence	Abstention from *ALL sexual activity*, vaginal, anal, and oral. One hundred percent effective.	X		
Outercourse	Oral genital sex and mutual masturbation.			X
The Pill	Also called oral contraceptive. The most widely used form of birth control.		X	
The Male Pill	Also called oral contraceptive. Newly developed for male usage.		X	
The Patch	Called the Ortho-Evra patch, it is a transdermal method of dispensing similar medicine found in The Pill. The Patch lasts for one week.		X	
The NuvaRing	A clear, flexible vaginal ring that is self-inserted in the vagina and releases a low dose of hormones. It lasts for a month.		X	
Diaphragm	Round, flexible disk inserted into the vagina to cover the cervix.			X
IUD	Also called intrauterine device. Must be inserted into the uterus by a physician.		X	
Male Condom	A sheath, generally latex, worn over the penis to prevent sperm from entering the vagina.	X		
Female Condom	A loose-fitting sheath inserted into the vagina to prevent sperm from entering the uterus.	X		
Spermicides	Inserted into the vagina to kill sperm. Comes in foams, jellies, suppositories, and creams.		X	
Withdrawal	Also called coitus interruptus. The penis is withdrawn from the vagina before ejaculation.		X	
Rhythm Method	Abstaining from sexual intercourse during the menstrual cycle when ovulation occurs.		X	
Norplant	Silicone tubes surgically embedded in a woman's upper arm to suppress fertilization.		X	
Sterilization	Male and female surgery. Male version is called vasectomy, and female versions are called tubal sterilization, tubal ligation, and hysterectomy.		X	
Cervical Cap	Much like the diaphragm, it is fitted into the vagina by a doctor. It is meant to be used with a spermicide and can provide up to 48 hours of protection.		X	

*Only total abstinence is 100% effective in preventing sexually transmitted diseases.

YOUR ACTION PLAN FOR WELLNESS... *Activity*

Throughout this chapter, we have tried to give you information that will be useful to you as you think about your overall wellness. The following activity will ask you to look at your life in more detail. You will be asked to identify one area of wellness, either in the mind, soul, or body, that you would like to improve.

Using the Change Implementation Model from Chapter 1, design a plan to bring this change in wellness into your life.

1. Determine what you need or want to change and why.

2. Research your options for making the desired change and seek advice and assistance from a variety of sources.

3. Identify the obstacles to change and determine how to overcome them.

4. Establish a plan by outlining several positive steps to bring about the change you identified.

YOUR ACTION PLAN FOR WELLNESS... *Activity*

5. Implement your plan for bringing about the desired change:
   a. Focus on the desired outcome.

   _____
   _____
   _____

   b. View problems as positive challenges.

   _____
   _____
   _____
   _____

   c. Turn your fears into energy by reducing anxiety through physical exercise, proper nutrition, and stress-management strategies.

   _____
   _____
   _____

   d. Associate with positive and motivated people.

   _____
   _____
   _____

Finally, think of a reward that you can give yourself once your wellness goal has been reached.

_____

BLUEPRINTS FOR CHANGE

NAME   DATE

REFLECTION

"For every action, there is a reaction." As we mature and grow, we find that what we do matters. How we treat others and ourselves has consequences for years to come. How we treat our bodies, what we put into our bodies, how we move our bodies, and who we let touch our bodies all have ramifications; our actions have reactions.

Consider how today's actions will determine your lifestyle tomorrow. If heavy drinking is involved today, what will that mean for your health in 10 years? If you smoke today, what will that mean for your health in 20 years? If you are full of stress and anxiety today and do nothing to reduce it, what will this mean for your future mental and physical well-being? If unprotected sex is a part of your life, will there be a tomorrow?

These are all choices that can positively or negatively affect your life years from now.

GET REAL

Below are a few questions to help you think about wellness, stress, and personal responsibility in college and in life. Study each question carefully and respond.

After researching and completing your Wellness Plan, where could you go on campus (or in the community) to find help meeting your wellness goal?

Phone # _____

How will reaching this wellness goal improve your quality of life in and out of the classroom?

Realistically, what do you consider to be the most dangerous effect of alcohol and drugs on your (or a friend's) academic career?

What do you consider to be the most negative effect of unchecked stress on your academic career?

If your best friend, romantic partner, son, or daughter confided in you that he or she had previously practiced or was still practicing unsafe sex, what realistic advice would you give him or her?

Case Study

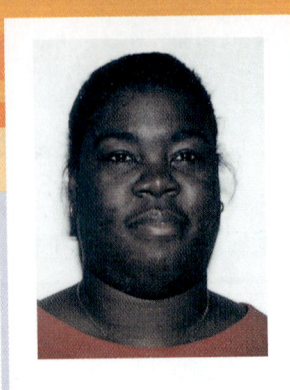

NAME: Natasha Yearwood
SCHOOL: The Community College of Southern Nevada, Las Vegas, NV
MAJOR: Electrical Engineering   **AGE:** 32

Below is a real-life situation faced by Natasha. Read the brief case and respond to the questions.

For years I watched my coworker and roommate, "John," struggle with his alcohol problem. If there has ever been any truth to the statement, "You can't solve the alcohol problem until you admit it," then John lived (and continues to live) that statement.

As college roommates, I watched him hide bottles of alcohol all over the house. I watched him deny his problem and try to convince everyone, "I can handle this." I watched him study drunk. I watched him as he continually performed below his capability because of his drinking problem. But most astoundingly, I watched him spend over $30,000 in lawyer and court fees to fight drunken driving charges.

I watched all of this as I stood by and begged him to get help. He did go to counseling a few times, but nothing seemed to help. I'm at a total loss as to what to do for John and how to help him. I don't even know if I should try to help anymore.

What advice would you give Natasha?

_____
_____
_____
_____

What advice would you give to John?

_____
_____
_____
_____

If one of your friends refused to listen to your advice and refused any type of help, what would you do? Why?

_____
_____
_____
_____

List at least five ways that excessive alcohol usage can damage your life.

_____
_____
_____
_____

What steps would you take if you saw one of your friends in John's position (i.e., hiding alcohol around the house)?

_____
_____
_____
_____

If you or someone you know has a drinking or drug problem, where could you go on your campus for assistance?

_____
_____
_____

Phone #
_____

at this moment journal

Refer to page 409 of this chapter. Having read and reflected upon the information in the chapter, consider how you might revise your goal to make it more:

REASONABLE

BELIEVABLE

MEASURABLE

ADAPTABLE

CONTROLLABLE

DESIRABLE

ONLINE JOURNAL

To complete an online journal entry, log onto the Companion Website at **www.prenhall.com/sherfield.** Go to Chapter 14 and click on the link to the Online Journal. You can respond to the questions provided or to questions assigned by your professor, or you may journal about your own experiences.

ADVICE TO GO
CORNERSTONES
for wellness & stress reduction

Understand that your choices have *consequences*.

Develop a way to *"decompress"* after school or work.

Eat a *balanced and regular* diet.

Take *time out* to be with friends or family.

Surround yourself with *positive* people.

Protect yourself at clubs and parties.

Keep yourself healthy with *exercise*.

Take care of your *spiritual* health.

Think before you drink.

Don't procrastinate.

LIVE

15 Dream

Hold fast to dreams, for if dreams die, life is a broken-winged bird that cannot fly.

—Langston Hughes

CHAPTER 15
DREAM

I met Wilma when she was a first-year student in college. I was director of student activities and of the Student Government Association, and she was a senator representing the first-year class. Her drive and enthusiasm distinguished her from other new students. She wanted to be a teacher. She had not gone to college immediately after high school; instead, *she had joined the armed forces and then entered the workforce.* During this time, Wilma had given her career a great deal of thought. She told me one day, *"I've had many jobs in my life, but I've never had a career."*

During the upcoming semesters, *Wilma made the president's list and the dean's list, was named to Who's Who Among American College Students, won several academic scholarships, was elected to the Student Government Association,* and even placed second in a dance contest. She was the envy of her peers and colleagues. In addition to energy and drive, she had a desire to have a career, *to do something that she loved—to teach.* She studied hard, tutored others, and graduated with honors. She received her associate's degree and transferred to a four-year college and became what she had planned for so many years to be—today, she teaches small children near her hometown.

Wilma's story does not seem extraordinary until you learn that Wilma began her career pursuit in her midsixties. *Today, in her seventies, she still teaches. She is an inspiration to all her students and colleagues who learn from her and love her dearly.*

> She told me . . . "I've had many jobs in my life, but never a career."

Career and Life Planning

The key to success is to keep company only with people who uplift you, whose presence calls forth your best. —EPICTETUS

QUESTIONS FOR REFLECTION

Consider responding to these questions online in the Questions for Reflection module of the Companion Website.

1. Why do you think Wilma had such amazing staying power when she started college so late?

2. What did Wilma mean when she said she had always had jobs but never a career?

3. Why do you think it is important that you start focusing on career goals even though you are just beginning your college education?

Where are you... AT THIS MOMENT

Before reading this chapter, take a moment and respond to the following ten questions. Consider each one carefully before answering, and then respond by circling the number in the appropriate box. When you have answered the questions, add your points and find your total score on the feedback chart below.

STATEMENT	STRONGLY DISAGREE	DISAGREE	DON'T KNOW	AGREE	STRONGLY AGREE	SCORE
1. To me, there is no real difference between a job and a career.	5	4	3	2	1	
2. I have given serious thought to what major I want to declare.	1	2	3	4	5	
3. I know what educational path I must follow to get to the career I want.	1	2	3	4	5	
4. I know where to go to get information about the various educational paths open to me.	1	2	3	4	5	
5. I could easily come up with a list of 10 words or phrases that describe my personality.	1	2	3	4	5	
6. My personality traits make little difference in the types of careers in which I'm interested.	5	4	3	2	1	
7. I am aware of the similarities and differences between my personality type and the personality types of other people in the fields in which I am interested.	1	2	3	4	5	
8. It is not important to me to make a connection with someone who can be a mentor to me in my educational path.	5	4	3	2	1	
9. In the end, the money I will earn in my future career is more important than the respect I will earn.	5	4	3	2	1	
10. I know where I can go to take interest and aptitude tests to help me decide what careers I may be suited for.	1	2	3	4	5	
TOTAL VALUE						

SUMMARY

10–17 Your level of direction and planning for a future career is low. You need to learn where to turn for help and guidance, and how your personality and interests will impact these decisions.

18–25 Your level of direction in career planning is somewhat low. You need to spend more time investigating your options and determining your interests and values.

26–34 You are average in your sense of career options. You may need to take advantage of the assistance available to you in charting your career options.

35–42 You have an above average sense of what you'd like to pursue as a career. You also have a sense of how your personality traits will help you in your future career.

43–50 You have an exceptionally tuned sense of how you'd like to integrate your life, personality, and career choices. You've probably already investigated many options and likely already have connections with others to help you learn even more about how to reach your career goals.

Goals . . . FOR CHANGE

Based on your total points, what is one goal you would like to achieve related to your career and life goals?

Goal _____
_____

List three actions you can take that might help you move closer to realizing this goal.

1. _____
2. _____
3. _____

Questions FOR BUILDING ON YOUR BEST

As you read this chapter, consider the following questions. At the end of the chapter, you should be able to answer all of them. You are encouraged to ask a few questions of your own. Consider asking your classmates or professors to assist you.

1. Explain the difference between a job and a career.
2. How will my personality traits impact my choice of careers?
3. How will I go about selecting a major?
4. How can I learn exactly what a specific job is like?
5. How important are the part-time and summer jobs that I have during college to my long-term career success? Explain.

What additional questions do you have about careers and life planning?

1. _____
2. _____
3. _____

What Am I Going to Do for the Rest of My Life?

"What am I going to do for the rest of my life?" is an overwhelming question for a beginning college student. You are having a hard enough time getting through classes, participating in extracurricular activities, dating, taking care of children, working part-time or full-time jobs, and meeting with teams to produce a project. How are you supposed to find time to make such an important decision in the midst of all this?

Well, first of all, you don't have to decide today. Of course, it's nice if you always knew you wanted to be an engineer or a broadcast major or a restauranteur or a teacher, but what if you just don't have a clue? Your advisor and your parents are pressuring you to make a decision, so what do you do?

Take your time. Research a variety of careers that you think might interest you. Talk to your advisor and to other professors. Read trade publications in a variety of work disciplines. Get a part-time job in a field that you think might interest you as a career. Shadow someone who is in a profession that appeals to you. Meanwhile, take general education courses that will apply to most majors until you can make up your mind. It's true that choosing a major and a career are very important decisions, but you don't have to rush into these decisions, and you must make your own choice.

The Coming Job Boom

YOUR FUTURE LOOKS INCREDIBLY BRIGHT

The job market is cyclical—up one day and down another. Some years, people are losing jobs all around you, while there are other years when companies are begging for employees and paying high salaries. Thanks to aging baby boomers, the job market is predicted to be outstanding for you in the coming years. There are 76 million baby boomers and only 46 million Gen Xers to take their places, says Eisenberg (2002). As the population ages, certain industries are desperately seeking qualified employees.

Hospitals need more nurses and many pay starting bonuses to attract applicants. Pharmacies are paying very high salaries to attract new graduates. Large numbers of teachers, professors, and administrators are retiring over the next decade. According to Eisenberg, schools will need 2.2 million more teachers over the next decade, not to mention librarians, counselors, and administrators. Further, we need more electricians, plumbers, and contractors. Engineers and accountants are in great demand. The service industry in this country is exploding with great demand for excellent managers in the hospitality, retail, and entertainment industries.

College graduates who have the right skills, work attitudes, and habits will be in the driver's seat. All of this is very good news for your generation of college students! A good job should be there waiting for you.

Your Career May Change Frequently

PREPARE FOR FLEXIBILITY

Regardless of your choice of careers, you may see your field change dramatically over the coming years. Technology is impacting everything we do. Since technology feeds on itself, computers and software are constantly doing tasks faster and better than ever before. Machines are taking over jobs that employees used to do. You might as well know this fact today: You have just begun to learn! As soon as you graduate and accept a job, the first thing you will probably have to do is go back to school in a corporate environment to learn how to do things their way.

Depending on the career you select, you might even see it totally disappear, making it necessary for you to re-tool and learn something new. Employment sources predict that today's young people will change jobs as often as seven times during a lifetime. The old days of going to work for a company and staying there forever are gone.

Your college career and all that you will learn during the next four years has to prepare you for the future. You need to be the captain of your own destiny, seeking the right career, the professors who can teach you the most, the temporary jobs that can prepare you for the real career path, and the extracurricular activities that will give you leadership experience.

You have probably grown tired of hearing, "These are the best years of your life." In many ways they are, but the truth is, they don't have to be the last great years of your life. If you are in college to really learn, grow, mature, and prepare for a great future, the best years may lie ahead. Years when you can put what you have learned to practice, years when you can find new solutions and lead other people to success, years when you can just enjoy the experience of continuing to learn and grow.

So, how do you learn to be flexible? Drink up knowledge like a sponge. Read, read, read! Learn to follow directions and think for yourself. Practice thinking creatively to solve new problems. Improve your writing and speaking skills. Become an expert with computer applications. Learn to work with a diverse population. Relate to people who are not just like you. Get comfortable with all age groups. Take risks and get out of your comfort zone. Study personal finance so you can manage your own personal affairs. Gain enough business skills to manage your own business, even if you plan to be a doctor. Getting an education is heavy stuff! After all, you are preparing for the rest of your life!

> went into the woods because I wished to live deliberately, to front only the essential facts of life, and to see if I could not learn what it had to teach, and not, when I came to die, discover that I had not lived. —HENRY DAVID THOREAU

Now, which career choice do you want? How do you find out? And how do you prepare? The following activity will help you answer these questions.

WHAT DO YOU KNOW NOW ABOUT WHAT YOU WANT TO BECOME?

Activity

1. What career do you think you want based on what you know now?

2. Why do you think you want to do this? What appeals to you about this particular career?

3. What most interests you today? Can you relate a career to this interest?

4. How important is prestige to you? Why?

5. How important to you is feeling that you are making a difference? Explain.

6. How important to you is making a lot of money?

7. Regardless of what you think about money, you have to have a certain amount to live. How much do you think that is? Does your career interest pay enough to support you and a family? Do you need to rethink your choice or modify it?

CONTINUED

8. Does your career interest relate to your values? Do you see any conflicts with your values? If so, explain.

9. For a good life, which values, people, places, and emotions do you feel you need?

10. Is there something you want to be remembered for that can be related to a career? Write a statement about what you think is the purpose of your life.

11. What is the difference between "making a living" and "living your life"?

12. Who is the person in your life who has the career that you want? Why do you admire that person and his or her career?

The answers to these questions hold some of the keys to deciding on the right major that would lead to the perfect career for you. You don't have to decide today, but you need to be closing in on what you want to do when you graduate.

Career Planning
WHERE THE JOBS ARE

While it may be difficult to make a decision today regarding your career, you might be interested in studying projections regarding the growth industries. According to Tieger and Barron-Tieger (2001), the service industries, along with health, engineering, business management and social services, will offer the best opportunities in the coming years. As shown in Figure 15.1, of the 10 fastest-growing industries, 9 belong to one of these industry groups.

Some of the occupations that are expected to grow the fastest are listed in Figure 15.2.

Other occupations expected to grow at a rapid rate include human service workers (55%); data processing equipment repairers (52%); medical records technicians (51%); speech pathologists and audiologists (51%); amusement and recreation attendants (48%); dental hygienists (48%); emergency medical technicians (45%); and engineering, mathematical, and natural sciences managers (45%) (Tieger and Barron-Tieger, 2001).

FIGURE 15.1 *Industries projected to experience the highest percentage of growth.*

Computer and data processing services	108%
Health services	68%
Management and public relations	60%
Miscellaneous transportation services	60%
Residential care	59%
Personnel supply services	53%
Water and sanitation	51%
Individual social services	50%
Offices of health practitioners	47%
Amusement and recreation services	41%

FIGURE 15.2 *The 10 occupations projected to grow the fastest.*

Computer engineers	109%
Systems analysts	103%
Personal and home care aides	85%
Physical and corrective therapy assistants	79%
Home health aides	77%
Medical assistants	74%
Physical therapists	71%
Occupational therapists and assistants	69%
Paralegal personnel	68%
Special education teachers	59%

Career and Life Planning 447

Plan for a Career— Not a Series of Jobs

Everyone at some time faces the age-old question, "Should I be what others think I should be or should I be what I want to be?" The life's work for many people turns out to be what other people think it should be. Well into the latter half of the twentieth century, women were expected to have traditional female careers, such as teaching, nursing, or homemaking. They had little opportunity to select a profession that suited them; society selected their professions for them. It was uncommon for women to enter the fields of engineering, construction, management, public safety, or politics; the avenues to such choices were not open.

> It is easy to live for others. Everybody does. I call on you to live for yourselves. —RALPH WALDO EMERSON

College students, male and female, still face pressures to be what others want them to be. Parents actively guide their children toward professions that suit their ideas of what their children should do. Some students have little choice in deciding what they will do for the rest of their lives.

For nontraditional students, spouses, time, and finances may dictate a profession. Many choose courses of study that can be completed quickly because finances and family considerations pressure them in that direction. Money is often another consideration when choosing a profession. Regardless of the pressures you have in your life, be careful to research your choices, talk with people already in the profession you are considering, and consider the long-term effects of your decisions. You want your career decisions to be well thought out, well planned, and carefully executed.

You are the only person who will be able to answer the questions, "How do I want to spend my time?" and "What is my purpose in life?" No parent, teacher, partner, counselor, or therapist can fully answer these questions for you. Another person may be able to provide information that can help you make the decision, but ultimately, you will be the person in charge of your career path, your life's work.

An informational interview is a useful way to research job options. These interviews can help you figure out how a career path can fit with your life goals.

What Do You Want to Be When You Grow Up?

YOUR CAREER SELF-STUDY

More people than you would imagine have trouble deciding what they want to be when they grow up. Studies indicate that more than 20 percent of all first-year college students do not know what their majors will be. That's all right for

Find a job you like and you'll never have to work a day in your life. —UNKNOWN

the time being, but before long you will need to make a decision.

The questions that follow are designed to help you make that decision regarding what you want to do with the rest of your life—your career.

WHAT IS YOUR PERSONALITY TYPE?

You can best answer this question by taking a personality inventory, such as the Myers-Briggs Type Indicator.® (An inventory based on the MBTI is located in Chapter 6 of this book.) This question is important, because your personality may very well indicate the type of work in which you will be successful and happy. If you are a real people person, you probably will not be very happy, for example, in a job with minimal human contact and interaction.

Describe your personality type.

_____
_____

How will your personality type affect your career path?

_____
_____

WHAT ARE YOUR INTERESTS?

Understanding your specific interests may help you decide on a career. If you love working on cars, you might consider becoming a mechanical engineer. If you love to draw or build things, you might be interested in architecture or sculpting.

What are your major interests?

_____
_____

How can these interests be transferred to a career choice?

_____
_____

DO YOU ENJOY PHYSICAL OR MENTAL WORK?

Many people would go crazy if they had to spend so much as one hour per day in an office. Others would be unhappy if they had to work in the sun all day or use a great deal of physical strength. The answer to this question will greatly narrow your list of potential career choices. For example, if you are an outdoor person who loves being outside in all kinds of weather, then you should probably avoid careers that are limited to indoor work. You should also consider whether you have any physical limitations that might affect your career choice.

Do you enjoy physical or mental work or both? Why?

_____

_____

What does this mean to your career path?

_____

_____

DO YOU WANT TO MAKE A LOT OF MONEY?

Most people, if asked, "Why do you work?" would respond, "For the money." There is nothing wrong with wanting to make money in your profession, but not all professions, regardless of their worth, pay well. Some of the hardest and most rewarding work pays the least. You have to decide whether to go for the money or do something that is personally challenging to you. Many times, you can find both!

Is your major goal in choosing a profession money or something else? What?

_____

_____

What does your goal mean to your career path?

_____

_____

WHERE DO YOU WANT TO LIVE?

Although this question may sound strange, many careers are limited by geography. If you are interested in oceanography, you would be hard-pressed to live in Iowa; if you love farming, New York City would be an improbable place for you to live. Some people simply prefer certain parts of the United States (or the world) to others. You need to ask yourself, "Where do I eventually want to live?" "What climate do I really enjoy?" "In what size city or town do I want to work?" "Where would I be the happiest?" "Do I want to live near my family or away from them?" "Do I want to be close to the ocean?"

Where do you eventually want to live? Why?

_____

_____

What does your preference mean to your career path?

_____
_____

DO YOU WANT TO TRAVEL?

Some jobs require travel; some people love to travel, some hate it. Ask yourself whether you want to be away from your home and family four nights per week, or whether you want a job that does not require any travel.

Do you enjoy travel? Do you want to do a lot of traveling?

_____
_____

What does this mean to your career path?

_____
_____

HOW DO YOU LIKE TO DRESS?

Some people enjoy dressing up and welcome the opportunity to put on a new suit and go to work. Others prefer to throw on an old pair of blue jeans and head out the door. Jobs have different requirements in terms of dress, and you will be affected by them every workday, so you will want to consider your own preferences.

How do you like to dress?

_____
_____

What does this mean to your career path?

_____
_____

There is often a typical style of dress or attitude associated with different professions. Will dress codes or other personal-behavior requirements affect your career decisions? Do you think they should?

WHAT MOTIVATES YOU?

What are the one or two things in your life that motivate you? Money? Power? Helping other people? The answer to this question is an essential element to choosing a career. You have to find that certain something that gives you energy and then find a profession that allows you to pursue it with fervor and intensity.

What is your motivational force and why?

How could this help you in deciding on a career path?

WHAT DO YOU VALUE?

Do you value relationships, possessions, money, love, security, challenges, or power? Once you have identified what you value in your life, you can identify careers that closely match your personal value system and eliminate careers that don't. If you have to constantly compromise your values just to get a paycheck, you may be unhappy.

What do you truly value in your life?

How might these values affect your career decisions?

WHAT ARE YOUR SKILLS?

Are you especially good at one or two things? Are you good with computers, a good manager of money, a good carpenter, a good communicator? Your skills will play a powerful part in selecting a career. If you are not good or skilled at manipulating numbers, then you will probably want to avoid careers that require their constant use. If you are not a good communicator, then you probably do not want a career that requires you to give daily presentations. Employers still stress the importance of three basic skills: writing, speaking, and listening. If you have these skills, you are ahead of the pack. If not, you need to enroll in a class that will help you to become better at all three.

What are your skills? What do you do well?

How could your strongest skills help you make a career decision?

DO YOU LIKE ROUTINE?

The answer to this question will narrow down your choices tremendously. If you like routine, you will want a career that is conducive to routine and provides structure. If you do not like routine and enjoy doing different things each day, certain careers will be unrealistic for you.

Do you like routine or do you prefer variety? Why?

_____
_____

How does this affect your career path?

_____
_____

ARE YOU A LEADER?

One of the most important questions you must ask yourself is "Do I enjoy leading, teaching, or guiding people?" If you prefer to be part of the crowd and do not like to stand out as a leader or manager, some careers may not suit you. If you like to take charge and get things done when you are with other people, you will find certain careers better than others. How you relate to leadership will be a part of your personality inventory.

Do you consider yourself a leader? Are you comfortable in a leadership role? Why or why not?

_____
_____

How will your feelings about leadership affect your career path?

_____
_____

How do you feel about managing other people?

_____
_____

Help Me: I'm Undeclared

No, it isn't a fatal disease. You're not dying. Being undeclared is not a disgrace or a weakness. It is a temporary state of mind, and the best way to deal with it is to stop and think. You should not declare a major because you are ashamed to be undeclared, and you shouldn't allow yourself to be pressured into declaring a major. Instead, you can take measures to work toward declaring a major and being satisfied with your decision. It is better to be undeclared than to spend several semesters in a field that is wrong for you, wasting hours that won't count toward a degree.

Nine Steps to Career Decision Making

Step 1—Dream! If money were not a problem or concern, what would you do for the rest of your life? If you could do anything in the world, what would you do? Where would you do it? These are the types of questions you must ask yourself as you try to select a major and career. Go outside, lie on the grass, and look up at the sky; think silently for a little while. Let your mind wander, and let the sky be the limit. Write your dreams down. These dreams may be closer to reality than you think. In the words of Don Quixote, "Let us dream, my soul, let us dream" (Unamuno).

Step 2—Talk to your advisor. Academic advisors are there to help you. But don't be surprised if their doors are sometimes closed. They teach, conduct research, perform community service, and sometimes advise in excess of 100 students. Always call in advance; make an appointment to see an advisor. When you have that appointment, make your advisor work for you. Take your college catalog and ask questions, hard questions. Your advisor will not make a career decision for you, but if you ask the proper questions, he or she can be of monumental help to you and your career decisions.

Use students in your program as advisors, too. They will be invaluable to you as you work your way through the daily routine of college. Experienced students can assist you in making decisions about your classes, electives, and work-study programs. They can even help you join and become an active member of a preprofessional program.

Step 3—Use electives. The accreditation agency that works with your school requires that you be allowed at least one free elective in your degree program. Some programs allow many more. Use your electives wisely! Do not take courses just to get the hours. The wisest students use their electives to delve into new areas of interest or to take a block of courses in an area that might enhance their career opportunities.

Step 4—Go to the career center. Even the smallest colleges have some type of career center or a career counselor. Use them! Campus career centers usually provide free services. The same types of services in the community could cost from $200 to $2,000. The professionals in the career center can provide information on a variety of careers and fields, and they can administer interest and personality inventories that can help you make career and other major decisions.

Step 5—Read, read, read! Nothing will help you more than reading about careers and majors. Ask your advisor or counselor to help you locate information on your areas of interest. Gather information from colleges, agencies, associations, and places of employment. Then read it!

Nothing is really work, unless you would rather be doing something else. —SIR JAMES BARRIE

DID YOU KNOW?

2010

The year in which a projected labor shortage of 4 to 6 million people may occur.

Source: Time.com. "The coming job boom." Posted at www.time.com/time/business/article/0,8599,233967,00.html.

Step 6—Shadow. Shadowing describes the process of following someone around on the job. If you are wondering what engineers do on the job, try calling an engineering office to see whether you can sit with several of their engineers for a day over spring break. Shadowing is the very best way to get firsthand, honest information regarding a profession in which you might be interested.

Step 7—Join preprofessional organizations. One of the most important steps you can take as a college student is to become involved in campus organizations and clubs that offer educational opportunities, social interaction, and hands-on experience in your chosen field. Preprofessional organizations can open doors that will help you make a career decision, grow in your field, meet professionals already working in your field, and, eventually, get a job.

Step 8—Get a part-time job. Work in an area that you may be interested in pursuing as a career.

Step 9—Try to get a summer practicum or internship. Work in your field of interest to gain practical experience and see if it really suits you.

Networking: The Overlooked Source for Career Development

We are often so concerned with books, computerized databases, and interest inventories that we forget to look in our own backyards when thinking about careers. Networking is one of the most important aspects of career development. Look at the person sitting beside you in your orientation class. That person could be a future leader in your field of study. You might be thinking, "No way," but you'd be surprised at how many people lose out on networking opportunities because they do not think ahead. The person sitting beside you is important. You never know where or when you may see this person again—he may be interviewing you for a job in 10 years, or she may be the person with whom you will start a business in 15 years. "Too far down the road," you say? Don't close your eyes—15 years will pass faster than you think.

> Not all who wander are lost.
> —J. R. R. TOLKIEN

You've all heard the expression, "It's not what you know, but who you know." Well, few statements could be more true, and college is the perfect place for making many personal and professional contacts. At this moment, you are building a network of people on whom you can call for the rest of your life. Your network may include people you know from:

> Friends do business with friends.
> —J. W. MARRIOTT, JR.

High school and college	Student government
Clubs and professional organizations	Newspaper staff
Sporting teams and events	Family connections
Fraternities and sororities	College committees
Community organizations	Volunteer work

Mentors

A mentor is someone who can help open doors for you, who will take a personal and professional interest in your development and success. Often a mentor will help you do something that you might have trouble doing on your own. It may be too soon for you to determine now whether you have found a mentor, and you may not find that person until you begin to take courses in your field of study.

The student–mentor relationship is unique. You help each other. Your mentor may provide you with opportunities that you might otherwise not have. You may have to do some grunt work, but the experience will usually help you in the long run. While you are helping your mentor, your mentor is helping you by giving you experience and responsibility.

As a young, uncertain first-year college student, Derrick applied for and was awarded a work-study position with Professor Griffon. His job was to help Professor Griffon ready a semester calendar of events from plays to lectures to

---

WORLD OF WORK

College provides tremendous opportunities for students to prepare for the World of Work. As a student, I was able to learn how to deal with competition in a non-monetary setting. This gave me the confidence to handle the competitive nature of my career as an attorney. College also provided me an opportunity to learn how to manage leisure vs. work/studying. Since time is my most important commodity, success in being able to prioritize my life issues is paramount to a successful career and home life. I have two wonderful daughters who have very active lives, which I don't intend to miss out on. I want to be able to spend time with them, attending their recitals, helping them with their homework, and introducing them to museums and the arts. I also have a husband who is not only my business partner but my soulmate, with whom I must spend time nurturing our relationship. I would not be able to manage all of my life goals if I had not learned how to prioritize my life and manage my time correctly.

If I could give one piece of advice to college students today, it would be to become active in extracurricular and co-curricular activities because it gives you a chance to become involved in the community. To be a successful career person you *must* give back. My work as an attorney cannot fulfill all of my needs. I've seen so many of my colleagues become so obsessed with work that they lose sight of the truly important aspects of life, family, friends, community. I'm very lucky that my career has provided me with skills that I can give back to the community through my work with volunteer organizations. Without this balance, my life would be incomplete.

QUESTIONS FOR REFLECTION

Consider responding to these questions online in the World of Work module of the Companion Website.

1. Why do you think Ms. Overdorf values balance in her life so much?
2. What do you think Ms. Overdorf and Wilma have in common?
3. How can you apply her beliefs to your own life while you are in college and beyond?

Tanya Stuart Overdorf, *Attorney,* Indianapolis, IN

How could a student assistant position with a professor help your career?

dances to speakers. One of his responsibilities was to prepare mailings and other advertising materials for the humanities series. The work was monumental, the pay minimal, and Professor Griffon was not always in the best of spirits. On some days, Derrick left the office swearing that he would never return. But he had little choice—the job paid more than unemployment. Derrick stayed with the job, and before too long, Professor Griffon began to give him more challenging work.

One day, an important member of the community came to the office. Derrick and the professor were both working at their desks. As the professor and the guest discussed a lucrative contract for an artist, Derrick overheard Professor Griffon tell the guest he could "bring the contract by tomorrow and leave it with Derrick, my assistant." "Assistant," Derrick thought, "that's interesting."

Before Derrick graduated with his two-year degree, he had a wealth of experience, knowledge, and, most important, contacts! He had learned how to run the lighting board in the theater, he had managed the box office, he had developed a marketing plan for one of the events, and he had been able to shadow many of the artists who came to the auditorium to perform. All this was possible because of his relationship with Professor Griffon. This student–mentor situation was rewarding for both of them. They helped each other, and both profited.

HOW TO FIND A MENTOR

You can't go shopping for a mentor; you don't advertise; you can't use someone else's mentor. You find a mentor through preparation, work, and a feeling of being comfortable. The following suggestions may help you find a mentor:

- Arrive at class early and work hard.
- Develop an outstanding work ethic.

Benefits of Having a Mentor

- Mentors teach, advise, and coach.
- Mentors serve as a sounding board for ideas.
- Mentors serve as constructive critics.
- Mentors can promote you among their peers and contacts.
- Mentors provide information to help with career development.
- Mentors can increase your visibility on campus and in the work arena.
- Mentors introduce you to people who can advance your career.

- Seek advice from many professors and staff members.
- Ask intelligent, thoughtful questions.
- Offer to help with projects.
- Convey the impression that you are committed, competent, and hardworking.
- Look for opportunities to shadow.
- If a professor or staff member gives you an opportunity, take it.
- Look at grunt work as glory work.

STRATEGIES FOR BUILDING ON YOUR BEST

Consider the following strategies for choosing a career:

- Observe people around you who have skills and qualities you admire and would like to emulate.
- Make your own choices based on your personal values and dreams.
- Choose a major that relates to your interests and long-term goals.
- Seek balance in your life by finding an outlet that allows you to use your best talents to benefit others.
- Begin building a network of people who can help you further your career.
- Use opportunities to shadow a professional in your chosen career.
- Above all, work toward a career that brings you joy, peace, and happiness.

Bringing It All Together

Throughout *Cornerstone,* we have tried to suggest that you can change your attitude, your behavior, your actions, and your life. If we did not believe this, we would not have spent 10 years of our lives writing and revising this book, nor would we have spent a collective 60-plus years teaching and working with students.

Change is possible and, in many instances, practical and necessary. However, change does not come without sacrifice, hard work, and much determination. But you already know that, don't you? You had to change to get this far in the text and in your college career. But change is not all that you face in the months, semesters, and years to come. You will also be faced with many hard, life-altering decisions that will affect you, your family, and your livelihood for many years.

One of the most important decisions that you will make, consciously or unconsciously, is deciding on what type of person you want to be, what you plan to do in your life, and what contributions you plan to leave this world when your time here is through.

> The world in which we live is full of roadblocks that can potentially cause us to lose focus and fall out of balance. Consider the following facts: Americans reporting that they were *"very happy"* were no more numerous in the early 1990s than in 1957. In 1993, only 21% of 18- to 29-year-olds thought that they had a chance at the *"good life"* as compared to 41% in 1978. Today, Americans spend 40% *less time* with their children than they did in 1965. Employed Americans spend 163 *hours more* per year on the job than they did in 1969. Sixty-nine percent of Americans would like to *slow down* and live a more relaxed life. (Sherfield, Montgomery, and Moody, 2001)

As a mature, rational, caring human being, you should realize that you are a part of a bigger picture. This world does not belong to us; we are only borrowing it for a while. Everything you do affects someone else in some way. You must realize that what you do—not just what you do for your career, but your daily actions—matters to someone. There is value in every job, and there is honor in all professions performed well and honestly. When making career and life decisions, you need to take into account the fact that other people, strangers and friends, will eventually be looking to you as a mentor, and a role model. This is a major responsibility that you cannot avoid; rather, you should relish the opportunity to inspire and teach. Embrace the moment. Finally, you must realize that unless you are out there, daily, creating a better future for yourself, you have no right to complain about the one that is handed to you.

Every time you make a choice, you determine your character.   —UNKNOWN

BLUEPRINTS FOR CHANGE

NAME

DATE

REFLECTION

Making a decision about your major or career can be difficult, but, fortunately, you still have a few months before you have to make this choice. Use this time to explore all avenues that will expose you to different possibilities. This is a growing time for you and you might discover new interests and directions that you have never considered before. Wilma followed her heart and after many years, finally pursued her dreams. If there is something you have always wanted to do or be, chances are your desires will not change even after you study other options.

The most important thing for you to remember is that this is your one lifetime. You need to prepare to do something you love. No matter how much money you make, you won't be happy unless you are doing something that matters to you, something that allows you to keep learning and becoming, something that provides you opportunities to give back—perhaps the best gift of all.

GET REAL

Below are questions to help you think about careers and life planning. Study each question carefully and respond.

What do you value most and how does this value relate to your primary career option at this time?

Discuss one experience you have had this semester that helped you think more positively about a particular career option.

Discuss one experience you have had this semester that caused you to think negatively about a particular career option.

How can you apply the information provided in this chapter to help you decide on a major and a career?

If you begin to build a network today, how will it impact your career when you graduate and begin a full-time job?

What can you learn from Wilma about following your dreams?

Case Study

NAME: Nailah Robinson
SCHOOL: Northern Virginia Community College, Annandale, VA
MAJOR: Nursing   AGE: 30

Below is a real-life situation faced by Nailah. Read the brief case and respond to the questions.

I started college right out of high school but because of my restlessness, lack of a major, and desire to be out in the world, I left college and moved to California. I worked in various jobs such as cosmetology and food service for many years.

I began college again in California to become a teacher. I quickly realized, however, that going back to college after being in the workforce was not very easy. You get used to a full-time salary and have full-time responsibilities, and those things stopped me once again.

About two years ago, I had my first child and during my stay in the hospital, I met the most wonderful nurse. She spent time with me and talked to me about my hopes and dreams, and it was in my conversations with her that I finally realized my place in this world. My grandmother used to say, "Sometimes, we can't see any further than where we are." That had been true with me, but my nurse helped me see down the road.

I knew that I wanted to be able to support and provide for my son, so I shadowed a nurse to make sure that my dream wasn't a nightmare. After my shadowing experience, I began college at NOVA. Just last week, I passed the entrance exam and was accepted into the nursing program. My dream is to work with at-risk, low-income children and give them the same care that my nurse gave me.

How can adversity affect your career decisions?

_____
_____
_____

Nailah spent 10 years away from college. Where do you hope to be 10 years from now?

_____
_____
_____

What role does your college degree play in your 10-year plan?

_____
_____
_____

How can other people (like Nailah's nurse) affect one's entire life perspective?

_____
_____
_____
_____

Has anyone ever touched your life like Nailah's nurse touched hers? Who? What "gift" did they give to you?

_____
_____
_____
_____

If the answer was no to the question above, do you feel that you have ever touched anyone's life in this way? Why or why not?

_____
_____
_____
_____

Where can you go on your campus to receive advice and assistance with your career goals?

_____
_____
_____

Phone # _____

at this moment Journal

Refer to page 441 of this chapter. Having read and reflected upon the information in the chapter, consider how you might revise your goal to make it more:

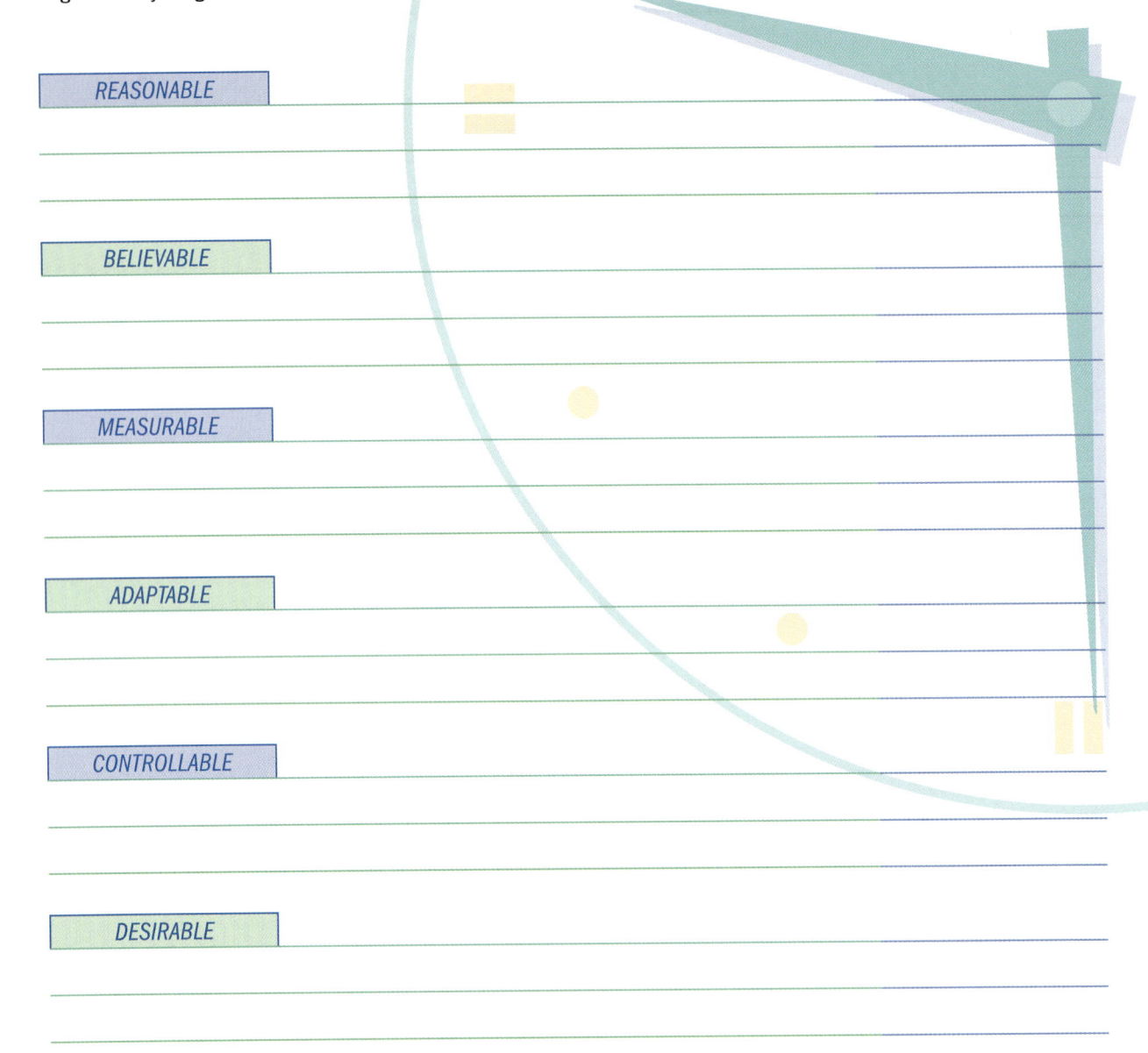

REASONABLE

BELIEVABLE

MEASURABLE

ADAPTABLE

CONTROLLABLE

DESIRABLE

ONLINE JOURNAL

To complete an online journal entry, log onto the Companion Website at **www.prenhall.com/sherfield**. Go to Chapter 15 and click on the link to the Online Journal. You can respond to the questions provided or to questions assigned by your professor, or you may journal about your own experiences.

ADVICE TO GO

CORNERSTONES

for career and life planning

Identify the assets you can offer a company.

Make *educated* and researched *decisions*.

Learn to *promote* and sell yourself in an interview.

Discover your personality type.

Shadow and do volunteer work.

Realize life is *more* than money.

Know your own *value* system.

Identify what *motivates* you.

Never be afraid to change.

Make your *own* decisions.

Pinpoint your *interests*.

DREAM

Glossary

Academic freedom Professors in institutions of higher education are allowed to conduct research and to teach that research, regardless of controversial issues or subject matter. Academic freedom allows the professor the right to teach certain materials that might not have been allowed in high school.

Academic integrity You have read, fully understand, and adhere to the policies, codes, and moral values of your institution. It implies that you will not cheat, plagiarize, or be unfair in your academic, social, cultural, or civic work.

Accreditation Most high schools and colleges in the United States are accredited by a regional agency. This agency is responsible for ensuring that a minimum set of standards are held at all institutions that are members in the accreditation agency. The Southern Association of Colleges and Schools is one example of an accreditation agency.

Adding Adding a class during registration periods or during the first week of classes means that you will be taking an additional class in your schedule.

Administration The administration of a college is usually made up of nonteaching personnel who handle all of the administrative aspects of the college. The administration is headed by the president and vice presidents. The structure of the administration at each college varies.

Advising To make sure that you will know what classes to take and in which order, you will be assigned an academic advisor—most often a faculty member in your discipline or major—when you arrive on campus. This advisor will usually be with you during your entire degree. She is responsible for guiding you through your academic work at the college.

African American studies This curriculum deals with the major contributions by African Americans in art, literature, history, medicine, sciences, and architecture. Many colleges offer majors and minors in African American Studies.

AIDS This acronym stands for Acquired Immune Deficiency Syndrome, a disease that is transmitted sexually, intravenously, or from mother to child. Currently, no known cure for AIDS exists, but several medications, such as AZT and protease inhibitors, help to slow the deterioration of the immune system.

Alumna, Alumni, Alumnus These terms are used to describe students who hold degrees from a college. The term *alumna* refers to a woman, *alumni* refers to a man, and *alumnus* refers to woman or a man. The term *alumni* is used most often.

Anti-Semitism Discrimination against people of Jewish or Arabic descent.

Articulation An articulation agreement is a signed document between two or more institutions guaranteeing that the courses taken at one college will transfer to another college. For example, if Oak College has an articulation agreement with Maple College, it means that the course work taken at Oak College will be accepted toward a degree at Maple College.

Associate degree The associate degree is a two-year degree that usually prepares the student to enter the workforce with a specific skill or trade. It is also offered to students as the first two years of their bachelor's, or four-year degree. Not all colleges offer the associate degree.

Attendance Each college has an attendance policy, such as "a student can miss no more than 10 percent of the total class hours or he will receive an F for the course." This policy is followed strictly by some professors and more leniently by others. You should always know the attendance policy of each professor with whom you are studying.

Auditing Most colleges offer the choice either to enroll in a course or to audit a course. If you enroll in a course, you pay the entire fee, attend classes, take exams, and receive credit. If you audit a course, the fee is usually lower, you do not take exams, and you do not receive credit. Course auditing is usually done by people who are having trouble in a subject or by those who want to gain more knowledge about a particular subject. Some colleges charge full price for auditing a course.

Baccalaureate The baccalaureate degree, more commonly called the bachelor's degree, is a four-year degree in a specific field. Although this degree can be completed in as few as three years or as many as six-plus years, traditionally the amount of academic work required is four years. This degree prepares students for such careers as teaching, social work, engineering, fine arts, and journalism, to name a few. Graduate work is also available in these fields.

Bankruptcy Bankruptcy is when a person must file legal papers through a lawyer to declare that she cannot pay her bills. Filing bankruptcy destroys one's credit history and it takes 10 years for the bankruptcy to disappear from one's credit report.

Binge drinking Binge drinking is defined as having five or more alcoholic beverages at one sitting.

Blackboard Blackboard is a delivery platform for distance education courses taken over the web. Several platforms exist, including WebCT and Course Compass.

Board of Trustees The Board of Trustees is the governing body of the college. The board is appointed by government officials (usually the governor) of each state. The board hires the president and must approve any curriculum changes to degree programs. The board also sets policy for the college.

Campus The campus is the physical plant of the university or college. The term refers to all buildings, fields, arenas, auditoriums, and other properties owned by the college.

Campus police Each college and university has a campus police office or a security office. You will need to locate this office once you arrive on campus so that, in case of emergency, you will be able to find it quickly. Campus security can assist you with problems ranging from physical danger to car trouble.

Carrel   This is a booth or small room located in the library of the college. You can reserve a carrel for professional use throughout the semester or on a weekly basis. Many times, the carrel is large enough for only one person. Never leave any personal belongings or important academic materials in the carrel because they may be stolen.

Case study   A case study is a story based on real-life events. Cases are written with open-ended conclusions and somewhat vague details to allow the reader to critically examine the story and develop logical solutions to resolve issues.

Catalog   The college catalog is a book issued to you at the beginning of your college career. This book is one of the most important tools that you will use in developing your schedule and completing your degree. The catalog is a legally binding document stating what your degree requirements are for the duration of your study. You will need to obtain and keep the catalog of the year in which you entered college.

Certificate   A certificate program is a series of courses, usually one year in length, designed to educate and train an individual in a certain area, such as welding, automotive repair, medical transcription, tool and die, early childhood, physical therapy assistance, and fashion merchandising. While these programs are certified and detailed, they are not degrees. Often, associate and bachelor's degrees are offered in these areas as well.

CLEP   The College Level Examination Program, or CLEP, is designed to allow students to "test" out of a course. CLEP exams are nationally normalized and often are more extensive than a course in the same area. If you CLEP a course, it means that you do not have to take the course in which you passed the CLEP exam. Some colleges have limits on the number of hours that can be earned by CLEP.

Club drugs   Club drugs are drugs taken at raves, parties, or dance clubs. Some of the most common club drugs are GHB (gamma hydroxybutyrate), Ecstasy, roofies, and meth.

Cognate   A cognate is a course (or set of courses) taken outside of your major. Some colleges call this a minor. For instance, if you are majoring in English, you may wish to take a cognate in history or drama. Cognates are usually chosen in a field close to the major. It would be unlikely for a student to major in English and take a cognate in pharmacy.

Communications   College curricula often state that a student must have nine hours of communications. This most commonly refers to English and speech (oral communication) courses. The mixture of these courses will usually be English 101 and 102 and Speech 101. This will vary from college to college.

Comprehensive exams   This term refers to exams that encompass materials from the entire course. If you are taking a history course and your instructor informs you that there will be a comprehensive exam, information from the first lecture through the last lecture will be included on the exam.

Continuing education   Almost every college in the nation offers courses in continuing education or community education. These courses are not offered for college credit, but Continuing Education Units are awarded in many cases. These courses are usually designed to meet the needs of specific businesses and industries or to provide courses of interest to the community. Continuing education courses range from small engine repair to flower arranging, from stained glass making to small business management.

Co-op   This term is used to refer to a relationship between business/industry and the educational institution. During a co-op, the student spends a semester in college and the next semester on the job. Some co-ops may be structured differently, but the general idea behind a co-op is to gain on-the-job experience while still in college.

Cooperative learning   In cooperative learning, learning, exploration, discovery, and results take place in a well-structured group. Cooperative learning teams are groups that work together on research, test preparation, project completion, and many other tasks.

Corequisite   A corequisite is a course that must be taken at the same time as another course. Many times, science courses carry a corequisite. If you are taking Biology 101, the lab course Biology 101L may be required as the corequisite.

Counseling   Most colleges have a counseling center on campus. Do not confuse counseling with advising. Trained counselors assist you with problems that might arise in your personal life, with your study skills, and with your career aspirations. Academic advisors are responsible for your academic progress. Some colleges do combine the two, but in many instances, the counselor and the advisor are two different people with two different job descriptions.

Course title   Every course offered at a college will have a course title. You may see something in your schedule of classes that reads: ENG 101, SPC 205, HIS 210, and so forth. Your college catalog will define what the abbreviations mean. ENG 101 usually stands for English 101, SPC could be the heading for speech, and HIS could mean history. Headings and course titles vary from college to college.

Credit   Credit is money or goods given to you on a reasonable amount of trust that you can and will repay the money or pay for the goods. Credit can come in several forms; credit cards and loans are the most common. Credit can be very dangerous to a person's future if he has too much credit or does not repay the credit in time.

Credit hour   A credit hour is the amount of credit offered for each class that you take. Usually, each class is worth three credit hours. Science courses, foreign languages, and some math courses are worth four credit hours because of required labs. If a class carries three credit hours, this usually means that the class meets for three hours per week. This formula may vary greatly in a summer session or mid-session.

Credit score   Your credit score is calculated by the amount of debt you have, your salary, your payment history, your length of residence in one place, and the number of inquires into your credit history, to name a few. Your credit score is used to determine if you will be extended future credit and the interest rate that you will be charged. A low score could mean that you cannot get credit or that you will pay a very high interest rate. Negative credit reports stay on your credit history for seven years.

Critical thinking Critical thinking is thinking that is purposeful, reasoned, and goal directed. It is a type of thinking used to solve problems, make associations, connect relationships, formulate inferences, make decisions, and detect faulty arguments and persuasion.

Curriculum The curriculum is the area of study in which you are engaged. It is a set of classes that you must take in order for a degree to be awarded.

Dean The word *dean* is not a name, but a title. A dean is usually the head of a division or area of study. Some colleges might have a Dean of Arts and Sciences, a Dean of Business, and a Dean of Mathematics. The dean is the policy maker and usually the business manager and final decision maker of an area of study. Deans usually report to vice presidents or provosts.

Dean's list The dean's list is a listing of students who have achieved at least a 3.5 (B+) on a 4.0 scale (these numbers are defined under GPA). This achievement may vary from college to college, but generally speaking, the dean's list is comprised of students in the top 5 percent of students in that college.

Default A default is when a person fails to repay a loan according to the terms provided in the original loan papers. A default on a Guaranteed Student Loan will result in the garnishment of wages and the inability to acquire a position with the government. Also, you will receive no federal or state income tax refunds until the loan is repaid. Further, a Guaranteed Student Loan cannot be written off under bankruptcy laws.

Degree When a student completes an approved course of study, she is awarded a degree. The title of the degree depends on the college, the number of credit hours in the program, and the field of study. A two-year degree is called an associate degree, and a four-year degree is called a bachelor's degree. If a student attends graduate school, she may receive a master's degree (approximately 2 to 3 years) and sometimes a doctorate degree (anywhere from 3 to 10 years). Some colleges even offer postdoctorate degrees.

Diploma A diploma is awarded when an approved course of study is completed. The diploma is not as detailed or comprehensive as an associate degree and usually consists of only 8 to 12 courses specific to a certain field.

Distance learning Distance learning is learning that takes place away from the campus. Distance learning or distance education is usually offered by a computerized platform such as Blackboard, WebCT, or Course Compass. Chat sessions and Internet assignments are common in distance learning.

Dropping When a student decides that he does not enjoy a class or will not be able to pass the class because of grades or absenteeism, he may elect to drop that class section. This means that the class will no longer appear on his schedule or be calculated in his GPA. Rules and regulations on dropping vary from college to college. All rules should be explained in the catalog.

Ecstasy Ecstasy, or "X," is a "club drug" that is very common at raves and dance parties. It produces a relaxed, euphoric state, which makes the user experience warmth, heightened emotions, and self-acceptance. It can cause severe depression and even death among some users. Ecstasy is illegal to use or possess.

Elective An elective is a course that a student chooses to take outside of her major field of study. It could be in an area of interest or an area that complements the chosen major. For example, an English major might choose an elective in the field of theatre or history because these fields complement each other. However, a student majoring in English might also elect to take a course in medical terminology because she is interested in that area.

Emeriti This Latin term is assigned to retired personnel of the college who have performed exemplary duties during their professional careers. For example, a college president who obtained new buildings, added curriculum programs, and increased the endowment might be named President Emeriti upon his or her retirement.

Ethnocentrism Ethnocentrism is the practice of thinking that one's ethnic group is superior to others.

Evening college The evening college program is designed to allow students who have full-time jobs to obtain a college degree by enrolling in classes that meet in the evening. Some colleges offer an entire degree program in the evening; others only offer some courses in the evening.

Faculty The faculty of a college is the body of professionals who teach, do research, and perform community service. Faculty members have prepared for many years to hold the responsibilities carried by this title. Many have been to school for 20 or more years to obtain the knowledge and skill necessary to train students in specific fields.

Fallacy A fallacy is a false notion. It is a statement based on false materials, invalid inferences, or incorrect reasoning.

Fees Fees refer to the amount of money charged by a college for specific items and services. Some fees may include tuition, meal plans, books, and health and activity fees. Fees vary from college to college and are usually printed in the catalog.

Financial aid If a student is awarded money from the college, the state, the federal government, private sources, or places of employment, this is referred to as financial aid. Financial aid can be awarded on the basis of either need or merit or both. Any grant, loan, or scholarship is formally called financial aid.

Fine arts Many people tend to think of fine arts as drawing or painting, but in actuality, the fine arts encompass a variety of artistic forms. Theatre, dance, architecture, drawing, painting, sculpture, and music are considered part of the fine arts. Some colleges also include literature in this category.

Foreign language Almost every college offers at least one course in foreign languages. Many colleges offer degrees in this area. For schools in America, foreign languages consist of Spanish, French, Russian, Latin, German, Portuguese, Swahili, Arabic, Japanese, Chinese, and Korean, to name a few.

Fraternities A fraternity is an organization of the Greek system in which a male student is a member. Many fraternities have their own housing complexes on campus. Induction for each is different. Honorary fraternities, such as Phi Kappa Phi, also exist. These are academic in nature and are open to males and females.

Freshman This is a term used by high schools and colleges. The term *first-year student* is also used. This term refers to a student in his first year of college. Traditionally, a freshman is someone who has not yet completed 30 semester hours of college-level work.

GHB, or gamma hydroxybutyrate GHB is a club drug that comes most often in an odorless, liquid form but can also come as a powdery substance. At lower doses, GHB has a euphoric effect and can make the user feel relaxed, happy, and sociable. Higher doses can lead to dizziness, sleepiness, vomiting, spasms, and loss of consciousness. GHB and alcohol used together can be deadly.

GPA, or grade point average The grade point average is the numerical grading system used by almost every college in the nation. GPAs determine if a student is eligible for continued enrollment, financial aid, or honors. Most colleges operate under a 4.0 system. This means that all A's earned are worth 4 quality points; B's, 3 points; C's, 2 points; D's, 1 point; and F's, 0 points. To calculate a GPA, multiply the number of quality points by the number of credit hours carried by the course and then divide by the total number of hours carried. For example: If a student is taking English 101, Speech 101, History 201, and Psychology 101, these courses usually carry 3 credit hours each. If a student made all A's, she would have a GPA of 4.0. If the student made all B's, she would have a 3.0. However, if she had a variety of grades, the GPA would be calculated as follows:

	Grade	Credit		Q.Points		Total Points
ENG 101	A	3 hours	×	4	=	12 points
SPC 101	C	3 hours	×	2	=	6 points
HIS 201	B	3 hours	×	3	=	9 points
PSY 101	D	3 hours	×	1	=	3 points

30 points divided by 12 hours would equal a GPA of 2.5 (or C+ average).

Grace period A grace period is usually 10 days after the due date of a loan payment. For example: If your car payment is due on the first of the month, many companies will give you a 10 day grace period (until the 11th) to pay the bill before they report your delinquent payment to a credit scoring company.

Graduate teaching assistant You may encounter a "teaching assistant" as a freshman or sophomore. In some larger colleges and universities, students working toward master's and doctorate degrees teach undergraduate, lower-level classes under the direction of a major professor in the department.

Grant A grant is usually money that goes toward tuition and books that does not have to be repaid. Grants are most often awarded by state and federal governments.

Hepatitis Hepatitis has three forms: A, B, and C. Hepatitis A comes from drinking contaminated water. Hepatitis B is more prevalent than HIV and can be transmitted sexually, through unsterile needles, and through unsterile tattoo equipment. Left untreated, hepatitis B can cause serious liver damage. Hepatitis C develops into a chronic condition in over 85 percent of the people who have it. Hepatitis C is the leading cause of liver transplants. Hepatitis B and C can be transmitted by sharing toothbrushes, nail clippers, or any item contaminated with blood. Hepatitis B and C have no recognizable signs or symptoms. Some people, however, do get flulike symptoms, loss of appetite, nausea, vomiting, or fever.

Higher education This term is used to describe any level of education beyond high school. All colleges are called institutions of higher education.

Homophobia Homophobia is the fear of homosexuals or homosexuality.

Honor code Many colleges operate under an honor code. This system demands that students perform all work without cheating, plagiarism, or any other dishonest actions. In many cases, a student can be removed from the institution for breaking the honor code. In other cases, if students do not turn in fellow students who they know have broken the code, they, too, can be removed from the institution.

Honors Academic honors are based on the GPA of a student. Each college usually has many academic honors, including the dean's list, the president's list, and departmental honors. The three highest honors awarded are Summa Cum Laude, Magna Cum Laude, and Cum Laude. These are awarded at graduation for students who have maintained a GPA of 3.5 or better. The GPA requirement for these honors varies from college to college. Usually, they are awarded as follows:

    3.5 to 3.7 Cum Laude

    3.7 to 3.9 Magna Cum Laude

    4.0 Summa Cum Laude

Honors college The honors college is usually a degree or a set of classes offered for students who performed exceptionally well in high school.

Humanities The humanities are sometimes as misunderstood as the fine arts. Courses in the humanities include history, philosophy, religion, and cultural studies; some colleges also include literature, government, and foreign languages. The college catalog will define what your college has designated as humanities.

Identification cards An identification card is essential for any college student. Some colleges issue them free, while some charge a small fee. The ID card allows the student to use the college library, participate in activities, use physical fitness facilities, and many times attend college events for free. They also come in handy in the community. Movie theatres, museums, zoos, and other cultural events usually charge less or nothing if a student has an ID. The card will also allow the student to use most area library facilities with special privileges. ID cards are usually validated each semester.

Identity theft Identity theft is when another person assumes your identity and uses your credit, your name, and your Social Security number. Identity theft can't always be prevented, but to reduce the risk, always guard your credit cards, your address history, and most importantly, your Social Security number and driver's license number.

Independent study Many colleges offer courses through independent study, meaning that no formal classes and no classroom teacher are involved. The student works independently to complete the course under the general guidelines of a department and with the assistance of an instructor. Many colleges require that a student maintain a minimum GPA before enrolling in independent study classes.

Internship An internship involves working in a business or industry to gain experience in one's field of interest. Many colleges require internships for graduation.

Journal Many classes, such as English, freshman orientation, literature, history and psychology, require students to keep a journal of thoughts, opinions, research, and class discussions. Many times, the journal is a communication link between the students and their professors.

Junior The term refers to a student who is enrolled in his third year of college or a student who has completed at least 60 credit hours of study.

Late fee A late fee is an "administrative" charge that lenders assess if a loan payment is late.

Learning style A learning style is the way an individual learns best. Three learning styles exist: visual, auditory, and tactile. Visual means that one learns best by seeing, auditory means that one learns best by hearing, and tactile means that one learns best by touching.

Lecture A lecture is the "lesson" given by an instructor in a class. The term usually refers to the style in which material is presented. Some instructors have group discussions, peer tutoring, or multimedia presentations. The lecture format means that the professor presents most of the information.

Liberal arts The liberal arts consist of a series of courses that go beyond training for a certain vocation or occupation. For instance, a student at a liberal arts college might be majoring in biology, but he will also have to take courses in fine arts, history, social sciences, math, "hard" sciences, and other related courses. The liberal arts curriculum ensures that the student has been exposed to a variety of information and cultural experiences.

Load A load refers to the amount of credit or the number of classes that a student is taking. The normal "load" for a student is between 15 and 18 hours, or five to six classes. For most colleges, 12 hours is considered a full-time load, but a student can take up to 18 or 21 hours for the same amount of tuition.

Major A major is the intended field of study for a student. The major simply refers to the amount of work completed in one field; in other words, the majority of courses have been in one related field, such as English, engineering, medicine, nursing, art, history, or political science. A student is usually required to declare a major by the end of the sophomore (or second) year.

Meal plan A meal plan is usually bought at the beginning of the semester and allows a student to eat a variety of meals by using a computer card or punch system. Meal plans can be purchased for three meals a day, breakfast only, lunch only, or any combination of meals.

Mentor A mentor is someone whom a student can call on to help her through troubled times, assist her in decision making, and give advice. Mentors can be teachers, staff members, fellow outstanding classmates, or higher-level students. Mentors seldom volunteer to be a mentor; they usually fall into the role of mentoring because they are easy to talk with, knowledgeable about the college and the community, and willing to lend a helping hand. A student may, however, be assigned a mentor when she arrives on campus.

Methamphetamine Crystal meth, as it is commonly called, is an illegal drug sold in pills, capsules, powder, or rock forms. It stimulates the central nervous system and breaks down the user's inhibitions. It can cause memory loss, aggression, violence, and psychotic behavior.

Minor The minor of a student is the set of courses that he or she takes that usually complements the major. The minor commonly consists of six to eight courses in a specific field. If a student is majoring in engineering, she might minor in math or electronics, something that would assist her in the workplace.

Multiple intelligences Multiple intelligences are the eight intelligences with which we are born. Howard Gardner, who believes that we all have one of eight intelligences as our primary strength, introduced the theory. The intelligences include Music/Rhythm, Logic/Math, Visual/Spatial, Naturalistic, Interpersonal, Intrapersonal, Verbal/Linguistic, and Body/Kinesthetic.

Natural and physical sciences The natural and physical sciences refer to a select group of courses from biology, chemistry, physical science, physics, anatomy, zoology, botany, geology, genetics, microbiology, physiology, and astronomy.

Networking Networking refers to meeting people who can help you (or whom you can help) find careers, meet other people, make connections, and "get ahead."

Online classes Used in conjunction with distance learning or distance education, online classes use the Internet as a means of delivery, instead of a traditional classroom.

Orientation Every student is requested, and many are required, to attend an orientation session. This is one of the most important steps that a student can take when beginning college. Important information and details concerning individual colleges and their rules and regulations will be discussed.

Plagiarism This term refers to the act of using someone's words or works as your own without citing the original author. Penalties for plagiarism vary from college to college, but most institutions have strict guidelines for dealing with students who plagiarize. Some institutions force the student to withdraw from the institution. Your student handbook should list the penalties for plagiarism.

Prefix A prefix is a code used by the Office of the Registrar to designate a certain area of study. The prefix for English is usually ENG; for Religion, REL; for Theatre, THE; for History, HIS; and so forth. Prefix lettering varies from college to college.

Preprofessional programs Preprofessional programs usually refer to majors that require advanced study to the master's or doctoral level to be able to practice in the field. Such programs include, but are not limited to, law, medicine, dentistry, psychiatry, nursing, veterinary studies, and theology.

Prerequisite A prerequisite is a course that must be taken before another course. For example, most colleges require that English 101 and 102 (Composition I and II) be completed before any literature course is taken. Therefore, English 101 and 102 are prerequisites to literature. Prerequisites are always spelled out in the college catalog.

President A college president is the visionary leader of an institution. She is usually hired by the Board of Trustees of a college. Her primary responsibilities involve financial planning, fundraising, community relations, and the academic integrity of the curriculum. Every employee at the college is responsible to the president.

Probation Many times, a student who has below a 2.0 in any given semester or quarter will be placed on academic probation for one semester. If that student continues to perform below 2.0, suspension may be in order. The rules for probation and suspension must be displayed in the college catalog.

Professor Many people believe that all teachers on the college level are professors. This is not true. A full professor is someone who may have been in the profession for a long time and someone who usually holds a doctoral degree. The system of promotion among college teachers is as follows:

adjunct instructor
instructor
lecturer
assistant professor
associate professor
full professor (professor).

Protease inhibitors Protease inhibitors are a series, or "cocktail," of drugs used to fight HIV/AIDS and slow the destruction of the immune system. They have been instrumental in extending the lives of people living with HIV and AIDS. However, a new strain of HIV has arisen that is immune to the protease inhibitors presently used.

Provost The provost is the primary policy maker at the college with regard to academic standards. He usually reports directly to the president. Many colleges will not have a provost but will have a vice president for academic affairs or a dean of instruction.

Racism Racism occurs when a person or group of people believes that their race is superior to another race.

Readmit When a student has "stopped-out" for a semester or two, he will usually have to be readmitted to the college. This term does not apply to a student who elects not to attend summer sessions. Usually, no application fee is required for a readmit student. He does not lose his previously earned academic credit unless that credit carries a time limit. For example, some courses in psychology carry a 5- or 10-year limit, meaning that if a degree is not awarded within that time, the course must be retaken.

Registrar The registrar has one of the most difficult jobs on any college campus. She is responsible for all student academic records. The registrar is also responsible for entering all grades and all drops and adds, printing the schedule, and verifying all candidates for graduation. The Office of the Registrar is sometimes referred to as the Records Office.

Residence hall A residence hall is a single-sex or co-educational facility on campus where students live. Many new students choose to live on campus because residence halls are conveniently located. They are also a good way to meet new friends and become involved in extracurricular activities. The college usually provides a full-time supervisor for each hall and a director of student housing. Each hall usually elects a student representative to be on the student council.

Residency requirement Many colleges have a residency requirement, meaning that a certain number of hours must be earned at the "home" institution. For many two-year colleges, at least 50 percent of the credit used for graduation must be earned at the home college. For four-year colleges, many requirements state that the last 30 hours must be earned at the home college. All residence requirements are spelled out in the college catalog.

Room and board If a student is going to live on campus, many times the fee charged for this service will be called "room and board." This basically means a place to stay and food to eat. Many students may opt to buy a meal plan along with their dorm room. These issues are usually discussed during orientation.

Root problem The root problem is the main issue, the core of the situation at hand. Most troublesome situations have several problems, but usually one major "root" problem exists that causes all of the other problems.

Scholar A scholar is usually someone who has performed exceptionally in a certain field of study.

Section code At many larger colleges, many sections of the same course are offered. The section code tells the computer and the registrar which hour and instructor the student will be in a particular class. A typical schedule may look something like this:

English 101	01	MWF	8:00–8:50	Smith
English 101	02	MWF	8:00–8:50	Jones
English 101	03	T TH	8:00–9:15	McGee

The numbers 01, 02, and 03 refer to the section of English in which the student enrolls.

Senior The term *senior* is used for students in their last year of study for a bachelor's degree. The student must have completed at least 90 credit hours to be a senior.

Sexism Sexism is discrimination based on sex and social roles.

Sexual harassment Sexual harassment is defined as any type of advance that is unwanted by the receiver, including touching another person, taunting a person verbally, denying promotions based on forced relationships, and so forth.

Social sciences The social sciences are courses that involve the study or interface with society and people. Social Science courses may include, but are not limited to, psychology, sociology, anthropology, political science, geography, economics, and international studies.

Sophomore The term *sophomore* refers to students who are in their second year of study for a bachelor's degree. A student must have completed at least 30 credit hours to be a sophomore.

Sororities Sororities are organizations of the Greek system in which females are members. Many sororities have on-campus housing complexes. Initiation into a sorority differs from organization to organization and campus to campus.

Staff Personnel in the college setting are usually divided into three categories: administration, staff, and faculty. The staff is responsible for the day-to-day workings of the college. Usually people in admissions, financial aid, the bookstore, housing, student activities and personnel, and so forth hold staff titles. The people heading these departments are usually in administration.

Student Government Association (SGA) This is one of the most powerful and visible organizations on the college campus. Usually, the SGA comprises students from each of the four undergraduate classes. Annual elections are held to appoint officers. As the "student voice" on campus, the SGA represents the entire student body before the college administration.

Student loan Unlike a grant, a student loan must be repaid. The loans are usually at a much lower rate of interest than a bank loan. For most student loans, the payment schedule does not begin until six months after graduation. This allows the graduate to find a job and become secure in her chosen profession. If a student decides to return to school, she can get the loan deferred, with additional interest, until she completes a graduate degree.

Suspension Suspension may occur for a variety of reasons, but most institutions suspend students for academic reasons. While GPA requirements vary from college to college, usually a student is suspended when his grade point average falls below a 1.5 for two consecutive semesters. The college catalog contains the rules regarding suspension.

Syllabus In high school, you may have been given a class outline, but in college, you are given a syllabus. This is a legally binding contract between the student and the professor. This document contains the attendance policy, the grading scale, the required text, the professor's office hours and phone number(s), and important information regarding the course. Most professors also include the class operational calendar as a part of the syllabus. This is one of the most important documents that you will be issued in a class. You should take it to class with you daily and keep it at least until the semester is over.

Tenure You may hear someone call a college teacher a "tenured professor." This usually means that the professor has been with the college for many years and has been awarded tenure due to his successful efforts in research, publication of books and articles, and community service. Usually, tenure ensures the professor lifelong employment.

TOEFL TOEFL is an acronym for the Test of English as a Foreign Language. This test is used to certify that international students have the English skills needed to succeed at the institution or to become a teaching assistant. Some colleges allow international students to use TOEFL to satisfy English as their foreign language requirement.

Tolerance Tolerance is the ability to recognize and respect the opinions, practices, religions, race, sex, sexual orientation, ethnicity, and age of other people.

Transcript A transcript is a formal record of all work attempted and completed at a college. If a student attends more than one college, he will have a transcript for each college. Many colleges have a policy in which all classes, completed or not, remain on the transcript. Some colleges allow D's and F's to be removed if the student repeats the course with a better grade. Many colleges, however, leave the old grade and continue to count the D or F in the GPA. Rules regarding transcripts vary from college to college. Many employers now require that a prospective employee furnish a transcript from college.

Transfer This term may refer to course work or to a student. If a student enrolls in one college and then wants to go to another, she is classified as a transfer student. The course work completed is called *transfer work*. Many colleges have rules regarding the number of credit hours that may be transferred from one college to another. Most colleges will not accept credit from another college if the grade on the course is below a C.

Transient   A transient student is someone who is attending another college to take one or two courses. If a student comes home for the summer and wants to enroll in a college near his home and maintain himself as a student at his chosen college, he is a transient student.

Transitional studies   Many colleges have an open admission policy, meaning that the door is open to any student. In these cases, the college usually runs a transitional studies program to assist the student in reaching her educational goal. If a student has not performed well in English, math, or reading, she may be required to attend a transitional studies class to upgrade basic skills in certain areas.

Veteran's Affairs   Many colleges have an Office of Veteran's Affairs to assist those students who have served in the military. Many times, a college will accept credit earned by a veteran while in the service. Most of the time, a veteran's financial packages will differ because of the GI Bill.

Vice president   Many colleges have several vice presidents who serve under the president. They are senior-level administrators who assist with the daily operations of the college. Most colleges have vice presidents of academic affairs, financial affairs, and student affairs, to name a few.

Volumes   This term is used by most libraries in the nation. A volume is a book or a piece of nonprinted material used to assist the student in his studies. You may read that a college library has 70,000 volumes. This means that it has 70,000 books and other pieces of media. Many colleges have volumes that range in the millions.

WebCT   WebCT is a delivery platform for distance education courses taken over the web.

Who's Who   This is a shortened title for *Who's Who in American Colleges and Universities,* a nationally recognized grouping. Students are nominated by the college because of their academic standing and their achievements in cocurricular activities and community service.

Women's Studies   Some colleges offer majors and minors in Women's Studies. The curriculum is centered around the major contributions of women to art, literature, medicine, history, law, architecture, and sciences.

References

ACT, Inc. *National Dropout Rates, Freshman to Sophomore Years by Type of Institution.* Iowa City, IA: ACT, 2000.

Adler, R., Rosenfeld, L., and Towne, N. *Interplay. The Process of Interpersonal Communication*, 2nd ed. New York: Holt, Rinehart and Winston, 2001.

Advanced Public Speaking Institute. "Public speaking: Why use humor?" Virginia Beach, VA: Author, www.public-speaking.org/public-speaking-humor-article.htm.

American College Testing Program. *National Drop Out Rates.* ACT Institutional Data File, Iowa City, 1995.

Amnesty International. Death penalty information, www.web.amnesty.org.

Anderson, D. *The Death Penalty—A Defence.* Sweden, 1998. Translated into English in 2001 at http://w1.155.telia.com/~u1550919/ny_sida_1.htm.

Armstrong, T. *Multiple Intelligences in the Classroom.* Alexandria, VA: Association for Supervision and Curriculum Development, 1994.

Astin, A. *Achieving Educational Excellence.* San Francisco: Jossey-Bass, 1985.

Bach, D. *The Finish Rich Notebook.* New York: Broadway Books, 2003.

Barnes & Noble and the Anti-Defamation League. *Close the Book on Hate: 101 Ways to Combat Prejudice*, 2000. Available online at www.adl.org/prejudice/closethebook.pdf.

Beebe, S. A., and Beebe, S. J. *Interpersonal Communication: Relating to Others,* 3rd ed. Boston: Allyn & Bacon, 2002.

Benson, H., and Stuart, E. *The Wellness Book.* New York: Fireside, 1992.

Benson, H., and Stuart, E. *The Wellness Book: The Comprehensive Guide to Maintaining Health and Treating Stress-Related Illness.* New York: Birch Lane Press, 1992.

Benson, H., and Stuart, Eileen. *Wellness Encyclopedia.* Boston: Houghton Mifflin, 1991.

Benson, H. *The Relaxation Response.* New York: Caral Publishing Group, 1992.

Berenblatt, M., and Berenblatt, A. *Make an Appointment with Yourself: Simple Steps to Positive Self-Esteem.* Deerfield Beach, FL: Health Communication, 1994.

Beyer, B. *Developing a Thinking Skills Program.* Boston: Allyn and Bacon, 1998.

Boldt, L. *How to Be, Do, or Have Anything.* Berkeley, CA: Ten Speed Press, 2001.

Bosak, J. *Fallacies.* Dubuque, IA: Educulture Publishers, 1976.

Boyle, M., and Zyla, G. *Personal Nutrition.* St. Paul, MN: West Publishing, 1992.

Bozzi, V. "A Healthy Dose of Religion," *Psychology Today,* November, 1988.

Brightman, H. Georgia State University Master Teacher Program: On Learning Styles, www.gsu.edu/~dschjb/wwwmbti.html.

Bucher, R. D. *Diversity Consciousness: Opening Our Minds to People, Cultures, and Opportunities.* Upper Saddle River, NJ: Prentice Hall, 2000.

Buscaglia, L. *Living, Loving, and Learning.* New York: Ballantine, 1982.

Business and Legal Reports, Inc. *Staying Safe on Campus.* Madison, CT: Author, 1995.

Cameron, J. *The Artist's Way: A Spiritual Path to Higher Creativity.* New York: Penguin Putnam, 1992.

Cardinal, F. "Sleep is important when stress and anxiety increase." *The National Sleep Foundation,* April 10, 2003.

Cetron, F. "What students must know to succeed in the 21st century." *The Futurist,* July–Aug 1996, v. 30, No. 4, p. 7.

Checkley, K. "The first seven . . . and the eighth." *Educational Leadership, 55,* no. 1, September 1997.

Chickering, A., and Schlossberg, N. *Getting the Most out of College.* Boston: Allyn and Bacon, 1995.

Chopra, D. *The Seven Spiritual Laws of Success.* San Rafael, CA: New World Library, 1994.

Christian, J., and Greger, J. *Nutrition for Living.* Redwood City, CA: Benjamin/Cummings Publishing, 1994.

Clegg, R. "The color of death." *National Review Online,* June 11, 2001, www.nationalreview.com/contributors/clegg061101.shtml.

Cloud, J. "The pioneer Harvey Milk." Accessed at www.time.com.

CNN Money. "More credit late fees paid." May 12, 2002. Accessed at http://money.cnn.com/2002/05/21/pf/banking/cardfees/.

Cohen, L. *Conducting Research on the Internet.* University of Albany Libraries, 1996a, www.albany.edu.

Cohen, L. *Evaluating Internet Resources.* University of Albany Libraries, 1996b, www.albany.edu.

Cojonet (City of Jacksonville, FL). "Consumer Affairs gets new tough law on car title businesses." Accessed at www.coj.net/Departments/Regulatory+and+Environmental+Services/Consumer+Affairs/TITLE+LOANS.htm.

Coldewey, J., and Streitberger, W. *Drama, Classical to Contemporary,* rev. ed. Upper Saddle River, NJ: Prentice Hall, 2001.

"Commonly Abused Drugs." National Institute on Drug Abuse. Accessed at www.nida.nih.gov/DrugsofAbuse.html.

Cooper, A. *Time Management for Unmanageable People.* New York: Bantam Books, 1993.

Cooper, M. "Alcohol use and risky sexual behavior among college students and youth." *Journal of Studies on Alcohol, 63*(2), 2002, p. S101.

Daly, J., and Engleberg, I. *Presentations in Everyday Life: Strategies for Effective Speaking.* Boston: Houghton Mifflin, 2002.

"Dan White." Accessed at www.findagrave.com/php/famous.php?page=name&firstName=Dan&lastName=White.

Daniels, P., and Bright, W. *The World's Writing Systems.* England: Oxford University Press, 1996.

Donatelle, R., and Davis, L. *Health: The Basics.* Englewood Cliffs, NJ: Prentice Hall, 2002.

Eddlem, T. "Ten anti-death penalty fallacies." *The New American, 18*(3), June 3, 2002.

Eisenberg, D. "The coming job boom." *Time Online Edition,* April 29, 2002, www.time.com/time/business/article/0,8599,233967,00.html.

Ellis, D., Lankowitz, S., Stupka, D., and Toft, D. *Career Planning.* Rapid City, SD: College Survival, Inc., 1990.

Elrich, M. "The Stereotype Within." *Educational Leadership,* April 1994, p. 12.

Equifax.com. "Glossary of terms." Accessed at www.econsumer.equifax.com/consumer/forward.ehtml?forward=credu_glossaryterms.

Equifax.com. "Identity theft and fraud." Accessed at www.econsumer.equifax.com/consumer/forward.ehtml?forward=idtheft_howitstrikes.

Equifax.com. "Teaching students about money and credit." Accessed at www.equifax.com/CoolOnCredit/parent1.html.

Facione, P. *Critical Thinking: What It Is and Why It Counts.* Santa Clara: California University Press, 1998.

Freshman Survey Data Report. Cooperative Institutional Research Program Sponsored by the Higher Education Research Institute (HERI). University of California, Los Angeles, 1999.

Fulghum, R. *All I Really Need to Know, I Learned in Kindergarten.* New York: Ivy Books, 1988.

Gardenswartz, L., and Rowe, A. *Managing Diversity: A Complete Desk Reference and Planning Guide.* New York: Irwin/Pfeiffer, 1993.

Gardner, H. *Frames of Mind: The Theory of Multiple Intelligences.* New York: Basic Books, 1983.

Gardner, H. "Reflections on multiple intelligences: myths and messages." *Phi Delta Kappan, 77,* no. 3, November, 1995, p. 200.

Gardner, J., and Jewler, J. *Your College Experience.* Belmont, CA: Wadsworth, 2000.

Gay, Lesbian and Straight Education Network. "Just the facts." New York: GLSE, 2000. Synopsis found online at http://msn.planetout.com/people/teens/features/2000/08/facts.html.

Gonyea, J. C. "Discover the work you were born to do." MSN.com Careers, 2002, http://editorial.careers.msn.com/articles/born.

Grilly, D. *Drugs and Human Behavior.* Boston: Allyn and Bacon, 1994.

Gunthrie, H., and Picciano, M. *Human Nutrition.* Salem, MA: Mosby, 1995.

Hales, D. *Your Health.* Redwood City, CA: Benjamin/Cummings Publishing, 1991.

Haney, D. "New AIDS drugs bring optimism." *The Las Vegas Review Journal,* February 12, 2003.

Hanna, S. L. *Person to Person.* Upper Saddle River, NJ: Prentice Hall, 2003.

Hickman, R., and Quinley, J. *A Synthesis of Local, State, and National Studies in Workforce Education and Training.* Washington, DC: The American Association of Community Colleges, 1997.

Hidden Menace: Drowsy Drivers, www.sleepdisorders.about.com/library/weekly/aa062902a.htm.

Jerome, R., and Grout, P. "Cheat wave." *People Magazine,* June 17, 2002, p. 84.

Kanar, C. *The Confident Reader.* New York: Houghton Mifflin, 2000.

Kirby, D. "The worst is yet to come." *The Advocate,* January 19, 1999, p. 57.

Kleiman, C. *The 100 Best Jobs for the 90's and Beyond.* New York: Berkley Books, 1992.

Konowalow, S. *Cornerstones for Money Management.* Upper Saddle River, NJ: Prentice Hall, 1997.

Konowalow, S. *Planning Your Future: Keys to Financial Freedom.* Columbus, OH: Prentice Hall, 2003.

Lecky, P. *Self-Consistency: A Theory of Personality.* Garden City, NY: Anchor, 1951.

Leinwood, D. Ecstasy–Viagra mix alarms doctors. *USA Today,* Sept. 23, 2002.

Lieberman, B. "1 in 5 new HIV cases is a drug-resistant strain, study finds." *The San Diego Tribune,* August 8, 2002.

Maker, J., and Lenier, M. *College Reading,* 5th ed. Belmont, CA: Thompson Learning, 2000.

Managing and Resolving Conflict, http://hr2.hr.arizona.edu/06_jcl/jobdesc/groundrules.htm.

Manisses Communications Group. *Alcoholism & Drug Abuse Weekly,* 13(36), September 2001, p. 7.

Mass, J. cited in Kates, W. "America is not getting enough sleep." *The San Francisco Chronicle,* March 30, 1990, p. B3.

McGraw, P. C. *Life Strategies Workbook.* New York: Hyperion, 2000.

McKay, M., and Fanning, P. *Self-Esteem.* Oakland, CA: New Harbinger, 2000.

National Association of College Employers. "Top ten personal qualities employers seek." *Job Outlook,* NACE, 2000.

National Foundation for Credit Counseling. "National Foundation for Credit Counseling announces study results on the impact of credit counseling on consumer credit and debt payment behavior." Press release, March 21, 2002. Accessed at www.nfcc.org/newsroom/shownews.Cfm?newsid=257.

Nelson, D., and Low, G. *Emotional Intelligence: Achieving Academic and Career Excellence.* Upper Saddle River, NJ: Prentice Hall, 2003.

Nevid, J., Fichner-Rathus, L., and Rathus, S. *Human Sexuality in a World of Diversity.* Boston: Allyn and Bacon, 1995.

Okula, S. "Protect yourself from identity theft." Accessed at http://moneycentral.msn.com/articles/banking/credit/1342.asp.

Ormondroyd, J., Engle, M., and Cosgrave, T. *How to Critically Analyze Information Sources.* Cornell University Libraries, 2001, www.library.cornell.edu.

Ormrod, J. E. *Educational Psychology: Developing Learners.* Upper Saddle River, NJ: Prentice Hall, 2003.

Pauk, W. *How to Study in College,* 7th ed. New York: Houghton Mifflin, 2001.

Paul, R. *What Every Person Needs to Survive in a Rapidly Changing World.* Santa Rosa, CA: The Foundation for Critical Thinking, 1992.

Popenoe, D. *Sociology,* 9th ed. Englewood Cliffs, NJ: Prentice Hall, 1993.

Powell, E. *Sex on Your Terms.* Boston: Allyn and Bacon, 1996.

Radelet, M. "Post-Furman botched executions." Accessed at www.deathpenaltyinfo.org/botched.html.

Rathus, S., and Fichner-Rathus, L. *Making the Most out of College.* Englewood Cliffs, NJ: Prentice Hall, 1994.

Rathus, S., Nevid, J., and Fichner-Rathus, L. *Essentials of Human Sexuality.* Boston: Allyn and Bacon, 1998.

"Retention Rates by Institutional Type," Higher Education Research Institute, UCLA, Los Angeles, 1989.

Rogers, C. *On Becoming Partners: Marriage and Its Alternatives.* New York: Delacorte Press, 1972.

Romas, J., and Sharma, M. *Practical Stress Management.* Boston: Allyn and Bacon, 1995.

Rooney, M. "Freshmen show rising political awareness and changing social views." *The Chronicle of Higher Education,* January 31, 2003.

Salmela-Aro, K., and Nurmi, J.E. "Uncertainty and confidence in interpersonal projects. Consequences for social relationships and well-being." *Journal of Social and Personal Relationships,* 13(1), 1996, pp. 109–122.

Schacter, D. *The Seven Sins of Memory: How the Mind Forgets and Remembers.* New York: Houghton Mifflin, 2001.

Sciolino, E. "World drug crop up sharply in 1989 despite U.S. effort." *New York Times,* March 2, 1990.

Seyler, D. *Steps to College Reading,* 2nd ed. Boston: Allyn & Bacon, 2001.

Shaffer, C., and Amundsen, K. *Creating Community Anywhere.* Los Angeles: Jeremy P. Tarcher Publishing, 1994.

Sherfield, R., Montgomery, R., and Moody, P. *Capstone: Succeeding Beyond College.* Upper Saddle River, NJ: Prentice Hall, 2001.

Sherfield, R. *The Everything Self-Esteem Book.* Avon, MA: Adams Media, 2004.

Silver, H., Strong, R., and Perini, M. "Integrating learning styles and multiple intelligences." *Educational Leadership, 55,* no. 1, September, 1997, p. 22.

Smith, B. *Breaking Through: College Reading,* 6th ed. Upper Saddle River, NJ: Pearson Education, 2001.

Southern Poverty Law Center. *Ten Ways to Fight Hate.* Montgomery, AL: Author, 2000.

Syemore, R., and O'Connell, D. "Did you know?" *Chatelaine,* 73(8), August 2000, p. 30.

"Ten credit card management tips." Accessed at www.aol1.bankrate.com/AOL/news/cc/20021218a.asp.

Texas A&M University. "Improve your memory." Accessed at www.scs.tamu.edu/selfhelp/elibrary/memory.asp.

The Chronicle of Higher Education, 49(1), August 30, 2002.

The Motley Fool. "How to get out of debt." Accessed at www.fool.com/seminars/sp/index.htm?sid=0001&lid=000&ref=.

The World Almanac and Book of Facts, 2002. New York: World Almanac Books, 2003.

Tieger, P., and Barron-Tieger, B. *Do What You Are: Discover the Perfect Career for You Through the Secrets of Personality Type,* 3rd ed. Boston: Little, Brown, and Company, 2001.

Uncle Donald's Castro Street. "Dan White: He got away with murder." Accessed at http://thecastro.net/milk/whitepage.html.

United States Department of Commerce. *2000 U.S. Census.* Washington, DC: U.S. Government Printing Office, 2001.

U.S. Bank. *Paying for College: A Guide to Financial Aid.* Minneapolis, MN: Author, 2002.

Warner, J. "Celebratory drinking culture on campus: Dangerous drinking style popular among college students." *Parenting and Pregnancy,* November 5, 2002.

Warnick, B., and Inch, E. *Critical Thinking and Communication—The Use of Reason in Argument.* New York: Macmillan, 1994.

Watson, N. "Generation wrecked." *Fortune,* October 14, 2002, pp. 183–190.

Wechsler, H., and Wuethrich, B. *Dying to Drink: Confronting Binge Drinking on College Campuses.* New York: Rodale Press, 2002.

Werner, R. *Understanding.* Newport, RI: TED Conferences, 1999.

Whitfield, C. *Healing the Child Within.* Deerfield Beach, FL: Health Communication, 1987.

Woolfolk, A. *Educational Psychology,* 8th ed. Boston: Allyn and Bacon, 2001.

Wurman, R. *Understanding.* New York: Donnelley & Sons, 1999.

Yale Study of Graduating Seniors. Yale University, New Haven, CT, 1953.

Young, J. "Homework? What homework?" *The Chronicle of Higher Education,* December 6, 2003.

Zarefsky, D. *Public Speaking: Strategies for Success,* 3rd ed. Boston: Pearson/Allyn & Bacon, 2001.

Zimring, F. *Capital Punishment and the American Agenda.* Cambridge, MA: Cambridge University Press, 1987.

Index

Abbreviations, note taking and, 231
Abstinence, 428
Academic:
    advisor, 77–78
    freedom, 68
    integrity, 296–298
    misconduct, 297–298
    services, 70–74
Acquaintance rape, 383
Acronyms, 266
Action steps, 44, 47, 48
Activities, college, 73
Ad baculum argument, 324
Ad hominem argument, 324
Ad populum argument, 324
Ad verecundiam argument, 324
Adler, Ronald, 209
Adversity, 39–40
Advisor, 77–78, 89
    career choice and, 453
Affixes, 144–145
Alcohol, 52, 420, 421, 423–424
Alcoholism, 52
Alternatives, developing/evaluating, 321
American Psychological Association (APA), 359
Analyzing, note taking and, 232
Anger, 19
Anxiety:
    reducing speech, 363–364
    test, 284–287, 296
Appeal to tradition, 324
Arguments:
    fallacious, 324–326
    seeking truth in, 323–326
Assessment:
    conflict management, 389–390
    of learning styles, 183–185
    of memory, 255, 256
    of stress, 418–419
    of test anxiety, 285
    personality, 186–188
    test taking, *see* Test taking
Assigning, listening and, 208
Assignments, 15
Attendance, 16
Attitude, 17, 23, 36–37
    stress and, 418
Audience:
    analysis of, 343, 345–346
    demographics, 345
Audiovisual aids, 343, 361–362
Auditory learning style, 185

Baliszewski, Robin, 148
Bandwagon argument, 324
Bauer, Andre, 82
Belonging, 51
Best, building on your, 7, 35, 39, 65, 70, 122, 137, 160, 175, 190, 205, 227, 251, 267, 283, 296, 309, 326, 339, 375, 388, 409, 416, 441, 457
Bhalla, Deepa, 330–331
Bicknell, Rebekah, 242–243
Birth control, 425, 428
Blood pressure, 414
Bloom, Benjamin, 160–164
Bloom's Taxonomy, 160–164, 261
Body:
    and food, 415–416
    cycles, 111–112
    its effect on wellness, 414–416
Body/kinesthetic intelligence, 181, 182
Bowser, Jr., Oscar, 300–301
Brainstorming, 268
Brain teasers, 316–317
Budgeting, 118–120

Caffeine, 421
Cameron, Julia, 326
Campus safety, 72, 87–88
Car title loans, 126
Cardiovascular fitness, 414
Career (*see also* Career choice):
    center, 453
    decision making, 453–454
    fastest growing occupations, 446
    geographical location and, 449
    industry growth and, 446
    need for flexibility in, 443
    planning, 446–454
    self-study, 447–452
    vs. series of jobs, 447
Career choice (*see also* Career):
    interests and, 448
    mentors and, 455–457
    networking and, 454
    personality type and, 448
    salary and, 449
    skills and, 451
    values and, 451
Catalog, college, 77
Cause–effect organization, 350
Change, 3–29
    attitudes that hinder, 20
    blueprints for, 25, 55, 91, 127, 165, 195, 217, 241, 273, 299, 329, 365, 399, 429, 459
    college attendance and, 10, 14–29
    goals for, 7, 35, 65, 101, 137, 175, 205, 227, 251, 283, 309, 339, 375, 409, 441
    how to, 20–24
    Implementation Model, 20–24
    process, 20–24
    reactions to, 18–20
Charts, 157
Cheating, 297–298
Chicago Manual of Style, 359
Children, studying with, 269–270
Choices, 13–14

Chronological organization, 350
Civic duties, critical thinking and, 312
Clarity, communication and, 216
Class, attending and participating in, 228–230
Classes, dropping, 76
Classroom:
    challenges, 69–70
    critical thinking beyond, 312
    etiquette, 73–74
Clubs, 73
College:
    activities/clubs, 73
    advisor, 77–78
    catalog, 77
    community, 4
    differences from high school, 15–17
    earning power and, 9–10
    expectations and, 15–17
    persistence in, 61–95 (*see also* Persistence)
    policies and procedures, 66–67
    primary reason to attend, 8
    professors, 67–70
    returning students, 62–63, 71, 107, 117, 134–135, 395–396, 447
    safety while in, 72, 87–88
    significance of, 10–13
    student services, 70–74
    things you need to know, 61–95
    transfers, 78–79
    why attend, 8–13
Comfort zone, 38–39
Communication, 335–369 (*see also* Speaking; Writing)
    listening and, 215–216
    steps to success, 343
    value of, 340, 342
Communities, 376–377
Community college, 4
Compare/contrast organization, 350
Comparing, 268
Compassion, 327
Competence, 51
Competition, 327
Comprehension:
    reading, 147–150 (*see also* Reading)
    testing, 160–164
Computer labs, 70
Concentration, 147–150
    memory and, 257, 258
Conclusions, writing, 357–358
Conflict, 388–390
Conscience, 297
Contrast/compare organization, 350
Cooperative learning, 267–269
Cornell method of note taking, 234–235, 236, 237
Cost of attendance, 85
Counselor, 77–78, 89
Courage, 327

I-0

Crafts, 269
Cramming, 270–272
Creative thinking, 326–328
Creativity, communication and, 215
Credibility, 17
    communication and, 216
Credit:
    cards, 119–122
    counseling, 119, 121
    rating, 120–121
Crimes, protecting yourself from, 87–88
Critical thinking, 305–333
    analyzing information, 317–318
    asking questions, 319–320
    beyond the classroom, 312
    defining, 310–311
    developing alternatives, 321–322
    distinguishing fact from opinion, 322–323
    fallacious arguments and, 323–326
    importance of, 311–312
    looking at things differently, 316–317
    making it work, 313–326
    restraining emotions and, 313–316
    seeking truth in persuasion, 323–326
    solving problems, 320–322
Cultural thoughtfulness, 216
Culture:
    celebrating differences and, 390–397
    components of, 385–387
    language and, 386
    relationships and, 384–388
    sanctions and, 387
    symbols of a, 385
    values and norms, 386–387
Curiosity, 327

Darwin's Theory of Evolution, 260
Date rape, 383
Debating, 306–307
Debt, managing, 118–126
Decision making:
    career choice and, 453–454
    critical thinking and, 312
Default, 85
Deferment, 85
Delivery, speech, 343, 362–364
Delph, Bryan, 177
Demographics, audience, 345
Depression, 19, 411–412
Dictionary, 146–147
Diet, wellness and, 415–416
Disabled student services, 72
Dishonesty, 67
Distance education, 80–81
Diversity:
    celebrating, 390–397
    conflict and, 388–390
    relationships and, 384–388
Documentation, 343
Doubt, overcoming, 38
Dow, Roger, 341–342

Dreams:
    achieving, 437–463
    creative thinking and, 327
Dress, career choice and, 449
Drilling, 268
Drinking, 420, 421, 423–424
Dropping classes, 76
Drug dependency, 52 (see also Drugs)
Drugs:
    chart of illegal, 422
    money and, 84–85
    prescription, 421
    use of, 52, 420–424
Dunn, Rita, 183
Dysfunction, levels of, 412

Earning power, education level and, 9–10
Ecstasy, 420,
Education (see also College):
    as privilege, 253
    culture and, 387 (see also Culture)
    distance, 80–81
    earning power and, 9–10
Electives, career choice and, 453
Emotional blocks, 105
Emotional reactions, 18–20
Emotions:
    listening and, 212–213
    restraining, 313–316
Employers, top qualities sought by, 342
Energy, communication and, 215
English, as a second language, 214–215
Environment, study, 252
Epps, Brian R., 12
Erikson's Stages of Development, 260
Essay questions, 294–295
Ethics, 17, 296–297, 352
Ethnicity, 387 (see also Culture)
Etiquette, classroom, 73–74
Evans, Forrest, 400–401
Evidence, writing and, 354
Exams, taking, see Test taking
Excitement, 19
Expectations, 16–17, 105
Extroversion vs. introversion, 189, 191
Extroverts, 188, 191

Fact, distinguishing from opinion, 322–323
Failing, fear of, 105
Failure, dealing with, 39–40
Family, relationships with, 380
Fear, overcoming, 38
Federal Privacy Act of 1974, 67
Federal Supplemental Educational Opportunity Grant (FSEOG), 83
Feeling vs. thinking, 190, 192
Finance, glossary of terms, 123
Finances:
    critical thinking and, 312
    managing, 118–126
Financial aid, 81–87, 122–123
    children and, 270

    eligibility for, 86
    glossary, 85
First-year history, writing, 75–76
Fitness, 414–416
    cardiovascular, 414
    fiscal, 119–120
Fixation, reading and, 149–150
Flash cards, 157
Flexibility, 414
    careers and, 443
Frames of Mind, 180
Frequency, of reading, 150
Friends:
    choosing, 37–38
    relationships with, 378–379

Gardner, Howard, 180
Generalities, in argument, 324
GHB, 420
Glittering generalities, in argument, 324
Goals, 54 (see also Goal setting)
    categories for, 46
    evaluation plan for, 46
    for change, 7, 35, 65, 101, 137, 175, 205, 227, 251, 283, 309, 339, 375, 409, 441
    how to write, 44, 46
    qualities of attainable, 43
    worksheet, 47–48
Goal setting, 41–48 (see also Goals)
    attitude and, 36–37
    critical thinking and, 312
    values and, 36
GPA, 76, 78–80
Grade point average, 78–80
Grades, 68–69, 78–80
Groups, studying, 267–269
Growth, 31–59
Gu, Zheng, 293
Gunnysacking, 388

H2 FLIB, 271
Harassment, sexual, 381–383
Hate, overcoming, 397–398
Headings:
    forming questions from, 156
    note taking and, 233
Health:
    defined, 410
    services, 72
    wellness and, 410 (see also Wellness)
High school, differences from college, 15–17
Highlighting, 271
HIV, 424–425
Hobbies, 269
Home, planning for, 116–117
Homesickness, 19
Homosexuality, relationships and, 392–393
Honesty, 296–298
    in relationships, 380
Hooks, Coretta, 128–129
Hope Scholarship Tax Credit, 84

Houston, Kevin Todd, 45
Human immunodeficiency virus, 424–425

Identity theft, 124–125
Importance/priority organization, 350
Income, sources of, 118
Independent study, 80–81
Individuality, 327
Industry growth, projected, 446
Information, analyzing, 317–318
Informational interview, 447
Innovation, creative thinking and, 327
Insomnia, 414
Integrity, 296–298, 352
Intelligences, multiple, see Multiple intelligences
Interests, career choice and, 448
International students, 71–72
Internet, research and, 349
Internship, 454
Interpersonal intelligence, 181, 182–183
Interview, informational, 447
Intrapersonal intelligence, 181, 183
Introduction, writing, 355–356
Introversion vs. extroversion, 189, 191
Introverts, 188, 191
Intuition vs. sensing, 189, 191

Jingles, 265
Job market, 442 (see also Career)
Johnson, LaDondo, 196–197
Journaling, 28, 58, 75–76, 94, 130, 168, 198, 220, 244, 276, 302, 332, 368, 402, 413, 434, 462
Joy, 52
Judging vs. perceiving, 190, 192
Juul, Jamie, 56–57

Kardon, Melpo, 218–219
Key words, 157
    listening and, 213–214
Kinesthetic intelligence, 181, 182
Knowing, vs. memorizing, 260–263

Lag-time response, 287–288
Language:
    culture and, 386
    labs, 71
    using effectively, 353
Latte Factor, The, 124
LEAD, 183–185
Learning, 172–199
    cooperative, 267–269
    multiple intelligences, 178–183
    styles, see Learning styles
Learning Evaluation and Assessment Directory, 183–185
Learning styles, 183–186
    multiple intelligences and, 185–186
Life plans, 442 (see also Career)
Linguistic intelligence, 180, 182
Listening, 202–221
    actively, 216
    Chinese pictograph for, 209
    communication and, 215–216
    constructively, 210
    defined, 209–210
    emotions and, 212–213
    English as a second language and, 214–215
    importance of, 206
    key words and, 213–214
    note taking and, 230
    obstacles to, 210–213
    prejudging, 210–211
    purpose for, 210
    ROAR, 206–209
    talking and, 212
    vs. hearing, 206
Listserv, 349
Loans:
    car title, 126
    payday, 126
    student, 122–123
Logic/math intelligence, 181, 182
Logodaedalian, 143
Loneliness, 378
Long-term memory, 255
Love relationships, 380–381
L-STAR note-taking system, 230–233
Luna, Joey, 166–167

Main ideas:
    reading and, 150–153
    selecting, 353–354 (see also Topic)
Major, career choice and, 452
Mapping system of note taking, 235–237
    group study and, 269
Maslow's Hierarchy of Needs, 260
Matching tests, 290
Math, centers, 71
Math, intelligence, 181, 182
Memorizing, vs. knowing, 260–263
Memory, 247–277
    aids to, 259
    assessment of, 255, 256
    attending to your, 259–260
    hindrances to, 260
    long-term, 255
    mnemonics and, 264–267
    rote, 260
    sensory, 254–255
    short-term, 255
    studying and, 263–269
    VCR3 and, 257–259
    working, 255
Mental health services, 72
Mental work, 448–449
Mentors, 455–457
Mind, its effect on wellness, 410–412
Mind maps, 157
Minority cultures, see Culture
Minority students, 72 (see also Culture; Diversity)
MIS, 178–180
Misconduct, academic, 297–298
Mnemonics, 264–267

Modern Language Association (ALA), 359
Money:
    career and, 449
    drugs and, 84–85
    management, 23, 118–126
Montgomery, Glenn E., 314
Motivation, 23, 36–41, 54
    attitude and, 36–37
    career choice and, 450–451
    finding, 90
    plan for, 49–50
    process of becoming, 40–41, 42
    self-esteem and, 46, 51
    source of, 41
    stages of, 42
    values and, 36
Movement, communication and, 215
Multiple choice questions, 291–292
Multiple intelligences, 178–183
    body/kinesthetic, 181, 182
    interpersonal, 181, 182–183
    intrapersonal, 181, 183
    logic/math, 181, 182
    musical/rhythm, 181, 182
    naturalistic, 181, 183
    survey, 178–180
    using to enhance studying, 181–183
    verbal/linguistic, 180, 182
    visual/spatial, 180, 181
Muscular:
    endurance, 414–415
    strength, 414
Musical/rhythm intelligence, 181, 182

Narrative statement, 44, 47, 48
National Association of College Employers (NACE), 352
National Foundation for Credit Counseling, 121
Naturalistic intelligence, 181, 183
Nervousness, 19
Networking, 454
Nontraditional students, 62–63, 71, 107, 117, 134–135, 395–396, 447
Norms, culture and, 386–387
Notes:
    outlining, 360–361
    taking, 155–158 (see also Note taking)
Note-taking, 155–158, 224–245
    abbreviations and, 231
    analyzing and, 232
    Cornell system of, 234–235, 236, 237
    L-STAR system, 230–233
    mapping and, 235–237
    outline technique, 233–234
    tips for effective, 228–238
    translating and, 232
    using a laptop, 238–239

Occupations, fastest growing, 446 (see also Career)
Open mind, relationships and, 384
Opinion, distinguishing from fact, 322–323

Optimism, 19
Organization:
    body of paper, 354–355
    of paper or speech, 350–352
Organizations, culture and, 387
Organizing, listening and, 208
Outlines, 157
Outlining, 343
    during note taking, 233–234
    notes for delivery, 360–361
Overdorf, Tanya Stuart, 455

PAP, 186–188
Paragraphs, main idea of, 150–515
Parents, culture and, 388
Part-time job, 454
Patriotism, in argument, 324
Pauk, Walter, 234
Payday loans, 126
Pegging, 266–267
Pell Grant, 83
Perceiving vs. judging, 190, 192
Perkins Loan, 84
Perry, Tomer, 26–27
Perseverance, 328
Persistence, in college, 61–95
Personal decorum, 73–74
Personality:
    Assessment Profile, 186–188
    learning about your, 186–193
    making it work for you, 190–193
    type, career choice and, 448
    types, 188–193
Persuasion, seeking truth in, 323–326
Peterson, Coleman, 253
Physical reactions, 18–20
Physical work, 448–449
Plain folks argument, 324
Planning, priorities and, 112–117
PLUS Loan, 84
Policies, college, 66–67
Practicum, 454
Prefixes, 144
Prejudging, listening and, 210–211
Preprofessional organizations, 454
Preregistration, 81, 89
Priorities, setting, 103–105
Prioritizing, 97–131 (see also Time management)
Priority management, 112–117
Problem solving:
    critical thinking and, 312, 320–322
    developing alternatives, 321–322
    identifying the problem, 320
Problems, solving, see Problem solving, 320–322
Problem-solving organization, 350
Procrastination, 103–105, 106–107
Professors, 67–70
    sexual harassment and, 382
Promises, keeping, 54
Public speaking, 336–337 (see also Speaking):
Punctuality, 16

Purpose:
    listening and, 210
    statement, 343

Question, SQ3R and, 155
Questions:
    asking, 319–320
    essay, 294–295
    matching, 290
    multiple choice, 291–292
    predicting test, 285–287
    short answer, 293–294
    true–false, 290–291
    types of responses to test, 287–288
Quick-time response, 287–288

Race, 387 (see also Culture)
Rape, 383
Reacting, listening and, 208
Reading, 133–169
    active vs. passive, 139
    career choice and, 453
    comprehension, 138, 160–164
    finding main ideas, 150–153
    for pleasure, 164
    note-taking and, 155–158
    purpose for, 143
    speed and comprehension, 147–150
    speed/rate, 140–142
    SQ3R, 154–160
    tools for, 138
    vocabulary and, 143–147
Receiving, listening and, 207
Recite, SQ3R and, 159–160
Rehearsal, 343
    for speaking, 362–364
Relationships, 371–403
    abusive, 52
    celebrating diversity and, 390–397
    conflict and, 388–390
    critical thinking and, 312
    going bad, 381
    homosexuality and, 392–393
    importance of, 376–377
    love, 380–381
    overcoming hate, 397–398
    rape and, 383
    sexual harassment and, 381–383
    types of, 377–381
    with diverse others, 384–388
    with family, 380
    with friends, 378–379
Religion, culture and, 387 (see also Culture)
Remembering, note taking and, 233
Repeating, memory and, 257, 258
Repetition, communication and, 215
Research, 343
    for speech or paper, 347–350
    Internet and, 349
Responses, types of, 287–288
Responsibility, 17
    personal, 419–430

Returning students, 62–63, 71, 107, 117, 134–135, 395–396, 447
Review, SQ3R and, 160
Reviewing, memory and, 257, 258
Rhymes, 265
Rice, Timothy Spencer, 104
Risk taking, 54, 327
ROAR, 206–209
Robinson, Nailah, 460–461
Roofies, 420
Rote memory, 260
Rudisill, Maritza E., 211

Salaries, education level and, 9–10
Salary, career and, 449
Sanctions, culture and, 387
Santos, Vanessa, 92–93
Scare tactic argument, 324
Scholarships, 86
School, planning for, 112–113
Security, 51
    campus, 72
    ensuring your, 87–88
Selective Service Registration, 85
Self-esteem, 12, 51–54
    attitude and, 36–37
    characteristics of, 51
    improving your, 52–54
    influences on, 51–52
    values and, 36
Self-talk, 53
Self-worth, 411
Sensing vs. intuition, 189, 191
Sensory memory, 254–255
Sentences, as mnemonics, 265
Sextasy, 420
Sexual harassment, 381–383
Sexually transmitted diseases (STDs), 424–427
Shadowing, career choice and, 454
Short answer questions, 293–294
Short-term memory, 255
Skills, career choice and, 451
Sleep, effective study and, 289
Soul, its effect on wellness, 412–413
Sources, exploring, 347–350
Spatial organization, 350
Speaking:
    anxiety about, 363–364
    audience analysis and, 345–346
    compared to writing, 343
    documentation and, 358–359
    organizing speech, 350–352
    outlining notes for, 360–361
    rehearsal for, 362–364
    research for, 347–350
    thesis statement and, 346–347
    topic selection, 344
    writing conclusions, 357–358
    writing introductions, 355–356
Spearman, Charles Steve, 417
Speech, writing, see Speaking; Writing
Spirituality, 412–413
Split page note taking system, 234–235

SQ3R, 154–160
  memory and, 263–264
Stafford Loan, 84
STDs, 424–427
Stock, Laren, 366–367
Story lines, as mnemonics, 266
Straw argument, 324
Strengths, understanding our, 176
Stress, 19, 416–419
  test of, 418–419
Stressors, 418
Student, success services, 70–74
Students:
  disabled, 72
  international, 71–72
  minority, 72
  returning, 62–63, 71, 107, 117, 134–135, 395–396, 447
Study habits, 23
Study, independent, 80–81
Studying, 15
  cooperative learning and, 267–269
  environment and, 252
  group, 267–269
  in a crunch, 270–272
  lack of sleep and, 289
  memory and, 252, 254–256, 263–269 (see also Memory)
  purpose for, 252
  with small children, 269–270
Style guides, 359
Success:
  academic services and, 70–74
  defining, 13
  persistence and, 66
  strategies for test taking, 288–296
Suffixes, 144–145
Summaries, 157
Survey, SQ3R and, 154–155
Syllabus, study and, 271
Symbols, cultural, 385

T system of note taking, 234–235, 236
Tactile learning style, 185
Talking, listening and, 212
Target dates, 44, 47, 48
Tate, Garcia Mills, 229
Teamwork, 16
Test anxiety, 284–287, 296 (see also Test taking)
Tests (see also Test taking):
  anxiety regarding, 284–287
  cramming for, 270–272
  placement, 67
  predicting questions, 285–287
  taking, see Test taking
  types of responses to questions, 287–288
Test taking, 279–303
  essay, 294–295
  matching, 290
  multiple choice, 291–292
  short answer, 293–294
  strategies for success, 288–296
  true-false, 290–291
Textbook, bringing to class, 230
Thesis, statement, 346–347
Thinking:
  creative, 326–328
  critical, see Critical thinking
  vs. feeling, 190, 192
Time:
  evaluating how you spend, 108
  sheets, 109–110
  taking control of, 102–103 (see also Time management)
Time lines, 157
Time management, 23, 102–131
  fun and, 105, 106–108
  procrastination and, 103–105, 106–107
  setting priorities and, 112–117
  using body's cycles and, 111–112
  work vs. play, 103
Tobacco, 421
Topic:
  communication and, 343
  reading and, 150–153
  selection, 344
  sentence, 150–153
Topical/categorical organization, 350
Transcripts, 71
Transfers, college, 78–79
Translating, note taking and, 232
Travel, career choice and, 449
Treasures, looking for, 176
True–false tests, 290–291
Truth:
  creative thinking and, 327
  seeking in arguments, 323–326
Tutoring, 71
Typology, personality, 188–193

Undeclared major, 452
Unsubsidized Stafford Loan, 84

Values, 36
  career choice and, 451
  culture and, 386
VCR3, memory and, 257–259

Verbal/linguistic intelligence, 180, 182
Veteran affairs, 71
Victory wall or file, 54
Visual learning style, 185
Visual/spatial intelligence, 180, 181
Visualizing, 271
  memory and, 257–258
Vocabulary, 143–147, 149, 152–153

Wellness, 410–435
  action plan for, 429–430
  alcohol use and, 420, 421, 423–424
  birth control and, 425, 428
  body's effect on, 414–416
  depression and, 411–412
  diet and, 415–416
  drug use and, 420–424
  fitness and, 414–416
  holistic approach to, 410
  levels of dysfunction, 412
  mind's effect on, 410–412
  personal responsibility and, 419–430
  soul's effect on, 412–413
  stress and, 416–419
Whining, 105
Win–win solution, looking for, 388
Words:
  as mnemonics, 265–266
  power of, 340, 342
Work (see also Career):
  balancing with play, 103
  expectations and, 16–17
  planning for, 115–116
Working memory, 255
Workload, 14
Work study, 84
Writing:
  audience analysis, 345–346
  centers, 70
  compared to speaking, 343
  conclusions, 357–358
  documentation and, 358–359
  introductions, 355–356
  organizing paper, 350–352
  process, 343
  research for, 347–350
  thesis statement, 346–347
  topic selection, 344

Yearwood, Natasha, 432–433

Zavala, Martin, 274

ST. CHARLES COMMUNITY COLLEGE

ORIENTATION TO COLLEGE

APPENDIX

St. Charles
COMMUNITY COLLEGE

TABLE OF CONTENTS

Student Profile 1A

Interview Exercise 2A

First Day of Class Checklist 3A

Plan for Success 4A

Information Scavenger Hunt 5A

Freshman Phrases 7A

SCC Academic Programs 11A

Educational Program Plan 13A

Course Scheduling Worksheet 14A

Holland Code Survey 15A

Definition of Holland Codes 18A

Career Center Activity 19A

Academic Locus of Control 21A

Student Library Guide 23A

SCC Case Studies 27A

SCC Connection Instructions 37A

Faculty Panel Summary 38A

Time Management Pages 39A

St. Charles
COMMUNITY COLLEGE

ST. CHARLES COMMUNITY COLLEGE
STUDENT PROFILE

NAME: Mr./Mrs./Ms. _____

TELEPHONE: Home _____ Cell _____

E-MAIL: _____

1) Are you a new or returning student?

2) Are you happy to be at SCC? Please explain.

3) What are your goals as a student at SCC?

4) What do you expect to learn from your experience in COL 101?

5) What other courses are you taking this semester?

6) Are there any circumstances that may impede your progress this semester? Please explain.

INTERVIEW EXERCISE

Spend about 10 minutes filling in the blanks below. Then pair off with someone whom you do not know. Spend 3 to 5 minutes interviewing that person, then switch.

1. I like _____

2. I really enjoy _____

3. I dream about _____

4. I look forward to _____

5. I'm a good friend because _____

6. One thing I've always wanted to do _____

7. Something I've recently learned is _____
   _____

8. I'm happiest when _____
   _____

9. I think it's funny when _____
   _____

10. One thing I'm proud of is _____
    _____

11. One thing I do well is _____
    _____

12. What I want people to remember about me is _____
    _____

13. One unique thing about me is _____
    _____

14. I chose to go to college because _____
    _____

15. I chose SCC because _____
    _____

16. One thing I hope to change between now and graduation is _____

FIRST DAY OF CLASS CHECKLIST

The following is a checklist of things you should expect to find out during the first class meeting for any course.

- ❑ What are the goals and objectives for the course?

- ❑ Is there a schedule or syllabus for the course? Get a copy, make sure you understand every detail on it, and keep it where you can refer to it regularly. Follow it!

- ❑ Are there research papers or projects? When are they due? Make a note of the dates and begin immediately to schedule time, on your semester planner, for this work.

- ❑ When and how will you be tested? Begin to plan now how you will take notes and what kinds of information you should be sure to include in your notes. Should your attention be focused on large concepts and theories or on many individual facts and details? Place these test dates on your semester planner.

- ❑ Does the instructor have special procedures that you should follow? Find out what they are and stick to them.

- ❑ What are the basic textbooks? Are there required readings in addition to the text? Are there recommended supplementary readings? Where can you find them? Make sure you read the assigned readings before going to class.

- ❑ What, if any, special materials will be needed to successfully complete the course? Do you need a dictionary, a thesaurus, a writing manual containing grammar rules, access to a personal computer, a calculator, or a special supplementary resource book?

- ❑ Does the instructor have regular office hours when s/he is available to meet with students who have problems or questions? When and where are these office hours held?

- ❑ What is the attendance policy? Is part of your grade based on attendance and participation? Does the instructor have a procedure to follow if you know you will miss a class? Is there a phone number you can call if an emergency arises and you will not be able to attend class?

- ❑ How will your grade be calculated? Your grade should never be a surprise, or mystery, to you. Keep track or your progress along the way.

Plan for Success!!

Maximum Credit Hour Recommendations

Job/Family Weekly Hours	Maximum Credit Hours in Fall/Spring	Maximum Credit Hours in Summer
0 - 20	15	8
21 - 29	12	6
30 - 39	9	4
40	6	3

To be a full-time student in the Fall or Spring, you must take 12 or more credit hours.

To be a full-time student in the Summer, you must take 6 or more credit hours.

Freshman Phrases
Glossary of Terms

ACE Center	The Academic and Career Enhancement (ACE) Center is a learning center with an attached computer lab.
Add	A way of putting another course on your schedule after initial registration has been completed.
Assessment Test	SCC's way of measuring student's ability in English, math & reading. The assessment is required for all first time students taking more than 5 hours.
Associate of Arts	Transfer program. The purpose of the Associate of Arts degree program is to provide the first two years of study for those students who plan to pursue a baccalaureate degree.
Associate of Applied Science	Career program. The primary purpose of curriculum leading to an A.A.S. is immediate employment. The requirements for this degree are designed so that students will receive appropriate course work preparing them to enter the job market upon completion of their program.
Certificate	Similar to a minor, but may be earned with a degree or independently of it.
Commuter Campus	Students at SCC commute daily to classes. SCC is not a residential campus that has student housing. The only cost you pay is tuition, fees, and textbooks!
Co-requisite	A requirement you must be meeting while you are taking a specific course.

Credit Hour	One unit of course work equivalent to 15 contact hours of classroom instruction. A typical college course is equivalent to 3 credit hours.
Department	A subdivision of a school or college that deals with a specified area(s) of study (i.e. Music).
Developmental Courses	SCC offers many courses to help prepare students for successful completion of college level course work. Any course below the 100 level is considered to be developmental.
Drop	A way of removing a course from your schedule.
Elective	Any course in the curriculum you wish to take AND for which you have met the prerequisite(s).
Finals	Finals refer to key examinations offered during the final week of a given semester or term. Finals usually weigh heavily in course grade determination.
Free Application for Federal Student Aid (FAFSA)	The application required for students to be considered for federal student financial aid (Federal Pell Grant, Federal Perkins Loan Program, Federal PLUS Program, Federal Stafford Loan Program, Federal Work-Study). Obtain a FAFSA from a high school or college for the appropriate year (usually available in November). The FAFSA is processed free of charge, and it is used by most state agencies and colleges. Note: Grants do not have to be paid back; loans do!
Freshman	Any SCC student who has completed fewer than 28 credit hours.
General Education	A component of the degree program that gives students an opportunity to explore areas outside of their majors.
Grade Point Average (GPA)	A calculation on all work taken at St. Charles Community College recorded on the student record and based on a 4.0 average (GPA) scale (i.e. A=4.0, B=3.0, C=2.0, etc.).

Grant	Awarded through the Financial Aid office, grants give qualifying students money for school that doesn't have to be paid back. (See FAFSA, above, for more information.)
Major	The subject of study in which a student chooses to specialize; a series of related courses, taken primarily at the transfer institution. Approximately 40 hours.
Midterms	Midterms refer to key college examinations usually offered midway through a given semester or term.
Minor	A smaller subject of specialization, also usually completed at the transfer institution. Approximately 20 hours.
Open Admissions	The admissions policy of SCC! We admit virtually all high school graduates, regardless of academic qualifications such as high school grades and admission test scores.
Prerequisite	Requirement which must be met before a related course may be taken.
Probation (Academic)	A student is placed on academic probation the second time his/her grade point average falls below satisfactory academic progress.
Registrar	Keeper of official student records.
Registration	A process by which students formally select classes for the next term.
Residency Requirements	A certain number of credits that must be completed at SCC for graduation (15 hours are required).
Scholarships	Awards to students based on merit or merit plus need, which do not need to be repaid.
Semester	A designated college term consisting of 16 weeks of class sessions in the fall or spring. The summer semester is usually an eight-week session.
Sophomore	Any SCC student who has completed 28 credit hours or more.

Student Aid Report (SAR)	Information received approximately 3-6 weeks after your FAFSA has been processed. It reports the information from student applications and, if there are no questions or problems with an application, the SAR reports the Expected Family Contribution (EFC).
Suspension (Academic)	A student is placed on academic suspension when his/her cumulative grade point average falls below satisfactory academic progress for the third time. The student will not be allowed to register for classes for the semester after being placed on suspension.
Syllabus	A detailed course outline often including instructor expectations for student attendance, assignments, and grading.
Transcripts	Official record of all coursework. May be obtained from the Registrar's Office.
Warning (Academic)	A student is placed on academic warning when his/her cumulative grade point average falls below satisfactory academic progress for the first time.
Withdrawal	A way to "quit" a course from the 3rd - 12th weeks of school without being academically penalized.

Academic Programs at SCC

Academic Transfer Programs

The **Associate of Arts degree** is designed to parallel the first two years of coursework at a four-year college or university. The Associate of Arts degree can be tailored to focus on many areas, including:

Accounting	Education	Music
Art	English	Physics
Biology	Foreign Language	Physical Education
Business Administration	History	Political Science
Chemistry	Journalism	Psychology
Communications	Law	Social Services
Computer Science	Mathematics	Sociology
Criminal Justice	Medicine	Speech and Drama

The **Associate of Science degree** can be a career degree or a transfer degree. If you choose the transfer pathway, you will transfer to a four-year school to complete your baccalaureate degree. SCC offers the Associate of Science degree in the following disciplines:

Engineering—transfer to specific institutions
Health Information Technology
Nursing

Career-Technical Programs

These career-oriented programs at SCC enable you to earn an **Associate of Applied Science degree** or a **Certificate of Achievement** in an area that prepares you for employment.

Associate of Applied Science Degrees

Business Administrative Systems

Business Administration
-Accounting
-Management
-Marketing
-Economic/Finance

Child Care and Early Education

Computer Aided Drafting/Manufacturing
-Architectural
-Industrial Technology

Computer Science
-Business Computing
-Multimedia/Web Design
-Telecommunications
-Networking
-Programming Languages
-Database Management

Criminal Justice
-Law Enforcement

Graphic Communications
-Graphic Design

Human Services
-General
-Gerontology
-Substance Abuse
-Victimology
-Youth Services

Occupational Therapy Assistant

Skilled Trades

Certificate of Achievement Programs

Business Administrative Systems
-Customer Service
-Business Administrative Systems Option
-Clerical Assistant
-Desktop Publishing

Business Administration
-Accounting
-Marketing
-Management
-Economics/Finance

Child Care and Early Education

Computer Aided Drafting/Manufacturing

Computer Science
-Computer Presentations
-Data Management
-Microcomputer Applications
-Multimedia
-Telecommunications
-Networking
-Web Design
-Programming Languages

Criminal Justice

Practical Nursing

Educational Program Plan

St. Charles COMMUNITY COLLEGE

Name of Student:_____ Date:_____

Major: _____ 1st Semester Enrolled at SCC:_____

Transferring to:_____ Anticipated Graduation Date:_____

Courses transferred from another college: _____ _____ _____

_____ _____ _____

_____ _____ _____

First Semester (WHEN:)   Second Semester (WHEN:)

_____   _____

_____   _____

_____   _____

_____   _____

_____   _____

Total Sem. Hrs. _____   Total Sem. Hrs. _____

Summer Session (WHEN:)   Total Sem. Hrs. _____

Third Semester (WHEN:)   Fourth Semester (WHEN:)

_____   _____

_____   _____

_____   _____

_____   _____

_____   _____

Total Sem. Hrs. _____   Total Sem. Hrs. _____

Summer Session (WHEN:)   Total Sem. Hrs. _____

13A

St. Charles Community College

| COURSE # | COURSE TITLE | CR HRS | SITE | \multicolumn{6}{c|}{TIME OF DAY CLASS MEETS} |
				MON	TUE	WED	THU	FRI	SAT
EXAMPLE: ENG 101/01	English Comp	3	Adm 1202	8-9:00		8-9:00		8-9:00	

THE ACADEMIC LOCUS OF CONTROL (LOC)

Locus of control is an individual's belief system regarding the causes of his or her experiences and the factors to which that person attributes success of failure. It can be assessed with the following Locus of Control Scale.

Directions: Mark True (T) or False (F)

____ 1. College grades most often reflect the effort you put into classes.
____ 2. I came to college because it was expected of me.
____ 3. I have largely determined my own career goals.
____ 4. Some people have a knack for writing, while others will never write well no matter how hard they try.
____ 5. At least once, I have taken a course because it was easy to get a good grade.
____ 6. Professors sometimes make an early impression of you and then no matter what you do, you cannot change that impression.
____ 7. There are some subjects in which I could never do well.
____ 8. Some students, such as student leaders and athletes, get free rides in college classes.
____ 9. I sometimes feel that there is nothing I can do to improve my situation.
____10. I never feel really hopeless-there is always something I can do to improve my situation.
____11. I would never allow social activities to affect my studies.
____12. There are many important things for me than getting good grades.
____13. Studying everyday is important.
____14. For some courses it is not important to go to class.
____15. I consider myself highly motivated to achieve success I life.
____16. I am a good writer.
____17. Doing work on time is always important to me.
____18. What I learn is more determined by college and course requirements than by what I want to learn.
____19. I have been known to spend a lot of time making decisions which others do not take seriously.
____20. I am easily distracted.
____21. I can be easily talked out of studying.
____22. I get depressed sometimes and then there is no way I can accomplish what I know I should be doing.
____23. Things will probably go wrong for me sometime in the near future.
____24. I keep changing my mind about my career goals.
____25. I feel I will someday make a real contribution to the world if I work shard at it.
____26. There has been at least on instance in school where social activity impaired my academic performance.
____27. I would like to graduate from college, but there are more important things in my life.
____28. I plan well and stick to my plans.

Scoring: Circle the answers that match your own answers. Add up the number of matches.

Total number of matches: _____

1) F	5) T	09 T	13) F	17) T	21) T	25) F
2) T	6) T	10) F	14) T	18) F	22) T	26) T
3) F	7) T	11) F	15) F	19) T	23) T	27) T
4) T	8) T	12) T	16) F	20) T	24) T	28) F

INTERNAL LOC (score 0)	LOC (score 14)	**EXTERNAL** LOC (score 28)
Correlates to a GPA of 4.0	2.0	0.0

If a person has an **internal locus of control,** that person attributes success to his or her own efforts and abilities. A person who expects to succeed will be more motivated and more likely to learn. This person will seek out information and is more likely to have good study habits and a positive academic attitude.

A person with an **external locus of control,** who attributes his or her success to luck or fate, will be less likely to make the effort needed to learn. People with external locus of control are also more likely to experience anxiety since they believe that they are not in control of their lives.

One study found that students with an internal locus of control showed better adjustment to college in terms of academic achievement and social adjustment. (See Njus, D.M. & Brockway, J.H. [1999]. Perceptions of competence and locus of control for positive and negative outcomes. *Personality and Individual Differences 26,* 531-548.)

Another study found that community college students who succeeded at distance education had high internal locus of control. (See Dille, B. & Mezack, M. [1991]. Identifying predictors of high risk among community college telecourse students. *American Journal of Distance Education 5 (1),* 24-35.)

A third study found that locus of control had a negative correlation with course withdrawal and failure, although the amount was not significant. In other words, the more students had an external locus of control, the more likely they were to withdraw from the course (See Pugliese, R.R. [1994]. Telecourse persistence and psychological variables. *American Journal of Distance Education, 8* [3], 22-39.

Student Library Guide

http://www.stchas.edu/library

General Library Information

Fall and Spring SCC Library Hours
Summer and Intersession hours vary; call 636-922-8434 for information

Monday-Thursday:	7:30 a.m.—10:00 p.m.
Friday:	7:30 a.m. — 4:30 p.m.
Saturday:	9:00 a.m. — 2:00 p.m.
Sunday:	closed

Contact Information

Reference Desk:	636-922-8620
Reference e-mail:	refdrop@stchas.edu
Circulation Desk:	636-922-8434

Checking Out Library Material

To check out materials from the library, a valid student ID must be presented at the Circulation Desk located on the first floor.

SCC Library Check-out Periods

General Collection:	3 weeks
Vertical File:	3 weeks
DVDs and Videotapes:	2 hours, in-library use only
Audio CDs:	3 days
Periodicals:	Library use only
Reference Books:	Library use only
Reserve Material:	Checkout time varies

Renewals

Books and materials which are not reserve items may be renewed as many times as needed during the semester if the material is not requested by another patron. Items may be renewed online in the Archway Online Catalog, at the circulation desk, or by phone at 636-922-8434. However, if the items are overdue, you must come to the library in person to renew them.

St. Charles COMMUNITY COLLEGE

Locating Books and Articles

To find books and articles in the SCC library, start at the library's home page http://www.stchas.edu/library, where links to our books, articles and other services are found.

Finding a Book, Video or CD:

Use the **Archway Online Catalog,** where you can locate the call number for SCC books, videos, DVDs, CDs and periodical holdings.

Go to http://www.stchas.edu/library
    Click on "**Find a Book**"
        Choose the type of search you want
        (**Keyword** is the broadest and most commonly used)

- Start with a **keyword** search in SCC's online catalog, **Archway**, or
- If you know the name of the book or video, start with a **title** search,
- If you are looking for books by an author, start with an **author** search, typing the last name first: Faulkner, William

Reference and Circulating Books:
- Reference books are for in-library use only and are located on the first floor.
- Circulating books can be checked out and are located on the second floor.
    - In the catalog record, circulating books will show the location as "StCharles Second Floor." If the status reads "AVAILABLE," write down the call number and go upstairs to find it.
    - If the status shows a date due, you can place a request on the title, or search MOBIUS.

LOCATION	CALL #	STATUS
StCharles Second Floor	HV 6789 .F45 2002	AVAILABLE

MOBIUS
- Search for and request books from other Missouri colleges and universities. (MOBIUS libraries rarely lend videos, DVDs and CDs).
- To search MOBIUS, click on the MOBIUS link from the library's home page, or go to http://mobius.missouri.edu/search/.
- You'll need your student ID in order to request books through MOBIUS.
- MOBIUS books are delivered in about 3 days. We'll call you when your book arrives. Simply show your student ID at the circulation desk to pick up your book(s).

24A

Obtaining Material from Other Libraries

Items not owned by the SCC library and books not available through MOBIUS may be borrowed from other libraries via **interlibrary loan**. You can borrow both books and articles. To borrow a book or article through interlibrary loan, see a reference librarian at the reference desk. Students are limited to borrowing five interlibrary loan items per semester. Items requested through interlibrary loan can take up to 10 days to receive.

Finding an Article:

Using Online Databases and Indexes

Articles are excellent sources for discovering valuable information on nearly all topics. A few advantages of articles are their currency and concise format.

Go to http://www.stchas.edu/library
    Click on "**Find an Article (Databases)**"
        If you're off campus:
            You will be prompted to enter your last name and your seven-digit student ID number (including the zero), followed by "sc," for example, 0123456sc
    You will see a list of the online databases available to you.

To help you locate an article by topic, an index is needed. The online indexes allow you to search for articles by keywords or subjects. The SCC Library has many online indexes, also referred to as online databases, which are available from any computer with Internet access. Most indexes provide the complete article, called full text, on the computer. These full text articles are electronic reproductions of articles from print publications; therefore, the articles that you access through the library indexes/databases are not considered Internet resources.

Choosing a Database

When beginning a search in an online database, it is important to choose one that best represents the subject to be searched. The SCC library has online periodical and newspaper databases covering a wide variety of subjects, and also has databases on specific subjects such as education and nursing. Read the database descriptions on the library web page to select the best one for your search.

Locations of Magazines, Journals and Newspapers in the SCC Library

Periodicals, such as magazines, journals and newspapers, may be found in various places in the SCC library, depending on their format. Periodicals from the current year are kept on the first floor, on the tall shelves in the back of the reference area, arranged by title. Back issues of periodicals, those before the current year, are kept on the second floor, arranged by title. To determine which periodicals SCC library has, consult the online SCC periodical holdings list at http://atoz.ebsco.com/home.asp?Id=5256. It includes not only the periodicals found in paper or microform in the library, but also includes those available in full text on our online indexes.

Other Library Resources

Computer Use

To ensure access for all students wishing to use the Internet, students are asked to use library computers and printers for research purposes only. You do not need to sign in to use the computers; however, during busy times students needing a computer for research take precedence over students using the computer for non-academic purposes.

Computers for e-mail, chat, or general entertainment are located in the College Center in Room 102 and near the cafeteria in the Student Center.

Study Areas

The first and second floors of the LRC offer study tables. The second floor study area, which shares space with the circulating books, is reserved for quiet study. If you are meeting with a group, use one of the second floor tutor rooms, or one of the study tables on the first floor. The second floor tutor rooms are across the hall from the classrooms and are available on a first come basis.

Reserve Materials

Instructors may place certain materials on reserve. This simply means that these materials are kept behind the circulation desk and may be checked out for short amounts of time to ensure that all students will have access to the material.

To check out reserve materials, give your instructor's last name at the circulation desk and show your student ID. You may also search under **Reserve Lists** on the Archway online catalog. By entering the instructor's name or course name, a list of materials placed on reserve for an instructor or course will be displayed.

Online Tutorial

An online library tutorial is available to orient students to the library and its various resources. You can view the tutorial at any time from any computer with Internet access. To access the tutorial, go to the library's home page, **http://www.stchas.edu/library**, and click **Online Tutorial**.

Updated Spring 2006
SCC Library Reference Department

COLLEGE 101
Case Study Exercise #1

FRED

Description: In order to stay in school, Fred needs to obtain a part-time job but has little work experience and doesn't know how to go about getting a job. Fred is presently thinking he'd like to enter the field of law enforcement but he really doesn't know what jobs are available in that career area. Fred would also like to get more involved on campus and meet new people.

Presently: Fred is enrolled in a class where he is having difficulty understanding material but finds that his instructor is seldom available during his posted office hours.

Assignment:

1. Bring in information about clubs and organizations at SCC. How can this information help Fred?

2. Bring in the ACE Center brochure. Get information about the ACE Center hours and the help that is available there for Fred.

3. Inquire about job placement information at SCC. Do they ever post part-time jobs?

4. Identify source of information on careers in the criminal justice field.

5. Suggest ways in which Fred can approach his instructor about getting help.

6. Talk to campus security about the services they provide on campus and how to reach them in case of an emergency.

COLLEGE 101
Case Study Exercise #2

KAREN

Description: Karen has decided to return to school now that her children are in school all day. Karen would like to pursue a career in allied health but can't decide between health information technology and nursing. She feels out of place with all of the young students in her courses. She would also like to work on her physical fitness and conditioning but can't afford membership in a health club.

Presently: Karen is taking general education requirements that will apply to either program; she needs to make a decision soon.

Assignment:

1. Bring in transfer guides or brochures from the HIT and RN programs.

2. Check with the Career Center and bring in information about careers in HIT and RN.

3. Bring in the college catalog and be ready to discuss course requirements for each major.

4. Where should Karen make an appointment to discuss her options?

5. Bring in information about the Returning Learner's Club on campus.

6. Bring in information about the college fitness center. What are the rules, procedures, and hours of operation?

COLLEGE 101
Case Study Exercise #3

JENNIFER

Description: It is the second week of school and Jennifer is feeling lost. She has a lot of reading to do for her history and sociology courses. In addition, she is taking beginning algebra and is having more difficulty recalling math facts than she thought she would. In high school, Jennifer was a member of several sports teams. She misses the discipline and competition of these activities.

Presently: Jennifer is undecided about her goals. She is taking courses that count as GEN ED requirements, but she would like to decide on a career path. She would also like to become involved in organized sports again.

Assignment:

1. Where on campus can she purchase her textbooks? Are there any supplemental materials she can purchase to help her with her beginning algebra? What are the open hours of the bookstore?

2. Bring in a list of resources available in the ACE Center to help Jennifer improve her reading, study skills, and basic math skills.

3. Bring in a brochure about ModuMath, a math software program offered in the ACE Center. How may this program be beneficial to Jennifer?

4. Visit the Career Center and talk to the career counselor to find out about the assistance available there to help Jennifer decide on a career.

5. Visit the college center and talk to the Student Activities Coordinator about SCC sports teams for both men and women.

COLLEGE 101
Case Study Exercise #4

NICOLE

Description: Nicole has been out of school for 16 years. She has just gotten divorced, has three children, and is worried that financially she won't be able to stay in school. She is interested in pursuing a career in the area of human services.

Presently: Although her assessment indicated that she should be in beginning algebra, Nicole placed herself in Developmental Math II. She is now finding that she is wasting her time.

Assignment:

1. Bring in the brochure about the Returning Learners workshop and explain the program to the class.

2. Explain the difference between grants and loans; bring in information about the FACTS tuition management program and be able to describe the program to the class.

3. Talk to someone on the Financial Aid office about scholarships available to SCC students. Share this information with the class.

4. Find out the process for dropping and adding classes, including the time restraints.

5. From the college catalog find the information about specific options available in the human services program.

6. Bring in information about the Child Care Center and be ready to explain how students can use this service.

COLLEGE 101
Case Study Exercise #5

JASON

Description: Jason has a history paper to do for his history class. It's been two years since he took an English class, so he does not recall how to do a research paper, especially citing sources. Furthermore, he is intimidated by the automated, computerized library at SCC. Jason is also very interested in art and wants to find out about art opportunities at SCC.

Presently: Jason wants to become a high school history teacher, but he is dreading driving all the way into St. Louis to complete his degree.

Assignment:

1. Find out what resources are available in the ACE Center to help Jason with the process of writing a research paper, and especially with citing sources.

2. Check with the reference librarians to find out what aids are available to help him do his research and cite his sources (including on-line sources).

3. Check into the on-campus UMSL office (ACAD 2123) for information about classes and programs available through UMSL that are held on-campus at SCC.

4. Visit both arts buildings on campus (FAB and VAB) and be able to tell where the art gallery is located on campus and a brief description of it.

COLLEGE 101
Case Study Exercise #6

SUE

Description: Sue works 20 hours a week and has already registered for 12 credit hours for the next semester. She plans a secretarial career and will be completing the Associate of Applied Science degree in Administrative Office Management next May.

Presently: Sue has found that she will have to work 40 hours a week because of unexpected expenses.

Assignment:

1. Look in the student handbook for information regarding working and going to school.

2. Bring in information, critical dates, and forms about dropping classes.

3. Find the open computer lab in the TECH building where Sue can practice the various software programs used in her degree program. What are the open hours for the lab?

4. Bring in information about degree requirements for her degree program.

5. Bring in information on applying for graduation at SCC and find out what steps Sue must complete to graduate.

COLLEGE 101
Case Study Exercise #7

PAUL

Description: Paul is transferring six credits from another community college to SCC. After completing an Associate of Arts degree at SCC, Paul plans to transfer to Maryville University to complete a bachelor's degree in business.

Presently: Paul wants to have his credits apply to his SCC degree. As a new SCC student, he also wants to find a place on campus to relax, "hang out," and meet other students.

Assignment:

1. Find out the procedure for having credits transferred from another college to SCC.

2. Bring in information on how Paul can have his SCC credits transferred to Maryville.

3. Bring in information on which classes will apply to his business major at Maryville.

4. Find out how many credits Paul needs for his associate's degree in business.

5. Visit and describe to the class the student lounge and student activity room located in the college center. What is available there for student use?

6. Visit and discuss the new café on campus; bring in information on the hours of operation and the types of refreshments available.

COLLEGE 101
Case Study Exercise #8

MAX

Description: Max has recently been laid off from a company which had employed him for 12 years. Max is thinking that he would like to change careers. He would like to limit his schooling at present to an associate degree in a vocational area. He has taken continuing education courses in computers and enjoyed them.

Presently: Max is unsure of financial aid options available to his as a laid-off worker. He also knows that his job search skills are rusty and that he will need help landing a job once he is out of school.

Assignment:

1. Check the course schedule for classes Max may take to pursue a technical degree in computers.

2. Check with one of the vocational counselors to determine available help through this office.

3. Check with the Continuing Education office or brochure to see if other classes may help Max in finding a job.

4. Discuss differences between college credit and continuing education classes.

5. Can the Career Center help Max with writing his resume and preparing for an interview?

COLLEGE 101
Case Study Exercise #9

KATHY

Description: Kathy has attended college for several semesters taking general education courses. So far she has maintained a "B" average. She has been accepted into the RN program starting this fall. Kathy is also interested in theater and loves to attend plays and concerts. She heard the college is presenting a couple of plays this semester and she would like to see them.

Presently: During the summer, Kathy had surgery on her right arm, and she has always written with her right hand. Currently she attends physical therapy twice a week. Doctor's orders restrict her to limited use of her right arm, which precludes writing.

Assignment:

1. Inquire about special services available for students with temporary or permanent disabilities.

2. Find out, from the assessment center if it is possible for her to have a scribe to help with her exams. Can she have extra time to complete her exams?

3. Where are copy machines available on campus for Kathy to copy the lecture notes of her fellow classmates?

4. What must she do to post signs on campus for typing help?

5. Bring in a list of plays and concerts being presented this semester. Are there any other events of interest?

COLLEGE 101
Case Study Exercise #10

JERRY

Description: Jerry always had difficulty in school. He was "passed" into the next grade year after year. He graduated from high school, but his learning problems were never investigated. Art and computer classes were the only ones that Jerry really enjoyed. He tried hard in other classes, but his studying never paid off. That was then, but Jerry feels that things will be different now that he is in college. He plans to pursue a Multimedia Certificate in the computer science field, but would like to confirm this decision by taking a vocational interest test.

Presently: He is having difficulty with his first two courses: Developmental Writing II and History 101. Jerry has trouble understanding what he reads and struggles with his writing class.

Assignment:

1. Bring in brochure and/or information explaining the First Alert program.

2. Find and bring in information about career choice assessments offered in the career center.

3. Check with the Coordinator for Accessibility Services to find out if Jerry is eligible for help, and what help is available.

4. Bring in information about the requirements for the Multimedia Certificate. In addition to his computer classes, what general education courses must he take?

Steps to Activate Your SCC Connection Account

1. **Have an e-mail address on file.**

   To activate your SCC Connection account, you must have a valid e-mail address on file. Many students already have this address on file because they put it on their application for admission. Stop by the Registration window (ADM 1113) if you need to update your e-mail address. If you do not have an e-mail address, you can get one free at www.yahoo.com or www.hotmail.com

2. **Go to SCC's homepage at www.stchas.edu**
3. **Click on the SCC Connection logo on the right side of the screen.**
4. **From the main menu, click on "Students".**
5. **Under User Account, click on "I'm new to SCC Connection."**
6. **Click on "Proceed to Step 1".**
7. **Enter your last name and either your Social Security number or your student ID number.**

   (Your student I.D. number is a seven-digit number. If yours is shorter, add zeros before the number to total seven digits. For example: If your ID is 1234, then enter 0001234.)

8. **Click on Submit: Your User ID will appear.**
9. **Click on "Proceed to Step 2".**
10. **Re-enter your last name and Social Security number or Student ID.**
11. **The next screen will ask you to use the drop box to display your** e-mail address. If the address is correct, click "Submit" and your temporary password will be e-mailed to you.

    (If you get an error message that says to contact your system administrator at this point, chances are good that we do not have an e-mail address on file for you. Stop by the Registration window to fill out a Change of Information form.)

12. **Exit the SCC Connection and check your e-mail for your temporary password. Write it here: _____**

    (Be sure to check any junk mail files you may have within your account. The return address is "stchas-scc connection".)

13. **Log on to the SCC Connection using your user ID and temporary password.** You will be prompted to change your password. You may also enter a password hint. Remember to keep this password secret.

14. **After you are completely logged in, you will be taken back to the Main Menu.** Click on "Students" and you will be able to access your personal information.

15. **If you forget your user ID, you may click on "What's my User ID?" under User Account.** If you forget your password, you may click on "What's my Password?" under User Account.

St. Charles COMMUNITY COLLEGE

COLLEGE 101
FACULTY PANEL SUMMARY

Name _____

Date of the panel you attended_____

A. Name the panel members:_____
_____
_____

B. Write two questions you would like to ask the panel.
1. _____

2. _____

C. What was discussed at the panel that surprised you?_____
_____
_____
_____
_____

D. How are the expectations of these college faculty members different from high school faculty members?_____
_____
_____
_____
_____

E. How will you, as a student, be able to utilize the information you heard at the panel?_____
_____
_____
_____
_____

F. Discuss any opinions, concerns, suggestions, reactions you have after hearing the panel.
_____
_____
_____
_____
_____

St. Charles
COMMUNITY COLLEGE

TIME	Monday	Tuesday	Wednesday	Thursday	Friday	Saturday	Sunday
7:00							
7:30							
8:00							
8:30							
9:00							
9:30							
10:00							
10:30							
11:00							
11:30							
12:00							
12:30							
1:00							
1:30							
2:00							
2:30							
3:00							
3:30							
4:00							
4:30							
5:00							
5:30							
6:00							
6:30							
7:00							
7:30							
8:00							
8:30							
9:00							
9:30							
10:00							
10:30							

St. Charles
COMMUNITY COLLEGE

St. Charles Community College

Month _____

Sunday	Monday	Tuesday	Wednesday	Thursday	Friday	Saturday